Lionel Trilling

D1568279

The Wisconsin Project on American Writers
A series edited by Frank Lentricchia

Lionel Trilling

THE WORK OF LIBERATION

Daniel T. O'Hara

THE UNIVERSITY OF WISCONSIN PRESS

The University of Wisconsin Press
114 North Murray Street
Madison, Wisconsin 53715

The University of Wisconsin Press, Ltd.
1 Gower Street
London WC1E 6HA, England

5   4   3   2   1

Printed in the United States of America

Library of Congress Cataloging-in-Publication Data
O'Hara, Daniel T., 1948–
    Lionel Trilling: the work of liberation.
    (The Wisconsin project on American writers)
    Includes index.
    1. Trilling, Lionel, 1905–1975—Criticism and
interpretation.   I. Title.   II. Series.
PS3539R56Z87   1988   818'.5209   87-37178
ISBN 0-299-11310-8
ISBN 0-299-11314-0(pbk.)

for Joanne

So by taking flight into the ego
love escapes annihilation.
                    —Freud

Contents

Preface

This book reads the career of Lionel Trilling as a single comprehensive work. The work's intention, from the beginning and throughout his intellectual life, is to create for Trilling a self that, when confronted by the great achievement of another mind, is capable of imaginative sympathy and not of resentful critique alone. The master figure in whose shadow the career takes its shape is that of the "subversive patriarch" of literary ethics, Trilling's ironic revision of the romantic stereotype of the Wandering Jew for his own critical purposes, first and foremost of which is ever to dissent from the orthodoxies of dissent. I theorize Trilling's defensive formation of this public persona in terms of the repressed or unconscious religious allegory of reading to be discovered in the classic Freudian conception of ego development. Through continuing responsiveness to the reality of loss and death, Trilling discovers that the ego can preserve the imaginative power of love. Freud was ever Trilling's hero of fate.

The result of this approach is a practical demonstration of a theory of reading as magnanimous self-creation: the shaped self arising from the performative ability to attribute noble motives realistically to the Other. To highlight this aspect of the book I mark my stages of response to Trilling's unfolding career by creating critical names for them based upon some of my subject's own more famous coinages. The literary ethics of "sincerity and authenticity," for example, become in my terms "the ethics of impersonation." Thus, the aim of this experiment in reading is, not surprisingly, to try out an ethics of criticism based upon an aesthetic appreciation of style that would define the essential function of the writer in the modern world as what Trilling sees the role of E. M. Forster or, later, Isaac Babel as being: to serve as the public figure, however marginal or well connected, for the personal life. In a time of rapacity and resentment run rampant, the magnanimous vision of the Other traditionally enshrined in literary study, and so rarely practiced now, may just prove to be subversively efficacious. Such, anyway, is my hope.

One additional prefatory note still needs to be sounded concerning the emphasis I place upon Trilling's radical ambivalence about being a Jew in America. Not only do I document this ambivalence, of course, but I deploy it as a theoretical category on the basis of Sander Gilman's comprehensive historical, psychological, and linguistic analyses in *Jewish Self-Hatred*. My point, like Gilman's, is that the psychology of resentment and self-hatred visible in the lives of certain Jewish intellectuals who aspire to assimilate, even partially, to the larger non-Jewish culture is a general human phenomenon that recurs when members of oppressed and marginalized groups try to free themselves from the confinements and constraints of any one set of social, cultural, and intellectual contexts. It is not, I assume, a phenomenon exclusive to Jewish-American intellectuals. In fact, it can be seen operating now in the broad context of the academic "celebrity" system as well. If I stress this "complex" in Trilling's case, especially in tracing the origins of the career, I do so because my focus is, after all, the character of the critic and because Trilling himself repeatedly recognizes its power, and works fiercely to free himself from it often in ways still exemplary.

Acknowledgments

To Frank Lentricchia, general editor of the Wisconsin Project on American Writers, Allen Fitchen, director of the University of Wisconsin Press, and Peter Givler, the former acquisitions editor of the University of Wisconsin Press, I am grateful for the opportunity to repay a considerable personal debt publicly. Trilling's work, especially his novel and stories, permitted me to see, at a particularly difficult period in my life, the imaginative possibilities of a critical response modeled upon Freud's conception of the work of mourning in everyday life. To Trilling's mediating spirit, I offer this libation.

Four friends have been of invaluable help by listening to my ideas about Trilling as they were forming. Donald Pease, critic, visionary, and comrade, literally inspired me in our many conversations about American literary culture. Similarly, Paul Bové and Alan Wilde, the one by generous criticism, the other by unfailing support, led me to compose my ideas more sharply and apply them more boldly than I otherwise would have done left to my own devices. Last but far from the least of these friends, Tina Barr, poet and sister in the spirit, has embodied in her vibrant poems and imaginative discussions the true creative voice, and so has reminded me why any of us comes to literary study in the first place.

Joanne Recchuiti-O'Hara, for nearly twenty years, has been my magnanimous companion and critic, for which good fortune I am deeply thankful every day of my life. This book about the magnanimous vision of our last major critic is thus most appropriately hers.

I want also to thank my research assistant, Mary Tiryak, for her great scholarly and critical help early in the book's genesis, and Nadia Kravchenko, Temple University's word-processing secretary for the humanities, and Susan Tarcov, copy editor for the University of Wisconsin Press, for their long-suffering struggle to eliminate my infelicities. I also want to express my gratitude to Susan Mellon for preparing an effective index. The precision and care of all four give "professionalism" its good name.

Unless otherwise noted, all references are to *The Uniform Edition of the Works of Lionel Trilling*, published by Harcourt Brace Jovanovich: © 1979–1981. I am grateful to Diana Trilling for permission to quote from *The Middle of the Journey:* © 1975, 1979.

Lionel Trilling

Chapter One

Sacred Mourning: The Work of Liberation and the Religious Unconscious

"But perhaps not": Fictions of the Magnanimous Mind

Lionel Trilling's preface to "Bartleby the Scrivener" discloses a great deal about his characteristic critical style.[1] It opens with Melville's summary letter of praise to his master Hawthorne delivered in the third person and the historical present tense. Hawthorne for Melville is ever he who "says No! in thunder" and not even "the Devil himself can make him say *yes*." It is a good thing, too, Melville adds revealingly, since "all men who say *yes*, lie . . ." (*PEL*, p. 74). Melville's radical ambivalence thus monumentalizes and memorializes his still-living master as the spirit of negation.

As Trilling admits, he reads Melville's judgment as it has customarily been read: For him, too, it represents the younger writer's idealized self-portrait. It is Melville as much as it is Hawthorne who refuses to suffer the moral or cultural conventions that make for social conformity in affirmation. In support of this established judgment, Trilling cites the following passage written by his own late disciple and colleague Richard Chase, from the authoritative introduction to the Melville selections in *Major Writers of America*, edited by Perry Miller:

> Although Melville was not exclusively a nay-sayer, his experiences and his reflections upon the quality of American civilization had taught him to utter the powerful "no" he attributed to Hawthorne. He learned to say "no" to the boundlessly optimistic commercialized creed of most Americans, with its superficial and mean conception of the possibilities of human life, its denial of all the genuinely creative or heroic capacities of man, and its fear and dislike of any but the mildest truths. Melville's "no" finds expression in the tragic-comic tale of "Bartleby the Scrivener." (*PEL*, p. 74)

3

Trilling concedes the general decorum of this customary reading. He then proceeds, however, to suggest that the "prim, genteel, rather finicking" refusal of Bartleby's "I prefer not to," with all its cultivated inadequacy, Dickensian formality, and Emersonian whimsicality, carries greater subversive weight in the long run than saying "No! in thunder" as Melville's own Ahab does so grandiloquently in his masterpiece *Moby-Dick*. Trilling is not only implying that this poor, antique-sounding phrase, "I prefer not to," may apply more centrally to Melville than does the latter's own revealing formula of the master who says "No! in thunder." Trilling is also implying that this uniquely haunting commonplace of the pathos of freedom in nineteenth-century America may apply more centrally to Hawthorne as well. In any event, in Trilling's eyes, both this topos and that sublime "No! in thunder" define between them the scope of oppositional response by contemporary readers, in which any middle ground has become a no-man's-land. Readers now emulate either Bartleby or Ahab, with nary an Ishmael to be found.

Melville, also according to Trilling, ironically foresaw this decadent development of critical mimicry from imaginative individuality to habitual opposition on a mass scale. What suggests to Trilling Melville's percipience is his taking great perverse "pains to point up the odd inadequacy of that word *prefer*," its lack of heroic pathos, in the passage where Melville "tells how it was [nevertheless] unconsciously adopted into the speech of the narrator and his office staff, and with what comic effect" (*PEL*, p. 75). In the contest of radical ironies Bartleby's verbal poverty, it seems, stands a better chance of spreading and taking root among people than Ahab's Shakespearean richness.

Thus, Melville's "Story of Wall Street," in which a clerk one day decides to respond to all societal demands and even to society's solicitude by saying "I prefer not to" until death supervenes an ending, becomes for Trilling a prophetic allegory of our adversary culture as it repeatedly discovers the latest model of the specious good. Ironically enough, this culture of opposition has been bred over the years by the education in modern literature, art, and thought provided the sons and daughters of the rather extensive American middle class by (among other critics) Lionel Trilling and his circle of New York Intellectuals.[2]

To introduce among its members a poignant credence in this fateful story, Trilling deploys subtextually their common knowledge of Richard Chase's tragic suicide. (Such sub-rosa tactics are what we tactfully call "good taste.") The initial equation of positions is thereby pointedly completed: Melville is to Hawthorne as Chase is to Trilling. Bursting out with "No! in thunder" does not subvert as extensively or survive as long as saying seriatim: "I prefer not to." Whether this is so for

Trilling's "Bartleby," it is certainly so for his "Hawthorne," who opposes all with his art subtly, instead of with his life self-destructively. What Mark Krupnick in *Lionel Trilling and the Fate of Cultural Criticism* correctly claims is Trilling's fate of being both gentleman and Jew, ironist and prophet—or neither one thing nor the other exclusively— has thus become the classic prototype of the personal dilemma of professional advancement.[3]

This phenomenon of critical impersonation of prior literary or critical models, which Trilling long addresses and ultimately divides into the competing ethics of sincerity and authenticity, constitutes the other, professional side of the borderline personality disorder of clinical narcissism widely noted over the last two decades by revisionary psychoanalysts, sociologists, and cultural historians.[4] Since the mid-sixties, an ever larger portion of the literate population in America appears to be suffering from an acute lack of stable identity. According to Hans Kohut, an increasing number of patients alternate between the episodic phantasmagoria of a grandiose self-conception and a more chronic state of deeply wounded self-esteem that precipitates periodically these nearly psychotic experiences. While resembling manic depression, clinical narcissism differs in that it does not (so far) possess a discernible physiological component and does not generally prohibit "normal" everyday functioning. In fact, many contemporary narcissists in their grandiose phases often are, while virtually sociopaths, also younger professionals said to show the greatest promise.

Trilling provides one significant perspective on this development in his remark, often repeated in his career, that we believe as readers so many different things from what we believe in our ordinary lives, things we would never dream of putting to the test of our personal experience—such as the total rightness of the critical negation of American society and culture, whether in Ahab's apocalyptic or Bartleby's whimpering style. Because from early on we are schooled in suspicion, in the profession of opposition, our critical judgments are automatic, abstract, and superficial—too *easy*: Not won by struggle against strongly established authority, they cost most of us really nothing and shortly feel worth about as much. Often we can even secure promotion in our fields for just such clever opposition. This kind of hollow irony eventually takes its toll, especially in a time when established authority appears more irrational and more popular than ever. For the narcissistic self is a bipolar self composed of a famished id and a muscle-bound superego. That is, the narcissistic self is a self without an ego, and so is incapable of reality testing or genuine criticism. In the age of Reagan, what could be worse?

Consequently, also according to Kohut, we have become and now reproduce a generation of unconscious hypocrites with no firm sense of identity, ever-willing victims of the latest intellectual fashion, impersonators of current critical beliefs as long as they advance our careers with little or no real cost to us. Trilling's "adversary culture" and the "culture of narcissism" of Christopher Lasch and Hans Kohut are thus two terms for the same ethical disaster of professionalism unbound in a modern society of apocalyptic consumers and purely interpretive communities.

Trilling often in his career cites John Dewey's *Ethics* where Dewey says that nowadays the final consideration in any proposed course of action not only entails our estimate of the effect such action will have on others but also—even primarily—entails our estimate of the effect such action may have on the "agent" (Dewey's word) or "self" (Trilling's word) one is and wants to be.[5] Repeatedly espousing sets of beliefs one does not or cannot live by is for Trilling an action that defines its habitual "agent" or "actor" (my word) as a hypocrite (God's word). Richard Chase at least had the decency to end a life he believed to be intolerable. The rest of us just say it is, and, when rewarded for doing so, buy a new car.

The essence of Trilling's pragmatism, in other words, is this concern with the morality, and not merely the rigor, of critical argument. His "antiprofessional" position (he loathed graduate teaching)[6] derives from the institutionalized separation of moral questions from the professed academic standard of systematic ratiocination that functions to rule out of court beforehand any serious or sustained consideration of the ethics of criticism. In sum, then, despite his own admiration for the "hardness" and "rigor" and "encompassing" progress of critical argument or of narrative development (see "The Meaning of a Literary Idea" in *The Liberal Imagination*), Trilling's ultimate concern is with the effect of discourse, fictional or otherwise, canonical or commonplace, on people as individuals.

The second part of Trilling's preface to "Bartleby the Scrivener" makes this "pragmatic" position perfectly plain. He invokes Marx and Freud as intellectual frame for and ethical elaboration of his highly personal moral reading of Melville's tale. Trilling reminds us that, insofar as labor is performed at another's will so as to accumulate more and more surplus value or *capital* and produce more and more marketable objects or *commodities*, people must feel increasingly alienated, perceiving themselves and their lives more and more as reified abstractions driven helter-skelter along the economic network. Similarly, Trilling recalls that, insofar as the ego forms and develops primarily through the fateful experience of the loss of love, ambivalence and guilt must accumulate more and more anxiety and produce increasingly painful neurotic symptoms until one day the person discovers the irresistible attractions of suicide. The chief although unconscious purpose of suicide for Freud is, Trilling also reminds us, to destroy not simply one's "hateful" self but also, even primarily, "some other person" whom the individual "has incorporated into his psychic fabric and whom he conceives to have great malign authority over him" (*PEL*, p. 77). The "good Son," for example, would thus kill off the "tyrannical Father" in his mind while maintaining the victim's outward pose of noble innocence. Franz Kafka's endless "Letter to His Father" comes to mind here.

Trilling in his preface thereby generalizes Freud's insights into suicide and combines them with those of Marx into alienation to conclude dialectically that "Bartleby, by his gradual self annihilation, annihilates the [patriarchal] social order as it exists within himself" (*PEL*, p. 77), in a mournful manner apparently exemplary for Trilling and his heirs— our Arnoldian high priest of the Religion of Culture and his cold-war, now neo-conservative disciples in postmodern America.

Perhaps so. But perhaps not. For Trilling's preface to "Bartleby the Scrivener" does not end here. It ends instead with an ironic afterthought occasioned by Melville's original highlighting of the nameless narrator's complicating point of view:

> An important complication is added to the story of Bartleby's fate by the character and the plight of the nameless narrator. No one could have behaved in a more forbearing and compassionate way then this good-tempered gentleman. He suffers long and is kind; he finds it hard, almost impossible, to do what common sense has long dictated he should do—have Bartleby expelled from the office by force—and he goes so far in charity as to offer to take Bartleby into his own home. Yet he feels that he has incurred guilt by eventually separating himself from Bartleby, and we think it appropriate that he should feel so even while we sympathize with him; and in making this judgment we share his guilt. It is to him that Bartleby's only moment of anger is directed: " 'I know you,' " says Bartleby in the prison yard, " 'and I have nothing to say to you.' " The narrator is "keenly pained at his implied suspicion" that it was through his agency that Bartleby had been imprisoned, and we are pained for him, knowing the suspicion to be unfounded and unjust. Yet we know why it is uttered. Bartleby's "I prefer not to" is spoken always in response to an order or request having to do with business utility. We may speculate about what would have happened if the narrator or one of

Bartleby's fellow-copyists, alone with him in the office, had had occasion to say, "Bartleby, I feel sick and faint. Would you help me to the couch and fetch me a glass of water?" Perhaps the answer would have been given: " 'I prefer not to.' " But perhaps not. (*PEL*, pp. 77–78)

Trilling thus seizes the opening in Melville's fierce story that this complicating ironic play of perspective creates. He does so in order to supplement subversively, complicate speculatively, his own extremely chilling and subtly egocentric reading of this "Story of Wall Street" with a gratuitous liberating horizon of moral possibility. This moral horizon suggests the idea, the impersonal imaginative ideal, of a magnanimous mind at its creative work of judicious modulation and select refinement. Trilling's own critical fiction is thus attached to Melville's story, the way the New Testament's "good news" of forgiveness of sins attached itself to the Old Testament's Jealous God of the Law and revised it into the Spirit of Self-Sacrifice, the Son of God's Love, in whom His Father was, of course, well pleased. What else, after all, is Trilling's final hypothetical dialogue but joyful Christian duty become humane neo-Aristotelian decency—the speculative appeal to Bartleby's compassion an expression of the god of the golden mean under the guise of the ideal Jewish mother? Perhaps an answer to my rhetorical question could be given as "just so." But perhaps not. For in the artful vacillation between ironically balanced perspectives, Trilling can simultaneously promote and subvert with equal magnanimity of mind all such interpretive potentials. It may be as Melville contends that "all men who say *yes*, lie," but what about the man who says, "Perhaps so. But perhaps not." As Sidney in his *Apology* noted, such a person must be a poet.

Such ironic poise on Trilling's part automatically suggests "the aesthetics of crisis" (as Alan Wilde terms it) of the high-modernist authors, the spiral of their imaginary overviews formally arising from the ironic impasses of desire and death.[7] Such irony is deployed here, however, in the critical domain and applied by Trilling to the reality of culture as a totalizing ideological and moral force that functions in society like death to contradict desire and in so doing provokes the magnanimous fictions of the critic. This view would suggest that Trilling is "nothing but" a New Critical humanist in New York Intellectual dress, rationalizing the capitalist order, or equally the last modernist in postmodern America and the prototype of the narcissistic personality he so despised.

While this is plausible, I would like to propose an alternative understanding of Trilling's ennobling desire for noble mind, via a reading of the "metapsychological" paper in which Freud first formulates the theory of suicide that Trilling cites. I focus on the Freudian instead of the Marxian theory (also cited, after all, in the "Bartleby" preface) because Trilling uses the former to contain and channel and transform the political impetus of the latter into an ethical imperative of his own invention. Although Marx accounts generally for our alienation well enough, it is Freud that demonstrates to Trilling precisely how such a material condition works itself out in a moral fashion for an individual in a way immediately useful to the critic as critic and as person. Trilling employs Freud thus as the ultimate "governor" of his critical world throughout most of his career, beginning formally in 1940 with the first version of "Freud and Literature" and continuing into the 1950s and 1960s until "The Authentic Unconscious," the sixth and climactic chapter in *Sincerity and Authenticity* (1972).

Loss, Ambivalence, Regression: The Ritual of Reading

"Mourning and Melancholia" (1917)[8] is the last of eight "papers on metapsychology" that Freud wrote over six years in an attempt, only partially successful, to revise his first wholly psychoanalytic theory of mind proposed in *The Interpretation of Dreams* (1899), in light of later clinical experience (his own and that of his disciples) and of the problems created by broader applications of the theory of the Oedipus complex as the cornerstone of the mind's functioning to larger cultural matters, such as in *Totem and Taboo* (1912) the origins of civilization itself. Like its companion pieces, this metapsychological essay on grief and depression (which so resembles grief in many ways) thus sums up Freud's theory and foreshadows the great if still controversial "discoveries" of the post–World War I years, that of the death instinct (see "The Uncanny" [1919] and *Beyond the Pleasure Principle* [1920]) and that of the new topology of the id, ego, and superego (see *The Ego and the Id* [1923]). Both of these "discoveries" or revisions in Freud's oedipal theory of the mind come to inform his argument in *Civilization and Its Discontents* against the radical prospect of any final social solution to human suffering and in behalf of the possible long-term therapeutic amelioration—for a fortunate few—of his era's psychic malaise, an over-severe superego.

According to Freud, the major features of grief and depression (or mourning and melancholia) are essentially the same: dejection, disinterestedness, lovelessness, severe inhibition of instinct, self-reproachfulness, delusional punishment ("MM," p. 153). The difference is that in the case of grief the person has suffered an objective loss of a beloved individual through death or the imaginative loss of "some abstraction which has taken the place of such a beloved individual, such as fatherland, liberty, an ideal, and so on" ("MM," p. 153). In the case of depression, however, there is no such readily observable loss, though a loss indeed is felt and finally avowed, as is another key feature that distinguishes depression from grief: what Freud sees as a great "fall in self-esteem" ("MM," p. 153). As Freud later notes ("MM," p. 169), the final and most important distinguishing feature, however, is that the mourner, after a due period of grieving, regularly gets well enough to function as if over the loss, but the melancholic rarely does so spontaneously and continues to suffer too long, except in those extremely rare cases where chronic depression suddenly, mysteriously, and without apparent psychological cause turns into the aggressive joy of mania. (Herein lies the ur-experience of the narcissistic personality type that has perfected itself in an era of permissiveness and that Kohut theorizes and Lasch laments.)[9]

Through a brilliant series of theoretical formulations comparing grief and the clinical experience of depression Freud draws ever closer to the conclusion: that the depressive has also suffered a loss but an unconscious loss of a love object with which his ego has identified. Rather than give up this expression of libido, this position of desire, the ego wholly internalizes the love object, setting it up as part of itself, against which it can begin to direct its (self-) reproaches for (its own) abandonment in a process that parodies demonically the work of mourning and its systematic disengagement from the beloved dead, the critical process by which the normal ego forms itself.

> Thus the shadow of the object fell upon the ego, so that the latter could henceforth be criticized by a special mental faculty like an object, like the forsaken object. In this way the loss of the object became transformed into a loss in the ego, and the conflict between the ego and the real person transformed into a cleavage between the criticizing faculty of the ego and the ego as altered by the identification. ("MM," p. 159)

Loss triggers total identification and internalization, which in turn permits the ambivalence present in any love relationship to make itself felt and come to the fore. This entire process constitutes an act of regression to ever-earlier stages of psychic life: "If the object-love, which cannot be given up, takes refuge in narcissistic identification, while the object itself is abandoned, then hate is expended upon this new substitute-object, railing at it, depreciating it, making it suffer and deriving sadistic gratification from its suffering" ("MM," p. 162). Via this circuitous path of self-punishment, Freud notes, depressives take their revenge "on the original objects" ("MM," p. 162) of their now unrequited love. The ultimate form of such revenge is, of course, suicide, which through its climactic expression of intense self-hate ironically mirrors the original situation of intense love in which the ego is also overwhelmed by the object of love—but not, of course, by a hated alienated self-object.

Freud aptly compares the dread complex of melancholia to an open wound drawing all the psyche's energies of identification into itself, making any relationship to reality progressively harder to sustain. But like the work of grief, which one by one dredges up the memories of the beloved dead and compares them with an empty reality, so the work of depression, which directs the superego's severest denigrations against the internalized love object, has as its usual goal not suicide but the loosening of the ego's fixation on this particular love object, all the while preserving the ego's capacity to love: "So by taking flight into the ego love escapes annihilation" ("MM," p. 169). The primary way, then, love can express itself for the time being is in narcissism. The return of this primal mental stage is at times accompanied by mania, as energies so long bound to the passionate work of *self-mourning* entailed in depression are now suddenly released all at once in a torrent of desire directed solely upon the only available "love object': one's own ego, which by this time has been transformed almost entirely into the sovereign ghost of the forsaken love. In this complex and paradoxical manner, the ego triumphs over the object by wholly impersonating it even at the risk of annihilation: "The ego may enjoy here the satisfaction of acknowledging itself as the better of the two, as superior to the object" ("MM," p. 169). As a way of life, such a cycle of depression and mania even in its milder forms would prove intolerable for the person and for society.

At the basis of Freud's metapsychological theory of mourning and melancholia lies, of course, the Oedipus complex and the inevitable dynamics of the family romance. The loss of the mother's breast, the threatened loss of the penis in castration anxiety, and the unconsciously desired and so guilty loss of the father compose the serial, trinitarian paradigm of the ego's subsequent experience of reality, which for Freud, as for Emerson, is ever the domain of loss. And as Freud reminds us in *The Ego and the Id* (1923), the ego constitutes itself by means of the abandoned object-cathexes it suffers. That is, the Freudian ego is akin to what Blake calls the Spectre of Urthona or, more appropriately, Los, the poet-prophet core of the human imagination. For me, this dialectical working-through of loss, ambivalence, and regression to a renewed capacity for love, whether consciously experienced in the process of grief, acted out unconsciously in its demonic parody, neurotic depression, or reflected in the theoretical interpretation of the analytic situation, suggests a repressed (or secularized) religious allegory of reading in which there are three different kinds of readers: the tragic realist (grief), the mythic visionary (depression), and the critical theorist (analysis).

The ritual of reading stages itself as the fall of the sublime into the experience of criticism. The aim of this ritual is the legitimation of sublime transport as the loving act of attributing nobility of mind to another. (It is this final response that Kohut's narcissists are not able to envision, let alone enact.) In this circuitous and paradoxical way the critical reader may imagine his chosen author magnanimously again, just as Trilling shares with Melville for a moment the magnanimous possibility of Bartleby's hypothetical compassion before finally turning against his own critical speculation; or just as Freud generously imputes to his whining depressive clients the project of preserving in their own perverse and painful manner the capacity for love, even when like Shakespeare's more truly tragic characters they too are destined to suffer the ultimate negation of self-destruction. Between them Freud and Trilling thus define the purpose of interpretation, the function of criticism, as this ability to imagine amidst the least fortuitous circumstances as noble a motive for the Other as one can imagine for oneself.[10]

Such imaginative power is in short supply these days, and it is always in danger of degenerating into condescending pity, noblesse oblige, mindless rah-rah-ism, or the Polyanna-like impressionism of the journalistic appreciator. For these reasons and after twenty or so years of critical suspicion in the American academy, it is no wonder that such liberal imagination is scarce.

One reason why such liberal imagination, such magnanimous understanding of the Other, is important in an avowedly pluralistic society should be self-evident: it preserves the ideological appearances of tolerance and fair play in a democracy. But this is not my reason, nor was it primarily Trilling's or Freud's. The ability—far from disinterested or spontaneous—to impute the possibility of magnanimity to the Other speaks well of the self that can do so. Recalling Trilling's endorsement of Dewey's ethics, we can say such fictions of the magnanimous mind in ennobling the Other ennoble the self as well, and so are ideal expressions of the literary ethics of the critic, since his or her rhetorical actions define the quality of the actor, as much as they identify with the subject of discussion. The least we can expect of the critic is a minimum decorum toward his or her chosen subject; otherwise the critic must appear as silly and resentful as does the author of a novel who argues with his own characters.

Granted this self-interested aesthetic basis for the moral code of the critic, what benefit or use can liberally imagining the potential nobility of the Other have for criticism as a profession—if it is a profession[11]—in postmodern America? As Bruce Robbins has wisely warned Stanley Fish in a recent essay, "Pragmatism, Professionalism, and the Public," to define the key concept of interpretative community too restrictively can result in overlooking the larger and quite differently structured and functioning interpretative communities to which the academic study of literature possesses mediated but still clearly recognizable relations of power and dependency. I certainly don't want to stand accused of narrowing precipitously the range of Trilling's psychoanalytically based literary ethics to the marginalized "public sphere" of the profession alone. But I do think such literary ethics can and ought to function now primarily as a necessary corrective to the excesses of critical suspicion in the profession often from the most unexpected quarters.

"Nutting" Ventured: A Wordsworthian Aside

Consider, for example, the reading Jonathan Arac gives of Wordsworth's "Nutting" (1798, 1800, 1845) in his section of *Critical Genealogies* on "the history of Romanticism in postmodern criticism." In this new volume, Arac attempts to do a new literary history, full of social bite, with reference to the historical situations of American criticism from 1950 to the present moment.[12] First, the poem.

It seems a day
(I speak of one from many singled out)
One of those heavenly days that cannot die;
When, in the eagerness of boyish hope,
I left our cottage-threshold, sallying forth
With a huge wallet o're my shoulders slung,
A nutting-crook in hand; and turned my steps
Tow'rd some far-distant wood, a Figure quaint,
Trick'd out in proud disguise of cast-off weeds
Which for that service had been husbanded,
By exhortation of my frugal Dame—
Motley accoutrement, of power to smile

At thorns, and brakes, and brambles,—and, in truth,
More ragged than need was! O'er pathless rocks,
Through beds of matted fern, and tangled thickets,
Forcing my way, I came to one dear nook
Unvisited, where not a broken bough
Drooped with its withered leaves, ungracious sign
Of devastation; but the hazels rose
Tall and erect, with tempting clusters hung,
A virgin scene!—A little while I stood,
Breathing with such suppression of the heart
As joy delights in; and, with wise restraint
Voluptuous, fearless of a rival, eyed
The banquet; —or beneath the trees I sate
Among the flowers, and with the flowers I played;
A temper known to those who, after long
And weary expectation, have been blest
With sudden happiness beyond all hope.
Perhaps it was a bower beneath whose leaves
The violets of five seasons re-appear
And fade, unseen by any human eye;
Where fairy water-breaks do murmur on
For ever; and I saw the sparkling foam,
And—with my cheek on one of those green stones
That, fleeced with moss, under the shady trees,
Lay round me, scattered like a flock of sheep—
I heard the murmur and the murmuring sound,
In that sweet mood when pleasure loves to pay
Tribute to ease; and, of its joy secure,
The heart luxuriates with indifferent things,
Wasting its kindliness on stocks and stones,
And on the vacant air. Then up I rose,
And dragged to earth both branch and bough, with crash
And merciless ravage; and the shady nook
Of hazels, and the green and mossy bower,
Deformed and sullied, patiently gave up
Their quiet being: and unless I now
Confound my present feelings with the past,
Ere from the mutilated bower I turned
Exulting, rich beyond the wealth of kings,
I felt a sense of pain when I beheld
The silent trees, and saw the intruding sky.—
Then, dearest Maiden, move along these shades

In gentleness of heart; with gentle hand
Touch—for there is a spirit in the woods.

(CG, pp. 35–36)

Arac argues at length that the key to understanding "Nutting" and indeed the development of literary modernity itself lies in the phrase "indifferent things" and its cultural history before and imaginative history within Wordsworth's poetry. The gist of Arac's argument is that the poem is not about what conventional Wordsworth scholars and critics say it is: how the compensatory would-be autonomous imagination arises from the guilt Wordsworth suffers over a symbolic act of rape or masturbation.[13] Rather, Arac claims, the poem stages in the destruction of the bower what Kristeva and other revisionary theorists of Freud would see as a literary reenactment of the symbolic castration of the pre-oedipal mother that every child in our patriarchal culture envisions, in order to get over the belief in the phallic resources of the mother and so imaginatively surrender authority entirely to the "real" father (*CG*, pp. 45–46). Feminist historians of this period in English history, meanwhile, would see such repressive symbolic action as socially significant too, specifically, as paralleling the general remasculization of society after the rise of women to cultural prominence in the eighteenth-century world of the salons.

> The insights of Margaret Homans [in *Women Writers and Poetic Identity*] and Julia Kristeva [in *La révolution du langage poétique*], emerging from current feminist commitments, help us to see that the erection of literary autonomy was accompanied both by the exclusion of women from the experience that makes literature possible and by the assumption of universality that fetishistically treats sexual differences as "indifferent things." Wordsworth offered the poet as "the rock of defence for human nature" . . . yet he was "a man speaking to men," or even to women, as in the address to the maiden, who emphatically asserted the right to speak both about women and for women. (*CG*, p. 48)

For all his careful, patient scholarship and qualified modulated critique, then, Arac's point is potentially devastating. For he is imputing to Wordsworth a generous share of responsibility—whether consciously recognized as such by Wordsworth or not—for the ideological disenfranchisement of women from the cultural life of the modern world, a fate Carol Kay cites Mary Wollstonecraft as clearly warning the English public was already beginning to overtake women in the 1790s (*CG*, p. 45).

Why read "Nutting" in this fashion? Does such a reading do anything for the poem or for Wordsworth? Does it help a reader—student or expert—understand the intention of this poem as any different from a polemical tract by Bentham or its current French parody by Lacan? Or does this reading, which summons the poem's Miltonic overtones only to leave them hanging as ornaments of revisionism, primarily do something for that interpretive community whose preestablished beliefs commit its members automatically to a politically suspicious reading of virtually any canonical text?

Let me say, again, that Arac's reading, like his book as a whole, is provocative and essential. I find his work important and useful.[14] What I'm pointing to here is how a prior commitment to the established ideological position of a ruling interpretative community in the profession of literary study causes an intelligent and committed critic to be blind to his own insights. For the key to "Nutting" is not the single phrase "indifferent things" and its place in the cultural archive. Rather, it is the array of the Miltonic allusions.

Arac himself notes how the poem's pastoral epithet "A virgin scene" echoes "A sylvan scene" in "Miltonic Eden as first approached by Satan, while making explicit the sexual suggestion many readers have found there":

As with a rural mound the champaign head
Of a steep wilderness, whose hairy sides
With thicket overgrown . . .
Access denied.

(*Paradise Lost*, 4:134-38)

I would add that in making explicit Milton's repressed sexuality, Wordsworth also makes his great original less sexy. However that may be, the Miltonic connection defines the intention of the poem, which is to have the poetic narrator internalize within himself all the roles assigned by Milton and Judeo-Christian myth to Satan, Adam, Eve, and God the Father. Instead of having as its one effect the repression of women, this massive repression of religious myth actually would lift the burden of primal guilt from the figure of Eve as it appears here under the guise of the listening maiden, who is undoubtedly Dorothy Wordsworth. And the passage that Arac cites as definitive for the birth

of literary modernity suggests an even greater act of internalization on
Wordsworth's part:

> and unless I now
> Confound my present feelings with the past,
> Ere from the mutilated bower I turned
> Exulting, rich beyond the wealth of kings,
> I felt a sense of pain when I beheld
> The silent trees, and saw the intruding sky.

Wordsworth has thus retold the myth of the Garden as a simple produce of his common day, going so far in sublime audacity as to represent the presence of the deity in the Garden after the Fall in his
projection of that grandly simple figure of "the intruding sky." This is
the first act in the drama of liberation from guilt that extends to
Nietzsche and Freud.

In terms of my earlier discussions of Freud and Trilling, one could
say that Wordsworth in "Nutting" enacts the dialectic of loss, ambivalence, and regression to primal narcissism, in the story he narrates of
the boy's sensed inadequacy vis-à-vis the huge hazelnut trees, to be
followed by the mutilation of the bower, and climaxed with the guilty
imagination of the spirit in the woods and the final moral injunction to
the "Dear Maiden." Furthermore, in recommending to the maiden
gentleness both of motion and of touch among "these shades" as if the
trees stood for the great dead, the speaker is attributing to her the
possibility of a greater nobility of mind, in which power expresses
itself as a transcendent refinement of style, than he himself has possessed. Thus, the speaker's systematic work of internalization and
repression in the poem frees the woman at last addressed for superior
magnanimity of mind—the central virtue of the Aristotelian and Ho-
meric hero—to which he himself still evidently aspires. Far from sim-
plistically participating in any rigidly defined remasculinatization of
culture, Wordsworth in this little poem takes woman as he takes nature
generally: as heroic muse of a revolutionary mode of imaginative influence in cultural affairs he desires for himself. Wordsworth thereby
ironically preserves this same possibility for subsequent generations of
readers, such as the authors of *Middlemarch* and *The Middle of the Journey*.
In short, Wordsworth plays aesthetic messiah to those who can read
him, a social role for the poet that we need some historical imagination
to conceive even if, owing to our critical suspicion of the pedestal style
of all such idealizations, we cannot fully appreciate its beneficial force
at this time.

"My Father Moved through Dooms of Love": The Figure a Career Makes

It may look as if my contrast of Trilling on Melville and Arac on Wordsworth, read in terms either of the way Freud's theory of mourning and melancholia may work to liberate the repressed religious unconscious, or of how prior professional commitments can hobble critical imagination, really reflects a generational shift in discursive styles, from what Nietzsche calls monumental to critical history. It may simply be that this earlier generation of critics needed tough-minded, realistic literary heroes after the failure of their revolutionary dream and so they "found" them; and what ours may require is to transform canonical authors into political scapegoats as grand testimony to our continuing commitment to a sixties-styled radicalism in an increasingly conservative era. Both critical actions entail distortions. And Shakespeare and company, after all, certainly can survive our free-floating distortions, as they have survived every other set that came before us, right?

There is, however, a crucial difference in the quality of distortion as it defines the agency of the critics involved. Critics in the past, on the whole, believed their Shakespeare, their Wordsworth, or their Melville to be the author himself; we begin from the knowledge that the author we promote at any particular moment is a self-conscious ideological fiction to further the cause (whatever it may be at the time). The only actual and avowed cause the author once continuously promoted, however, was the spontaneous imaginative health of his critic. Trilling repeatedly praises "the force of style" as what elevates and energizes the mind. The function of criticism in Trilling is ultimately therapeutic in this sense: it permits the critic and through the critic his readers to attain a momentary stay against the confusions of resentment, in the fictions of the magnanimous mind that the critic creates through his readings of authors who thereby either become or continue to be canonical.

The following poem by e. e. cummings, which Trilling discusses sympathetically in his 1967 *Prefaces* (see Chapter 5), best exemplifies, I think, this fundamentally reverential attitude of the monumental critic:

> my father moved through dooms of love
> through sames of am through haves of give,
> singing each morning out of each night
> my father moved through depths of height
>
> This motionless forgetful where
> turned at his glance to shining here;

that if (so timid air is firm)
under his eyes would stir and squirm

newly as from unburied which
floats the first who, his april touch
drove sleeping selves to swarm their fates
woke dreamers to their ghostly roots

and should some why completely weep
my father's fingers brought her sleep:
vainly no smallest voice might cry
for he could feel the mountains grow.

Lifting the valleys of the sea
my father moved through griefs of joy;
praising a forehead called the moon
singing desire into begin

joy was his song and joy so pure
a heart of star by him could steer
and pure so now and now so yes
the wrists of twilight would rejoice

keen as midsummer's keen beyond
conceiving mind of sun will stand,
so strictly (over utmost him
so hugely) stood my father's dream

his flesh was flesh his blood was blood:
no hungry man but wished him food;
no cripple wouldn't creep on mile
uphill to only see him smile.

Scorning the pomp of must and shall
my father moved through dooms of feel;
his anger was as right as rain
his pity was as green as grain

septembering arms of year extend
less humbly wealth to foe and friend
than he to foolish and to wise
offered immeasurable is

proudly and (by octobering flame
beckoned) as earth will downward climb,
so naked for immortal work
his shoulders marched against the dark

his sorrow was as true as bread:
no liar looked him in the head;
if every friend became his foe
he'd laugh and build a world with snow.

My father moved through theys of we,
singing each new leaf out of each tree
(and every child was sure that spring
danced when she heard my father sing)

then let men kill which cannot share,
let blood and flesh be mud and mire,
scheming imagine, passion willed,
freedom a drug that's bought and sold

giving to steal and cruel kind,
a heart to fear, to doubt a mind,
to differ a disease of same,
conform the pinnacle of am

though dull were all we taste as bright,
bitter all utterly things sweet,
maggoty minus and dumb death
all we inherit, all bequeath

and nothing quite so least as truth
—i say though hate were why men breathed—
because my father lived his soul
love is the whole and more than all[15]

In dealing with cummings, one is always aware of R. P. Blackmur's famous devastation of the early poems, claiming that they were characterized by a sentimental, egotistical, imprecise, and sensationalistic abstractness papered over by the novelty of typographical tricks and infused by "the thrill of substance" while possessing little or no substance itself.[16] "Notes on E. E. Cummings' Language" (1930) is dense with such powerful and often self-reflective deprecation. Yet one of Blackmur's remarks, in scoring off cummings, actually opens a perspective appropriate to this later poem, "My Father Moved through Dooms of Love" (1940): "But what Mr. Cummings does, when he is using language as thrill, is not to resurrect a word from the dead: he more often produces an apparition, in itself startling and even ominous, but still only a ghost: it is all a thrill, and what it is that thrilled us cannot be determined" (*Blackmur*, p. 65). Having defined one of the central functions of the imagination to be resurrecting dead metaphor so as to incarnate our living consciousness in traditional form, Blackmur denies cummings this power in a way suggesting a sharp contrast like that operative between the serious specters in Henry James and those in Poe. Blackmur, of course, is the Dr. Johnson of the New Critics, most often sublimely brilliant when he is most suggestively idiosyncratic, as Johnson on Donne or Milton is, as Blackmur is here on cummings.

For "My Father Moved through Dooms of Love" is a visionary allegory in the tradition of Blake presented in cummings' new idiom. Like Whitman or Wordsworth, the sublime father of the first and fifth stanzas is one for whom loss and gain are nothing but the movements of his spirit *through* them (in both senses of the word). "Singing each morning out of each night" and "Lifting the valleys of the sea" not only echo Genesis; these tropes allude as well to both the avowed aspiration of the speaker in "Song of Myself" and the apocalyptic scene on Mount Snowdon in *The Prelude* when Wordsworth looks toward the Atlantic main and beholds the moon, like the emblem of a mighty mind, feasting on eternity: the god image of all the prophets of nature to come. Similarly, the second stanza alludes to Lucifer's fate in Milton—this Son of God ever compelled to shine with borrowed light from the Father. For "this motionless forgetful where" (the wandering space or commonplace of the Son) can turn to "shining here," this "if" can "stir or squirm" or become a definite figure only "at his glance," only "under his eyes," "timid air" being "firm" in its self-fixation.

Yet the poem, whatever else it may be, is not a demonic lamentation of belatedness, but the exuberant celebration of the dead father now fully alive as and in the Son's memory: "the pinnacle of am" where "love is the whole and more than all." Here the Shelley of *Prometheus Unbound* and the Goethe of his treatise *Nature* join hands in the transumptive diction of cummings. The work of mourning has made a messiah of joy out of the original Satan: "singing each new leaf out of each tree." No more nobler vision of magnanimity could be imagined for another than this renewable power of self-creation.

The poem thus represents the principle, as well as the person, of the Father as if nature were patriarchal and there were no greater act of subversive will than simply being what one is.[17] Our modern culture must ceaselessly transform what is, and so finds such figures of being and of masculine authority opague, impenetrable, resistant—*expendable*. Moving "through sames of am" can sound only like death to us, a fixed form of imaginative motion: "conceiving mind of sun will stand."

Only by conceiving oneself as if a little dead in this way may one ever conceive of another's greater life. And this is the curious function and perverse fate of the monumental critic.

Blackmur's contribution to Robert Spiller's *Literary History of America*, collected in *Selected Essays*, is another instructive case in point.[18] "Henry James," after the introductory obeisance and ironic counterpoint to its celebrated subject, proceeds to discover the reasons for James's great achievement as a novelist of the second order, not quite up to Flaubert, Balzac, Tolstoi. At his best James, like the narrator of "The Pupil" in his own way, could only produce a self-destructive "prodigy . . . of the novel." For Blackmur, James transforms the genre into "dramatized fairy tale" (*Blackmur*, p. 291). The reason for this more limited achievement derives from James's being too much his father's son:

> What we can see in these novels [*Washington Square* and *The Tragic Muse*] which relatively fail, and indeed in a full ten of the nineteen novels which he published in his life-time (as perhaps a greater proportion of his hundred-odd shorter pieces) is that James's work constitutes a great single anarchic rebellion against society—against the laws of society—in the combined names of decency, innocence, candor, good will, and the passionate heroism of true vocation. His work as a body is the dramatized or pictured exhibition, at those chosen points most familiar to him in his own society, of the revolt implied in the title of his father's book, *Society of the Redeemed Form of Man*. Both Jameses were basic dissenters to all except the society that was not yet; and in both cases the rebellion or dissent was merely eccentric or extravagant in life and manners, but central and poetic in work and insight. (*Blackmur*, p. 297)

The "luxury of perception and expression" (*Blackmur*, p. 310) that James possessed was accidental to the ordinary things of his society, and so his work makes only for an exquisite loneliness, crushed by the first catastrophe of civilization in this century, World War I.

The loss of that mode of life, of that privileged accident which afforded James "the luxury of perception and expression," inspires Blackmur's nostalgia and resentment. T. S. Eliot's sublime author, the James who possesses a mind so fine no idea could ever violate it, experiences a fall in his disciple Blackmur's stylish parody and ironic critique. But in discussing *The Sacred Fount* Blackmur magnanimously reverses himself and, neither coerced by convention nor compelled by unconscious forces, *chooses* to imagine his subject's peculiar nobility as a moment of self-critical apotheosis:

The one occasion on which James at all successfully tried for full articulation by direct means was in that testamentary novel *The Sacred Fount*. There the nameless narrator records the passage of the force of life through half a dozen people, with himself as the medium whereby they become conscious of the exchange, and, gradually, conscious of the nature of the force exchanged. He is their conscience and their creator because he is their intelligence; he makes them see what they are. In the end they reject his intelligence, and the reader is left with the ambiguous sense either that the author is crazy and had merely invented his perceptions or that he was right but his creations had now taken over the life with which he endowed them, with a quite human insistence on mutilating and battening on each other as they themselves chose. The halves of the ambiguity shade into each other interminably in that indestructible association of the moral life in which evil is ignorance but actual, and good is knowledge created real. Such success as *The Sacred Fount* has is by tour de force; but it is the essential tour de force of James's sensibility; it is the represented hallucination of what, as artist and man, he wanted to do for life; it is the poetic equivalent, the symbol and example, of what, on his own shaking ground, he wanted to stand for. If he could not say what it was, that is because it was so deeply himself that he could only show it in action, like a man in love or deadly fear. But read with good will and with a sense of the title kept turning in the mind, *The Sacred Fount* becomes the clue to the nature of the intent and to the quality of the achieved substance of the novels and tales, and then in turn becomes clear itself. If there is a secret in Henry James and if there is a way in which we can assent to that secret, both may be found in *The Sacred Fount*. It is the secret of why he was obsessed with the story of the story, the sense of the sense, the passion of the passion. He wanted, in all the areas of life he could reach, to be the story, the sense, the passion not just of the life itself but of the conscience he could create for it. So deep and hidden were the springs of conviction within him, and at the same time so sure the credit he gave to his actual perception, that he could not help believing what he created to be the conscience of truth as well as the reality of art. The being was one with the seeming. (*Blackmur*, pp. 306–307)

"But read with good will . . ." Thus Blackmur correctly characterizes the critic's job as being, as it clearly is here in "Henry James," "the formal discourse of an amateur" (*Blackmur*, p. 19).

So as love takes flight into the ego to escape annihilation, it offers a kiss to the emerging vacancy in the form of such fictions of the monumental writer as those in Blackmur's James essay or the cummings poem. The career of reading is thus ever a work of mourning, of imaginative sharing in the experience of loss, the series of "little deaths" that constitutes our passional life and prepares for the final romance. Such a work, as Trilling comments, liberates "those aspects of art which are gratuitous, which arise from high spirits and the impulse to play" that in turn result from this psychic work.

Yet, as Trilling also comments in citing his "great master Rousseau" on the topic of art, such ludic impulses may not always be "totally a benefit in our life."[19] As a result, modern art and the adversary culture it has spawned inspire in Trilling a final ambivalence. Nevertheless, in the conflict of interpretation between the categorical and dialectical modes of thought, between the imperatively moral kind of judgment and the anthropological or culturally relative kind, Trilling, good critical humanist that he is, always recommends that we judge only our own conduct categorically. We should always assume for ourselves "a fixed and permanent law," while generously reserving for others the relativistic and situational forms of aesthetic judgment.

In this ironic and complex critical fashion, Trilling remains loyal to the original literary and naturalistic impulses of pragmatism. For Trilling, as for William James whom he knowingly follows in this matter, the meaning of any theoretical or abstract critical "concept may always be found, if not in some sensible particular which it directly designates [by convention], then in some particular differences" of loss and gain "in the course of human experience which its being true will make" to the person or persons concerned.[20] For Trilling, therefore, the literary culture of pragmatism construes criticism as, in Blackmur's formula, the formal discourse of an amateur, whatever else it may become when professionalized in theory or in the discourses of today's self-proclaimed neo-pragmatist adversaries.[21]

Both Blackmur's James essay and the cummings poem can thus function rather nicely as visionary allegories of the patriarchal principle, their subject the mythic figure or giant form that is cast in the mind of the poet or critic. As Blackmur might say, the writer's "job of work" is to make the figure of the Father necessary to the reader in some particularly resonant way. This book is the imaginative critical story of Trilling's career in terms of the master figure that the developing shape of that career casts in the mind of its revisionary critic. My "job of work" is to make this master figure, the subversive patriarch of critical opposition, necessary to the minds of my readers through the critical appreciation of my chosen subject's potential for magnanimous influence. Blackmur, this time from "The Expense of Greatness: Three Emphases on Henry Adams" (1936), can be directly helpful again in providing the best, virtually aphoristic definition of this mode of monumental history: "We make the man focus upon himself, make him achieve—as he never could for himself in the flux and flexion of life—his own persuasive form. To make such a focus is the labor and the use of critical appreciation" (*Blackmur*, pp. 229–230). And, I would add, of critical intelligence as well in these hypersuspicious and polemical postmodern days. Certainly this kind of critical appreciation is what I have attempted to achieve in what follows with respect to Lionel Trilling. In "an adversary culture," for an established oppositional figure like Trilling to entertain affirmative notions of responsible authority constitutes, perhaps, the most subversive act imaginable today.

"Why, one is bound to ask, should anyone get excited about all this sackcloth?" is the way Mark Shechner, in a rave review of Mark Krupnick's intellectual biography *Lionel Trilling and the Fate of Cultural Criticism*, puts the question about Trilling's resurgent popularity as a cultural critic and celebrator of the tragic vision of life.[22] Why, in other words, should any would-be American cultural critic celebrate anyone now, especially Lionel Trilling given his former great fame as cold-war America's literary critic and his subsequent eclipse? Isn't our role as critics to negate, especially given the return of the cold war under Reagan? Does returning to Trilling necessarily signal a return to cold-war culture as well? After all, thanks to *The Liberal Mind in a Conservative Age* by Richard H. Pells and *Prodigal Sons: The New York Intellectuals and Their World* by Alexander Bloom, we know that Trilling's role in the "family" of New York critics (as Norman Podhoretz, that ever born-again neo-conservative editor of *Commentary*, calls it in *Making It*) was to provide the glitter of irony and complexity, just that right touch of class, to cold-war liberal attitudes and domestic policies. Trilling, for example, did head the faculty commission at Columbia in 1953 that "supervised" Communists on the staff, with the result that "only" one Columbia anthropologist's contract was not renewed (see Bloom, p. 249). One could argue that such measured, tactful scapegoating and tasteful internal housekeeping prevented the kind of faculty purges and institutional bloodbaths instigated by state legislatures around the country in the heyday of the McCarthy era, as in the infamous case of the University of California. Nonetheless, Trilling's role in this incident at Columbia is significantly revealing because it cuts through the habitual ironic complexity to some core personality that was, since at least the late thirties, staunchly, even blindly anti-Communist and antirevolutionary. Diana Trilling, as Bloom reports (p. 47), claims her

husband was seriously involved in radical politics for at most a year or
so in the early 1930s, although the evidence in this matter remains
conflicting. Whether our sympathies are engaged with radical causes
or not, Trilling's record in politics is far from heroic or wholly admira-
ble, to say the least.

So why *promote* Trilling, with this and all his other faults, as in some
way exemplary? This is what Krupnick, for instance, is doing simply
by tracing Trilling's career, as the jacket description so succinctly puts
it, "through its many torturous phases—exponent of positive Jewishness in the 1920s and radical politics in the thirties, liberal critic of the
liberal imagination in the forties, defender of orthodox Freudianism in
the fifties, opponent of the adversary culture of the sixties and spokes-
person for humanist "sincerity" against modernist "authenticity" in
the seventies." I find this career breakdown highly problematic. Can
one really be an exponent of radical politics during the entire thirties
for only one year, or a defender of orthodox Freudianism in the fifties
when one's best and most extensive revisions of Freud occurred in the
early and mid-forties and were to occur again only in the late sixties?
Or can one really be an exponent of humanism in the seventies when
at that time one was turning against the very idea of the social efficacy
of a liberal education in any conceivable form? Beyond these questions
of the actual nature and shape of the career, however, about which
Krupnick and I clearly disagree, there still remains what we share in
common: our more or less reverential turn back to Trilling (and his
circle) now, in a spirit (in my case) of critical appreciation as Blackmur
(on Adams) defines it.

Cornel West in "Lionel Trilling: Godfather of Neo-Conservatism"[23]
gives the most incisive brief analysis for such returns, when he argues
they are "symptomatic of the prevailing crisis of those who take seriously the life of the mind." West continues, revealingly:

> This crisis principally takes the form of searching for an intellectual
> vocation which shuns the encapsulating bureaucratic life of the acad-
> emy and eschews the narrow ideology activity of defending the status
> quo. Intellectual life in America has become a rather dull affair—with
> highly specialized academicians talking and writing to one another
> and busily engaged writers primarily serving as legitimating man-
> darins to the powers that be. (*West*, p. 233)

Consequently, West concludes, "recent attention given to the New York
intellectuals is often fuelled by a nostalgia for a time when ideas really
mattered, when intellectuals were engaged in intense cultural and

political affairs of this nation and when the man or woman of letters was relatively free of academic institutionalized captivity" (*West*, p. 233).

The problem for West is that "like most nostalgic quests, this interest in the New York intellectuals has produced a mythology—an uncritical acceptance of the mythic (and often self-serving) self-descriptions of the New York intellectuals themselves" (*West*, p. 233). Overall, I agree with West's reading of the general motivation and the prevailing danger for "returns" to Trilling and his circle. I also agree with his critique of Trilling's career, although my emphases are not his (I prefer, as I argue in Chapter 5, the late Trilling to the earlier). I agree that if we look in all seriousness to Trilling's career as a guide for the "intellectual vocation" in our time, what we face, if we are honest with ourselves, is "a dead-end" (*West*, p. 234). After all, Trilling and the particular circumstances that made him possible have passed away or become something radically alien. (On this last point, I agree with both Krupnick and Robert Boyers in his review of *Lionel Trilling and the Fate of Cultural Criticism* that Trilling would have disowned Podhoretz in this neo-conservative incarnation as he did in his disciple's previous phase, that of guru of radical chic.)[24] My disagreement with West, as to a somewhat lesser degree with Arac, my *Boundary* 2 colleagues, really concerns a general critical insensitivity to the personal dimension of motivation, to what Boyers, after Trilling, sees as those "aspects of experience utterly beyond the reach of a narrowly pragmatic political discourse" (*Boyers*, p. 19), which has lately captured all too many of us—and has made the free expression of the personal virtually impossible in professional circles.

The fundamental reason I decided to work on Trilling rather than Freud, for example, was that after I had already blasted in an essay his revisions of Freud that appear in *The Liberal Imagination, Beyond Culture, and Sincerity and Authenticity*, I read his novel and short stories and the collection *The Opposing Self*. Surprisingly, I felt restored to imaginative health and energy rather than the reverse. This unexpected response had much to do, I am now certain, with his generally magnanimous style of mind in dealing with his experiences, his own abilities and limitations, and those of his intellectual opponents. So I decided I owed him one. That essay has now become this book. Whether or not I still owe him one is not for me to say.

For me, as I argue in what follows at considerable length, Lionel Trilling was—in Boyers' apt formula—"a deeply original and radical thinker by virtue of his having adopted an adversary perspective on the full range of questions to which he turned his attention" (*Boyers*,

p. 19). Trilling's radical originality, what I characterize as his work of being—from early on and throughout his career—a "subversive patriarch," consists in his repeated personal exposure of "the false way in which certain views were held by intellectuals in his days," especially "the best of views" when "held and promoted by people with no feeling for the consequences" of those views for themselves or for others, "by the very fact of their holding" them (*Boyers*, p. 19) in the first place.

In other words, my concern is not with the practical potential for galvanizing mass political movements that the example of Trilling's career might contain. Neither Lenin's model of the vanguard party nor Gramsci's idea of organic intellectuals affiliated to revolutionary subaltern groups travels well to an American context. To look for utopian promise in Trilling or his critical circle is self-evidently doomed to failure and a "dead end." My concern instead is for the moral and therapeutic value in critically appreciating the development of another person's style of mind, his creation, throughout the course of his career, of himself as a figure of capable imagination:

> It has been some time since we in America have had literary figures—
> that is, men who live their visions as well as write them, who *are*
> what they write, whom we think of as standing for something as
> men because of what they have written in their books. They preside,
> as it were, over certain ideas and attitudes . . . . But in modern
> English literature there have been many writers whose lives were
> demonstrative of the principles which shaped their writing. They
> lead us to be aware of the moral personalities that stand behind the
> work. The two Lawrences, Keats . . . Shaw . . . Wells . . . [even] E.
> M. Forster, who makes so much of privacy, acts out in public the role
> of the private man, becoming for us the very spirit of the private life.
> He is not merely a writer, he is a figure.[25]

Trilling, in his work of subversive patriarch, becomes for me just such a figure: the public guardian of the personal life, and so the American—*our*—Montaigne.[26]

Chapter Two

Spectral Politics: Literature, Power, and Reading in the Early Work

The Apocalyptic Bell: Liberal Self-Hatred
and the Power of Repression

"What a miserable dog you are!" is the abrupt exclamation that concludes Lionel Trilling's first professional work, "Impediments."[1] The
story, prefaced by the Shakespearean tag "Let me not to the marriage
of true minds admit impediments," actually enacts its author's undis-
guised psychomachia; set in a realistic academic situation, it also dramatizes the question of identity in "liberal" America. "Impediments"
originally appeared in 1925 in the *Menorah Journal*, an organ of H.
Hurwitz's Menorah Society. The journal, under the editorship of Elliot
Cohen (1925–1931), future founder of *Commentary*, was devoted to discovering a "positive" place for secular Jews in the modern world. Predictably, then, the story stages a confrontation between two New York
college students over their shared if largely unaddressed sense of conflict between ethnic origins and cultural aspiration. Neither "naturally" American nor actual "aliens," these sons of Eastern European
Jewry have turned, at their mothers' injunction, to the idea of education
to "liberate" themselves.

A certain Hettner is the exasperated utterer of the story's climatic
judgment on its own unnamed narrator. Hettner is the uncouth manifestation of advancement anxiety and represents one of the educated
anti-Semite's more lurid racial slurs: the Jew as intellectual hunger
incarnate, a repulsive creature fiercely drooling over the cultural wealth
of nations. As such, he is the specter that is haunting the more refined
Jewish narrator, himself a spectatorial prig and defensively reserved
assimilator. This narrator is a sort of passive-aggressive echo of Iago.
He gets his perverse kicks from baiting his blunter but braver alter ego
with pointedly irrelevant questions, open-ended remarks, and ivory-
tower silences. His is an all-consuming ironic manner initially per-

fected as a defense against the goyim. He fears that he is at heart too much like the Hettner he hates.

Trilling's first work thus sounds the dominant theme certainly in his early career: the agonizing opposition between a relentlessly oppressive world and a desperately aggressive self—an opposition that the process of education, it is hoped, will dialectically refine if not somehow resolve. This familiar liberal theme appears here in the context of the perceived conflict in modern America between suspect communal origins and desired individual end.

Such bitter early works as "Friend of Byron" (1926) about Isaac Nathan's betrayal of his tradition and of himself and "Chapter for a Fashionable Jewish Novel" (1926) about the pretentious eccentricities of aspiring Jews who are "patriotic by perversity"[2] disclose the deep vein of Jewish self-hatred and defensive irony that oppresses the young writer of brief reviews and often briefer sketches for stories published in self-consciously sophisticated journals for upwardly mobile intellectuals. Recently published notebook entries from the time put the case most clearly. Trilling at the beginning of his career was, as we shall see in detail, a greatly divided man struggling for self-expression against the threatening backdrop of a world in which the sense of fatal anticlimax had become habitual.[3]

Four notebook entries in particular, one from 1927, the other three from 1928, give an especially good sense of Trilling's further plans for the story line in "Chapter for a Fashionable Jewish Novel" published the year before in the *Menorah Journal*. For Trilling desires, above all else, "to win freedom" for his hero, and so complete a comic novel. The irony of Trilling's intention resides not simply in his failure to follow through and fulfill it but more significantly in his notion of the nature of his putative hero's desired goal: "freedom, *of some sort*."[4]

In the first entry we have from 1928, we get a glimpse of what sort of freedom Trilling is beginning to envision for himself: "To become a friend to yourself! Emerson addressed himself as 'dear' in his journals" ("Notebooks," p. 14). Any form of tender self-regard, even transcendental self-love, is apt to appeal to a not-so-secret self-hater. Yet I think Trilling reveals more here than that truism. To be self-conscious about origins and ends without being, as in "Impediments," a miserable alienated majesty seems to Trilling a highly prized form of self-possession to imagine for oneself in any age.

Each of the final two entries from 1928 once again records the "why" underlying this goal of self-trust and then prefigures something new: the "how" by which Trilling will now try to achieve his "freedom." "Being a Jew," Trilling reveals in a common yet striking image, "is like walking in the wind or swimming: you are touched at all points and conscious everywhere" ("Notebooks," p. 15). This exquisitely precise and comprehensive sense of self and world in dynamic yet monumental opposition results in part from its author's being a first-generation American Jew during the Jazz Age. The oversensitive image suggests its own poignant alleviation—not to be conscious at every point of resistance. Either one can attain such worldly status as to enable one, as it were, to glide through air or over water, or one can become selectively unconscious, pointedly repressed. And, perhaps, one can achieve the former stature only by first inducing in oneself the latter state of stoic *apatheia*.

The longest and last of these entries projects the method for this inspired "madness" of self-discipline, as it elaborates a theory for educating "a son." Sounding a bit like a cross between James Mill and a super-Platonic Sigmund Freud, the twenty-three-year-old Trilling focuses in good humanist fashion on his hypothetical son's literary enlightenment. In this way Trilling uses his growing mastery of style to transform the original situation of self-hate in "Impediments" into this ascetic prospect of ironic self-education.

Intelligent love (what Trilling learns to call that refinement of self-hate which education is for him) will be the pedagogic measure that evaluates books, for instance, according to the perverse criterion of bad "taste," as it were, or unpleasure. If one wants to be the hero of the book, then, clearly, the book is no good. Only books that don't make one dream but retain the harsh anxious feel of reality (i.e., of "being a Jew" in America), are truly educational:

> The great books taught me, they never made me dream. The bad books made me dream and hurt me: I was right when . . . I said that the best rule-of-thumb for judgment of a good novel or play was— *Do you want to be the hero? If you do, the work is bad.* ("Notebooks," p. 15)

More is involved here than the young man's idea of education as medicine: if it tastes awful, it must be good for you. For one thing, Trilling realizes that as he comes to understand himself better via his chosen curriculum of reading, he can become his own ideal reader, he can play refining narrator to his gentler Hettner. And since the Hettner character represents Trilling's fear of uncouth origins, the son that Trilling already is here can educate the father, as if the latter were in turn to be reborn as a "son." In short, the dilemma of self-hatred and self-division as staged in "Impediments" is not to be done away with:

it is to be revised into the displaced, imaginatively refined master-slave dialectic built into the traditional humanistic ideal. That is, this dialectic becomes massively internalized as the spectral politics of reading. In narrating the story or idea of a great writer's force of style, Trilling can play his resentful self-hatred out as mourning self-division and magnanimous self-criticism. He can replay, in other words, the psychomachia of "Impediments" from the greater imaginative point of view ironically shared by the implied author and his reader, as they mirror in a finer tone the endless struggle of ego and specter.

To be a Jew, a writer, and a liberal intellectual in society is, for young Lionel Trilling, then, ever to be a battleground where ultimate victory will take the apocalyptically anticlimactic shape of public recognition of his private agony, as a distinctively individual yet ironically representative figure: the critic as a gentleman-amateur, the Jew as last man of letters. Trilling envisions himself as the essential author/reader of his own education. He is to accomplish this feat via stylish critical readings of the historical conjuncture of literature and power in imperial America from the heyday of high modernism to the emergence of the postmodern condition. Two early stories that I will examine, "A Light to Nations" (1928) and "Notes of a Departure" (1929), also published in the *Menorah Journal*, imagine such a career for Trilling in more particular ways. First, however, another formerly unavailable document sheds considerable light on Trilling's precarious psychic state at this time. It will also provide further motive for his revisionary project of becoming a sublime figure of unaffiliated freedom in our literary culture by repeatedly repressing another part of himself, "reading" it as a new species of "original nature" so that the discipline of refinement, of self-education through acculturation, can ironically continue without apparent end.

As one of several regular contributors to the *Menorah Journal*, Trilling writes a letter to its board of directors (December 2, 1929) in support of Elliot Cohen's stewardship. Although this collective effort is momentarily successful, the real significance of Trilling's letter lies elsewhere. It functions as a general guide to the prevailing—and recurrent—psychology of assimilation and revisionism among this representative group of "freethinking" New York intellectuals for whom Cohen plays Socratic guru as later Philip Rahv, an editor of *Partisan Review*, will also do.[5]

In describing the expressive impasse the *Menorah Journal* relieved, Trilling testifies to the important services the "little" magazine performs, especially for the ironic heirs of a tradition-bound community in America:

My family is orthodox, with a pretty sound tradition of learning and piety behind it. But, like most families with such a tradition and with sincere and not unintelligent intentions of continuing it, it was losing out. I see its Jewish gestures as the swing of the clapper of a bell: with the clapper hung in the bell it was intended for, it struck the sides and gave forth a sound. But now the clapper had been hung in a bell that was too big for it. It swung but it could never reach the side of the new environment. No sounds came.[6]

So long as one repeats the ritual gestures within the community's original context, one can expect to ring true. But once one and a part of one's original community have been displaced to the more expansive confines of the New World, the same patterns of individual or communal self-expression don't even ring false, they never manage to sound at all, unable to strike home.

The implications of this passage extend Trilling's ostensible argument in Cohen's behalf. Embedded in the sublime figure of the castrat(ed/ing) bell lies a vision of modernization (and the appropriate response to it) actually arising out of the experiences of Trilling's own father, about which the son had only recently learned.[7] Modernization greatly empowers social mobility, even as it drastically constrains original expression.

David Trilling, the critic's father, was destined, as befits the family's original patriarchal namesake, for the rabbinate back home in Bialystok (then in Lithuania, now in Poland), until he blew some lines at his own bar mitzvah. Consequently, he was packed off to an uncle in America to start a new life in the land of second chances. Haunted by this early failure, in which he simply failed to strike home, Trilling's father ruined every subsequent revisionary venture he projected for himself, encouraged as he was by the American ideology of success not just to do "good" but to dream (and fail) "big." His harried son, the ubiquitous reviewer and part-time teacher early in his career, ended up having to support his parents and his hyperthyroid wife, while working eleven years on his Ph.D. degree.[8]

Trilling's sublime vision of the castrat(ed/ing) bell thus generalizes his father's story into a representative allegory of the perils of modernization, revisionism, and assimilation, as faced by his entire ethnic community and its self-conscious offspring. Conveniently glossing over the possibility of failure "back home," Trilling nonetheless makes a telling point. Once a portion of the traditional community has been displaced to America, making the same gestures of expression as before, only on a grander scale, becomes a futile ritual, a glaring exercise, on the symbolic level at least, in unconscious self-castration. The lesson is also clear enough concerning the *Menorah Journal*, as far as Lionel Trilling cares to see it: to survive imaginatively in America, one must create (as Trilling does) via selective assimilation and conscious restraint an appropriate context for oneself at each stage of a career, in which one can bring forth an authoritative sound ("son") of one's own, and then move up and on to the next phase in development, but one must never go simply straight to the "expanse" of "beyond," if one is to avoid repeating the father's fate of perpetual anticlimax.

This passage reveals and anticipates much about Trilling's career. First of all, it is not surprising (if a bit disappointing) that as he is giving memorable expression to the reasons for associating with Cohen and his version of the *Menorah Journal*,[9] Trilling is in the process of severing his close ties with both, and is beginning to expand his horizons to include the *Nation* and the *New Republic*.[10] Having served its original purpose of providing a forum for him to find a "voice," the *Menorah Journal* and the Jewish world it represents is now proving too restrictive.

Second, the passage makes use of literary language, the apocalyptic figure of the revolutionary bell that Poe, Shelley, Baudelaire, and Hart Crane imaginatively revise in their poetry to produce an allegorical reading of the very real American fate of modernization, in which that fate is ironically presented as essentially past, an apocalyptic if also anticlimactic fait accompli suffered by the preceding generation. Trilling thereby represses this experience of modernization by reading it as an original nature to be ironically avoided or sublimely evaded by the perfection of a flexibly defensive revisionary style of irony. Trilling memorializes the memory that would repress him by remaking it into an instructive myth of repression he has himself authored and now would authorize for representative use.

This critical exploitation of literary language becomes the vehicle enabling him to contain the vision of modernization as a revisionary transformation of original nature that went too far in the past and now must be restrained, even as the discipline of refinement must be continued, so as to give him the power to "restyle" himself for further possibilities of expression. The literary tradition thus provides and will repeatedly provide him with ever-encompassing figures, scenes, moral exempla, and representative actions to encapsulate fate as essentially past, in a memorable revision of traditional formulae that makes possible the critical vision of further development in imaginative freedom. Trilling's imagination of freedom, of the momentary possibility of a perfect fit between new environment and displaced self that would "sound great," must master the seductive fixating extremes of divine aspiration and demonic self-punishment. It must do so by retaining as the critical measure for career success the human image of self-over-coming through the development of a classic style that has been en-shrined by Western tradition, especially since the Enlightenment.[11]

The Imagination of Freedom: An American Fate

"A Light to Nations" and "Notes of a Departure," stories, respectively, of 1928 and 1929, portray an early version of this imagination of free-dom and the vicissitude it may often suffer. The stories are based on the year Trilling spent at Alex Meiklejohn's experimental college in Wisconsin (1926–1927), a period when Trilling experienced the true reality of America and discovered once and for all that New York, that last outpost of Europe, really had to remain his home—for imaginative survival's sake.

For, as depicted especially in "Notes," the heartland of America is the place of the uncanny, a place on the one hand forever young and fresh and new, "an unceasing vortex of youth" (*OTT*, p. 44), and on the other, an intimidating hollow gyroscope of death that could make Trilling do things he must not do, like attempt to "spin out of himself" a world entirely of his own making, a living, exact replica not of Trilling and his specific concerns but of America itself, as he fearfully envisions it—the imperious tyrant-dream incarnate: "It would have no direction save round about itself, and it would whirl, slowly or swiftly, and in the center of the vortex would be the hollow, the spot of death which he had sensed" (*OTT*, p. 44).

It is understandable for an anxious assimilator to experience Amer-ica as the country of the sublime. Its great expanses suggest, to a writer especially, the grandest prospects of self-revision, divine aspiration. A New York Jew of Trilling's generation would reflexively dread the pos-sibility of his total assimilation to America's uncanny whirl. Such a prospect naturally precludes the exercise of conscious individual will. Here, then, in this apocalyptic vision of America, the Uncanny is the great original of all Trilling's subsequent nightmare images of a tempt-ing, totalizing dream, to be rediscovered in Stalinism, the adversary culture of modernism, and the "madness" of postmodern orthodoxy, all of which would obviate the need for further personal development or struggle, and so put an end to the basis of and purpose for "liberal" culture.

Trilling's defense against this prototypically "totalitarian" vision of the American sublime, as "Notes" dramatizes, becomes the strategic reassertion of his racial origins. The narrator of "Notes," clearly Trilling himself, learns to take the Wisconsin town lightly once he first "de-

stroys it" and "makes it as nothing." By saying "I am a Jew" he is
immediately "free," "the embodiment of an antique and separate
race," the imaginative critic as the Wandering Jew. This ancient innocence of permanent exile—the town thinks of Jews as a consecrated
people curiously exempt from personal guilt—becomes the narrator's
companionable solitude, his ironic "guardian angel" (*OTT*, p. 43) with
which he periodically wrestles to protect himself from the goyim dream
of spinning out of himself world after unreal world, as his student
McAllister does; or of wooing and winning the town's perfect beauty,
Enid, as she wishes him to do; or of finding, as he himself desires, a
home in the enfolding center of the nation, his New-Found Land
"spreading on all sides of him" (*OTT*, p. 51), seductively.

Yet in successfully resisting such dreams of divine aspiration, whose
realization would mean his complete and actual transformation into
another, self-made person, into the Platonic conception of himself like
Fitzgerald's Jay Gatsby, solely the effect of an alien land, the narrator
must face the prospect of returning to New York and a life of demonic
"worry" like "a constant incipient wretching." In this state of free-
floating anxiety, the narrator's mind is repeatedly all but engulfed by
"the image of blank, deep, black rest . . . the mind leaning always
toward it from the tight bleak fatigue," defensively shrinking itself to
an "integral" if "invisible . . . point" (*OTT*, p. 52). But just as his
Jewishness saves him from sublime prospects in Wisconsin by becoming a companionable, angelic solitude, so it rescues him from this
abysmal vision of New York by becoming now a "murderous comedian," the Harpo Marx-like puppet in the mind's eye upon whose
traditional head of red curls the narrator can heap his anxious psychic
blows of frustration and despair as he prepares to leave for New York
(*OTT*, pp. 53–54). Since "mythical characters are [comic] careerists,"
like Satan or Ulysses, repeatedly beginning high and ending low, the
narrator reasons that this sudden revision in his sense of Jewish identity is entirely acceptable.

The narrator of "Notes" thus masters the extremes of divine aspiration and demonic self-punishment, ironically enough, by means of
his "hated" Jewish defensiveness. He is left with, however, a blank
future when he tries to imagine what he is now to do and be; for he
feels no better than an "unformed word" without "a weapon" or even
"an adversary" truly of his own selection (*OTT*, p. 55).

> From the angel he had got solitude. From the comedian he had got
> naked freedom, had got a clean-wiped slate, had got the readiness
> and ability to receive reality. (*OTT*, p. 55)

And such "freedom" is "not enough," for "freedom must act, a *tabula rasa* exists for marks to give meaning to its virgin blankness." Similarly, the narrator concludes, "the readiness to receive and the ability to receive wither if soon they do not receive" (*OTT*, p. 55). As this scriptural image of identity makes clear, Trilling's revisionism will be one of style, of reading the transcription of social reality his mind receives once he finds "his own weapon, his own adversary, his own thing to do" (*OTT*, p. 55). His Jewish defense in this light will occasionally serve at best as comic relief from the quest to realize his dream of classic style (rather than that of the American sublime or the nightmare of urban anxiety), much as Gérard de Nerval's lobster, led about on a blue ribbon, ironically served his master's creative purposes: "[Nerval] said that it did not bark and knew the secrets of the deep" (*OTT*, p. 56).

"Notes of a Departure" does not conclude with this comic picture of classical resolve. Rather, it concludes with a sudden illumination, with the human image of the self most appropriate for Lionel Trilling to imagine as his ego ideal. Beyond all his other possible responses of "elation, happiness, eagerness, heroism, and even beyond that of a deflating anxiety like a wrinkled toy balloon," a new feeling emerges that name after name can only point to but not finally explain, a new feeling upon which the comment most pleasing to him is "Well, it's about time it came. It's about time" (*OTT*, p. 57).

This new feeling, as the comment suggests, has disclosed who in time Lionel Trilling will be recognized as essentially being quite *literally*—a man *wholly* of letters in the liberal humanistic mode:

> He felt not happy, not eager, not sternly strong, but complete. He was complete not as a story is complete that a writer sends to the printer, but as the idea for that story becomes complete in the mind of the writer over many months; for the idea will come to the writer perhaps as a bold sentence, a mere static situation, and as it rests in his mind it begins to take on little additions of significance, dropping some and cultivating others, growing and forming itself until the writer finds it sufficiently full to begin to translate on paper. (*OTT*, p. 57)

Unable and unwilling simply to give birth to his literary father, as Harold Bloom argues American revisionism proposes the writer try to do, Trilling proposes here to conceive the self as a "son" that he can begin to educate through his own interpretive writing:

And as the writer sits down to the paper he knows and is afraid that, however complete and promising seemed the idea, words will perhaps betray it, will probably expose it cruelly, will certainly change it, and so he writes with the probability of failure on his pencil.

That is, rather than hysterically revise the father, *one functions as the father*, failure and all, and envisions the reader-self as one's student-offspring, the prime albeit spectral candidate for the intelligent love operative in the Socratic model of education. It is that humanistic revision of crude political will into the aesthetic effects of culture upon the individual impressionable mind which Trilling critically accepts in conclusion here:

> But as [the writer] sits down, though he is not elated nor happy, nor has he time for any posture of heroism in the face of this fear [of failure] he knows that his thus sitting down and beginning his first paragraph is the only thing he can do and the best moment of his life. (*OTT*, p. 57)

As Marcus Klein in *Foreigners: The Making of American Literature, 1900–1940* reminds us, this humanistic culture of writing serves an avant-garde ideological function in the America of the Jazz Age, giving déclassé, expatriate modernists like Eliot, Pound, and Hemingway and immigrant scions like Trilling and his circle of New York intellectuals a utopian aesthetic base for their opposition that in the latter instance will shortly begin to inspire the radical movement of the 1930s. To become, if only at first in one's own mind, a recognized public figure representing the then widely valued idea of freethinking intellectual life in the modern Babylon, is one liberal aim for the critic that had political consequences once—and we should not forget it simply because our own times have precluded this liberating function of the idea of the writer.[12]

Exactly what the liberating function entails, especially for a Jew, is the theme of "A Light to Nations" (1928).[13] This story, also published first in the *Menorah Journal* and based on Trilling's year in Wisconsin, dramatizes the "subtler effects" upon others in our democracy of being a Jew for whom higher education is the panacea for most problems, social and personal. The perverse messiah complex haunting the Jewish teacher receives wickedly ironic attention here.

"Nations" opens with the bitterly comic vision of "the whirling rabbi," the celebrant of ritual, appealing first to the right and then to the left, repeatedly chanting, with varying emphasis upon each word, the question for today's solemn harangue, "What does it mean to be a Jew?" Trilling proposes to answer the question by reflecting on how two Wisconsin students, one the daughter of Italian immigrants and the other her Wasp friend, react to learning that their romantically idealized teacher is a Jew. But before doing so, Trilling describes what happens any time two Jews meet when out "passing" amongst the goyim:

> a sort of hot flare of something deeply familiar yet frightening [passes] across the front of their brains, much the same hot rush that I used to get when, as a little boy, my eye would catch the very word Jew in the opposite page of a book, standing forth from all the other words and exciting me to a quick desire to know what words were being used to modify it; or when, in a great space of calm of Anglo-Roman letters, a few in Hebrew type lay twisted and uneasy, dignified in incomprehensibility. ("Nations," pp. 402–403).

The dramatic purpose of this revealing reflection is to prepare the reader for the narrator's subsequent smoldering response, on the first day of class, to his Italian-American would-be disciple and imaginative emanation, a bright female student who obviously suffers from the same alien complex of self-hatred and aspiration occasioned by passing as one of the "real" Americans. Yet this passage, repeated, as we shall see, in only slightly revised forms later in his career, has a central importance for understanding Trilling.

The language about language or writing shows that the authentic unconscious—the sexual sublime—is an uncanny sense of awful recognition which addicts of any kind of suffering often experience when they first meet. Only here the secret passion is Trilling's representative romance of self-interpretation as his own ideal reader. The dignified incomprehensibility of the Hebrew letters amidst the calm space of Anglo-Roman type allegorize Trilling's own social situation. It also provides the needed indeterminate ground of possible meanings necessary for the formal production of himself as a sublime text, a "figure" of his own choice set off against such a ground and within the great calm space of Anglo-Roman type—an image which serves as a perfect emblem for a monumentally conceived tradition or canon. This promising figurative recognition between Jews depends upon a prior self-recognition of sublime difference that will inform any future experience of reading, whether of self or of other: "a sort of hot flare of something familiar yet frightening across the front of their brains" ("Nations," p. 402). The passionately immediate response the narrator suffers when he sees his Italian beauty arises, despite ethnic differences, from their shared sense of sublime difference, from their alien complex of self-hatred and aspiration. She, too, as we soon see, would like to become a figure within yet set off from the larger cultural world. As such, she is a perfect candidate for the literary salvation the teacher-narrator can offer. To anticipate a bit, she can become with his help the bride of the humanistic sublime.

For the teacher-narrator possesses the power of reading into every representational indeterminancy an allegory of that power of self-revision which belongs, preeminently, to Lucifer Amor. Consider, for example, his ironic reflections on his favorite student's seductively uncertain appearance of decadent beauty:

> Were I to say that her face was vulpine and were the reader to send his mind after the accurate picture of a fox, my purpose would be defeated, for a fox has something gay and well-natured about its face. But if I were to say of her face that it was vulpine and only the word (and not the image) were to act, to produce not visual but literary connotations, then I might be successful with it. Or if I said vulturine I might be even more successful, for there is a sort of debased nobility in the vulture; he seems to befoul to hurt himself with a terrible perverse purpose and to do evil that he might suffer. Lucifer sat a cormorant, on the tree. ("Nations," p. 403)

Kierkegaard's seducer couldn't have put it better.

What makes his student's face, with its "febrilely" burning black eyes, tender sallow skin "cross hatched with tiny lines," and surmounting "turban of heavy black hair" ("Nations," p. 403), so interesting is what these self-conscious signs of pathos suggest to the narrator. They suggest, as does the entire face, that suffering was not the girl's original fate but became so because her life "was being shaped so by an immediately present force within" that drew her repeatedly back from "the verge of beauty" ("Nations," p. 403) and the adolescent joy that should have been her lot by natural right, as it were. Because, as it turns out, the girl believes in the American dream of liberal education, that she may advance socially if she works hard at school, she is terribly ashamed of and frustrated by her tradition-oriented Italian family, who when she comes home a little late, for example, lock her out for the night, to her intense embarrassment and the neighbors' imagined universal delight. In short, she is as artificial and unnatural as sex or writing.

By disclosing to this student that her teacher is a Jew and shares a

similar past of shame, aspiration, and artificial self-division, the narrator makes his earlier advice to her to make such experience "material
for [critical] thought" ("Nations," p. 407) and literary inspiration much
more than plausible. This self-revelation in connection with such advice has a positively "thaumaturgic" ("Nations," p. 407) effect, releasing her from self-conscious bondage. She now can begin writing an
increasingly competent prose. For if her "secret sharer" is a *Jew* and he
could become a college instructor of literature and publish stories and
reviews, surely she—more of a real American than he—could do likewise, if not even better. Similarly, her Wasp friend, once she learns the
secret identity of her professor, also begins to write better, also out of
an ambivalent complex of ironic emulation, joining "all those who write
prose decently" and so are "somewhat saved" ("Nations," p. 408).
Racism can serve a critical purpose after all.

The Alien Complex: Truth in Myth?

This story stages the perversely messianic function that the literary
figure of the Jew as would-be leading intellectual can play in liberal
America. Clearly, Trilling's repressed Italian beauty plays scapegoat
muse to his satanic majesty. For the narrator is able to represent
through her his own sublime sense of literary language as both mi-
metic and allusively revisionary. But he, in turn, also plays scapegoat
muse to his transgressive romance-daughter. He facilitates her quest
for aesthetic liberation via the perfection of an individual style. Such a
style would encompass her origins of self-interpretation even as it
would occupy the "great space of calm" amidst the tradition of letters.
It would, in short, empower her to stage, as he has here done, a
revisionary modification of identity, however "twisted and uneasy"
the latter may appear to be. For in the modern world, as Trilling experienced it, such ironic and perverse pathos strangely dignifies the victim of self-abuse (as it were), by its seductive "incomprehensibility"
("Nations," p. 403) beyond the pleasure principle, beyond economic
interest. It is as if the American intellectual is an Oedipus anxious for
a Sphinx at all costs.

The answer to the question of Jewish identity in the literary culture
of liberal America is therefore that the man of letters can become the
master-scapegoat in the society of sacrifice, the priest of creative resentment. "By the end of the week I was not surprised that she liked
me, "Trilling's narrator revealingly observes, "for I saw how she lived:
she fastened hard to some superior and took on that person's color all
day until she thought she was being shaken off, and then she would

snap hard in revenge, perhaps at the other person, more likely at
herself" ("Nations," p. 404). The specular drama of cultural aspiration
and shameful regression to origins has here enacted its hermeneutic
spiral once more, as Trilling succinctly characterizes the pattern of
critical response he comes to recognize explicitly as his own, a pattern
he calls "the alien complex."

This phrase occurs in "Flawed Instruments," a 1930 review in the
Menorah Journal of two works by Ludwig Lewisohn, *Adam*, a play, and
Stephen Scott, a novel, and it refers initially to "that carefully rationalized sense of personal and racial apartness which animates so much"
of this author's writing.[14] As such, it can prove debilitatingly provincial,
and yet Trilling's own sublime conception of liberal culture, as we have
just seen in "Notes of a Departure" (1929) and "A Light to Nations"
(1928), would appear to be a perfect instance of a "carefully rationalized sense of personal . . . apartness" at least. Therein lies the difference. Lewisohn's error occurs in limiting the sense of apartness as a
basis for a sense of identity to members of his race alone, condemning
the rest of his characters to the status of pure examples of social determination of one sort or other without any perverse, individualizing
qualities of their own. Lewisohn thus exhibits what Trilling in "The
Promise of Realism," another 1930 review in the *Menorah Journal*, calls
the distinctively "American fate" (*SLS*, p. 28).

Citing Nietzsche's witticism from the 1887 "Attempt at Self-Criticism" of *The Birth of Tragedy*, that in slaying dragons one may become a
dragon, Trilling claims that since the "liberal renaissance" in American
literature of Anderson, Lewis, and Dreiser, writer after writer in "fighting their environment" have now become "scarcely distinguishable
from the foe" (*SLS*, p. 28). America, in this ironic light, truly is "a
tragedy," like "a god" or "mad father" you fight with because he "will
never grow up," but whose loving will in the end defeats you by
replicating in the very career of your stubborn opposition to him the
essence of his "dangerous innocence" (*SLS*, p. 28). Fighting "against
the pattern that society imposes" and "against the ideal pattern" one
thinks one "should impose" upon oneself, the leading writers of each
generation in turn reincarnate the original "alien complex" that constitutes "the American fate" (*SLS*, p. 30). The adoption of "foreign"
ideologies or archaic points of view, as "The Social Emotions," another
early review, argues, merely permits the "unconscious" work of Amer-
icanization in this modern tragic sense to occur, a tragedy of identity
which the unspoken stresses of style can especially disclose (*SLS*, p.
36) and so help the critical reader aesthetically to overcome. Since, as
"D. H. Lawrence: A Neglected Aspect" argues in praising *The Psychol-*

ogy of the Unconscious and Fantasia of the Unconscious, the modern experience fragments rather than synthesizes our powers of response, dividing against each other thought and feeling, memory and desire; thus literature via the perfection of style as Schiller and Arnold recommend must provide us with the changes to respond with "all of ourselves at once," "integrally, completely" (*SLS*, p. 39).

One consequence of this aesthetic ideology in its modern American context appears to be that the liberal critic not only must be willing to engage in a Gramsci-like self-inventory of the traces of cultural repression but must learn to accept the distasteful possibility that there may be more than a little truth in the mythical stereotypes that mark each of us and our origins. "The Changing Myth of the Jew," a previously unpublished treatise from 1930 or 1931 originally written for the *Menorah Journal*, ruefully concludes on just this ironic note:

> The question may be asked: What importance has an account of material which is confessedly merely mythological? The importance, to the historian, the psychologist, the sociologist, the political thinker is obvious. But to one interested chiefly in literature, the answer is not so plain. However, one answer may be found in almost any modern Jewish novel by a Jew. When the Jew, at the Emancipation, entered into the life of the Western world he found the myths awaiting him. Sometimes he fought them, sometimes he accepted them to his own advantage, often he went off and contemplated them in great confusion of mind. When he came to write of himself he was not able to free himself from them. Some one of them had become a Doppelgänger of his moving by the side of the real person we suppose he must be. And the task which every Jewish novel presents to the critical reader—and the serious writer—is that of disentangling what is mythical from what is actual. And that task is difficult, for in the mythical there is usually, of course, a little of what is true. (*SLS*, p. 76)

As we have seen in these early stories and reviews, Trilling chooses as his truth from these myths of the Jew the figure of the Wandering Jew, which he reincarnates in the form of the critic as permanent exile. The salient features of this stereotype for Trilling were that "the eternal Ahasverus" of Jerusalem, who had forbidden Jesus, on his way to Golgotha, to rest before his house, was "to be the instrument of a history." The Wandering Jew is a man who, marked like Cain on his forehead for his crime, is condemned to live in exile until the end of time. He is "a man who speaks seldom and smiles never; he moves gravely and nobly." Permitted few personal belongings, he is ever "generous," even to the goyim. "Dark, powerful, and majestic," he has seen "every country" and "talks familiarly of races long dead." "His knowledge is only less vast than his misery" (*SLS*, pp. 61–62). The Wandering Jew is thus Trilling's master figure for the alienated intellectual in liberal America, in whose shadow Trilling conducts his often mournful if also magnanimous work of liberation from critical self-hatred through revisionary readings of the force of another's style.

Trilling in this conclusion to "The Changing Myth of the Jew" summarizes the situation that each formerly excluded people confronts at its emancipation and entry upon the historical stage of Western culture, particularly in modern America at least during the reign of liberalism (1914–1980). Cultural aspiration and ethnic or racial guilt combine to produce a species of self-hatred and imagined freedom that testifies to the enabling (as well as constraining) power of repression, especially for individuals with literary ambitions, whose primary condition of self-realization, after all, is sustained solitary work on formal matters of language and interpretation.

Trilling's conclusion, however, also outlines the beginnings of a revisionary psychoanalytic reading of general cultural production that resembles William Blake's myth of creation more than it does Freud's myth of the primal murder in *Totem and Taboo*. Blake, you recall, divides the creative psyche into four basic parts: the imaginative function per se; its estranged and fallen emanation in the world; its demonic shadow or spectral parody; and its guiding vision of a reintegrated and organized innocence. Through imaginative creation the writer or artist overcomes his regressive and ironic alter ego, the specter, in order to recover his powers of autonomy always already disseminated in the social world. Such recovery or "divine" convalescence is symbolized in Blake by the reunion of self and other staged as a visionary marriage of artist and emanation that signals the return of the Golden Age for all humankind.

Trilling's conclusion sketches out a similar prospect, as far as the first part of Blake's myth goes. The specter of Jewish self-hatred haunts him, and insofar as it does so Trilling must admit, as in "Impediments," the truth contained in anti-Semitism that accuses Jews of being quintessential self-haters. Yet, as "Notes of a Departure" and "A Light to Nations" dramatize, such spectral self-hatred can be turned to one's advantage.[15] It can become the ironic shield of one's mind, saving it from the perils of the American sublime ("Notes") and the potential disasters of self-victimization ("Nations"). It can even become the basis for the literary intellectual's self-conscious role as the reluctant messiah of liberal culture, in a manifestation of the alien (or alienated) majesty complex par excellence. Trilling can effect these transformations thanks to his growing mastery of prose, the model for which is the classic ideal of the English plain or middle style. Spectral politics thus means for him the politics of reading the ironic conjunctions of literature and power as betrayed by an individual's style. Trilling's self-education early in his career consists, then, in learning how to disentangle what is usefully mythical (or "actual") from what is not of use in literary language: "for in the mythical there is usually, of course, a little of what is true." That is, a little of what can be still *made* true.

Literary Ethics: The Canon of Style

The first half of the 1930s was a difficult time for Trilling. As Alan Wald and others have shown, the struggling Columbia instructor was emotionally drained by the daily fratricidal battles of the literary left. Trilling usually sided with the Trotskyite contingent seeking to develop that alliance of modernism and Marxism which after the debacle of the Moscow trials Philip Rahv and William Phillips would exploit as the intellectual basis for revamping the *Partisan Review*. Aside from signing protest letters, however, Trilling never thought to use his critical writing at the time—mostly literary reviews for the *Nation* and the *New Republic*—in a directly polemical fashion for radical political ends. One could see this aversion to open engagement as personal timidity or strategic reticence. Yet, as a young man doing two teaching jobs and taking on hack reviewing to support his sick wife and financially ruined parents, Trilling had enough trouble staying sane to worry overmuch about his radical purity. For Trilling now suffered from a highly selective writer's block that permitted much other writing and even many poor drafts of his dissertation but horribly inhibited him when he attempted seriously to work on what he hoped would be the book on Arnold. The coup de grace came in the spring of 1936 when Trilling was told he would be let go from Columbia at semester's end, because as "a Marxist, a Freudian, and a Jew" it was self-evident that he surely must be unhappy after more than a decade at dear old alma mater.[16]

Trilling responded uncharacteristically to this subtler form of anti-Semitism and disinterested assault on "liberal" ideas by the guardians of the Anglo-Saxon traditions in literary study: he fought back fiercely, searching out and verbally destroying each member of the committee of full professors who spoke "for" him and his humane termination. The result, now the stuff of fables, was that his prediction of future distinction persuaded this "old gang," rather than waste such heroic promise, to give him another shot. He then fulfilled his own prophecy by writing what still is considered the standard intellectual biography of Matthew Arnold. I think we can see better what is actually happening here by examining two notebook entries of the time and an excerpt from a contemporaneous review.

The first entry, from June 13, 1936, reflects on the psychological effects of his recent success in reversing Columbia's decision to fire him:

> Going through [a] change of life and acquiring a new dimension. Principally a sense that I do not have to prove anything finally and everlastingly. A sense of life—of the past and present. Am no longer certain that the future will be a certain—Marxian—way. No longer measure all things by linear Marxian yardstick. But this is symbolic. A new emotional response to all things. New response to people, a new tolerance, a new interest. A sense of invulnerability. The result of my successful explosion at Columbia? The feeling that I can now write with a new illumination, getting rid of that rigid linear method that has irritated me in my reviewing for so long. . . . An easier understanding of poetry and painting—and of opinion—less responsibility put on people—Sense of my own stature and less concern with it. Effect visible in O'Neill essay. ("Notebooks," p. 21)

The "successful explosion at Columbia" has apparently affected a revolution in sensibility and style that is as close to a personal apocalypse or conversion experience as the habitually worldly Trilling could ever approximate. By impersonating the heroic character, by so interpreting the situation and composing the perfect kind of prophecy for consumption by an English department—one of *pure* distinction—Trilling found his true voice: defensively tolerant and ironically humane yet self-assertive and sublimely expansive in the classic style of the critical essayists he most admired at the time: Montaigne, Pascal, Hazlitt, Arnold (of course), and, surprisingly to today's tastes, George Santayana, that last aesthetic puritan.

In proposing an essay on the "ambivalent moments" in reading, Trilling's second notebook entry of the time confirms this sense of his recent "successful explosion" at Columbia and also develops further the therapeutic conception of self-education already introduced:

> an essay on the "ambivalent moments"—those moments in our reading when we neither hate nor love what the author is saying but hate and love together: when our mind is poised over a recognition of a truth which attacks other truths, or when the author has brilliantly

caught half the truth, and denies the other half. These are the most fertile moments. They are the moments of the critic: Santayana, Arnold, Carlyle, Nietzsche, etc. ("Notebooks," p. 21)

As in the earlier case of the antiromantic, psychoanalytically correct curriculum of reading designed for a hypothetical "son," Trilling is here elaborating the irony of his represssive theory of education. He recognizes the "truth" of what he reads only when it is an experience of painfully complex totality, like "being a Jew" in America and feeling eyes etching their stares into each point of one's body. This "awful" complexity is clearly akin to the radical ambivalence enshrined in the New Critical and deconstructive definitions of irony as "absolute." Such irony appears in either context as that self-consuming figure used to represent equally stressed yet imaginatively opposed meanings. This irony formally (New Criticism) and so repeatedly (deconstruction) gives a local habitation and a name to the semantic void at the heart of all such unavoidable aporias of possible meanings by narrating the theoretical allegory of its own many erroneous readings.[17] But in this passage Trilling identifies these "ambivalent moments" psychologically, even phenomenologically, as the most fertile for producing both the critic as the name for, and his reading as the local habitation of, such irony: those "ambivalent moments . . . in our reading when . . . our mind is poised over a recognition of a truth which attacks other truths, or when the author has brilliantly caught half the truth, and denies the other half." That is, Trilling's theory of self-education depends on a tragically sacrificial, rather than comically romantic, vision of the hero. The great authors provide the occasion for complexity by provoking us to produce the other half of the truth that they have artfully aspired to revise, while the mere second-raters leave no room for such a possibility; they possess little or no semantic indeterminacy, being the flat ideological reflex of their readers' fantasies, no matter how extravagant. "The great books taught me, they never made me dream" ("Notebooks," p. 15). If you want to be the hero of a work, even if it is your own career conceived as a work, then "the work is bad." In this ironic manner, authors are great because they prophetically sacrifice themselves to become the sublime stimuli of our most imaginative (because most ambivalent) moments. That is, like David Trilling, they both appall and call forth their "son's" critical love. Trilling's famous "moral realism" is thus another formula for this liberal self-education, which depends on the discovery of such "fertile" moments of radical ambivalence in each text read, so as to produce a sense of identity as the tragic critic of the textual wars of modern culture.

Literary ethics, in other words, not only inform Trilling's understanding of reading, the critic's nature and role, and the shape of a career; they also inform his vision of culture as sublimated and individuated war, what I characterize as his education in the ironic refinements of spectral politics. (I suppose this vision is what makes him a "liberal" critic.) Although difficult theoretical issues of representation and agency are not often discussed by Trilling, a self-described liberal, pragmatic, and critical naturalist of the modern mind,[18] I think his fundamental sense of such things has been made clear enough for now. By reading the accepted and newly christened classics—those works one at first resists and then must ambivalently accept as great because of the power of their style to anticipate and so transcend by provoking our defenses—the critic, according to Trilling, can freely choose one or another "genius" as his or her provisional representative in the cultural arena, provided the critic in question possesses the requisite ironic subtlety to impersonate successfully such sublime authority.

Consider, for example, the opening of the 1936 *New Republic* essay on Eugene O'Neill, then still a darling of the liberal imagination. Trilling singles out this essay, you recall, in the previously discussed June 13 notebook entry as evidence for his new sense of critical stature and range.

> Whatever is unclear about Eugene O'Neill, one thing is certainly clear—his genius. We do not like the word nowadays, feeling that it is one of the blurb words of criticism. We demand that literature be a guide to life, and when we do that we put genius into a second place, for genius assures us of nothing but itself. Yet when we stress the actionable conclusions of an artist's work, we are too likely to forget the power of genius itself, quite apart from its conclusions. The spectacle of the human mind in action is vivifying, the explorer need discover nothing so long as he has adventured. Energy, scope, courage—these may be admirable in themselves. And in the end these are often what endure best. The ideas expressed by works of the imagination may be built into the social fabric and taken for granted; or they may be rejected; or they may be outgrown. But the force of their utterance comes to us over millennia. We do not read Sophocles or Aeschylus for the right answer; we read them for the force with which they represent life and attack its moral complexity. In O'Neill, despite many failures of his art and thought, this force is inescapable.[19]

Trilling begins "The Genius of O'Neill" in typical humanist fashion by subsuming his topic under some suitably resonant, subject-oriented abstraction, one of what Hemingway curses in *A Farewell to Arms* as the "big words," like family, nation, or race, that sanctify wars. Here the lofty denomination is, of course, "genius." By using such terms, Trilling is able to become sublimely expansive, in the mode of the history of ideas and of "great books" education, in what Irving Howe characterizes as the New York Intellectuals' "style of brilliance," which combines immense scope of reference with intense, if often allusive, polemic, all in the name of the creation of a distinctive voice. Trilling, in noting the modern change of attitude toward genius, nevertheless reaffirms this traditional category of aesthetics and literary criticism, purely on the basis of "the force of style" ("O'Neill," p. 179), and anticipates Howe's critical definition of the literary (rather than political) achievement of the New York Intellectuals.[20]

But this reaffirmation of a traditional literary category does serve a generally therapeutic end. Since the spectacle of the human mind in action, what Emerson calls "the active soul," is, as dramatized here, revivifying by a natural kind of sympathetic magic or mental music, then the sublimely expansive utterance, however questionably based or reaffirmed, can stage this very drama of imaginative transcendence of chronic passivity. "The force of style" thus retains aesthetic value as a creative stimulus that inspires and enacts the moments of radical ambivalence eloquently suffered by the critical reader, even if the specific content of such utterances and the particular courses of potential action they entail no longer pertain—for one reason or another—to current forms of life.

Although O'Neill is the alpha and omega of the paragraph, for example, he, like the other authors Trilling will put to the test of style, is more an occasion for Trilling's "essay" (in miniature here) then a substantial unchangeable "subject." In a few short years, O'Neill will dwindle considerably in Trilling's estimation. (See the discussion of the essay "Reality in America" in Chapter 3.) And yet, "the force of style," like the passion of love, still animates Trilling's second thoughts about O'Neill as about other figures he continues to address.

The motive for Trilling's revisionism should be evident from all that has been said so far. The critical victim of self-hatred can ironically impersonate a current literary favorite (canonical or otherwise) and thereby effect a classic union of imaginative sympathy, "a marriage of true minds," that involves a narcissistically motivated self-overcoming of radical ambivalence, in a quest for the perfection of an individual style. Fulfillment of the representative quest would rescue (among other things) liberal culture from the worst excesses of our American fate of replicating in our opposition the very authoritarian "madness"

of the country we lament, by promoting a sacrificial critical consciousness as the necessary corrective to our grandiose idealisms. Such "success" would also ensure a niche in the Western pantheon of classic
writers for Lionel Trilling, son of an immigrant Jewish tailor who could
never "strike home" and "ring true" in anything he ever attempted,
even if the authors used to facilitate this end thereby become, in the
intellectual equivalent of serial monogamy, the scapegoat muses of the
quest.[21] These "spectral politics" of Trilling's self-education in reading
thus define the psychic mastery of the formal conjunctions of literature
and power in the early work as "literary ethics."

While this analysis is correct intellectually, emotionally its terms are
a bit loaded, one-sided. After all, is it so wicked of Trilling to desire
fame as a man of letters in his time? One can envision far more destructive pursuits of happiness. More significantly, however, "the style of
brilliance," perfected by Trilling in a characteristically English-sound-
ing mode, does manage to achieve, as Irving Howe himself is forced to
note, representative status in middle-class literary culture for members
of a formerly excluded racial/ethnic group:

> The real contribution of the New York writers was creating a new,
> and for this country, almost exotic, style of work . . . . The kind of
> essay they wrote was likely to be wide-ranging in reference, melding
> notions about literature and politics, sometimes announcing itself as
> a study of a writer or literary group but usually taut with a pressure
> to "go beyond" its subject, toward some encompassing moral or
> social observation. (Howe, p. 41)

To make an original contribution to the modern development of an
admittedly minor genre, the critical essay, is something, even if the
style of brilliance—self-consciously "knotty or flashy," professionally
antiprofessional with its "free-lance dash," "daring hypothesis," and
"knockabout synthesis" (Howe, p. 41)—easily falls prey, in Mailer and
Podhoretz, to its own striving after success by becoming dilettantish
and self-parodic, a ridiculous parrotlike echo of its own straining to
become or remain sublime. Any mode of discourse can be equally
abused or perverted by weaker minds.

The question really goes beyond how we judge Trilling's representative stylistic achievement, as anticipated in microcosm by the opening of his 1936 O'Neill essay. For, as Bruce Robbins and his authority
Magli Larson both argue, the moment of cultural history in which
Trilling and "the style of brilliance" flourish is an early moment in
the professionalization of literary criticism. This is the time when the

model for the critic's activity is the gentleman amateur, the "natural" aristocrat in the liberal republic of letters, for whom the commodity to be monopolized and administered is a form not of scientific or technical expertise but of critical experience in imaginative survival. What Larson tells us in effect, Robbins claims, "is that academics is *not* a profession—if by profession we mean doctors and lawyers . . . we are closer to social workers than to doctors."[22] Consequently, Trilling's achievement of representative status does have a historic and moral as well as formal significance. It means, most generally, that he provided many people with what they perceived to be a species of wisdom.[23]

"Wisdom"? What can that word possibly mean now? I know what it used to mean for literary critics with the Arnoldian gleam in their eyes. It meant a flexibility of mind that when faced with what appeared to be the facts admitted as much, no matter how adverse they were to one's own position. The classic example of this sort of thing occurs in Arnold's "The Function of Criticism at the Present Time" when he praises Edmund Burke for confessing, in the midst of his conservative critique of the French Revolution and long before the signs of the times revealed the certain course of history, that further resistance to its egalitarian principles would be perversely obstinate and ironically self-defeatist. This act of self-overcoming—imaginatively gratuitous as it is—defines the nature of the wisdom critical humanists like Trilling and Arnold assumed as both their object of study and subject of instruction. One could christen it for convenience sake "prophetic irony."

Several conditions make faith in such critical power possible. As Trilling's 1937 essay on Willa Cather suggests, one was the strangely captivating vision of American literature as a series of heroic defeats suffered by writer after writer from one generation to the next, due to our "pioneer" mentality that prefers to experiment with "the idea of things than to perfect any one experiment" (*SLS*, pp. 92–93). This complex fate of being an American requires the realistic guidance of the critic; in addition, the new progressive spirit, as "The America of John Dos Passos" (1938) argues, also runs to excess by all but overwhelming the individual, for good or ill depending on the scenario, with the power of social forces rigidly to determine even the most imaginative writer's prospects. Americans, for either reason, would appear to relish being defeated before they have begun. In this context, the ironic flexibility, self-conscious complexity, and transcendent style espoused by critical humanism naturally seem to Trilling the perfect antidote to the customary self-defeat of Americans.

"The America of John Dos Passos" gives the most ample expression to Trilling's early Arnoldian faith, so much so that he repeats portions of its formulation throughout *Matthew Arnold* (1939) and, indeed, throughout his career (see, especially, the conclusion to "Wordsworth and the Rabbis" in *The Opposing Self* [1955] and *Sincerity and Authenticity* [1972], passim). I quote the relevant passages in toto here for clarity and convenience sake.

> The moral assumption on which Dos Passos seems to work was expressed by John Dewey some thirty years ago [in his *Ethics*]; there are certain moral situations, Dewey says, where we cannot decide between the ends; we are forced to make our moral choice in terms of our preference for one kind of character or another: "What sort of an agent, of a person shall he be? This is the question finally at stake in any genuinely moral situation: What shall the agent *be*? What sort of character shall he assume? On its face, the question is what he shall *do*, shall he act for this or that end. But the incompatibility of the ends forces the issue back into the questions of the kind of self-hood, of agency involved in the respective ends." (*SLS*, p. 109)

The early stories for the *Menorah Journal* anticipate Trilling's aesthetic turn to Dewey's pragmatist axiology. In an age of conflicting interpretive communities, such a literary test of uncertain moral codes makes sense, since the quality of personality is the last albeit embattled value left in liberal America. And it is the modern novel that has become our "singe-ing" school, the source of the most relevant touchstones of value—particularly for the progressive middle class, Trilling's chosen readership despite its often debilitating effects on its writers.[24]

> The modern novel, with its devices for investigating the quality of character, is the aesthetic form almost specifically called forth to exercise this modern way of judgment [that Dewey recommends and Dos Passos in *USA* practices]. [For] the novelist goes where the law cannot go; he tells the truth where the formulations of even the subtlest ethical theorist cannot. He turns the moral values inside out to question the worth of the deed by looking not at its actual outcome but at its tone and style. He is subversive of dominant morality and under his influence we learn to praise what dominant morality condemns, he reminds us that benevolence may be aggression, that the highest idealism may corrupt. Finally, he gives us the models or the examples by which, half unconsciously, we make our moral selves. (*SLS*, p. 110)

It is sometimes forgotten that Trilling began his career intending to become a novelist and not a critic. For such an author criticism often functions as a laboratory for developing his notions of the kind of imaginative work he wants to write and for creating the taste by which that work will be judged. Trilling's celebration of the novel's exemplary realization of the modern way of judgment is one case in point. In addition, however, these remarks on the aesthetic foundations of moral evaluation in modern culture embody the literary ethics of the critic who would attain the status of a leading intellectual, the prophetic ironist in the Arnoldian mold par excellence. As such, Trilling in characterizing the modern way of judgment assumes centrality for the critic he desires to become as well as for the novelist he discusses. The advantage to the profession of literary study entailed by this position appears luminously clear. That this striking clarity also extends to our critic's self-interested motive goes without saying. Such are the politics of reading with a vengeance.

Yet an essay entitled "Literature and Power," published in 1940 though conceived at the same time as the final version of *Matthew Arnold* (1939), would seem to give the lie to such natural conclusions. The essay is prompted by H. V. Routh's *Toward the Twentieth Century*, a book in the tradition of Arnold's famous inaugural lecture of 1859 as professor of poetry, "On the Modern Element in Literature." Of the several distinguishing traits of modernity that Arnold distinguishes— its maturity, its urbanity, its gratuitous refinement, and so on—Routh, Trilling observes, seizes on modernity's power to provide through the agency of literature an intellectual synthesis of cultural contradictions as an ideological replacement for the great coordinating mythologies of the Judeo-Christian tradition now in ruins. Consequently, Trilling concludes, "Mr. Routh is committed to the teaching of a subject-matter" which he himself must consider "inadequate and mistaken" (*SLS*, p. 100), since literature, Routh finds, has not taken the place of religion, despite the Arnoldian prophecy of its power to grant us an "intellectual deliverance."

If this is so, Trilling rightfully inquires whether literary study is "anything more than pious," the performance of "levitical chores in the temple of the respected forgotten dead," and universities anything other than the churches of the secular Word, enclaves of a new mystery religion, with "secret magics," picked up in the course of the scholar's "mortuary duties" (*SLS*, pp. 146–148). In other words, Trilling asks the appropriately "hard" questions of the genteel tradition in literary study in an essay originally published in John Crowe Ransom's New Critically oriented journal, the *Kenyon Review*.

Trilling, however, accomplishes more in this move than cleverly promoting his career among theoretical opponents. For he also proposes to say what, since it cannot save the world by an "intellectual deliverance," literature can do. Drawing on a familiar analogy with music, Trilling claims that reading literature is an encounter with the voice of genius and so "insists on being a self-explanatory experience even for its least learned lover" (*SLS*, p. 153). That is, literature provides its appreciators with a self-validating contemplative experience in which can be found "a deep absorption," "an appreciation of style" and "an almost mystical interest in technique" (*SLS*, p. 153) that otherwise can be provided only in less complexly intense forms by sports, play, and games. The Coleridgean ghost of romantic organicism obviously haunts these claims.

Trilling would wish to revise this judgment somewhat, to be sure. As the most Wordsworthian of modern critics, he repeatedly embraces the famous credo from the preface to *Lyrical Ballads* that pleasure is the primary principle of our being, and the surest guide for literary creation. The politics of reading thus involve the elementary pleasure taken in style, even in the most refined or speculative of styles. If we continue to require that literature save the world by becoming the new intellectual synthesis of morality, science, and politics, then we are in danger of losing sight of what literature really can do, grant to us "an independent, contemplative experience . . . a pleasure, a 'gay knowledge' . . . an experience justified in itself, of nearly unconditioned living" (*SLS*, pp. 154–155) that he believes is "a social necessity" since it passes on to the reader, professional or not, the artist's "awareness of the qualities of things" (*SLS*, p. 155). Such awareness, like the transcendent self-overcoming style of Edmund Burke for Arnold, should shape our critical understanding of art, ethics, and politics. For, as Trilling ironically adds in closing, "after survival," the question of quality is "the great social concern" (*SLS*, p. 155). Self-hatred thus becomes free play.

Apocalyptic Anticlimax: America and the Spirit of Criticism

Could it be that in "Literature and Power" Trilling simply reaffirms in the end, albeit in a more modest tone, that redemptive function of literature which he so judiciously denies at the outset, much as in "The Genius of O'Neill" he restores to critical usage, in the form of "the force of style," the traditional aesthetic category of genius after initially taking note of its suspicious nature to us? Perhaps it would be sensible to read the solemn Lionel with more of Stevens' "Sleight-of-Hand Man" in mind. Yet if he is revising Arnold's prophetic prescription for literature, Trilling is also transforming its proposed critical function from an ideological to a psychological one. The critic, by meditating upon the experience of literature, summons "the force of style" informing a particular text, career, or period and so provides the reader with a new pleasure—conscious, ascetic, *intellectual* but pleasure nonetheless—that otherwise may be overlooked. Taking Nietzsche instead of Arnold as our guide in this context of *"gaya scienza,"* Trilling is turning the Arnoldian critic in the wilderness into the ascetic priest of intellectual pleasure, the textual administrator of potentially explosive affects in times of crisis. The truly representative victim of self-hatred, who is equally ashamed of his origins and his end, would thus envision a freedom from his classically American fate, in the form of a mythic literary hero who ironically measures his (and anyone's) moral vision by the canon of style he has internalized and its venerable promise of "the paradise within." Trilling's "subjects" are the various avatars of this utopian-sounding prospect. Self-hatred would thus become sublime.

"The Altar of the Dead," a 1895 *nouvelle* by Henry James, conveniently dramatizes the revisionary psychology of the modern writer. The plot is deceptively simple and, on its face, singularly unpromising. An old man, George S. Stransom, and a middle-aged woman, discreetly left unnamed, devote themselves to memorializing the great loves of their otherwise empty lives. They virtually transform their passion of mourning into a sacred career after they meet in a London chapel and agree to tend a blazing shrine of votive lights dedicated to their great dead.[25]

It is Stransom's hope that the woman will survive him to become the priestess of the altar, who in also servicing his memory will thus ironically replace his dead beloved, Mary Antrim, the woman he failed to marry owing to a cruel stratagem on the part of his one-time best friend, now his long and bitterly despised enemy, Lord Acton Hague. Unfortunately, however, his candidate for self-sacrifice still carries a torch for the man who betrayed her and murdered their love, the same now-deceased Hague. The climax of the story occurs as Stransom, about to die, must choose either to forgive his spectral other who robbed him of the actual and imaginative possession of the only woman he really loved, or go to his death ritualistically repressing the past and so lay waste to the last few spontaneous moments of life left to him. Stransom, in the end, decides to forgive and embrace life even as he suffers a final stroke and starts to die in the loving arms of his new priestess for the altar of the dead.

The beauty of this late Victorian melodrama lies in its allegorical allusiveness as the emblematic inscription of James's own family ro-

mance, of the age's religious decadence, or of the aristocracy's continuing cultural hegemony. As usual, the wonderfully vicious Jamesian
narrator exploits these imaginative possibilities to the hilt by his artful
use of figurative language. The primary reference of the story, however,
is the absolutely ironic effect of the revisionary quest for the sublime,
a quest to reread one's experience in such a way as to overcome one's
spectral alter ego and to be reunited with the repressed emanation of
the Father's androgyny in "the fields of light" ("Altar," pp. 286–288).
That is, the aim of the modern writer is to be that "echo" of the past
which becomes "more distinct than the original sound," "a masterpiece of splendour," "a mountain of fire" ("Altar," p. 260) that would
thus "reconstitute a life in which a single experience had reduced all
others to nought" by effacing "the disfigurement of a possible gap,"
by filling up the resultant "central hollow" of the self, with "passion
of light" ("Altar," pp. 269, 287, 289). In "The Altar of the Dead" James
revises the revisionary quest by showing how only in finally giving it
up may it be successfully completed.

Trilling, a discreetly psychoanalytically inclined disciple of James,
follows his master's lead in his critical career by repeatedly opposing
the sublime quest of the apocalyptic imagination as it manifests itself
in modernism, Marxism, or, as the Willa Cather essay suggests, the
American pioneer mind-set. In doing so, however, Trilling, also like
James, reenacts the sublime quest by narrating in his fiction and critical
essays the story of its repeated failure or anticlimax. Trilling, in short,
would master the possibility of the sublime quest imaginatively by ·
having his subjects, characters, and narrator *play at it*, as "Literature
and Power" suggests, and so *play the sublime quest out*. In this ironic
fashion, Trilling would save from themselves the other aspiring New
York intellectuals, the liberal culture at large, and, of course, himself
from the blind fate of anticlimax that destroyed his father and would
haunt any son's entire life. The work of the career would then become
a work of liberation in the therapeutic sense of lifting, via the process
of mourning, the burden of this hated past.

Being a Jew and being the son of a lovable but ineffectual father
marked Trilling profoundly. As most of his early work shows, and
"Notes of a Departure" dramatizes, the young critic moves between
self-hatred expressed as temptations to total assimilation and defensive
Jewishness formally or comically masking the psychic wounds. Literature, writing or reading it, appears to Trilling as the playing and
replaying of the dialectic of grief for this founding double loss of autonomy, however narcissistically fantasized the latter may be. Such
grief constitutes, as we know from Freud's "Mourning and Melan-

cholia" (1917), a work releasing, bit by bit, an ever-increasing capacity for renewed identification, sympathy, and love. For the critic, as we shall see in Trilling's case, this development in responsiveness makes possible the genuine recognition of the genius of another mind's imaginative achievement. That is, loss and the complex work of liberation it sets in motion define between them the conditions of possibility for critical response. The making of a critic entails a recovery from loss through the conflicts of resentment and self-hatred to magnanimity.

Loss, ambivalence, regression, renewed capacity for love—these are the stages of response in reading experience and in the experience of reading. As the notebook entries especially clarify the matter, Trilling begins immediately from a sense of loss, of wounded self-regard and of self-hatred. Like Eliot's Prufrock, the Jew in America originates in a pinning and wriggling world and wishes, above all else, for the power to hold himself "dear," by seeing himself, like the displaced Hebrew letter of "A Light to Nations," burning fiercely in the great calm space of Anglo-Roman type, a classic of our letters nonetheless. And in his early reviews of Lawrence and the "liberal renaissance" in this country before the Great War ("The Promise of Realism"), Trilling underscores his sense that this entire experience is not unique to him or his "people" but is constitutive of that complex fate of being an American. America, you recall, is "a tragedy," like "a god" or "mad father" "whose dangerous innocence" is the weak point in his rule (*SLS*, p. 28), since every generation of opposing selves still aspires to the status of literary success.[26] "An echo . . . more distinct than the original sound . . . a masterpiece of splendour . . . a mountain of fire" ("Altar," pp. 269, 287, 289). In short, the remounted and well-hung bell of the apocalypse.

Although Trilling, too, feels the pull of this American fate—our penchant for apocalypse—and, at the end of his career, gives full credence to his own sense of radical change and cultural mutation, here at the beginning of his career, as "Notes of a Departure" makes clear, and for some time to come, he resists the spectral vortex of American world-spinning, in favor of the anxious ambivalences of modern urban life, where the possibilities for the critical appreciation of the force of style of another's personality or work are greatest. This resistance to apocalypse, in favor of the customary complexities of human agency, constitutes Trilling's choice of traditional literary ethics over revolutionary politics, the work of liberation over utopian polemics, and apocalyptic anticlimax over final judgment.

To act this intentionally anticlimactic messiah complex out *as* his work, however, Trilling needs to discover and, when necessary, refine the ironic models of self-revision appropriate to him and his chosen audience of liberal, would-be middle-class intellectuals. Matthew Arnold, of course, is the first major figure of his ideal type. For Trilling, Arnold is in fact the classic spirit of criticism in the modern world.

Trilling puts the case for the educational efficacy of his spectral politics in the 1949 preface to the second edition of *Matthew Arnold*, his celebrated Ph.D. thesis from a decade before.[27] There he argues that this century's totalitarian "assault on mind," by which he means the intellectual elements of the progressive middle class, has "the power both to attract and to weary what seems to oppose" it (*Arnold*, p. 3), since, as he reiterates in his introduction to *The Portable Arnold*, also published in 1949, "the extremity of our condition makes us value extremity in ourselves, for men adopt as their own the nature of whatever overawes and oppresses them."[28] To counteract this sublime danger "in a time of change" our culture needs Arnold's fine example of that "openness and flexibility of mind" which attempt to see the object as it really is (*Arnold*, p. 3)—by which Trilling means not a mythical scientific objectivity but the effort of the sympathetic imagination to transcend momentarily our own interests and adopt the declared perspective of another, however alien that other may appear at first to be. What matters is that the attempt be sincerely made, even though it must always fail, perfect understanding being a regulative ideal.

This imaginative form of disinterestedness is, for example, what made it possible for Arnold "to speak for or against the [French] Revolution at any particular time," depending upon "how much of the Revolutionary principle" he thought "England at that time required" (*Arnold*, p. 10). The selective, dialectical, and historical nature of Arnold's mind is, for Trilling, exemplary.

What makes this strategic position possible for Arnold or any critic is, of course, the ability to view everything *aesthetically*. Not only does this literary vision entail for Arnold seeing the world critically as a work of art, oneself and other people as literary characters and, as even John Dewey recommends in *Art as Experience*, life as the material for drama, it also means appropriating for oneself the celebrated genius of the artist who, as Arnold approvingly quotes Schopenhauer as claiming, can repress self-interest so that he may "lose" himself in the perception and so become "pure knowing subject" (*Arnold*, p. 25) by an act of will which transcends the normal functioning of the will—which is unceasingly to desire and immediately to consume the objects of desire rather than ever to pause to contemplate general ideas, such as justice and freedom. Following Arnold who, as Trilling sees him, follows Schopenhauer, Trilling understands the force and genius of style and its critical appreciation to be singular examples of this moment of self-overcoming or, in Schopenhauer's terms, of aesthetic transcendence. The magnanimous sympathy that arises from the Freudian work of mourning, which serves as my theoretical model of the reading experience, corresponds to that power of mind that informs Arnold's famous ironic interpretation of Edmund Burke's surprising volte-face, in "The Function of Criticism at the Present Time," when Burke recognizes the inevitable victory of the forces of the French Revolution in the modern world.

Not unsurprisingly given Trilling's liberal position, he reads Arnold's influential career—the early phase of world-weary dandy, through the middle years as Victorian Hellene and inspector of schools, to the final phase of critical gadfly and religious demythologizer— entirely by means of this aesthetic vision of the intellectual quest for imaginative release from the all-consuming Will. Arnold, like his Scholar Gypsy (for Trilling the paradigmatic figure for the modern intellectual), waits perpetually for the spark from heaven to fall:

> Like Wordsworth before him, like T. S. Eliot after him, [Arnold] wrote for a small group of saddened intellectuals for whom the dominant world view was a wasteland, men who felt heartsick and deprived of some part of their energy by their civilization. (*Arnold*, p. 79)

Here and really throughout his career, Trilling writes the situation of his contemporaries, whom he would represent, larger than life through such monumental figures as Arnold, bestowing in the process on all around "character and style," that "quality of emotion made apparent" which constitutes for him (as for Dewey) "ethics" and "government" (*Arnold*, p. 30) in the fullest sense.

For Trilling, style as aesthetic transcendence, as the grand style, is all in all, virtually definitive of the writer as a man (hence "the *force* of style"), since such sublime style is "the saying in the best way *what you have to say*," "*The what you have to say*," Trilling adds revealingly, "depends on the age in which one lives," just as the best way of saying depends on an individual's unique appropriation of classical canons of taste (*Arnold*, p. 31). Given the catastropic alienation of modern life caused by the economic system and the evident failure and betrayal of revolutionary hopes (*Arnold*, p. 111), the only course left open, Trilling argues, is the one Arnold recommended, the "conscious tragedy" (*Arnold*, p. 96) of working upon the self to perfect that power of self-overcoming which at least holds some promise of giving to one's life and to the lives one may touch through one's work a pleasurable order.

As the famous 1853 preface to his new poetry suggests to Trilling, Arnold, in espousing Greek clarity and condemning romantic confusion, "stood ready to sacrifice poetic talent, formed in the solitude of the self to the creation of a character, formed in the crowding objectivity of the world" (*Arnold*, p. 135). In short, Arnold, like the narrator of "Notes of a Departure," chooses the "conscious tragedy" of inventing a public self, in a heroic decision to repress poetry and apocalyptic longings and face reality (that "crowding objectivity" of the modern world), an act which in Trilling's eyes is certainly Arnold's greatest work of art.

To develop this ironic idea of the discipline of style Trilling adduces Arnold's comments on Gobineau's *The Pleiads* and, as well, a substantial quotation on the subject from the once-popular novel. Engaging in "an energetic self-cultivation," Arnold observes, encourages "sensitive young men" to fly the modern world to distant lands or to the past in an attempt to "revolutionize their souls" (*Arnold*, p. 116). I cite now the passage from Gobineau for the illumination of Trilling's aestheticism it provides:

> My opinion is that the honest man, the man who feels himself possessed of a soul, is more than ever imperiously bound to concentrate upon himself and, being powerless to save others, to strive for his own improvement. It is the only thing to do in such a time as ours. All that society loses does not disappear, but takes refuge in the lives of individuals. The whole surroundings are petty, wretched, shameful, and distasteful. The isolated individual remains, and as amongst the rubbish and mutilated fragments of Egyptian ruins, hard to recognize with walls broken down, fallen in, there survive, towering to the heavens, colossal statues or obelisks testifying to noble ideals, perhaps transcending even the town or temple razed to the ground, so isolated human beings, finer or nobler than ever their ancestors were, testify to the sublimity of God's creatures. To work upon oneself, to cultivate whatever good qualities one possesses, to suppress one's bad qualities, stifle one's worst ones, or, at the very least discipline them—that henceforth is one's duty and the only form of duty that is also of any use. In a word, so to contrive [a self] as to count among the Pleiads. (*Arnold*, p. 116)

This passage from a once-popular early-nineteenth-century novel not only summarizes the romantic ideal of aesthetic education as well as anything in Schiller's more celebrated *Letters* on the subject, it also prefigures much that is to come in its description of the ascetic ends to which the refinement of pleasure will be usefully put in the cultural sphere from Arnold and Nietzsche to the New Critics and, most recently, Michel Foucault. Predictably, Trilling's generalizing commentary appears to question but does not discard this Faustian pursuit of experience in a decadent society for self-cultivation's sake. Yet in so doing, Trilling ironically discloses the central problem of any humanistic discursive practice: "Self-cultivation in loneliness, in the face of the degeneracy of the world, with reference to some eternal but ill-defined idea—it is a familiar burden" of the modern writer's "communion with himself" (*Arnold*, p. 118).

It is this essential uncertainty, this radical "indetermination" at the heart of critical humanism ("self-cultivation . . . with reference to some eternal but ill-defined idea"), that makes the aesthetic morality that Trilling discovers in Dewey's *Ethics* (*Arnold*, p. 131) so necessary. For without the sublime measure provided by the Western canon of style, in which the individual is represented, according to Arnold and his heirs, as overcoming mere self-interest through heroic sacrifice and magnanimous attributions of nobility to the Other, literary critics would be completely lost, at sea for sure: "The sentiment of sublime acquiescence in the course of fate," Arnold claims, defines the tragic mode (*Arnold*, p. 154). I would suggest that such tragedy defines for Trilling the nature of the sublime style as much as does that famous list of traits—"rapidity," "plainness and directness of diction and syntax," "plainness in thought," and "nobility"—which Arnold in *On Translating Homer* claims mark the grand style from the Greek classics to Shakespeare and the finest European modern writers (*Arnold*, p. 168).

For Trilling, in other words, the sublime fundamentally is a psychological experience, rather than a purely rhetorical or grammatical effect of linguistic performances. Such an experience is best characterized for him by the report Sir Joshua Reynolds makes about the nature of Bouchardon's response on first reading Homer—a formula for the sublime to which Trilling returns in "The Fate of Pleasure" (1963): "[Bouchardon's] whole frame appeared to himself to be enlarged, and all nature which surrounded him, diminished to atoms" (*Arnold*, p. 174). Filled, finally, by the chosen literary Father's stylish transcript of self-overcoming, the critical Son, thanks to the work of liberation from oedipal resentments and guilty self-hatred, is himself likewise transported beyond the constraining structures that are always taken for "all nature." The spectral vortex, the spot of death, of the would-be American dreamer is thus healed momentarily by a symbolic action of social dimension: under the cover of his defensively adopted critical persona Trilling and the canonical tradition can once more contract the sublime—now *at his pleasure*, however.

But there is one irony in Trilling's use of Arnold to endorse this liberal sublime, the spectral politics of education. If we reflect on the passage from Reynolds, especially in light of the revealing disgust with the actual public sphere found in Gobineau's novel, we realize that to experience the sublime moment as a sympathetic meeting of minds between the Great Dead and the skeptical son, one must already be an isolated, transported reader for whom the "whole frame" of things dwindles to tiny atoms, even as the sense of the self enlarges to assume the world. Or, as Northrop Frye has envisioned, the reader at the highest reaches of vision (or anagogic symbolism) becomes a Giant Human Form Divine in whose fiery lineaments the universe is contained.[29] Yet Trilling, in desiring to preserve this aesthetic possibility of the will, also desires to avoid the extremes of divine presumption and demonic deflation inherent in any experience of the sublime, so as to carve out a middle ground of commonplace or conventional authority. To achieve this end, he must follow Arnold in contradictorily positing aesthetic transcendence as the primary guarantor of the "ideal" or "best," that is, public, self.

As the parabolic racial theories in Arnold's *On the Study of Celtic Literature* suggest to Trilling (*Arnold*, pp. 190 and 232), this self can balance its various elements (rather than exclude any), and so is mature, magnanimous, and well-rounded or "modern" enough to indulge ironically (rather than fixate permanently) in the quest for the sublime. For this self there are deep down "only duties and no rights" (*Arnold*, p. 285). Even the great myths of the traditional religions serve only to compose for such a self the "moral theater" (*Arnold*, p. 322) in which this self has been schooled by the ages to see "renunciation as the Aristotelian entelechy or final form of its being" (*Arnold*, p. 342). Performing what St. Paul called a Necrosis, dying like Jesus to the flesh that "one may live in the mind" (*Arnold*, p. 350), this self, like the narrator of "A Light to Nations," helps to make up the saving remnant in liberal culture (*Arnold*, pp. 395–399), for whom "the saying of a small thing well may make human speech and human life important" (*Arnold*, p. 329).

The subject of Lionel Trilling's work is the education of the will in a time when anything is possible and so nothing has meaning. Given such a nihilistic prospect, Trilling deliberately represses the extremes of experience, whether of origin or of end, in an ironic version of the sublime quest to imagine a freedom for the self beyond *ressentiment* that will permit the aesthetic use of pleasure, as measured by the canonical models (like Arnold) enshrined in tradition. The spirit of criticism for Trilling, therefore, arises from the condition of a will that wills its own heroic anticlimax, short of apocalypse of any sort. In this displaced fashion, Trilling recovers the "style" of his real father.

I want to be clear on this central topic of Trilling's ironic hero worship and monumental criticism. His several later disavowals of exclusive affiliation with the American Jewish community—"for me it could now only be a posture and a falsehood"[30]—follow from the "castrat(ed/ing) bell" letter written in support of Elliot Cohen's stewardship of the *Menorah Journal*. All these statements of independence testify to Trilling's fear that achieving representative status within one selective context, however vociferous and influential, might compromise intellectual integrity. This is why the heroic role for Trilling must always conform to the educational model of literary ethics he derived in part from Dewey and in part from the Columbia University mystique of intelligence, which in the 1920s "was directed to showing young men how they might escape from their lower-middle-class upbringings by putting before them great models of thought, feeling, and imagination, and great issues which suggested the close interrelation of the private and personal life with the public life, with life in society."[31] For Trilling and his generation, we should remember, the canon of the grand style proved liberating. In the contemporary critical rush to oppose the traditional canon, we would do well to reflect, especially in light of the growing conservative reaction, on its liberalizing function. If Edwin Meese had experienced the force of style in Paul Valéry's critical appreciation "The Method of Leonardo da Vinci," how could he ever hold the views and promote the policies he tried to stuff down the country's throat?

Self-conscious detachment from any position he might passionately adopt defines Trilling's ironically heroic stance. Trilling thereby protects his imaginative freedom from suffering the uniquely American fate of willing self-defeat, even as the patriarchal figure is restored to a judicious measure of authority. To accomplish this feat, Trilling must read the moral dialectic of the individual in society aesthetically, as fundamentally a cultural matter, that is, as essentially a matter of public style: "My own interests lead me to see literary situations as cultural situations, and cultural situations as great elaborate fights about moral issues, and moral issues as having to do with gratuitously chosen images of personal being, and images of personal being as having something to do with literary style."[32] The circle of interpretation of the monumental critic thus encloses all of experience within a literary world in which "great elaborate fights" over the "gratuitously chosen images of personal being" define the form of life that Trilling can recognize.

One obvious danger of this point of view occurs when Trilling must confront the revolutionary conflicts of the decade, which he can do, significantly enough, only after the fact, as we shall see when discussing *The Middle of the Journey* (1947). Seeing human experience in terms of the criterion of style tends to hollow out in advance the revolutionary potential of political issues, transforming them into what the narrator of "A Light to Nations" advises his student they must now become for her, too—namely, "material for thought," the resources from which marketable stories, however moral, are made. The sense of "dryness and deadness," the spiritual "desiccation," that according to Trilling was the legacy of the decade of the 1930s to American intellectual life may actually result more from this prior decision on his part and that of his circle to view life as literature or at least putative literature, than from the much-lamented radical politics of the Popular Front. For as Tess Slesinger charactizes the failure of American radicals in *The Unpossessed* (1934), a brilliant first (and only) novel that Trilling in 1966 will both rediscover and downplay, the problem afflicting her leftist friends, including her husband, Herbert Solow, and Trilling himself, is that their sense of style makes them "too deliberate to be unconscious" enough to act on their passionately held abstractions for any length of time. Like the artist-hero of Henry James's "The Real Thing" for whom déclassé aristocrats beg to pose as servants, and members of the underclass make perfect lords and ladies, the liberal writers will use their increasingly influential work to get even with the powers-that-be, especially via the education of their children, but beyond this ironic prospect of spectral politics with a vengeance they will not go. It would be in bad taste to do so.

In this context, Arnold's famous praise of irony in "The Function of Criticism"—"that return of Burke upon himself has always seemed to me one of the finest things . . . in any literature"—comes back to haunt Trilling and his kind, even as such a flexible frame of mind once helped to defend him against the "murderous comedians" of his own Jewish self-hatred, the anti-Semitic specters he both resisted and made use of to secure for himself a place in American literary culture: the first Jewish professor of English literature at Columbia University. As Raymond Williams remarks in his new preface (1983) to his classic *Culture and Society*, culture in the sense of ironic personal style replaces the religious form of salvation, and this secular displacement of an ascetic discipline helps to explain "the two extraordinary centuries which have so greatly changed the world" since the Industrial Revolution, especially in the intellectual sphere.[33]

Lest this conclusion simply make Lionel Trilling over into the priest of the scarifice, let's return to Blake on this topic of spectral politics, in order to complicate as well as underscore the aesthetic problem of self-representation in monumental criticism.

According to Blake's vision in *Jerusalem*, one of the Prophetic Books Trilling knew well,[34] the Spectre (that shadowy, often demonic alter ego of Los the imaginative creator) manifests itself in symptoms. It is that which transforms every source of pleasure into a reason for pain:

"Every . . . joy forbidden as a crime,
. . . buried alive in the earth with pomp of religion;
Inspiration denied, genius forbidden by laws of punishment.
                    . . . .
   I behold the soft affections . . .
Condense . . . into forms of cruelty,
   Arise, spectre, arise!"[35]

This classic neurosis results from the Spectre's principal work of self-hatred: the repression and renaming of one part of the psyche as evil by another part renamed as good. "A murderer of its own body but also a murderer / Of every definite member" (Blake, p. 644). For the Spectre desires as its highest and finally only pleasure the ghostly reflection of its imagined glory, the perverse splendor of self-mutilation. The pain of the mind's willing derangement thus induces a spectral vision as a kind of overcompensating side effect, the way a wave-battered body creates the dream of a dolphin gliding over the sea alone at dawn.

The "dread" Spectre in every person, Blake says, anticipating Freud on the diseased superego, takes the two "contrary states" or "qualities" of innocence and experience which clothe every substance and now calls them "good and evil." From this invented opposition, the Spectre makes an abstraction of sublime proportions that negates by objectifying the minute particulars of perception. "This is the spectre of man," Blake concludes satirically, "the holy reasoning power; / And in its holiness is closed the abomination of Desolation" (Blake, p. 644).

Corresponding to this spectral dialectic of redefinition, invented opposition, and critical negation is the work of liberation (loss, ambivalence, regression, and renewed capacity for love), as practiced by Blake's fallen yet resisting creator figure. Los first lifts the secret "sighs and tears" and "bitter groans" of the spectres themselves (Wordsworth's "still sad music of humanity," Trilling's anxious urban wretches), and then places them into his furnace of creation to form "the spiritual sword / That lays open the hidden heart" (Blake, pp.

642–643). Next, despite his own pain, Los persists in his analytic probing ("I drew forth the pang / Of sorrow red-hot"), in order to disclose his own unconscious hypocrisy: "That he who will not defend truth may be compelled to defend / A lie" (Blake, p. 644). Finally, after self-discovery of this analytic kind, Los renews the dialectic of liberation by putting his Spectre to work, compelling the latter to build a system, a place and plan, a style of future self-education all his own: "trembling in fear / The Spectre weeps but Los unmoved by tears or threats remains. / 'I must create a System or be enslaved by another man's; / I will not reason and compare; my business is to create'" (Blake, p. 644). The power of repression, that is, can become the work of liberation when dramatized, played out in the creation of a self-critical text.[36]

So far, anyway, Trilling's ironic pattern of reading the conjunctions of literature and power resembles as much the spectral as the creative dialectic (as elaborated in *Jerusalem*). His spectral politics of self-cultivation, derived from self-hatred, internalize the alien culture as an ideal that then both wounds and wins one over, redefining ("modernizing") interpretive context, inventing radical oppositions of style, all so that such critical negation may repeatedly give rise to the sublime spectacle of tragic self-sacrifice in place of revolutionary politics. From the earliest stories and reviews on the Jewish question, through his critique of the complex fate of being an American and his development of the literary ethics of style, to the selection of Arnold as the perfect incarnation of the critical character in a decadent time for an essentially middle-class audience of well-intentioned liberal intellectuals, Trilling would appear to be the "realistic" (if not "demonic") parody of any liberation, apocalyptic or anticlimatic, that one could authentically call a "work." As we shall see in the following two chapters, however, the way this tragic doctrine of self-sacrifice can evade the charge of neurotic pathology and ideological complicity to emerge as the critical creation of a new nobility of mind composes the story that occupies the next decade or so in Lionell Trilling's representative career as America's monumental critic of liberal culture.

Chapter Three
Worldly Messiah: The Work of Maturity

Perverse Majesty: The Sacrifice of Genius

In the 1940s Trilling continues his representative movement away from radical politics to the cultural politics of personal development. Trilling will argue that only the prior recognition of the immense weight of institutions, customs, and values can form the intellectual basis for any conceivable change in things as they are. This acceptance of "reality," of the "fact" of the individual, biological, *and* social conditions of existence, becomes for him the ground for all projected configurations of private or public life. In so stressing the moral quality of this vision of reality, Trilling expresses a common liberal sentiment. What makes his notion of "reality" different is the large and central place it grants to mind and its complex energies. Like Wallace Stevens in this same decade, Trilling envisions a dialectic of reality and mind that is meant to school his ideal reader in the variety of ways the *discipline of style* in a very bad time can keep the imagination alive. One recalls Trilling's early fondness for Nerval's pet lobster. To this end of imaginative survival—his own primarily and that of the culture only slightly less pressingly—Trilling, also like Stevens during these years, develops a literary conception of the heroic character, one more tragic than comic in cast, that is indebted to the self-conscious "points of view" in the novels of the mature James rather than to the poetic comedians of Stevens. Trilling's tragic conception of the hero is therefore traditionally "aesthetic" or "monumental." Yet for it to be appropriate to "realistic" times, it must also appeal to his generation's radical sense of belatedness and contingency. Born too late for the Great War and its accompanying artistic and political revolutions, Trilling and his circle of New York intellectuals are also generally too old, too married, or otherwise too alienated for the Good War and its pervasive hoopla. (Irving Howe, who serves his hitch at an Alaskan radar station, is a notable exception.) Trilling, as we shall see in greater detail, modernizes the militant features of the traditional hero by following James's lead in spiritualizing them via their internalization. The new "science" of psychoanalysis provides a heroic model of "normal" development (the "ego" being the sovereign ghost of forsaken loves) and a classical doctrine of achieved maturity (the sincere recognition of guilt) that will aid in making his revisionary project influential in a self-consciously "tough-minded" time. By decade's end, Trilling will find himself cast in the role of messiah of mental health, in difficult ironic fulfillment of the 1927 story "A Light to Nations."

Trilling's literary "allegiance" to "the intellectual middle-class, which believes it continues" the tradition of "humanistic thought," makes it practically inevitable that Trilling will participate in what Philip Rieff terms "the triumph of the therapeutic" in modern culture. For liberal humanism seeks to define a middle realm between the sphere of religion and the world of nature in which reason may operate freely, both unconstrained by dogmatic belief and uninhibited by the vision of necessity entailed by conventional science. This in-between realm is fit for both imaginative and material production in the control of the middle class. For freedom to such a class is essentially an economic and ethical issue. And modern psychology, particularly psychoanalysis, provides a defense of freedom in a strong form, precisely because Freud admits so much of the case for the negative while reaffirming a rational ideal of ego development toward a "balanced" maturity. So the American intellectual middle class does indeed continue the tradition of humanistic thought by giving it a Freudian twist that preserves the idea of freedom—which is required as a "rule" or regulative ideal—a freedom from the prospects of religious revivals and political revolutions, developments which usually are inspired by a deterministic vision of human nature and history.

In order to express his allegiance to the intellectual middle class, what Grant Webster in *The Republic of Letters* rightly calls the bourgeois avant-garde, Trilling must repeatedly adopt positions that provoke his audience by opposing its current beliefs and values. Standing ahead of and in opposition to—"beyond"—what he sees as his class's prejudices and fixed ideas becomes Trilling's "transcendent" therapeutic stance as Babbitt's Socrates. This is why in 1940 he will praise T. S. Eliot's politics as the perfect conservative corrective to the pieties of liberalism, casting Eliot in the gadfly part of Coleridge to his solemn impersonation of John Stuart Mill. Trilling focuses particularly on Eliot's critique of "the diminished ideal" of liberal culture which now, unlike in its prerevolutionary days, cannot project "a great character for man" (*SLS*, p. 164). Trilling agrees here with Eliot (from *The Idea of a Christian Society*) that "the social imagination, when it was fresher, gave the worlds of the future a quality which our projected visions can no longer have" (*SLS*, p. 165). As Trilling puts it years later looking back on the 1930s, "the diminished ideal" of liberation suffers its diminishment owing to a now-familiar failure in self-knowledge on the part of modern radicals who, ironically enough, reconstitute in both the conduct of their personal lives and the implementation of their revolutionary schemes the very idols of the cave their savage critiques of existing society have supposedly destroyed for good (*LD*, p. 30). In short, while Eliot's "positive" Christian views on politics are in Trilling's eyes useless, his critical negation of progressive humanism has a tonic effect, is "good medicine."

The first part of "Reality in America," also in 1940,[1] questions the liberal domination of American studies exercised by Parrington and his disciples exactly on these grounds. The liberal imagination no longer has a social vision of human possibility that can both admire self-consciousness and recognize reality. Insofar as Parrington in *Main Currents in American Literature* can endorse individual will he "suspects mind," that is, "the electric qualities" of spirit, imagination, playfulness, ambiguity, and complexity that mark the work of such writers as Hawthorne and James. "To speak" of James "as an escape, especially as an artist similar to Whistler, a man characteristically afraid of stress," Trilling concludes, is not only "to be mistaken in aesthetic judgment," it is also to criticize the great achievements of literary genius "from the point of view of a limited and essentially arrogant conception of reality" (*LI*, p. 10). Trilling goes Eliot one better in accusing liberalism of resentfully adopting a perversely reductive metaphysics which in the name of enlightenment and democracy condemns original imaginative insight per se as socially retrograde and escapist. Parrington, in Trilling's revision of *Hard Times*, becomes the modern avatar of Gradgrind.

"Reality in America" (pt. 1) accomplishes more than this famous demolition of liberal historiography. It also announces a new conception of the hero, vaguely Hegelian in its philosophical antecedants, that owes as much to the examples of James and Freud in their careers as it does to fictional protoganists and the developmental model of the mind. But before bringing this good news, the essay redefines the context of debate by ridiculing the deterministic image of culture as irresistible "currents" memorialized in Parrington's title. Trilling instead proposes for culture the revisionary, agonistic images of struggle, debate, conflict, contest: "[culture]," Trilling remarks, "is nothing if not a dialectic" (*LI*, p. 9). In this fashion, Trilling can more realistically claim that the representative figure or hero expresses the dialectic of his cultural moment in the sublime story of his psychological growth toward ever greater autonomy:

> [In] any culture there are likely to be certain artists who contain a large part of the dialectic within themselves, their meaning and power lying in their contradictions; they contain within themselves, it may be said, the very essence of the culture, and the sign of this is that they do not submit to serve the ends of any one ideological group or tendency. (*LI*, p. 9)

Trilling goes on to claim that the very writers Parrington condemns—Hawthorne, James, Emerson, Poe, etc.—are to one degree or other just "such repositories of the dialectic of their times," containing "the yes and the no of the culture, and by that token" becoming "prophetic of the future" (*LI*, p. 9). However insufficiently representative specific imaginative heroes may prove to be, their authors, Trilling adds, possess in this full way "the force of style."

Trilling's dialectic of genius proposes to resolve cultural contradictions by representing them in the exemplary histories, the heroic careers of major writers. Whatever the oppositions of the time, canonical authors symbolically contain them in the imaginative developments of their ironic works. A current conflict is thereby temporized, projected back into an encompassing past and then made to prefigure in its central figures a future time beyond this conflict that is still enmeshed in its own "unmaking." In this double-minded way, the past struggle and its present heir are utopianly repressed, displaced literally to the "nowhere" of an idealized self-consciousness momentarily "shared" by privileged author and perfect reader alike: "a marriage of true minds." Yet to maintain this romance of reading Trilling must assume that the heroic unconsciousness turns critically against it own self-interests so as to embody in its dialectic work both sides in the cultural debate. Moreover, if successful, such genius sacrifices its present moment to become "prophetic of the future" it makes possible, but Moses-like, can never actually profit by. It is thus no accident that Trilling often repeats James's famous exclamation to a young correspondent, "Life is nothing if not heroic and sacrificial."

From Hegel and Schiller through Carlyle, Arnold, Pater, and beyond, this monumental vision of history, as Nietzsche characterizes it, functions to transform the dialectic of cultural contradictions into the creative development of the leading intellectual whose "work"—in the extended sense of life, career, and corpus of texts I have been invoking—represents these contradictions critically, self-consciously. Crucial to this heroic reading of history is the assumption of the cultural critic's freedom—however conditioned by circumstances—to transcend, at least partially, the ideological constraints of his time in a manner felt to be pregnant with possibility. How the critic who aspires to this sublime condition achieves the status of exemplary opposition is another question, one that Trilling confronts directly in his first influential reading of Freud.

In the original version of "Freud and Literature" also published in 1940,[2] Trilling examines the ideas and influence of psychoanalysis on literary study without developing his own idea of "classic tragic realism" to any significant degree. Instead, he debunks the reductive method of reading that resulted from Freud's comparison of creative work with daydreaming by recalling Freud's own reservation concerning the power of such a comparison to account fully for the formal achievement of the artist. Beyond this clever move, Trilling not only places Freud and his ideas in their historical context in the development of Western culture and science, a defensive strategy that takes some of the sting out of Freud's biological determinism; he also gives a specific example of how, as Freud himself claimed, the poets discovered the unconscious ahead of him. Trilling cites one of Freud's favorite texts, Diderot's *Rameau's Nephew*, as his example of how literature has anticipated, in this instance, the founding insight of psychoanalysis, the Oedipus complex itself: "If the little savage [the Nephew's expression for 'child'] were left to himself, if he preserved all his foolishness and combined the violent passions of a man of thirty with the lack of reason of a child in the cradle, he'd wring his father's neck and go to bed with his mother" (*LI*, p. 36). In this context, Trilling can afford to agree with Freud—that the neurotic and the artist respond to reality not by choosing "the way of the ego" and transforming reality according to their desires but by choosing "the antithetical way" of fictional compensation and transforming the self. Trilling then reminds us that the artist, unlike the neurotic, gives a public shape to this work and life that testifies to his possession, in the form of the career, of a strong ego drive as well as the power of creating memorable fantasies, or acceptable hallucination. Finally, Trilling concludes, "of all mental systems, the Freudian psychology is the one which makes poetry indigenous to the very constitution of the mind" (*LI*, p. 52). Poetry materializes the mind. It is, for Freud, "a pioneer settler" there and "a method of thought" by which the mind seeks to master reality (*LI*, p. 53). Every person is thus his or her own potential genius.

Trilling in these measured ways refines the Freudian genius, assimilates it to literary culture, and democratizes it for his middle-class American audience. Moreover, in his commendation of Franz Alexander's reading of *Henry IV* (pts. 1 and 2) as a paragon of psychoanalytic discrimination, Trilling endorses the model of psychic development that the Freudian analyst finds exemplified in the play:

> Dr. Alexander undertakes nothing more than to say that in the development of Prince Hal we see the classic struggle of the ego to come to normal adjustment, beginning with the rebellion against the father, going on to the conquest of the super-ego (Hotspur, with his rigid notions of honor and glory), then to the conquests of the *id* (Falstaff, with his anarchic self-indulgence), then to the identification with the father (the crown scene) and the assumption of mature responsibility. An analysis of this sort is not momentous and not exclusive of other meanings; perhaps it does no more than point up and formulate what we all have already seen. It has the tact to *accept* the play and does not, like Dr. Jones's study of *Hamlet*, search for a "hidden motive" and "a deeper working" which implies that there is a reality to which the play stands in the relation that a dream stands to the wish that generates it and from which it is separable; it is this reality, the "deeper working," which according to Dr. Jones produced the play. (*LI*, p. 52)

Trilling cannot stomach Jones' deterministic understanding of a literary work's relation to the idea that animates it. Shakespeare's original intention, whatever it may have been, finds its "instrument of thought" in the creation of *Hamlet*. As far as Trilling can see, this means that in the process of composition the original intention develops, refines, and transfigures itself into the objective formal reality of art. Trilling's fixation on the normal pattern of mature development, as we shall see in discussing his classic novella "Of This Time, of That Place" (1943), reinforces such defensive blindness.

As "Freud and Literature" makes clear, Trilling's intention is to see Freud as his greatest hero whose discovery—psychoanalysis—combines scientific rigor and imaginative insight in a "realistic" (or "tragic") manner that reconciles the rationalist and romantic strains in the culture. Yet, as it also makes clear, Trilling can see Freud and psychoanalysis in this way only after he has sacrificed those features— particularly Freud's biological determinism—which define his genius as eccentric rather than central to the humanistic tradition of thought. In essence, Trilling rehabilitates Freud by assisting him to become one of Trilling's heroic characters, to complete the act of self-overcoming that the shape of the career prefigures. The sacrifice of genius that Trilling speaks of in "Reality in America" and that he finds underwritten here by the psychoanalytic model of mature development—the ego accepts loss—entails not only the heroic sacrifice performed *by* the genius in his work but also the sacrifice performed *upon* the genius in the reading of that work by his critical heir. Heroes, like gods, are thus ever consumed, as the "son" comes to occupy the place of the "father" in a new cultural context.

The "cost" of this oedipal mode of reading, as Harold Bloom demonstrates at great length, is guilt and a gothic inability to appreciate or to achieve the sublime effect—the rhetorical basis of all authority—except in proximity to the grave. This is the point of Trilling's savagely hysterical diatribe in "The Progressive Psyche" (1942) against Karen Horney's blasphemously competitive *Self-Analysis* for its daring to suggest a less exclusively tragic view of our fate. Similarly, this is the point in his more discriminating critique in "An American in Spain" (1941) of Hemingway's *For Whom the Bell Tolls*, which is guilty of narcissistic,unrealistic and un-Donne-like posturing in the face of death and the hero's self-sacrifice. Both pieces suggest that animating them and related examples of his cultural politics of the time is the specter of an oedipal motivation for his own work. Informing the force of style of the magnanimous mind is murderous rage that monumental criticism must sublimate in raising the heroic image.

Trilling's essay on Wordsworth's "Immortality Ode," which still exercises considerable influence today,[3] exemplifies this strategy. Exploiting the model of psychic development and normal maturity posited by classical psychoanalysis, Trilling argues, unconventionally, that Wordsworth really finds the loss of the visionary gleam to be a good (as well as necessary) thing, since to acquire the greater humanization that attainment of the philosophic mind permits entails that one put away the solipsistic illusions of childhood and youth (*LI*, pp. 137–144). As in "Reality in America" and "Freud and Literature," Trilling here would both lead and oppose (when required) the war-obsessed public mind, and in summoning some gloomy special effects can achieve this end all the better: trailing clouds of glory after the sacrifice, too.

What I have shown so far would modify Mark Sheckner's contention that it was only "in the post-war climate of stalemate and reassessment" that Trilling "came to prominence as a spokesman for ambivalence, moral realism (that is, the acceptance of 'good-and-evil'), ideas in modulation and the tragic view of life."[4] Trilling begins to come to prominence somewhat earlier, and as a spokesman for what all these catch phrases tend often to obscure, the sacrifice of genius: the creation and exploitation of "great writers" for the critic's own purposes. The category of genius exists, in other words, to permit such spectral politics to function "normally" in literary study, so as to enable one generation of scholars to shape another in its own monumental image.

Trilling, as early as 1940, is beginning to develop that critical focus on "the pedagogic example," that psychological "dialectic" of mind, and that selective "fashioning" of "a prosthetic identity" by means of "tragic" disassociation and "loyal" opposition, which Sheckner sees as resulting only at decade's end in the transformation of "the rhetoric of liberalism from one of social progress and justice to one of sensibility and depth, all the while tidying up the depths by purging them of whatever was embarrassing, childish, and undignified."[5] More is involved in this development, however, no matter when it first begins, than another repetition of romantic disillusionment at the failure of revolutionary hopes, or than the cultural assimilator's bad-faith myth. For the experience of Trilling and his generation dramatizes that, as T. J. Jackson Lears has recently suggested,[6] any conception of a leading role for American critics, including Gramsci's idea of organic and traditional intellectuals, can rarely apply to the American scene. Except in extreme crises, such as the Civil War and the Vietnam War or the Depression, American intellectuals scarcely exist for the rest of the nation. In addition, as Trilling's case exemplifies, members of the same generation rarely develop at the same pace or in the same ways. Even their commentators cannot agree on the curve of their careers. Just as American culture encourages a general heterogeneity of personal styles and attitudes, a radical cultural lag in which many apparently historically superseded forms of life coexist along with the latest developments; so, too, it promotes this essentially disjunctive form of temporality among members of the intellectual class. Should Trilling, for example, in the 1940s, as a representative New York writer affiliated with the Trotskyite *Partisan Review*, be seen as an organic intellectual expressing in modern terms the introspective bent of his "people," and in 1950, when these essays are collected in *The Liberal Imagination* to great éclat, as having suddenly become a traditional intellectual translating revolutionary politics into mental theater? What if, in other words—as used to be the case for group after previously excluded group in liberal America—the "revolutionary" end is to be recognized and included within the dominant systems of representation in American culture and that end is largely being achieved?

Given the peculiar situation of repressed groups in America, repeatedly aspiring to and attaining middle-class status, the Leninist rhetoric of leading intellectual and vanguard party and all the rest cannot simply be put to work here. R. P. Blackmur's relatively early analysis, "Lionel Trilling: The Politics of Human Power" (1950), however, contains some suggestions for an effective perspective on this problem of the successful American intellectual in liberal America.[7]

Blackmur begins by noting the prophetic stance that Trilling adopts in the essays written in the 1940s and collected in *The Liberal Imagination* in 1950. This stance is doubly prophetic. Trilling in these essays not only "cultivates a mind not entirely his own" (Blackmur, p. 32) by ironically impersonating the public mind and correcting or opposing its views when necessary; his own views expressed therein tend always to cultivate as well a further "meaning that is not yet" (Blackmur, p. 32), a final revelation ever more about to be. Trilling, according to Blackmur, searches out "special forms of reality" in the literature he discusses in order to control by instructive or cautionary example how the middle class of teachers, politicians, doctors, government employees, and other members of the emerging professions respond to a projected public realm, defined negatively as "what's there and cannot not be known" (Blackmur, p. 33) if these people are to survive and flourish. For Blackmur, Trilling always knows "the human price" of culture because he is constantly made aware by his own critical method of impersonation of the cost in energy and effort of cultivating this Mind "not entirely his own." "He has," Blackmur concedes, "the fortitude, in his essays, to act by choice as a public (*res publican*) mind." As such, Blackmur explains, it is "his business to take a position, to react and to respond, between incommensurable forces," however defined. Trilling is, Blackmur therefore concludes, "an administrator of the affairs of the mind" (Blackmur, p. 34). He is ever on guard lest this public mind fall victim to what Kant called the "Radical Evil" of unconscious hypocrisy, that peculiar corruption of liberal intellect that hides its pride in and lust for power under the mask of the most solicitous concern imaginable for the welfare of others. For Blackmur, then, Trilling's subject is "the politics of human power," and "his platform" is the independent liberal imagination "of middle class professionals" so far as it "survives in him and us" (Blackmur, p. 37).

Blackmur follows up this brilliant reading of Trilling as the liberal messiah—or is it Pilate?—with a close analysis of "Tacitus Now" (from *The Liberal Imagination*), focusing on this essay's characteristic abuse of general terms, in this case the word *human*. Blackmur argues that Trilling's "liberal" project of discovering "a living value" in a classic often depends, as here, on little knowledge of the text in its original historical contexts and, at times, on even less knowledge of its original language. Trilling's kind of critical humanism instead depends on "the noble lie" of a common transcendent human nature which licenses a tradition of sensibility in criticism productive of inspired feelings and impressionistic judgments about works only half understood and hardly read. The typical response of such humanistic criticism is "like the nostalgia for the unknown" (Blackmur, p. 39). And another familiar reaction of critical humanists is an equally impressionistic appreciation for "extraliterary systems" that prompts, as in "The Meaning of a Literary Idea," a call on Trilling's part for the "hardness" of rhetorical argument in poetry and fiction. The gush of enthusiasm and the girding of mental loins are the critical humanist's habitual dialectical gestures.

Blackmur's point, however, is not merely to defend philology or its technocratic professionalization in the New Criticism from the latest devotee of Arnold's touchstone reading. Rather, it is to highlight how critical humanism always entails a cultural politics that demonstrates relevance by ignoring differences, all in the name of greater human power for the critic and the community he would represent. The principle that informs Trilling's project, in short, has informed and will continue to inform many apparently very different projects, some of which may even claim to be "antihumanistic" critiques of humanism warring in behalf of the "liberation" of one group or another.

For what Blackmur in "The Politics of Human Power" describes transcends the case of Lionel Trilling. Blackmur isolates the prophetic stance of the postromantic critic of culture in the Anglo-American tradition. Whether one thinks of Arnold and Carlyle, Emerson and Whitman, or even Raymond Williams and Edward Said, the critic in question assumes a position in advance of and in opposition to the interpretive community he addresses and whose needs he would administer to by means of correction, refinement, or provocation. Unlike the scholar whose first concern is his subject, the prophetic critic's first and often only concern is with the present moment in cultural history and how it may be influenced in order to revise the course of public opinion—at times, primarily for the sake of acquiring or exercising this power over the future. Whatever the particular instance may suggest, the true mark of this kind of critic is the absence of any immediate clearly definable practical political or scholarly aim. As Blackmur's critique suggests, Trilling is just such a critic because his politics of human power appear to mean, in the final analysis, nothing more specific and determinate than preserving the mind's freedom to criticize itself and its products—what Edward Said calls "critical consciousness." While laudable-sounding as a general aim, what can it mean, strictly speaking? Two essays from 1942, "The Sense of the Past" and "Tacitus Now," in elaborating Trilling's representative attitude toward the past, may help to clarify if not answer this question.

At first glance, "The Sense of the Past" would appear to contradict Blackmur's conception of Trilling as an impressionistic critic of the present moment. Trilling recognizes formally the achievement of the New Criticism in reestablishing literature "as the agent of power" (*LI*, p. 183) in the culture by excusing it from the scientific standard of historical fact "as transferred in a literal way to the study of literature" (*LI*, p. 183). Yet he thinks there is a virtue in examining literature as an "object of knowledge" (*LI*, p. 183), that responding to it solely as the subject of power ignores at its own risk. Citing Professor Cornelius of Mann's "Disorder and Early Sorrow" as his authority, Trilling characterizes the historical sense he admires in a way that resembles more Hemingway's desire for "a clean well-lighted place" than either Mann's or Eliot's "mind of Europe." "There inheres in a work of art of the past," Trilling advises, "even in our own culture with its ambivalent feeling about tradition," "a certain quality, an element of its aesthetic existence, which we can identify as *its pastness*." This sense of the past, Trilling reassures the New Critics, exists "side by side with the formal elements of the work" (*LI*, p. 184). Adjacent and supplemental to and yet incorporated by the work's form lies this dimension of "pastness." In however mysterious and attenuated a manner, surely in this quietly moving passage Trilling asserts a "sense of the past" that complicates if it does not contradict the idea that he is simply a prophetic critic of the present moment in cultural history. Although he identifies this "sense of the past," the "pastness" of the work of art, in aesthetic terms and categories (a typical critical procedure), what Trilling is pointing to is that disruptive textual dimension of radical indetermination—always already not-meaning—which Paul de Man, for one, wrestled with for most of his career.[8]

"Tacitus Now," Trilling's 1942 introduction to a new English translation of *The Annals*, suggests a level of significance that Blackmur has missed. The living value Trilling discovers in this classic arises out of the response the critic self-consciously makes to the original trope deployed by Tacitus to describe the sublime effect the rebel Sabinus, as he is led to his own execution, has had on the people. "Wherever he turned, wherever his eyes fell," the translated passage correctly reads, "there was flight and solitude" (*LI*, p. 203). So great is Trilling's response to this sense that he momentarily imagines that with such a superb translation one no longer needs the original text, a naive remark, perhaps, which calls forth that Blackmurian scorn of Trilling's scholarly credentials mentioned earlier. In any event, Trilling elaborates this response, transferring now to Tacitus himself the admiration occasioned by the imaginative characterization of Sabinus:

> The tragedy [of Rome's great decline] had ended long ago [before Tacitus began to write]; what he observed was the aftermath which had no end, which exactly lacked the coherence of tragedy. His subject is not Rome at all, not Rome the political entity, but rather the grotesque career of the human spirit in a society which, if we may summarize the whole tendency of his thought, appeared to him to endure for no other purpose than to maintain the loud and lively existence of anarchy. From this it is easy, and all too easy, to discover his relevance to us now, but the relevance does not account for the strange invigoration of his pages which is rather to be explained by his power of mind and his stubborn love of virtue maintained in desperate circumstances. (*LI*, p. 204)

Now we can see wherein lies the sense of the past for the critical humanist. The semantic and topical indeterminacy that the passage of time effects in "the classic" invites imaginative response to its more memorable figures, a response which reads into the work an allegory of the reader's own mental and historical conditions. The above remarks interpreting the relevance of "Tacitus Now" ironically reflect the imperial anarchy and psychological alienation of Lionel Trilling's liberal imagination. These are spectral politics indeed, intended to colonize that aesthetically conceived dimension of the past which, like Benjamin's ecstatic aura, canonical works carry along, as it were, "beside themselves." The myth of the golden age and the dream of paradise regained haunt the therapeutic precincts of such classical indeterminacy. In short, Trilling's "sense of the past" is, as Blackmur would suggest, a prophetically revisionary one, as part of the struggle by each generation over the spaces of representation or sites of power in the culture. Clearly an "unprofessional" activity, even for Blackmur, the least scientific and technocratic of the New Critics, but an activity that the profession exists to regulate.

As is the case in Jonathan Arac's reading of Wordsworth's "Nutting," so here, too, with Trilling's reading of Tacitus: the space of indeterminacy that marks any text owing to the action of time and the unstable play of grammar, logic, and rhetoric is being seized by the critic and coopted to his purposes. In Trilling's case, the process occurs under the shadow of his familiar compound ghost, the Byronic figure of the Wandering Jew dressed up in Roman costume: "Wherever he turned, wherever his eyes fell, there was flight and solitude" (Shakespeare's *Coriolanus* also sounds here). The difference is that Trilling is able to attribute, on the plausible basis of this figure, a compatible, indeed noble motive to his chosen author, for anticipating his own views, whereas Arac cannot do so and must chide his author for being blind to what his critics now see. Whether or not either professional reader can stand up to Blackmur's measure of scholarly precision and rigor is not the issue for me. What is, however, is this difference between the magnanimous and unmagnanimous styles of critical response.

As in the case of the latter-day feminist critic "rediscovering" the significance of some long and wrongfully neglected popular "classic," such interpretive procedures directed at objects of neglect can prove to be ruefully provocative and so productive of more critical work. Trilling's *E. M. Forster* (1943), the founding text in the serious study of this author, is a curiously relevant case in point.[9]

"I had a quarrel with American literature at that time," Trilling opens his 1964 preface to the Forster study, clarifying its original polemical motive for a later audience.[10] Directed against the "childishness" and "pious social simplicities" of the then-established liberal culture in America, Trilling "enlisted Mr. Forster's vivacity, complexity, and irony" (*EMF*, pp. 3–4) as appropriate pharmakon, to show how "a generation charmed by the lugubrious" in O'Neill, Dreiser, and Anderson was then turning to Steinbeck, Van Wyck Brooks, and Hollywood, vainly "fleeing from the trivial shape of its own thoughts" (*EMF*, pp. 8–9). Instead of trying to escape the idea of death, Trilling argues, we should learn from Forster how it can save us by relaxing the imperious will and catching "the truth" of "the human heart by surprise" (*EMF*, pp. 9–10). Trilling, as in his first book on Arnold, would educate the will to its own negative transcendence primarily by incorporating the lesson of his chosen hero's ironic style:

> The comic manner . . . will not tolerate absolutes. It stands on the barricades and casts doubt on both sides. The fierce plots move forward to grand simplicities but the comic manner confuses the issues forcing upon us the difficulties and complications of the moral fact. The plot suggests eternal division, the manner reconciliation, the plot speaks of clear certainties, the manner resolutely insists that nothing can be so simple. "Wash ye, make yourselves clean," says the plot, and the manner murmurs, "If you can find the soap." (*EMF*, p. 12)

This uncharacteristically mocking style mimics Forster's own, of course, but depends intellectually on a prior acceptance of tragedy,

what Trilling, after James, also calls "the imagination of disaster." For
without it, the liberal critic tends to wax apocalyptic and "eschatolog-
ical" (*EMF*, p. 22), being discontented—as most of us are, Trilling
assures us—"with the nature rather than the use of the human faculty" (*EMF*, p. 22). Our disenfranchized ascetic will hungers fiercely
after final judgment upon the fact of being human itself, and so falls
easy prey to the terrible beauty of totalitarian solutions. Forster, the
prototype of the modern academic mind, recommends the perfect corrective: "not becoming better," Forster says, "but by ordering and
distributing his native goodness can man live as befits him" (*EMF*, p.
23)—that is, as art and culture allow.

Trilling calls this quality of mind that Forster represents "worldli-
ness," by which he means a certain urbane insouciant "acceptance of
man in the world" that avoids the extremes of Jacobin rationalism and
romantic cynicism by being "positive" about the nature in human
nature: Forster is, Trilling notes, "one of the thinking people" who
never is led "by thought to suppose they could be more than human
and who in bad times, will not become less" (*EMF*, p. 24). Forster's
adoption of the "middle style" of personal discourse that presupposes
a reader to be won over without bullying clinches the argument for
Trilling (*EMF*, p. 33). In essence, then, we should read Forster to become more like him.

Trilling is using Forster to get American liberals off the streets and
into the academy—or at least into the academic frame of mind. Accusing them of apocalyptic rather than specific political longings is the
first step. Providing them with an attractive goal—the perfection of the
transcendent comic manner—is the next.

Finally, discovering in Forster a more liberally acceptable (because
more personally sympathetic) and openly accessible form of modernism is Trilling's way of ushering his circle into the petit bourgeois
academic fold under the militant-seeming banners of aesthetic revolution. For once convinced that education of the individual sensibility is
the answer, they can be "saved" by their worldly messiah, with his
ironic "specular" genealogies of this very class:

> Perhaps the intellectual first came into historical notice when Burke,
> attacking the French Revolution, spoke with contempt of the many
> small lawyers and small priests in the assembly. They were, he said,
> merely men of mind, therefore, ill-suited to the management of a
> state. . . . The French Revolution was the first great occasion when
> Mind—conscious, verbalized Mind—became an important element
> in national politics. Interest, of course, was also in play, and force,

too, but mind had the new function of generalizing interest and justifying force. And since Burke's day mind has played an increasing part in politics. (*EMF,* pp. 122–123)

Simply by using Mind, in other words, simply by functioning in society to shape public opinion, whether in the classroom or in newspapers and magazines, or in some other professional context, we will liberate succeeding generations, as reading Forster has liberated, as we have seen, the usually solemn Lionel into some uncharacteristic Trilling wit.

What Trilling does in the Forster book—light the way for fellow New York intellectuals into the American mainstream—depends upon his ability to discover in Forster and his major works the sense of the past, that seductive aesthetic quality of textual indeterminacy so productive of new texts. Particularly in *Howards End*, of course, Trilling finds his example, since the novel does clearly propose to "only connect" "the prose and poetry of life" along the lines he has already found so attractive in Arnold—via the sensible relaxation of the fierce opposi-tional will, that is, its refinement through culture, into the worldly grace of an ironic style.

Richard Chase, Trilling's colleague at Columbia and "father" of "*The American Novel and its Tradition*," has caught his spiritual mentor's mind-set perfectly when he contrasts the English novel's habit of "absolving all extremes into a normative view of life" with "the profound poetry of disorder" that attends our fictional romances. Unlike Hawthorne's *Scarlet Letter* or Melville's *Moby-Dick*, for example, English novels, such as George Eliot's *Middlemarch* or Jane Austen's *Pride and Prejudice*, pro-pose this normative view of life and, in doing so, reveal their origins in "the two great influences that stand behind the genre"—"classic trag-edy and Christianity," according to which "character moves through contradictions to forms of harmony, reconciliation, catharsis, and trans-figuration."[11] (If Trilling is our liberal Eliot, then surely Chase is our American Leavis). I quote Chase here to highlight the relations be-tween Trilling's Arnold, Freud, and now Forster. Trilling sees at work in these heroic characters a normative vision of life as a classical drama of mature self-sacrifice and adjustment to reality that is symbolized by the magnanimous attribution of noble motives to the Other in the form of the Great Dead.

Trilling discerns in all these sources a normative vision of life as the balanced development of the individual mind amidst the imperial an-archy of modernity. He stands in relation to the texts he cites and the world he addresses, much as he envisions Tacitus in his *Annals* address-ing the Empire, in the name of a form of life noble and all but a fading memory, in stubborn loyalty to what is principled rather than popular. The human price of this vision, however, is considerable.

"Of This Time, Of That Place," his 1943 novella, is Trilling's finest performance in the English fictional mode of espousing "the normative view" of life. This once frequently anthologized and much commented upon novella is a work of liberation and sacrifice related more clearly to "Impediments," his first bitter tale of spectral politics and self-aberration, than to the comic polemic of his contemporaneous celebration of Forster. The four parts of this classically balanced and beautifully framed "tragedy" (Trilling's greatly disputed word for it)[12] tell the sad story of a very talented but deeply troubled student who is "betrayed" into the necessary psychiatric care by the teacher of poetry he eulogizes. Although, for dramatic effect, set in the "fishbowl" of a Midwestern college town rather than in New York and focused closely on the teacher's unconscious motivation rather than on any sensational details of the case, the story is clearly based on Allen Ginsberg's career at Columbia College, a fact confirmed by Ginsberg's reading of a forgiving "love poem" to Trilling, "Lion in the Room," on the triumphant return of the Prince of Beats to the Columbia campus for a reading in 1959[13]. "Of This Time, Of That Place" (Trilling ironically selects one of the "mad" student's memorable phrases as his own title) functions equally well as a "realistic" fiction and as its author's revealing psychomachia, since the underlying emotional conflict between sympathy and symptomatology, guilt and duty, gives rise to "the idea" for this story, Trilling himself admits, as an imaginative form of "resolution" to an otherwise "irreconcilible contradiction."[14] For me, the story crystallizes the perverse majesty involved in the sacrifice of genius so necessary to Trilling's work of liberation in becoming the worldly messiah of his liberal time and middle-class place.

Of central importance in this context is the scapegoat psychology that informs the plot throughout. The story opens with Joseph Howe, poet and assistant professor at Dwight College, after teaching his first class of the new school year, responding to a savage review of his second book of self-conscious "modern" poetry. Written by Frederic Woolley, now ex-champion of formalism, the review uses Howe as a whipping boy to effect its author's transformation into a social critic, and thus renew a faltering career. The threat to Howe's position at Dwight—the publisher of the literary journal in which the review appears is influential with the school's board of trustees—pains him almost as much as the injury to his reputation. What hurts Howe most, though, is that he has been made into a scapegoat so as to better advance the older man's narrow self-interest but all in the name of the highest virtue—social concern for the plight of the masses during this latest crisis of capitalism (World War II). Woolley makes the laughable argument that the "people" need the clear and strict Dorian mode of Thomas Wormser's bucolic wonder in *Corn under the Willows* and not the "self-possessed Phrygian music" of "the Howes": "this becoming the multiform political symbol by whose creation Frederic Woolley gave the sign of a sudden new life, this use of him as a sacrifice whose blood was necessary for the rites of rejuvenation, made him feel oddly unclean" (*OTT*, p. 819). The point of the story could not be made more graphically—to advance in society and to renew personal growth, however inadequately these are conceived, appears to require the sacrifice of the spectral Other, whether that Other possesses recognized genius or not. This scapegoat psychology explains, I suppose, Trilling's use of the slippery term "tragic" to describe the story's plot. For Howe in turn scapegoats the student-innocent Tertan by the story's end.

Without belaboring either this point or the story's classically simple form, I would like to focus on its most interesting aspect, the role language plays in determining the outcome, in fact the power language has to determine that Tertan is "a case" to be dealt with by therapy in the first place.

"The question was, at whose door must the tragedy be laid," is the way the second section of the story ironically opens, both anticipating what is to come and referring to the situation in Ibsen's *Ghosts*, about which Howe is unsuccessfully interrogating his callow class. The better students respond by blaming, first, specific characters—Pastor Manders, Mrs. Alving—and then more general forces: heredity or society. (Stettenhover, the football player, sulks.) Only Tertan hits on what Howe believes is the correct answer, but he does so only amidst the most incredible word-salad imaginable. "Mr. Tertan says," Howe obligingly translates for the discussion's sake, "the blame must be put upon whoever kills the joy of living in another" (*OTT*, p. 91). That is, upon everyone in the play, and so Howe makes it a masterpiece of man's fate in our fallen world, Ibsen's perverse self-revision of his earlier penchant for the radical solutions of socialism. Or so Howe wants his students to see it.

While Tertan is careening to the desired conclusion, Howe reflects abruptly: "Oh, the boy was mad. And suddenly, the word, used in hyperbole, intended almost for the expression of exasperated admiration, became literal" (*OTT*, p. 90). Using the word, Howe finds, makes it true of Tertan and of his strange career at college:

It was a monstrous word and stood like a bestial thing in the room. Yet it so completely comprehended everything that had puzzled

Howe, it so arranged and explained what for three months had been
perplexing him that almost at once its horror became domesticated.
With this word Howe was able to understand why he had never been
able to communicate to Tertan the value of a single criticism or correction of his wild, verbose themes. (*OTT*, p. 90)

If the seduction of semantic indeterminacy grants the aura of relevance
to the classics, the power of words to define, to identify, to fix and
determine a "reality" can create the conditions for the perception of "a
classic case": "that is to say, without a doubt, perfect in its way, a
veritable model, and . . . sure to take a perfectly predictable and inevitable course to a foreknown conclusion" (*OTT*, p. 104). Suddenly,
Tertan becomes for Howe, "because of a word" (*OTT*, p. 92), just such
a sublimely arresting "classic case" as the other associations of the
term classic—"the Parthenon and the form of the Greek drama, the
Aristotelian logic, Racine and the Well-Tempered Clavichord, the blue-
ness of the Aegean and its clear sky"—now serve uncannily to testify
and domesticate at once, striking an all too resonant tragic note: the
terrible beauty of sacrifice.

But Howe resists any easy scapegoating of his alter ego, deciding to
delay taking the action he knows must finally be taken on Tertan's case:
"Some pure instinct told him that he must not surrender the question
to a clean official dash in a clear official light to be dealt with, settled,
and closed" (*OTT*, p. 94). No sooner are these thoughts of his formulated, however, than he is blurting out the matter before the Dean: "it
would always be a landmark of his life that, at the very moment when
he was rejecting the official way, he had been, without will or intention,
so gladly drawn to it" (*OTT*, p. 14). The explanation for this climactic
recognition of his own complicity with established authority lies reflected in the scene in which it occurs, one of the Dean's old-fashioned
committee rooms:

It was designed with a homely elegance on the masculine side of the
eighteenth-century manner. There was a small coal fire in the grate
and the handsome mahogany table was strewn with books and magazines. The large windows gave on the snow lawn and there was
such a fine width of window that the white casements and walls
seemed at this moment but a continuation of the snow, the snow but
an extension of casement and walls. The outdoors seemed to be taken
in and made safe, the indoors seemed luxuriously freshed and expanded. (*OTT*, p. 95)

The sense of the past, that aesthetic quality of uncertainty accompanying the productions of culture like another dimension into which we anxiously project ourselves and our circumstances, pervades this eighteenth-century-styled earthly paradise. The apocalyptic image of the union between nature and culture recalls the works of many masters: Wordsworth's preface to *The Excursion*, Keats's "Eve of St. Agnes," Joyce's "The Dead"—to name but a few obvious echoes. It is for the possession of this academic scene of worldly glory—muted, tame, and ghostly—that Trilling's Howe so easily, as if sleepwalking, sacrifices the pathetic doppelganger and mad heir of his own modernist aspirations, thereby consumating the scapegoat cycle begun at the story's opening by betraying "not only a power of mind" (Tertan's at least) "but a power of love" (*OTT*, p. 100).

Howe, made self-conscious by his knowledge of secret identity with Tertan (*OTT*, p. 100), allows "the strange affirming power of a name" (*OTT*, p. 106) to convert a student of promise into "the hard blank of a fact" (*OTT*, p. 107), even as he must permit the more socially acceptable but no less mad students like Blackburn—a malicious, ignorant, grade-grubbing manipulator—to pass and graduate with honor (*OTT*, pp. 107–108). In other words, sociopaths are welcomed in society. Howe pays for his key part in "the metamorphosis of Tertan from person to fact" (*OTT*, p. 105) by being caught between Blackburn and the Dean at the graduation ceremony in a camera buff's formally staged picture, upon the precise snapping of which Tertan, now a figure of taboo like Coleridge's thrice-encircled demonic poet, repeatedly pronounces the terribly apt phrase "instruments of precision" (*OTT*, p. 115). Attired in the large panama hat and shabby white suit of his crazy wastrel father, Tertan possesses for Howe at this point a "perverse majesty" (*OTT*, p. 115) not to be withstood, and so Howe's heart now overflows with universal sympathy for this uncommon image of the common fate before hurrying off "to join the procession" (*OTT*, p. 116).

Although neither Tertan nor Howe possesses the moral stature of the traditional hero, together they do indeed enact a tragedy. It is the modern tragedy of betraying the human-all-too-human in the pursuit of the more than human. This is the sublime aesthetic effect of traditional order and beauty upon our world, the effect for which Trilling longs. The sense of glory dooms the most sensitive to madness and betrayal. The academic vision of transcendent order—that apocalyptic marriage of snow and fire found by Howe in the Dean's committee room—bears a terrible pricetag: the scapegoating of Howe's only muse, the mad Tertan. As Woolley and Blackburn would do to Howe, so Howe does to Tertan: transforms him into a figure representing his own antithetical imaginative proclivities, by passively suffering and acquiescing in the institutional power of language to do so. The crushing irony of this story is that when we last see Tertan he is doing likewise to all and sundry: "Instruments of precision" indeed!

Underlying "the normative view of life" in the English novel, in Freudian psychology, and in critical humanism (Arnold and Forster), therefore, is this ritual structure of repression and sacrifice, what I have been calling "spectral politics," in order to suggest the weird combination of hero or ancestor worship, social defensiveness, and sublime aspiration of the will that informs both the ironic conjunction of liberal argument and tragic figure in Trilling's mature texts and the developing shape of his representative career as a leading intellectual prophet of internal exile. This constellation of opposing drives constitutes the priestly or religious unconscious of Trilling's lifelong work. It bears a striking resemblance, of course, not only to Nietzsche's portrait of the ascetic will in *On the Genealogy of Morals*, but also to Blake's Prince of Spectres, Urizen, the great original of all would-be worldly messiahs who imagine that they can work a liberation and a revolution upon culture, for others or themselves. "I have searched for a joy without pain," Urizen says in his First Book, and Trilling's grand vision of the committee room demonstrates exactly what it means to do so. " 'The question was, At whose door must the tragedy be laid?' " "Mr. Tertan says the blame must be put upon whoever kills the joy of living in another." Mr. Tertan, of course, speaks more truly than he can know.

My point is that as Trilling moves from assistant to associate to full professor from 1940 to 1951, oedipally espousing one heroic character after another (Arnold, Freud, Forster, etc.) as corrective to the pieties of American liberal culture, his work reveals the ironic dialectic of *ressentiment* and scapegoating that Neitzsche characterizes so succinctly: "The slave of *ressentiment* is deprived of the proper outlet of action, and so forced to find compensation in an imaginary revenge."[15] Imaginary, that is, until such time as the slaves of *ressentiment* rule and can make more noble natures embody this revenge literally in their own personal fates. Yet, as Nietzsche goes on to show, the noble temper must seek "its antithesis in order to pronounce a more grateful and exultant *yes* to its own self" (*GM*, p. 35). That is, noble and slave moralities are equally literary ethics constitutive of the spectral politics of sacrifice that René Girard analyzes in *Violence and the Sacred* and that Trilling's work, especially the fictions of these years, represents so tellingly. Is it any wonder then, as Diana Trilling puts it so well to her famous husband and a few of his more rancorous colleagues on her return home from the partially boycotted performance of the Beats at

Columbia, that "Allen Ginsberg read a love-poem to you, Lionel. I liked it very much."[16] Perverse majesty—yes?

Tragic Beauty: The Beauty of the Commonplace

Spectral politics, literary ethics, the sublime psychology of sacrifice, the tragic critique of liberal culture for lack of heroic imagination: all these revisionary names function to demarcate and structure from different angles—political, moral, psychoanalytic, and aesthetic—the same ironic quest for what Trilling in *Sincerity and Authenticity* terms finally "the authentic unconscious." Trilling means by this phrase to refer neither to the anarchic dreams of the id nor to the visionary desires of the ideal ego, but to the savage civilities and bitter defenses of the superego—what I would characterize as the empowering repressions of the religious unconscious. If, after Lacan, it is appropriate to read the unconscious like a text, then, as Lacan's own major formulas suggest—"mirror stage," "the imaginary, symbolic, and the real," "the discourse of the other," and "the name of the father"—the text of the unconscious that such readings produce must "naturally" possess, as Trilling's mature work dramatizes, a decidedly priestly cast. In other words the "theory" that Trilling practices in his representative career, his "ideology" or "system of beliefs," is a critical internalization of the Judeo-Christian heritage.

Put in this way, my claim appears both surprising and not surprising: not surprising since the idea that almost everything in modern culture is a secularization of religion has a long history in philosophical, theological, and literary circles, to the point now of inspiring apocalyptic yawns even in the authors who still make use of this topos. Yet surprising, too, since Lionel Trilling, liberal, freethinking writer on religous and modern cultures alike, hardly leaps to mind as the spiritual fellow traveler of Billy Sunday or Jimmy Swaggart. Could the urbane champion of the Forsterian comic manner actually be a closet zealot? Hardly. As the rest of his mature work in the 1940s demonstrates, however, particularly his novel *The Middle of the Journey*, the imaginary matrix of his various positions, the subtext of his texts, as it were, embraces a vision of ritual sacrifice as terrible as any in D. H. Lawrence, the modern writer Trilling invariably invokes for his authority on that subject. The nature of the sacrifice differs, of course, with Trilling representing in his heroic scapegoats and ironic surrogates not primarily the sexual possibilities of the individual but rather the various social or intellectual bodies to which he has affiliated himself in the past. The free-floating American intellectual fears becoming fixated in a single community, fears the specter of the apocalyptic bell. So he or she must anxiously reinvent his or her sense of identity via opposition for dissociation's sake, over and over again, especially when the career becomes truly representative.

Consider, for example, his contribution to a 1944 symposium "Under Forty: American Literature and the Younger Generation of American Jews" sponsored by the *Contemporary Jewish Record*: "As the Jewish community now exists, it can give no sustenance to the American artist or intellectual who is born a Jew."[17] Yet, in the same statement, Trilling also admits that especially for a Jew of his generation "it is never possible to 'escape' his Jewish origin" ("Under Forty," p. 198). The reason that Trilling feels this is so sheds a familiar light on the curious basis of his affiliations generally:

> In order to be sure of this [impossibility of "escape"], I have only to remember how, when I was a child beginning to read for pleasure, certain words would leap magnetically to my eye from the page before I had reached them in the text. One such word was "snake"; others were words of such sexual explicitness as a child is likely to meet in his reading; and there was the word "Jew." These were words, that is, which struck straight to the unconscious, where fear, shame, attraction and repulsion are indistinguishable. Yet there was no dramatic or even specific reason why the word "Jew" should produce (as it still produces) so deep, so visceral, a reverberation. ("Under Forty," p. 198)

First of all, that Trilling could phrase the question of Jewish identity in terms of "escape" at all, however self-conscious the scare quotes, truly marks him as a man of his generation. But, as we have already seen in "A Light to Nations," what always animates Trilling's sense of identity with another person or a larger group is the uncanny reverberations of the words read in association with the Other. The passion of such "textual" affiliations possesses the romantic intensity of espousing an abstraction, what Trilling goes on in this passage to confess is really an intellectual "point of honor," that is, the "social" passion of an academic professional in the making. Finally, this passage discloses how the transport of the sublime style depends originally upon the critical reader's prophetic anticipation of shock, the shock of more than mild surprise, in which alienated self-recognition, sexuality, and radical ambivalence give rise to a sense of identity primarily with the repressive judgments that create the unconscious where all such responses are "indistinguishable." The reverberating penumbra of semantic associations repeatedly produces the spectral self of the critic. When not reading in this militantly ironic sense, Trilling, like any other critic, does not exist: "the moments of the critic . . . when our mind is poised over a recognition of a truth which attacks other truths . . . moments in our reading when we neither hate nor love what the author is saying but hate and love together."[18] In short, to read critically constitutes an act of holy war.

A holy war—for what? "There is, in sanest hours, a consciousness, a thought that rises, independent, lifted out from all else, calm, like the stars, shining eternal. This is the thought of identity—yours for you, whoever you are, as mine for me. Miracle of mircles, beyond statement, most spiritual of earth's dreams, yet hardest basic fact, and only entrance to all facts" (*SLS*, p. 210). Thus Trilling cites *Democratic Vistas* in "Sermon on a Text from Whitman," the first of several key uses of this passage in the critic's long career. To what end? In justification of his holy war for identity against what he sees in 1945 and increasingly thereafter as the epidemic flight from and wish to lose individuality in larger causes (*SLS*, p. 215). "The thought of identity," Trilling argues, makes true democracy possible, because it focuses our energies on our "relation to nature" and gives the highest value to "the biological crises" of "birth, love, death" (*SLS*, p. 211), and so pragmatically creates a common developmental vision of life liberally available to all good Americans. In his 1915 essay "Repression," Freud remarks that repression, constitutive of the unconscious, occupies a position midway between "flight and condemnation."[19] I would suggest that Trilling's holy war for identity requires the progressive intensification and elaboration of repression in this sense, in order to maximize and stabilize both the intellectual recognition of conflict, however painful, and the potential of definitive response. For in this condition even the critic can become creative—if ever at another's expense. Negative capability requires the examples of those who are not even that. Howe and Tertan project this sublime power for their implied author, who would hover imaginatively between and over his creations.

Two stories of the same year, "The Other Margaret" and "The Lesson and the Secret," graphically dramatize this sacrificial aesthetic. "The Lesson and the Secret" recounts the experiences of Vincent Hammell as he tries to teach "creative writing" to older women students in the Midwest, all of whom he considers "the failures and misfits" of their social class; otherwise, he perversely reasons, "they would not have to meet weekly to devote themselves to literature" (*OTT*, p. 62). Hammell finds their desire to uncover "the secret of writing," in the sense either of how to write well or of how to sell big, extremely irritating. So one day in class he decides to read an "exemplary" story by "Garda Thorne." He hopes to revenge himself upon his class with this tale of two young and beautiful American girls, who on a visit to an Austrian village end up frolicking in the local priest's wine vat while he is away attending the dying. They then must "scramble to get themselves decent" before his return, "their legs still sticky under their stockings" (*OTT*, p. 69). Clearly, whatever his conscious pedagogical intentions may have been in reading this story, unconsciously Hammell intends it to work as a more or less "realistic" parable that reflects ironically on the situation of these aging, small-town, imperious "misfits." He rightly begins to feel "sorry" and "uncomfortable" for selecting it, growing increasingly aware of the full significance of his choice:

> But, as he read, he felt that it had been a cruel mistake to read this story to these women. As it went on through its narration of the flash of skirts and underskirts, of white stained thighs, the grave silence of the girls and their giggles and the beautiful prints of their naked feet on the stone floor, it seemed to him that his own youth had been thoughtless to have chosen the story. He felt, too, like an intruder into feminine mysteries and the sweat came to his forehead. (*OTT*, p. 69)

Like the protagonist in Lawrence's "Tickets Please," Hammell suspects "something latently dangerous" as he faces all these aroused women, fearing that they will suddenly see him, as he now momentarily sees himself, as "the author of the story," a story that celebrates the things that once were "their peculiar possessions; their youth, their beauty, their femininity" (*OTT*, p. 69). They may turn on him, as Lawrence's fiercer women do, and take retribution for his violation of their "feminine mysteries."

Aside from the "lovely shifting of skirts" back down over their knees, however, the women in his class responded initially with amused and pleased silence, and then with expressions of gratitude to literature for its temporary ability to lift (by symbolically representing them) their secret repressions. That is, the secret of writing that they now learn is its therapeutic power to make repression palpably visible, to embody it in the reader who can thereby forget it and find herself:

> In the sunlit room, in the soft spring air, there was a moment of musing silence as the quest for the precious secret was abandoned. Despite himself, Vincent Hammell experienced a sense of power, in all his months of teaching the class the first he had felt. Yet in the

entrancement of the women, in their moment of brooding relation, there was something archaic and mythological, something latently dangerous. (*OTT*, pp. 69–70)

Hammell continues, speculating that "it was thus that the women of Thrace must have sat around Orpheus before they had had occasion to be enraged with him" (*OTT*, p. 70). Hammell would like to break the spell by reminding them that "he had merely read aloud to them the story" which a woman had written. Before he can do so, however, "old Mrs. Pomeroy" memorializes the occasion by observing, "such a story makes one truly glad there is literature. We should be grateful" (*OTT*, p. 70). And they are, for as long as they can recall "the moment of contemplation" (*OTT*, p. 71). That is to say, not for long: "At the question ["does this writer sell well?"] there was a noisy little murmur of agreement to its relevance as the eyes turned to Vincent Hammell to demand his answer" (*OTT*, p. 71).

Literature, as represented in "The Lesson and the Secret," is the power of repression to memorialize by transcription the condition of being "in between" flight and condemnation, the condition that most resembles the dreaming of the hysteric as interpreted in the analytic situation. What Hammell's use of Garda Thorne's tale suggests is that the teacher of literature, unlike the professional therapist, takes possession of the unconscious of his students by permitting what he has read to take possession of him just enough to provoke critical judgment. The teacher functions like the imagination's priest, prophet, and shaman rolled into one—for as long as the ambivalent moment of literary contemplation lasts or can be ironically recalled. That is, he functions as if he were the superego or, more broadly, the conscience of his class. In this priestly fashion, the critic as leading intellectual can play "king"—but at the cost of greater repression for his readers and himself: "When the priest returned they had to sit there demure with their legs still sticky under their stockings. The priest served them the wine they had bathed in and their manners were perfect as they heard him say that never had he known the wine to be so good" (*OTT*, p. 69).

The several layers of sexual significance here resonate all the more authoritatively because of Trilling's intentionally commonplace style. The critic, devouring and refining his literary masters, reproduces the perverse spectacle of tragic beauty in his clientele: "It was thus that the women of Thrace must have sat around Orpheus before they had had occasion to be enraged with him." And in so envisioning the teacher of literature's position, Trilling prefigures his sacrificial role in modern culture. This is "the thought of identity" with a vengeance.

"The Other Margaret," also a story of 1945, stages the modern critical consciousness as the universal tragedy of cultural life. The story focuses ostensibly on the conflict engendered in Stephen Elwin's teenage daughter, Margaret, by her stubborn espousal of the liberal piety learned in school, that society is responsible for all evils. Margaret Elwin, to her father's mind, refuses to face reality and recognize what she cannot not know, that all of us, even the worst victims of social injustice, are to be held morally accountable for the actions we commit. Occasion for this conflict of "illusion and reality" arises when the open hostility of the Elwins' new black maid, the other Margaret of the title, is left unchecked out of permissive deference to the girl's progressive attitudes. Spite escalates then to a climactic incident of resentful violence, the deliberate smashing of the beautiful green porcelain lamb that Margaret Elwin made herself as a birthday gift for her mother.

"The Other Margaret" is as much Stephen Elwin's as his daughter's story. We see all that happens through his eyes, and his experiences and reflections inform and interpret every scene. It is as if a Jamesian center of consciousness were recording a Forsterian domestic melodrama in a mournful rather than mocking style—all primarily for a surprising effect. For instance, the purchase and changing appreciation of a painting—a reproduction of a Rouault King—formally contains and comments upon the action. What begins as the portrait of "a fierce quality that had modulated, but not softened, to authority" ends up as a cheap print of "quaint, extravagant," and irrelevant "romance" dressed up in its overshadowing gilt frame. Stephen Elwin thus discovers his spectral alter ego.

Similarly, one of the story's major motifs, a sentence about death by Hazlitt, reflects the conflict between spoiled innocence and spiteful experience as understood by Margaret Elwin's father. As he purchases the Rouault King from his dealer-designer friend, Mark Jennings, another customer, a young lieutenant, comes in to disturb their "community of feeling" (*OTT*, p. 11), delicately poised as they are in contemplation of the strangely attractive cruelty of this tragic profile in wisdom. Elwin envies the younger man's decision to go off to war in order to share "the experience of his generation" (*OTT*, p. 14). It is now that Elwin recalls and reflects on the Hazlitt line, "No young man believes he shall ever die," from "On the Feeling of Immortality in Youth." First heard in Mr. Baxter's high school classroom, the line, then and repeatedly thereafter, defines the nature of the sublime for Elwin, crystallizing the wisdom he would live by and impart to his daughter.

The Hazlitt sentence, once it had been remembered, had not left Elwin. Every now and then, sometimes just as he was falling asleep,

> sometimes just as he was waking up, sometimes right in the middle
> of anything at all, the sentence and the full awareness of what it
> meant would come to him. It felt like an internal explosion. It was
> not, however, an explosion of force but rather an explosion of light.
> It was not without pain but it was not wholly painful. (*OTT*, p. 15).

The sublime, the gratuitous power of literature and art to transport
and recreate receptive minds, depends on "the dark illumination"
(*OTT*, p. 33) contained in Rouault's portrait and in this imperious
touchstone from the radical Hazlitt. Culture, as the Arnoldian prophecy foretold, can indeed transform life, even during the Second World
War.

Or so Elwin believes. Three incidents now test this belief, however,
as he returns home. His bus driver, an older man, deliberately closes
the door on a young boy and his brother for no apparent reason. Elwin
only supposes that he is displacing onto these strange boys a desire for
revenge for filial ingratitude he has suffered. Lucy Elwin, his wife,
retells with ironic disdain an anti-Semitic joke picked up on her bus
ride home, and young Margaret jumps to the mistaken conclusion that
her own mother has been a closet bigot. And finally, the family debates
the difference between the old black maid and the new one, discovering
their Margaret's relish for reading expressions of decency and compe-
tence from victims of life's injustices as nothing but examples of "slave
psychology" (*OTT*, p. 34). Creeping resentment and critical suspicion,
abroad in the land, even in the schools, have thus invaded the home.
After such a blow, Elwin recognizes the end of innocence in summoning the image of "the great chain of the world's rage" (*OTT*, p. 19), in
which each of us is a secret link. So much for the liberal compensations
of culture.

In this troubled context, however, Stephen Elwin observes suddenly
how his daughter argues her point in all "the innocence of her passion"
(*OTT*, p. 24). He just as suddenly recalls now her innocent self-delight
in learning to play the recorder. It dawns on him, as Margaret gives
Lucy her birthday gift, that this gift is as much her idealized self-
portrait as the Rouault King is his own. Culture may have its limited
compensations after all:

> The . . . present was . . . a green lamb, large enough to have to be
> held in two hands, with black feet and wide black eyes. The eyes
> started out with a great charming question to the world, expressing
> the comic grace of the lamb's awkwardness. Elwin wondered if Mar-
> garet had been at all aware of how much the lamb was a self-portrait.
> When Elwin, some two years before, had listened to his daughter
> playing her first full piece on the recorder, he had thought that noth-

ing could be more wonderful than the impervious gravity of her face as her eyes focused on the bell of the instrument and on the music-book while she blew her tune in a daze of concentration; yet only a few months later, when she had progressed so far as to be up to airs from Mozart, she had been able, in the very midst of a roulade, with her fingers moving fast, to glance up at him with a twinkling, side-long look, her mouth puckering in a smile as she kept her lips pursed, amused by the music, amused by the frank excess of its ornamenta-tion and by her own virtuosity. For Elwin the smile was the expres-sion of gay and conscious life, of life innocently aware of itself and fond of itself, and, although there was something painful in having to make the admission, it was even more endearing than Margaret's earlier gravity. Life aware of itself seemed so much more life. (*OTT*, pp. 28–29)

This long and central passage of the story concerns less the conflict between innocence and experience in the lives of Margaret and Ste-phen Elwin than the struggle for representation among several differ-ent levels of authority. For the action of "The Other Margaret," as we have seen, repeatedly questions the liberal patriarchy represented by Elwin. Even more tellingly, the language of the text, as here in this vision of "radical innocence," betrays the specular desire simultane-ously to praise and repress the autoerotic play to be found at textual origins. (The incestuous wish in this sublime passage makes a more basic self-reflection.) Similarly, the various allusions, especially to Ha-zlitt and Rouault, serve the same reflexive end in a story of intended social significance. Who's in charge here—daughter, maid, father, or author—and to what ends are some of the representational questions raised? The tragedy of "The Other Margaret," in short, is not so much the spectral confrontations of white princess and her demonic alter ego, a black maid, as it is Trilling's sacrifice of his Jamesian center of consciousness to the "dark" forces that would wrest the narration from its author's control.

In saying all this, it seems that I am ignoring the calm commonplace style and moral realism for which Trilling has become justly famous. After all, for him, culture (repression's other name) is precisely an intermediate realm between (yet still informed) by the anarchic desires of the self and the political struggles endemic to the social world. Critical humanism of the kind practiced by Trilling, as we have seen in some detail, arranges the associative dimension of words to produce culture as an earthly paradise where power temporarily overcomes itself in reflexive play and yet retains its very real potential for violent transgression or equally violent repression. "The Sense of the Past," "Tacitus Now," and "Of This Time, Of That Place" are just three memorable examples of this vision of culture in Trilling's mature work. Could it be that I am too hastily processing "The Other Margaret" into a "deconstructive" touchstone for purposes of my critical argument?

While this result of interpretive labor is always possible these days, what I am finding in Stephen Elwin's vision of his daughter at play is not so much Trilling's "unconscious" as his intentionally compromising revelation of patriarchial authority. Trilling, in other words, is disclosing here and throughout this story the spectral profile of the sexual and political foundations of culture. That he does so suggests to me that Trilling wants to indulge desire and evade guilt by playfully attributing both to his fictional hero who is to be sacrificed as an inadequate point of view in fulfillment of the formal requirements of the "tragic" action. In short, if Elwin, as we shall see even more emphatically, scapegoats his daughter-muse as well as his willful maid, he suffers in turn the same fate at the hands of his creator. It is as if Trilling in "The Other Margaret" completes the sacrifice of the kind of mind that made possible the tragedy of Tertan and Howe in "Of This Time, Of That Place." The developmental model of psychic maturity that shapes Trilling's career requires such "progress." The vision of culture as an earthly paradise where power can play and yet still be power always depends upon the inspiration or provocation of some scapegoat muse or other for its defensively narcissistic impetus, even as the serene middle-class style of discourse that Trilling deploys is really what Freud in his 1914 essay describes as the "pure" defense mechanism of repression. Trilling's style requires an ironic surrogate's espousal of the "heroic" ideology of self-sacrifice. From Hettner and Isaac Nathan to Tertan, Howe, Hammell, and Elwin—Trilling has been rewriting in various ways Conrad's "Secret Sharer" or the specter portions of Blake's *Jerusalem*.

Consider, for example, how Elwin, knowing that his daughter prides herself on possessing a mind "unable to resist a fact," seizes "the vacant moment" in the debate over individual versus social responsibility for evil, in order to parade facts appropriate to his argument that there can be "no exemption" from one's responsibility, even though we all recognize that society is guilty too (*OTT*, p. 31). Elwin ruefully catches his cruel King's soft gaze, as he propounds, on the basis of "the dark illumination" contained in the Hazlitt sentence, "the double-truth" of such tragic wisdom (*OTT*, p. 31). Which is that, upon entry into adulthood and the larger cultural life, each of us assumes a share in the guilt of society, because we all make up the secret links in that "great chain of the world's rage," no matter how hard we try to deny this moral fact. We are complicitous in culture by our very existence. Unable to resist the temptation to push his daughter into a painful recognition, Elwin abruptly recognizes himself as an heir of Melville's Claggart, that demonic insister upon radical evil. Elwin recoils from this recognition, to realize why his daughter is defending "the other Margaret," at first so vehemently and then so mournfully:

> Yet wisdom, a small measure of it, did seem to come. It came suddenly, as no doubt was the way of moments of wisdom, and he perceived what stupidly he had not understood earlier, that it was not the other Margaret but herself that his Margaret was grieving for, that in her foolish and passionate argument, with the foolish phrases derived from the admired Miss Hoxie [her teacher], she was defending herself from her own impending responsibility. Poor thing, she saw it moving toward her through the air at a great rate, and she did not want it. Naturally enough, she did not want it. And he, for what reason he did not know, was forcing it upon her. (*OTT*, p. 35)

"Mirror upon mirror, all's the show" as Yeats in "High Talk" says. The dark illumination of human finitude that is moving toward Margaret Elwin reflects the tragic wisdom of her father and his broodings, even as the passionate innocence of her handmade lamb and her makeshift defense of the maid reflect her and her desire to remain always capable of becoming "so much more life."

The "climax" comes as Margaret Elwin watches —over the heads of her solicitous parents—the other Margaret, apparently out of everyone's line of sight in the kitchen, gleefully smash the beautiful green lamb to bits. The story concludes now quickly with the girl assuming the burden of true vision and asserting incessantly what she really saw despite her father's weak refrain of liberal exculpation that it was an accident. This final reversal destroys the pretentions to a hard wisdom on the part of Rouault's King and its cultured idealizer, Stephen Elwin, and diminishes, intentionally, any aspirations to the sublime effect of authentic tragedy. A cheap reproduction indeed.

Trilling in this story generalizes the modern penchant for absolute irony—that critical consciousness which would even subvert itself— into a universal human condition that marks the passage from innocence to experience in the moral life of culture. Moreover, the way that he does so betrays the spectral replication of the psychology of sacrifice among his scapegoat characters and between them and the authorial mind that creates only to destroy them. Finally, "The Other Margaret" subverts all points of view within the story. It thus permits the reader to imagine that its omnipotent author, in seeing and understanding all that he artfully posits and demolishes, represents the most comprehensive position available. This would make him the perversely self-delighting majesty that contains, as Rouault's King only appears to do, the conflicts of this fictional critique of liberal culture. This ironic policy of containment symbolically reproduces Trilling's vision in the reader's mind. In the name of ever-lost innocence, that "insupportable fact" of our moral life, Trilling would leave his reader as Stephen Elwin must leave his daughter, hysterically broken and in bitter tears, enwombing herself in the sound of her own weeping and open now only to her father's liberal "stroking": "Elwin . . . [was] quite unable . . . to give her any better help than that" (*OTT*, p. 37).

Whether it is a class or a crusading daughter, Trilling's fictional heroes function in their stories to propagate that tragic culture which requires, as Tertan's case makes particularly clear, the sacrifice of "genius," so as to reproduce *as lost* the vision of innocence to be found in literature and art, for ironic consumption by the "belated" middle-class moderns he represents. The images of playing the recorder and stroking one's hysterical daughter define the limits of Trilling's culture. The pattern of loss, ambivalence, and regression visibly played out in Elwin's case and compressed, climactically, in his daughter's final recognition also defines Trilling's ritual of reading as the culture of mourning: that "dark illumination" to be spread to all.

Two other works of 1945, "Art and Neurosis" (preliminary version) and "F. Scott Fitzgerald" make this perfectly clear. This shorter version of "Art and Neurosis" continues Trilling's earlier attack from "Freud and Literature" (pt. 2) on the reductive uses of psychoanalysis in literary study. It does so, however, not so much by defending Freud from himself as by defending him from his disciples, particularly Edmund Wilson in *The Wound and the Bow* and a Dr. Rosenzweig who would clarify Wilson's speculative thesis for greater diagnostic precision when treating dead authors. Wilson (and Rosenzweig after him) use the Philoctetes "pattern" as a key for understanding the creative process. This ancient Greek story appears to suggest that Ulysses-like power to bend a great bow depends upon paying a great price: Philoctetes' fetid suppurating wound which isolates him from his fellow man. Trilling sees in this psychoanalytic appropriation of classical culture another instance of the romantic myth of the sick artist, which he, in emulation of Charles Lamb's "On the True Sanity of Genius," will here debunk once and for all by showing how useful this myth is both to the Gradgrind bourgeoisie and the Scholar-Gypsy avant-garde and how mistaken it is as an explanation of genius. In "Art and Neurosis," then, Trilling would appear to have anticipated and answered the original prototype of the argument I am here laying out.

Both onslaughts on the myth of the sick artist would also appear to subvert the argument that he is the priest of tragic culture whose mature work propagates, in an ironic play upon the old commonplace "misery loves company," the sublime necessity of sacrificial pain.

> the whole economy of the neurosis is based exactly on this idea of the *quid pro quo* of sacrificial pain: the neurotic person unconsciously subscribes to a system whereby he gives up some pleasure or power, or inflicts pain on himself in order to secure some other power or some other pleasure. . . . And this idea would seem to explain, if not the origin of the ancient mutilation of priests, then at least a common understanding of their sexual sacrifice. . . . But if genius and its source are what we are dealing with, we must observe that the reference to neurosis tells us nothing about . . . architectonic skill. . . . We cannot, that is, make the writer's inner life exactly equivalent to his power of expressing it. Let us grant for the sake of argument that the literary genius, as distinguished from other men, is the victim of a "mutilation" and that his fantasies are neurotic. It does not then follow as the inevitable next step that his ability to express these fantasies and to impress us with them is neurotic, for that ability is what we mean by his genius. . . . For, . . . what is surely not neurotic, what indeed suggests nothing but health is his power of using his neuroticism. He shapes his fantasies, he gives them social form and reference. (*LI*, pp. 167, 174)

One—someone—should feel devastated by this "liberal" polemic.

Trilling himself goes on to provide the basis of my rebuttal, when he recalls correctly that "the activity of the artist, we must remember, may be approximated by many who are themselves not artists" (*LI*, p. 124). That is, for such dilettantes, the myth of the sick artist expresses the true insanity of nongenius. The Philoctetes pattern applies to them— to all only would-be partakers of the creative life. Trilling is absolutely right, and in his fiction of this period he ironically dramatizes their self-made tragic plight, just as a good critical representative of the public mind should do. In essence, then, I am claiming that Trilling is of the dilettante's demonic party but, unlike them, knows it.

This is why, I would suggest, Trilling in another essay at this time envisions F. Scott Fitzgerald as the Samson Agonistes of self-creation who needs to aspire to be great even if he doesn't have all the makings

(*LI*, pp. 244, 250). For in *The Great Gatsby* at least Fitzgerald passes his own test for a first-rate intelligence—"the ability to hold two opposed ideas in the mind at the same time and still retain the ability to function" (*LI*, p. 245)—even if this negative capability of the artist cannot protect him from succumbing at last to the quintessentially American dream of his own tragic character: the dream of "Platonic self-begetting" (*LI*, p. 251), as Trilling calls it. Trilling means that romantic vision of suddenly recognizing and then realizing perfectly the idea of oneself through the adoption of the creative voice: "In the novel no less than in the poem, the voice of the author is the decisive factor" (*LI*, p. 253).

Here we come upon one of the central paradoxes of liberal culture. It is the Arnoldian mission of humanistic education to promote "the best that has been thought and said" among the classes and masses alike, in order to create a new class of "humane aliens" who form the utopian vanguard of the ideal future state, in which the principle of aesthetic pleasure will replace the reality of politics as the final measure of success in life. The function of the little magazine, for example, is to contribute to this mission by organizing "a new union between our political ideas and our imagination" (*LI*, p. 100). Similarly, the critique of reality in America aims to move us from "the dark and bloody crossroads where literature and politics meet" (*LI*, p. 11), to a place in our thinking where it is not always "a little too late for mind" (*LI*, p. 18) to avert oedipal crises, nor always a good thing to picture reality as too "hard, resistant, unformed, impenetrable, and unpleasant" (*LI*, p. 13) to support "the electrical qualities of mind" (*LI*, p. 14) for more than an idle moment or two. And finally, to this same cultural end of maturity, Trilling's dithyrambs in praise of "classic tragic realism" (*LI*, p. 57) mean to defuse—in the manner of Sherwood Anderson and his book of grotesques (*LI*, p. 27)—dread of suffering the complex fate of being an American.

And yet, as Trilling's fiction and remarks in "Art and Neurosis" dramatize, when liberal culture begins to succeed in its mission it suffers one of its biggest failures, by making essentially Anderson's mistake of recommending generally what by definition only a few can ever achieve—a distinctive life: "Certainly the precious essence of personality to which Anderson was so much committed could not be preserved by any of the people or any of the deeds his own books delight in" (*LI*, p. 33). That is, liberal culture would substitute for oedipal politics an adolescent aesthetics that, as the preface to *Winesburg, Ohio* bluntly puts it, permits rather than prohibits an anarchy of "truths" and their accompanying "life-styles": "It was the truths that made the people grotesques. . . . the moment one of the people took one of the truths to himself, called it his truth, and tried to live his life by it, he became a grotesque and the truth he embraced became a falsehood" (*LI*, p. 27). Consequently, Trilling, like any humanist, is caught in the contradiction between his promotion of culture and his dismay at seeing culture reproduced in adulterated form among a great number of people, many of whom, like perhaps Trilling himself, would aspire to the highest achievements no matter what the costs or how uncertain the talent. Hence the "solution" of Tertan's "sacrifice" or the polite diatribe in "Art and Neurosis" against modern dilettantes for their inability even to face what the artist transforms into his art, all "the chaotic and destructive forces" that the psyche "contains" (*LI*, p. 178). Instead, they glorify their own neurotic pain in the myth of the mad genius and his tragic beauty, this myth being their one "sick" creation. In other words, Trilling needs the myth of sane genius in order to separate sheep from goats in cultural affairs.

Two entries from Trilling's notebooks of these years (1945–1946) demonstrate how central to the project of critical humanism is this distinction between normal and abnormal development. The first entry reflects on Kafka's *The Trial* as a psychomachia as well as a novel:

> Kafka: *The Trial*—what is the mystery here when we remember that every neurosis is a primitive form of legal proceeding in which the accused carries on the prosecution, imposes judgment and executes the sentence: *all to the end that someone else should not perform the same process.* In writing about Kafka—whenever—it is important to remember the function of this *sui-trial* (See *Ancient Mariner* at the very opening of our era). ("Notebooks," p. 26)

The neurotic, fearing castration at the father's hands, repeatedly castrates himself symbolically in advance. What mastery he thereby gains over the dread power he must pay for in ever greater repression. We recall that *The Castle* comes after *The Trial* in Kafka's career, or, as Trilling's last remark reminds us, Joseph K. is all that is left of the Ancient Mariner, and K. in turn is all that is left of the former:

> This is very important in making a judgment of tendencies of modern culture. The masochistic character of the estimate of survival—to adopt a form of being that will differentiate oneself from the dominant father-culture—to take str[ength]-w[ea]k[ness] from that—to indict the Philistine-father by str[ength]-w[ea]k[ness]—the str[ength]-w[ea]k[ness] of the legal process of the neurosis. ("Notebooks," p. 26)

The avant-garde, whether political or aesthetic, depends for its sense of unique identity upon oedipal conflict and "the str[ength]-w[ea]k[ness] of the legal process of the neurosis." As the self-diminishing style of this entry underscores, there appears to be no escape from this inevitable fate of modern cultural life.

The second entry, however, from the period when Trilling composes *The Middle of the Journey* (1946–1947), suggests the critical humanist's traditional avenue of "escape"—ascension to the "spirit" of irony.

> *Spirit.* The modern feeling that spirit should find its expression *immediately* in the world of necessity and that all that falls short of the full expression of spirit is repulsive. I see this often in gifted students of a particular kind who, when they find that, say, a graduate school is not up to their standard and expectation, cannot endure staying and abandon their projects. They have, one might say, no irony—for irony, perhaps, is the awareness with acceptance of the breach between spirit and the world of necessity—institutions, etc. They insist that spirit be wholly embodied in institutions. If what I have just written were put to them, they would say, why of course, why not? Yet the fact is that there is a weakness of spirit within that keeps them from enduring—they do not believe that they really exist and can exist if what they recognize as good within themselves is not matched by external forms, received and established by something. They do not understand the *tragic* choice. They want the reign of spirit immediately. ("Notebooks," p. 26)

Maintaining the contradiction between liberal culture and its degradations becomes here an instance of that spirit of Emersonian self-reliance which perseveres in the breach between freedom and necessity by means of its ironic acceptance of social forms. The tragic choice between culture and self-development makes one a *teacher*, and it entails seeing all those others who aspire to but fail to endure in their choices as weak. They are those "artistic" students who, like Tertan, voluntarily or otherwise, should enter the madhouse. How else can Trilling and company see themselves as normal, and true genius as sane?

If the many "weak" students of modern culture need their romantic myth of the sick artist, then Trilling and critical humanism need all the more the myth of the normal genius or worldly messiah and its corollary, the myth of the many false messiahs. In the conclusion to the final version of "Art and Neurosis" (1947) Trilling claims as much when he says that although "we are all ill," through "a universal accident," the artist gives a pleasing form to our condition despite, not thanks to, his own pain. Consequently, the symbol of the artist should not be the Philoctetes of Wilson or Rosenzweig but Pan, Dionysus, Apollo—or best of all, that figure who is originally the symbol of the critic's art of interpretation, "the baby Hermes":

> that miraculous infant who, the day he was born, left his cradle to do mischief: and the first thing he met with was a tortoise, which he greeted politely before scooping it from its shell and, thought and deed being one with him, he contrived the instrument to which he sang "the glorious tale of his own begetting." These were gods, and very early ones, but their myths tell us something about the nature and source of art even in our grim, late human present. (*LI*, p. 180)

This is the vision of innocence—self-delighting, other-affrighting— with a vengeance. Under its guise Trilling attacks the myth of the sick artist and proposes his own myth of the "mature" or "normal" genius. The genius possesses the power of embodying his psychology more intensely, distinctly, and memorably than other people can, within the possible modes of representation available to a culture at any one time. The price of genius is a perpetual borderline condition of alienation, and appropriation and exploitation by those who would live the life of the artist as their moral protest against the middle-class world, without earning the right to do so by their imaginative accomplishments, not even by their accomplishment of survival. Failing to become geniuses, such "other" people either resentfully deny the category of genius in the name of reason and revolution, or opportunistically deploy it for their own professional purposes. In this strategic fashion Trilling would "save" Freud and psychoanalysis from reductiveness and also permit literary critics to make use of Freudian ideas without succumbing to a crude and deterministic materialism every bit as mistaken about the mind's freedom as that of Stalinist Marxism and its American fellow-traveling avatars. Moreover, the myth of normal genius, by focusing on the artist's creative power to objectify his experience in great imposing public forms of tragic beauty, facilitates the defensive translation of progressive social attitudes into the triumph of the therapeutic and of individual maturity. Consequently, a psychological principle of sublime judgment can now resolve the contradiction between the official democratic mission of culture and its secret aristocratic promise of individual distinction, in favor of those few "strong" liberal masters who endure the discipline of style to become latter-day "classics" of the language and so deserve to instruct and judge those many "weak" others who aspire and fail, pathetic victims all of their too-fierce "castration anxiety." These few "teachers" are themselves to be "led" in turn by the representative literary intellectual who possesses the most ironic consciousness, the worldly messiah of critical humanism, the priest of heroic self-sacrifice amidst imperial anarchy, the prince of scapegoats whose kingdom *is* of this world and who, for our own good, knows precisely when to prescribe to his fellow professionals the appropriate "dose" of savage civility or unctuous appreciation. Many are called to culture, but few indeed are chosen, as Blackmur knew, to administer it.

It would be an easy game to "deconstruct" this liberal ideology of critical humanism by showing, as Neil Hertz has done, how it exemplifies "a recurrent turn of mind" in post-Enlightenment culture, "the representation of what would seem to be a political threat as if it were a sexual threat,"[20] and thereby write it off from a neo-feminist perspective as "male hysteria under political pressure." Trilling's major stories of the period—"Of This Time, Of That Place," "The Lesson and the Secret," and "The Other Margaret"—as well as his notebook entries and essays on Freud and the heroic reality of mind all proclaim, as we have seen, his continuing, perhaps increasing, concern with what, after Henry James, he calls "the masculine character" and the modern threats to its survival. Similarly, one could show how, underlying his psychological principle of critical judgment on aesthetic matters or the manifestations of "The Female Will" (Blake), lie the vestiges of imperialism, racism, and Social Darwinism that, as Edward W. Said has generally argued about liberal culture, have been dressed up and refined "endlessly" into the discipline of style by succeeding generations of literary humanists, with the result that Reagan and William Bennett have been "allowed" to rule the country.[21] It is not that such critiques of "patriarchal politics" from the left of Lionel Trilling and liberal culture are too implausible or simplistic to be even countenanced. It is that they are not comprehensive enough for my taste. I do think, however, that they point out the dimensions of a larger, more pervasive problem that effects virtually everyone who wants to advance him or herself via education: viz., the repressed religious unconscious of cultural assimilators who suffer from the radical guilt of their doubly alienated position. Cut off (for better or worse) by imperious aspiration from their traditions and reflexively repelled by disgust from modern culture, American intellectuals whatever their origins—déclassé elites, repressed peoples home and abroad, or the remnants of the feminine mystique—have become some of the major sources of a new militancy of the spirit, prophetic in intensity, to be found on the right and on the left. Such militancy belies analyses that suggest our critical culture is "religious" primarily in the sense of its being "otherworldly" and "gnostic," or "monkish" and "hermetic."[22] My point is that "the work of liberation" to be found in Trilling and his time—so secular in appearance, liberal in rhetoric, and repressive in some of its real tendencies—derives directly from the Judeo-Christian unconscious, from the ascetic will, animating the modern world still after all these years since Hegel first announced the death of god: This is the "unconscious, where fear, shame, attraction and repulsion are indistinguishable" ("Under Forty," p. 198). In other words, that place created in our minds by repressive memories where, for safe keeping, Freud inserted the god of his—and our—fathers.

A Vast Idea: The Encompassing Mind

"The figure of that first ancestor, invested by family tradition with a dim and dusky grandeur, was present to my boyish imagination as far back as I can remember."[23] This is the tentative way Nathaniel Hawthorne—who added the w to the family name—speaks of its American founder, William Hathorne, in "The Custom House," the introduction to *The Scarlet Letter*. Hawthorne continues with greater assurance as he recreates the memory of this distinguished ancestor from the early days in the history of Salem, Massachusetts:

> [The figure of the first ancestor] still haunts me, and induces a sort of homing-feeling with the past, which I scarcely claim in reference to the present phase of the town. I seem to have a stronger claim to a residence here on account of this grave, bearded, sable-cloaked and steeple-crowned progenitor—who came so early [in 1635], with his Bible and his sword, and trod the unworn street with such a stately port, and made so large a figure as a man of war and peace—a stronger claim than for myself, whose name is seldom heard and my face hardly known. He was a soldier, legislator, judge; he was a ruler in the church; he had all the Puritanic traits, both good and evil. He was likewise a bitter persecutor, as witness the Quakers, who have remembered him in their histories, and relate an incident of his hard severity towards a woman of their sect which will last longer, it is to be feared, than any of his better deeds, though these were many. (*NH*, pp. 323–324)

A tender rancor suffuses this comparison of Hawthorne with his earliest relative. It gives way to more purely negative features when he speaks of John Hathorne, a second-generation persecutor whose specialty was the Salem "witches": Whether these ancestors repented their persecutions or not, their heir formally takes upon himself "for their sakes" all the "shame." Since, for better or worse, he cannot measure up to their stern ideal, that's the least he can do. This symbolic expiation permits Hawthorne to envision a final reunion with his disapproving patriarchs.

> Either of these stern and black-browed Puritans would have thought it quite a sufficient retribution for his sins that after so long a lapse of years the old trunk of the family tree, with so much venerable moss upon it, should have borne, as its topmost bough, an idler like myself. No aim that I have ever cherished would they recognize as laudable; no success of mine, if my life, beyond its domestic scope, had even been brightened by success, would they deem otherwise than worthless, if not positively disgraceful. "What is he?" murmurs one grey shadow of my forefathers to the other. "A writer of story-books! What kind of a business in life, what manner of glorifying God, or being serviceable to mankind in his day and generation, may that be? Why, the degenerate fellow might as well have been a fiddler!" Such are the compliments bandied between my great grandfathers and myself across the gulf of time! And yet, let them scorn me as they will, strong traits of their nature have intertwined themselves with mine. (*NH*, p. 325)

In other words, their spirit lives on in his "letters."

I take this excursion into Hawthorne for an explanatory purpose. For this passage provides us with a comprehensive and concrete portrayal of the religious unconscious in the process of formation. Haunted by a heroic vision of origins, alienated from a present reality that feels like an end, the mind in question establishes its ironic priority in present alienation by recognizing personal guilt for not measuring up to the ancestral ideal of communal service, and by proposing, since it feels unworthy already, to take upon itself and symbolically expiate any ancestral shame as well as its own. If the ancestors, to be truly whole, scapegoated others, then their heir will have them remain in authority by envisioning their scapegoating of him, their heir, in recompense for the family's sins. A sublime judgment thereby emerges that while the heroic ancestors had to act their persecution complexes out on others, their ironic heir, however otherwise unlike them, can imagine the reinternalization and greater repression of their repressive impulses within his own work. Thus, the religious unconscious both informs and results from this great work of liberation that makes American democracy so effective: Every man and woman his or her own self-punishment.

My sacrificial formulation echoes, of course, Nietzsche, Frazer, Freud, Girard, and Harold Bloom (among others) on the repressive origins of memory, will, desire, and the revisionary will to write in Western culture. The passage from Hawthorne, however, as I try to suggest, adds or highlights a dimension of the argument often overlooked. Our mind-forg'd manacles can individualize a subject of repression only on the basis of the continuation of the communal ideal in a new form. In other, more familiar terms, the original formation and subsequent operations of what we generally call "conscience" remains fundamentally the same, even as its expressions must change over time, with changing circumstances. In short, whether our ancestors persecuted others, or we persecute ourselves, the subjects of repression in either case represent in deed and word the creation of the religous unconscious. While we, unlike Hawthorne, may prefer to be less "whole" and more humane—toward others at least—we, like him, would live our lives for some fostering vision, progressive or traditional, larger than mere self-interest permits. And those who do so have "strong traits" of their ancestors' "nature . . . interwined" with their own. Or, to modify Trilling's vision from "The Other Margaret," life that sacrifices itself is so much more life—and more to sacrifice.

Sacrifice, if not heroic sacrifice, marks *The Middle of the Journey*, Trilling's only novel and the most complete expression of his mind we possess. Three recently published notebook entries, although apparently made after the novel's publication, reflect back on its informing point. The first entry, from 1948, summarizes in an epigram Trilling's disgust with liberal culture: "We are at heart so profoundly *anarchistic* that the only form of state we can imagine living in is *Utopian*; and so cynical that the only Utopia we can believe in is authoritarian" ("Notebooks," p. 28). That is, American liberals secretly love the idea of absolute power and, to see it in action for themselves, are quite willing to hypocritically suffer the abuse—of others.

The second entry, also from 1948, continues the motif of sacrifice, but in a more personal vein. Reacting in advance to the negative reviews of his novel that are surely to come (the early ones were mildly favorable), Trilling explodes in rage over those who envy him his achievement: "Suppose I were to believe that one could be a professor and a man! and a writer!—what arrogance and defiance of convention" ("Notebooks," p. 29). And so what attacks he provokes upon himself.[24] Again, the idea of scapegoating—this time oneself as opposed to other people or one's entire culture—pervades Trilling's thinking. Interestingly, this entry shows how intimately connected and uncertain are his roles of teacher, critic, and man. For Trilling, one must ever aspire to be what one already ideally is. And the risk of all aspiration is the resentful attacks it inspires in other aspirants, especially in life's many "failures."

The third and final entry relevant to *The Middle of the Journey* comes from early 1949. Although Ginsberg will return to alma mater in semi-triumph a decade later, he visits the campus at this time to show his old professors that they were correct in recommending commitment, for he is now better if not cured. Trilling reflects later on Ginsberg's gentle strangeness and high praise for Jack Kerouac's novel with characteristic honesty: "[Ginsberg is] like a different kind of humanity. . . . But later I saw with what bitterness I had made the prediction [of failure for Kerouac's novel]—not wanting [it] to be good because if the book of an accessory to a murder is good—how can one of mine be?—The continuing sense that wickedness—or is it my notion of courage—is essential for creation" ("Notebooks," p. 31).

As Freud in *Moses and Monotheism* also notes, the production of any text involves a "murder": the "sacrifice" of some projected hero and of one's passion, in order to "fulfill" in repressed form the original parricidal lust. The courage to create, for Trilling, likewise entails the power to transgress—ultimately against oneself.

The action of this 1947 novel (set a decade earlier after the debacle of the Moscow trials) melodramatically embodies Trilling's sacrificial ethic. John Laskell, the protagonist and author surrogate travels from New York to Westport, Connecticut, to spend the last month or so of the summer with his friends, Nancy and Arthur Croom, in the final phase of his long recovery from a near-fatal attack of scarlet fever. On arrival, Laskell tries to share his feelings about escaping death with this otherwise sensitive and generous young couple (they paid for his private nurse, for example), only to discover to his resentful dismay that they resist all approaches to the topic. It is as if, Laskell suspects, the very idea of death for them is in bad taste, even politically reactionary. Laskell and his "official" hosts (they have actually put him up with their neighbors, the Folgers) are "liberal" nonliterary intellectuals. Arthur Croom is soon to join the New Deal bureaucracy in Washington, Laskell is the author of a "radical" critique of modern architecture, *Theories of Housing*, and Nancy Croom, wife and mother, expecting another child, is secretly working for the Communist Party. Much of the novel consists in extensive debates among these three characters and their friends about the best way to save mankind from the self-destructive syndrome endemic to what we now call "late capitalism" in its endless, crisis-ridden death throes. Unbeknownst to the Crooms, Gifford Maxim, professional revolutionary and hero of all their hopes (it was he who had induced Nancy to go against her husband's wishes and help with clandestine work), has broken with the party of the angels and gone over to the other side. Although Laskell already knows about this revolting development when he arrives, he angrily keeps the information to himself, preferring to wait for the proper moment of maximum effect to deliver the bad news and so exact sweet revenge on the Crooms for their refusal to allow him to discuss his shadow-bout with death.

As he recovers his strength and begins to tire of the endless discussions with the Crooms that are really trials of will, Laskell gets entangled with their neighbors, the Cadwell family; Emily, suburban wife and mother and would-be bohemian in the gaslight Greenwich Village style; Duck, her wastrel husband and the town handyman whose irresponsible ways the Crooms indulge as proletarian chic; and Susan, their daughter, beautiful, inquisitive, so alive, who wants to be a dancer when she grows up. Laskell eventually has an affair with Emily and becomes a second father to Susan, going so far as to spend hours instructing her in the proper way to recite the introductory lyric of Blake's *Milton* for the annual pageant, the centerpiece of the town's charity bazaar. Laskell is playing at adulthood with another man's wife and daughter. His only lover, Elizabeth Feuer, died unexpectedly before he had to face the reality of marriage. Nonetheless, he is able to discover that Emily's quaint carpe diem philosophy covers true depths of feeling. She cherishes a secret that she can share only with her sensitive lover: Susan has a bad heart and will not live long.

Into this resonant disaster waiting to happen comes Maxim, erstwhile "measure" of human heroism and secret agent of enlightenment, who, thanks to Laskell's reluctant intervention, has a platform for his revisionary Christian aesthetics of universal tragedy in the pages of Kermit Simpson's *New Era*, a libertarian journal blandly devoted to including in its promiscuous vision of the world every conceivable shade of opinion. For the first time in his life, Maxim has a public existence, something he desperately hopes will protect him from violent reprisals for his betrayal of the party. Maxim plans to visit Laskell and the Crooms in Westport near summer's end both to convert them to his latest views and to warn Nancy, whose secret involvement in his former work he does not disclose, that she faces a danger beyond her experience to comprehend if she continues in her path. It is at this point that Laskell tells all about Maxim's defection. The effect on the Crooms is, as it had been at first on Laskell, devastating: their great leader has self-destructed, leaving a monumental vacancy in their mighty forecasts of a better future. While everyone, even Laskell, wrestles with this intellectual catastrophe, the real tragedy occurs. Duck Cadwell, drunk and jealous of Laskell's intimate authority with both his women, takes it out on his daughter, striking Susan hard twice after she has had to be prompted by Laskell in her performance of the Blake poem at the talent show. The sick girl collapses immediately, the shock of the cruel blows of her own father's hands bursting her weak heart. Maxim, neither cause nor catalyst of this tragedy, is nevertheless its brilliant critic, teasing out with incisive dialectical irony every nuance of motive and guilt in all concerned. John Laskell, despite these many threats to his recovery, at last returns to New York alone yet a new man.

In *The Middle of the Journey* Trilling has superimposed a Forsterian melodrama of anticlimax upon a Jamesian romance of self-consciousness and Dostoyevskian novel of ideas, in a style as precisely observant of manners among the intellectual class of the time as Proust's or Lawrence's. John Laskell, the Jamesian center of consciousness, stands poised between Gifford Maxim, former revolutionary now religious fanatic, and Nancy Croom, princess of the radical will. The real conflict in this novel thus arises not so much from the plot as from the pragmatic choice of selves the plot makes available for responding to the world. The question, in other words, is: which kind of subject can Laskell, as he completes his convalescence, choose to emulate? Is he, in other words, constrained to only these two models of human agency? The posthumously published introduction to the 1975 reissue of the novel and the great 1948 essay on *The Princess Casamassima* clarify and enhance the argument of his novel as Trilling intended it to be seen.

Originally, according to the posthumous introduction, Trilling wanted to write a *nouvelle*, in the Jamesian mode, that would focus exclusively on John Laskell's discovery of the politics of death in American radical culture of the 1930s. "The enlightened consciousness of the modern age," Trilling writes, can perceive death only as a self-indulgent, debilitating idea that inspires regression from the rigors of the struggle for revolution. Trilling planned, therefore, to demonstrate the falsity of this ideology by revealing the classic American immaturity entailed by such a naive judgment of death:

> In short, the Crooms might be said to pass a *political* judgment upon Laskell for the excessive attention he pays to the fact that he had approached death and hadn't died. If Laskell's preoccupation were

looked at closely and objectively, they seem to be saying, might it not be understood as actually an affirmation of death, which is, in practical outcome, a negation of the future and of the hope it holds out for a society of reason and virtue? Was there not a sense in which death might be called reactionary? (*MJ*, pp. xii–xiii)

Fellow travelers of Stalinism are really good old Americans at heart: imperial adolescents wishing to command the future, forget the past, and make their empty presents dramatic, on the basis of the imposition upon all of a simple, rigid, monolithic scheme that would abolish the incessant conflict of individual wills in a final day of utopian judgment.

With the introduction of Gifford Maxim, however, Trilling's rather simple plan for a *nouvelle* had to be scrapped, in favor of that full-scale treatment only a novel could provide. The reason for this change was not that Trilling wanted to base a character on Whittaker Chambers, an acquaintance from college days, and capitalize on the publicity of the infamous Hiss-Chambers pumpkin imbroglio. Rather, the character of Maxim took on a life of his own in his author's mind, acquiring a weird stature, that of the quixotic intellectual "whose commitment" to an idea—in this instance, first radical politics and then ascetic religion—becomes "definitive of his whole moral being, the controlling element of his existence" (*MJ*, p. xiii). Such a figure—"a tragic comedian of radical politics" (*MJ*, p. xviii)—is the modern form of personal sublimity, and possesses the fascination of the abomination. Besides, the novel's genesis predates the Hiss-Chambers case. When Trilling recalls Chambers, he cannot help but focus on that physical feature symbolic for him of such catastrophic sublimity, even though he never exploited this feature in creating his portrayal of Maxim: "When the mouth opened, it never failed to shock by reason of the dental ruin it disclosed, a devastation of empty sockets and blackened stumps . . . the aggressive toothlessness . . . [and] desolate mouth of a serf" (*MJ*, p. xiv). Playing upon the Shakespearean formula of all-devouring time, Trilling tropes here the self-consuming pathology of the sublime in which the life becomes mere material for realizing the idea of self-transformation presupposed in the work of liberation. For Trilling, then, American radicals are patrons of the sublime, conspicuous consumers of the idea of the apocalypse in whatever forms it takes, who seek thereby to assume characters, isolated by a vast idea of themselves, however conceived, which may engross the present and dominate memory (*MJ*, p. xx). Chambers-Maxim, in short, is another one of Trilling's spectral comrades and murderous comedians who, like Hettner or Tertan, embody the temptation to live solely by the conception of oneself that obsessively occupies their minds at the moment, just as do Fitzgerald's Gatsby, Flaubert's Saint Anthony, or Lenin's Lenin in their respective fictional and ideological works. Gifford Maxim is thus Trilling's most comprehensive representation of the man who would father himself. And, as his famous introduction to James's *Princess Casamassima* strongly suggests, Nancy Croom, as we shall see in detail, is his fullest realization of the modern woman who would mother herself and the radical future into existence no matter what the cost.

Of the celebrated essays on the novel collected in *The Liberal Imagination* (see "Manners, Morals, and the Novel" and "Art and Fortune"), Trilling's introduction to *The Princess Casamassima* is the most successful in carrying out his intention to create an audience for *The Middle of the Journey*. For Trilling combines historical, biographical, generic, and thematic approaches in a unified theory of the novel as a vision of the world redeemed in art, a theory that is also a particularly brilliant reading of this novel. The essay illuminates the major elements in Trilling's writing at the time, but especially the characters Gifford Maxim and Nancy Croom in his novel, who are two sublime instances of the modern will.

The essay, part of the James revival, envisions itself as the fulfillment of the prophecy James made after the failure of *The Princess Casamassima* and *The Bostonians*, that all his works, even these "failures," would eventually enjoy "a general resurrection, kicking off their gravestones in furious new life" (*LI*, p. 85). The essay then assumes that James and his true readers can accept the overripe decadence of Europe as an alluring imaginative possibility (*LI*, p. 61), however much they must finally resist it. For such capacity for suspending disbelief thus enables James to employ effectively the romantic convention of "the young man from the provinces," that nineteenth-century fixture of the novel (see Stendhal's Julien Sorel or Dickens' Pip), which mixes the changeling myth with Horatio Alger ideology, in a variety of curious ways, and which animates the story of Hyacinth Robinson, the Keatsian hero of *The Princess Casamassima*, as well. The novel tells the story of this apparent orphan who is raised to be a bookbinder but who discovers his real desire to write books at the moment when his anarchist involvements have led him to contemplate the murder of an aristocrat believed to be his own father. Although *The Princess Casamassima* is, Trilling argues, "a brilliantly precise representation of social actuality" (*LI*, p. 74), even down to the details of the anarchist's secret organization and terrorist methods, its plot, derived from the heroic convention of romance, experiments with reality, "to force or foster a fact into being"

(*LI*, p. 65), and so represents the world as "experience liberated . . . . disengaged, disembodied, disencumbered, exempt from the conditions that usually attach to it" (*LI*, p. 65). This pragmatic, experimental exemption is, of course, only provisional as far as Trilling is concerned, never absolute or permanent.

The new fact that James in his novel would force or foster into being, like a scientist in his laboratory experimenting with natural law, is what Trilling sees as the multifaceted law of human nature, the literary ethics of advanced intellectuals. This is the law that says, "an adult can die like a child from the withdrawal of love" (*LI*, p. 76), or can choose to revel in "the fruits of the creative spirit" (*LI*, p. 78) and still possess "a true knowledge of society" (*LI*, p. 80), or "can use an art-form to settle a long-running familial dispute" (*LI*, p. 89) over the choice of vocation and yet can still intend to criticize all modes of the modern "imperious will" (*LI*, p. 82), precisely in the name of art's ironic power to manipulate into existence (*LI*, p. 89) that "perfect ambivalence" (*LI*, p. 89) which constitutes "the truth of life" (*LI*, p. 86). By this fine formula, Trilling means to refer to the Shakespearean, almost godlike recognition that people love their "enemies" as well as their friends for the energies a world of conflict releases in them. "Life aware of itself is so much more life," as "The Other Margaret" puts it, echoing Keats on the ardor of pursuit.

Trilling bases this aesthetic vision of moral complexity upon the self-conscious sacrifice that the tragic hero makes in behalf of the human paradise of culture. James's Hyacinth Robinson, for example, pays with his life for this vision. Forced to choose between the world "raised to the noblest and richest expression" by art (*LI*, p. 84) and the murderous oedipal consequences of revolutionary action, James's hero commits suicide with the very weapon given to him to shoot his suspected father. And Trilling defends, even honors Hyacinth for doing so:

> Hyacinth's death, then, is not his way of escaping from irresolution. It is truly a sacrifice, an act of heroism. He is a hero of civilization because he dares to do more than civilization does: embodying two ideals at once, he takes upon himself, in full consciousness, the guilt of each. He acknowledges both his parents, as it were. By his death he instructs us in the nature of civilized life and by his consciousness he transcends it. (*LI*, p. 86)

Hyacinth, like Trilling's own heroes, justifies existence by the quality of his consciousness. To possess a fully developed psyche, according to Trilling, means one is able to sacrifice revolutionary dreams and espouse things as they are, learning to enjoy what otherwise would oppress one, even to the point of relishing heroic self-destruction, so long as an exquisite consciousness can in the process be produced to appreciate the irony of it all. Here, in a nutshell, is the ideology of sacrifice pervading Trilling's mature work.

Under the militantly quietistic banner of his aesthetic messiah, Trilling would do battle against the only enemy of this vision, that imperious modern will so insistent on its own innocence and freedom from all complicity with things as they are, which pursues the quest for a reality corresponding to its insistence, a reality without pain or sacrifice, or guilt. Arnold had said the romantics didn't know enough, and Trilling adds, so, too, American radicals; and what they all fail to know is their own desperate spirits. For, in the end, the imperious modern will must reject every claim of civilized life and look upon all its great heroes as silly scapegoats:

> The Princess, as some will remember, is the Christina Light of James's earlier novel, *Roderick Hudson*, and she considers, as Madame Grandoni says of her, "that in the darkest hour of her life, she sold herself for a title and a fortune. She regards her doing so as such a terrible piece of frivolity that she can never for the rest of her days be serious enough to make up for it." Seriousness has become her ruling passion, and in the great sad comedy of the story it is her fatal sin, for seriousness is not exempt from the tendency of ruling passions to lead to error. And yet it has an aspect of heroism, this hunt of hers for reality, for a strong and final basis of life. "Then it's real, it's solid!" she exclaims when Hyacinth tells her that he has seen Hoffendahl and has penetrated to the revolutionary holy of holies. It is her quest for reality that leads her to the poor, to the very poorest poor she can find, and that brings a light of joy to her eye at any news of suffering or deprivation, which must surely be, if anything is, an irrefrangible reality. As death and danger are—her interest in Hyacinth is made the more intense by his pledged death, and she herself eventually wants to undertake the mortal mission. A perfect drunkard of reality, she is ever drawn to look for stronger and stronger drams.
>
> Inevitably, of course, the great irony of her fate is that the more passionately she seeks reality and the happier she becomes in her belief that she is close to it, the further removed she is. Inevitably she must turn away from Hyacinth because she reads his moral seriousness as frivolousness; and inevitably she is led to Paul who, as she thinks, affirms her in a morality which is as real and serious

as anything can be, an absolute morality which gives her permission
to devaluate and even destroy all that she has known of human good
because it has been connected with her own frivolous, self-betraying
past. She cannot but mistake the nature of reality, for she believes it
is a thing, a position, a finality, a bedrock. She is, in short, the very
embodiment of the modern will which masks itself in virtue, making
itself appear harmless, the will that hates itself and finds its manifestations guilty and is able to exist only if it operates in the name of
virtue, that despises the variety and modulations of the human story
and longs for an absolute humanity, which is but another way of
saying nothingness. In her alliance with Paul she constitutes a striking symbol of that powerful part of modern culture that exists by
means of its claim to political innocence and by its false seriousness—
the political awareness that is not aware, the social consciousness
which hates full consciousness, the moral earnestness which is moral
luxury. (*LI*, pp. 90–92)

In this extraordinary passage, Trilling transforms James's Princess into
the mirror image of his own willful practice of revisionary reading. He
does so, however, self-consciously to clear a space not so much for such
spectral politics as for the celebration of "the imagination of love" that
he has teased out of James's novel and has hoped to put into his own
work:

The fatal ambiguity of the Princess and Paul, the revolutionary
leader, is a prime condition of Hyacinth Robinson's tragedy. If we
comprehend the complex totality that James has thus conceived, we
understand that the novel is an incomparable representation of the
spiritual circumstances of our civilization. I venture to call it incomparable because, although other writers have provided abundant
substantiation of James's insight, no one has, like him, told us the
truth in a single luminous act of creation. If we ask by what magic
James was able to do what he did, the answer is to be found in what
I have identified as the source of James's moral realism. For the
novelist can tell the truth about Paul and the Princess only if, while
he represents them in their ambiguity and error, he also allows them
to exist in their pride and beauty: the moral realism that shows the
ambiguity and error cannot refrain from showing the pride and
beauty. Its power to tell the truth arises from its power of love. James
had the imagination of disaster and that is why he is immediately
relevant to us; but together with the imagination of disaster he had

what the imagination of disaster often destroys and in our time is daily destroying, the imagination of love. (*LI*, p. 92)

In order to let "the imagination of love" prevail, Trilling first must discipline "the imagination of disaster," and this he would do in *The Middle of the Journey* and particularly through the portrayal of Nancy Croom, Trilling's version of James's Princess, and of Blake's Female Will.

"I'll thank you to step out of the cosmos, John" is the way Nancy Croom, cultivating these plants in her garden, responds with amusing because unintended irony to Laskell after the first of their many debates on politics and death. Increasingly, her unconscious wish that Laskell abstract himself from her world becomes the substance of her conscious arguments, until she actually identifies Laskell, who has confided to her his great pleasure in contemplating a rose during his illness, with Ferdinand the sissy bull who refuses to fight the matador in the ring, preferring instead to drowse in his green and pleasant fields. (This liberal bull, forever enshrined in a Disney cartoon, comes from the folklore surrounding the Spanish Civil War). Finally, in a self-conscious assault on Laskell for his celebration of the limits of human will, Nancy Croom solicitously summons his reverence for the past, in the form of his mourning for an old love, as the definitive feature of his now superannuated personality. So skillful is Nancy in her motherly assault that it is all that Laskell can do to resist the "deep voluptuous emptiness" that mournful formula of hers opens up in him:

"You live for yourself, you don't know how real certain things can be to other people. It's simply that your mind is turned in a different direction. I never realized it, I suppose. But the way you love the past, for instance—"her voice was now indefinitely kind, so kind that it destroyed him. "I do think you care more about the past than you do about the future, John." (*MJ*, pp. 202–203)

As she continues by asserting her own future-orientation, so filled with promise and new life, Nancy suddenly closes off the subject by placing a hand on her own prominent belly in testimony to her growing authority, and for a moment Laskell is more devastated by her than he ever is by Maxim, master dialectician:

There was nothing more to be said. Not that Laskell could have said anything. He did not speak for the destruction that was going on within him, a soft destruction, almost voluptuous. . . . Nancy's

gentle definition of him was at work, making a deep voluptuous
emptiness in him. It frightened him, but it also drew him. Something
within him was cooperating with Nancy's definition to dismiss him
from the world of men. (*MJ*, pp. 203–204)

To regain the field from Nancy, Laskell discloses how he had read from
her manner alone the secret she has been concealing all these months
from her husband: that, against his wishes, she has been facilitating
the Party's clandestine work of subversion, spying, and assassination
by receiving under her own name "letters" to be forwarded to others
in the covert network of agents.

One can see from this passage why "manners," "the hum and buzz"
of a culture's unconscious tastes ("Manners, Morals, and the Novel"),
would matter so much to Trilling, as much as does the disciplining of
the will through the perfection of a self-consciously masculine style of
writing ("Art and Fortune"). For the real war here takes the form of
debate, victory in which assures imaginative survival as a mind de-
serving of aggressive respect rather than condescending indulgence.
The danger facing the liberal John Laskell is that in recoiling from
Maxim's impersonation of the mad father he may fall easy prey to
Nancy Croom's terrible mother routine, and, Prufrock-like, be fixed at
last in a formulated phrase as a quaint object of solicitous pity: Bartleby manqué. Yet Laskell evades this fate by his ability to read between
the lines. His greater sensitivity to the nuances of things becomes the
basis for his own project of demystification. "To unmask the unmaskers" is the way Trilling defines this central project: "to show that the
very ideas they were committed to were betrayed to very death by their
way of dealing with ideas: as if they were totems, in the way of piety"
(*LD*, p. 24). In this light, the revolutionary dialectic of a better future
replicates, in its manner of execution, the very corruptions that had
led to condemnation of the present society (*LD*, p. 20). Given such a
bleak prospect, the intellectual legacy of modern radicalism in America
would appear to be at best "the dessiccated spirit" (*LD*, p. 31) of pure
resistance embodied in John Laskell.

From what position, however, historically grounded and socially
affiliated as it must be, can Laskell and his author possess such a
demystified perspective on the radical dialectic? The vision that Laskell
offers on arrival in Westport when Duck Cadwell, drunk once again,
fails to meet the train, provides a clue.

There was no sound save the chatter of the telegraph machine and
then the wirelike sound of cicadas rising and falling in the late after-

noon, a sound like a mode of silence. The sky was blue and immense. The sun was hot. Laskell saw a little knot of buses and stores, not far from the station, and a row of red filling pumps. He saw a man at the pump, but the man went away. The vertigo of fear began in his stomach and rose in a spiral to his brain. He did not know what he was afraid of. He was not terrified by anything, he was just in terror. It had the aspect of movement, of something rushing at him, or in him, like a brown wind. Some alien intelligence wanted desperately to shriek, yet knew that if it should utter a sound, it would be lost; and wanted blindly to clutch, yet dared not move. (*MJ*, p. 8)

Laskell is not really able to recall what has happened to him during these "terrible moments." But like a victim of hysterical repression, in psychoanalysis, he can reconstitute the sense of the experience if not the experience itself via retroactive interpretation, a later reasoning that here analogously associates images of reading with symbolic castration (*MJ*, p. 8). This "act of intelligence" (*MJ*, p. 9) judges that it is the mind itself and not the world which is the source of its terror, and so it is the mind that can learn to discipline its "unreasoning parts" to the point where they can express themselves in appropriate utterance rather than in some alien compulsive shriek. Laskell confronting Nancy Croom's gentle devastation, Trilling's other heroes, even Trilling himself as represented by the figure of the paralyzed bell in the 1929 letter for Elliot Cohen, all embody Trilling's vision perfected in this exemplary sublime passage identifying the primal evil as the dread necesssity of self-expression. The psychoanalytic model of human existence, therefore, sustains Trilling in his representative faith in the therapeutic power of critical reading. Borrowed light from his own Freud would make Trilling the worldly-wise messiah of all once and would-be radicals: "At last he was able to ask himself, strictly and with an educated man's knowledge of the devious craft of the mind's unreasoning parts, what effects his weeks in bed could have had that, like an infant deserted, he had been overwhelmed by hysteria because the Crooms, for some reason they could not help, had not met him" (*MJ*, p. 9). Granted the dismissive formula for his own repression, Laskell anticipates and preempts our derisive judgments of his perpetually aspiring author.

Ever at the forefront of intellectual developments, Trilling bases his critical enterprise on the sublime vision of the mind's terror to be found in Freud and modern literature, and given wide sanction by the tragic experiences of the Second World War, the Holocaust, and their "existentialist" aftermath. The critic's function is to express the unreasoning voice of the world protesting the pains of present existence in a finer because more traditional tone, much as Mr. Folger before supper conducts for Laskell's enthralled amusement the eery baying of his hungry hounds, so that it sounds as if they are suffering from the general fate of not being human more than from any specific injustice capable of remediation (*MJ*, p. 131). In other words, the critic's job is to give us lessons in what it means to be human in this world of pain and not act as the prophet of a paradise to be regained for all on earth in some utopian time. If this world is a vale of soul making, as Keats suggests, then Trilling proposes that the literary critic become headmaster in any such finishing school, providing the classic curriculum of noble self-expression so that a precious few of us may learn to emulate our betters in tragic song. "Nor is there singing school," as Yeats says, "without studying monuments" of the soul's "magnificence." In this humanistic manner every dog will potentially have his great day.

The wisdom that Laskell discovers in his convalescence and that Trilling would impart to his readers is, again in Yeats's language, that "the innocent and beautiful have no enemy / But time." In "the white empty peace of illness" Laskell becomes fascinated with the lone surviving rose of the three dozen the Crooms originally sent him. For it is such natural beauty that truly classic form as symbolic compensation for death tries to duplicate in the dance of words:

> [One] could become lost in its perfection, watching the strange energy which the rose seemed to have, for it was not static in its beauty, it seemed to be always at work organizing its petals into their perfect relation with each other. Laskell, gazing at it, had known something like desire; but it was a strange desire which wanted nothing which was its own satisfaction. . . . Yet what strange love it was that was satisfied by its own desire and wanted nothing. It puzzled him, but even the puzzle was a happiness—for it was a puzzle that did not need solution and he did not try for one. He rested content with the contentment this harmless activity gave him, a kind of fullness of being, without any of the nagging interruptions of personality. (*MJ*, pp. 16–17)

Many reverberating allusions—to Yeats, to Dante, to the Song of Songs—trail in the wake of this Keatsian vision of the will's playful self-sacrifice. The expert summoning of such marmoreal excellence, in refinement of the will's self-destructive delight, becomes the liberal critic's representative pleasure.

Laskell's climactic discussion with Nancy Croom about politics and death clarifies Trilling's therapeutic understanding of the critic's role in modern society. At this point, Laskell and Nancy are debating the difference between fishing with rod and fly and fishing for food with whatever means available, as Duck Cadwell always recommends, including the odd stick of dynamite or two. But Laskell, like a Hemingway hero, finds playing by self-imposed rules of the game appealing for what such discipline and restraint disclose about the agent's noble conception of the kind of self he can be. Nancy cannot begin to fathom such literary ethics, preferring instead results at all costs, even when Laskell extends the argument by adducing the example of poor farmers in the Smokies who, despite gnawing hunger, often express when fishing this innate sense of decency.

Laskell now realizes that Nancy's radicalism merely glorifies Duck Cadwell's essential nihilism as natural appetite unjustly constrained by social circumstances and moral codes. So he tries once more to explain his position by appeal to life's art. "Life," he reluctantly contends, always seeks to "overcome" itself by first "conforming" to and then transcending the "conventions" it itself invents, the way a masterful poet makes use of the sonnet form to immortalize his particular love. For Trilling, then, as Laskell's argument suggests, renouncing radical politics and accepting things as they are is akin to working within the established forms of language and making them express one's own intention, rather than inventing alone, or with a select group of fellow initiates, an entirely new language. The critic in this context thus functions, as Laskell here attempts to do with Nancy Croom, to recall to the public mind great arresting images drawn from the cultural tradition that depict the tragic nobility of self-sacrifice, even as they simultaneously call into guilty doubt the disability of radical politics. Whether "unmasking the unmaskers" or not, the critic would thus play the part of the cultural memory, the censor of all communal dreams, whose opportune impersonation of a mnemonic device means the sacrifice of original productive power for greater productive facility and a spirit of savage civility. The worldly messiah of historical change, the critic's heroic position of willed exile—leading the public mind—is as literally utopian as his political affiliation, despite appearances to the contrary. It is in fact spectral—that is, with the great dead alone, literary martyrs or otherwise. In this ironic fashion, the public mind can experience through the critic's sublime interventions the liberating catharsis of its resentful wishes for absolute power within the confines of culture and oppositional discourse. In short, conscience thus makes critics of us all.

The price of becoming a priest of culture, however, is considerable. For the birth of the critic entails the death of every muse. For Laskell, the first to go, of course, is Maxim. Where he once stood in Laskell's mind, always accompanied by two great mural figures, naked faceless young men representing Power and Justice, there is only a great vacancy and Laskell's sadder but wiser stance in the resultant void (*MJ*, p. 209). Similarly, lovely, vital, inspiriting Nancy Croom now goes, no more than the castrating princess of proletarian chic, stripped bare by Laskell's penetrating gaze. Emily Cadwell, the Demeter of Laskell's sexual dream and her Persephone-like daughter, Susan, also "die"— the latter quite literally so that the critic in Laskell, once born, may repeatedly suffer his difficult rebirth. But the greatest scapegoat–muse is the vision of the future itself—the prophetic memory of the middle-class revolutionary becoming the obsessive present of the bourgeois avant-gardist:

> The sound of the crickets filled the Crooms' room and to Laskell it suddenly seemed that the sound no longer spoke with the sweet melancholy of the end of summer. It seemed to him that it was the sound made by the passing of time, a very different thing. It was not like an elegy heard with pleasure in its sadness, but like the inexorable ticking away of life itself. The Crooms in their house together had shut themselves off from it as snugly as they would have shut themselves off against a storm. They had made everything tight, seen to all the windows, looked in on their child to see that he was undisturbed, and now were the happier for what was going on outside. But Laskell could not share the shelter which they had together. He felt suddenly exposed to the whole force of the movement that was indicated by that ceaseless noise of time rushing away. He had a desire, not for shelter—he could not hope for that much—but for something he could hang on to as standing against the movement of time he now heard around him. Summer spoke of its end but did not go on to speak of new beginnings. It spoke only of the end of all other summers. Laskell, standing there while Nancy counted, had the sense—and he wondered if it came eventually to every man and if it always came so early in life—that there was really no future.
>
> He did not mean that *he* had no future. He meant that the future and the present were one—that the present could no longer contrive and manufacture the future by throwing forward, in the form of expectation and hope, the desires of the present moment. It was not that he had "lost hope," but only that he did not make a distinction between what he now had and was and what he expected to have and be. The well-loved child of the middle class is taught about the future by means of the promises made to him—the birthday gifts

will come and the Christmas gifts will come, and the performances at the Hippodrome, and camp and college and the trip to Europe. And all the promises and their fulfillment are symbolic of the great promise, made to him by everyone, that he will grow and change. This great promise he takes into himself in the form of a pledge—made to himself and to everyone—that he will grow and change for the better. He takes it into himself too in the particular form of his vision of time, in which the future is always brighter and more spacious than the present. How the mind of the fortunate young man of the middle class is presided over by the future! It is his mark, his Muse—for it is feminine in its seductiveness—and sets him apart from the young men of the truly lower class and from the young men of the truly upper class.

What happened to Laskell, all at once, was that he realized that you couldn't live the life of promises without yourself remaining a child. The promise of the future might have its uses as a way of seducing the child to maturity, but maturity itself meant that the future and the present were brought together, that you lived your life *now* instead of preparing and committing yourself to some better day to come.

His new perception of the nature of time struck him with very great force. Yet it was not especially startling. . . .

It was not a gay feeling, this change in the character of the relation between present and future, but it was certainly not an unhappy one. The well-loved child of the middle class had always done everything with an exemption granted, for the future was made not only of promises but also of opportunities for forgiveness, and redemptions, and second and third chances. As Laskell looked back on this evening, he found that his odd idea about the future and the present being one brought its own heroism. It had a kind of firm excitement that was connected with his feeling that at this very moment he had the full measure of existence—now, at this very moment, now or never, not at some other and better time that lay ahead. If at this moment he did not have the simplicity of character he wanted, he would never have it; if he was not now answerable for himself, he would never answer. (*MJ*, pp. 154–157)

The psychoanalytic model of mature identity that Trilling develops in his essays on Freud, Whitman, and the novel and that he dramatizes so memorably in his stories of the time envisions a world where sacrifice—of others, of one's future hopes—is all. Quite simply, to attain and preserve the priestly role of meditation for a group or an entire culture requires that the critic curtail any detailed positive vision of the future, in favor of the darkling plain of a present moment haunted by all the specters of the past. In this manner, the critic can become the place of judgment in a culture.

The novel's final tableau, as insightfully read by Maxim, underscores this curious development. Maxim sees Emily Cadwell embrace Laskell after the funeral and wipe the tears from his eyes in an unmistakable maternal gesture of forgiveness for his part in her daughter's tragic death. In Maxim's guilt-obsessed mind—he feels responsible for several "assassinations"—this scene of forgiveness is as if Billy Budd's mother were excusing Captain Vere for his awful judgment. However extreme Maxim's conclusion may be, this scene does permit Laskell to realize his "middle" position between the Crooms, for whom all men are potentially angels condemned by unjust social conditions to lives of quiet desperation, and Maxim, for whom all men are "beasts" redeemed only by divine grace from their living hells. Moreover, Laskell can now attack these positions with dialectical cogency and a vigorous irony: "an absolute freedom from responsibility—that much of a child none of us can be. An absolute responsibility—that much of a divine or metaphysical essence none of us is" (*MJ*, p. 333). He can even admit the cogency of his friends' criticism that he would like to remain above the battle between their opposing extremes. This prompts Maxim's ultimate assault—an appeal to the sacrificial ethic of the critic: "The supreme act of the humanistic critical intelligence—it perceives the cogency of the argument and acquiesces in the fact of its own extinction" (*MJ*, p. 338). Laskell's response (as his earlier encounter with Nancy Croom foreshadows) is to correct Maxim on one point by asserting with ferocious tenacity the fact that he does not acquiesce. That is, Laskell occupies the place of judgment where the extremes of cultural opinion may do combat and be judged. A walking psychomachia, Laskell can write the wars of culture as if they are the history of the present moment.

One of the bowls that Emily Cadwell makes for the fatal bazaar and gives to Laskell enacts the final transformation of time into a perpetual historical present. At first an object of patronizing indulgence for its memory of many recent masters, the bowl by the novel's end gathers into its symbolic recesses the brooding darkness at the heart of modern culture. More significantly for Laskell now, it also discloses "some particularity of the individual who had made it." Laskell reads in the bowl's formal dimensions what Trilling intends the reader of his novel to envision: a "deep awareness of nullity" and a "knowledge of darkness." Consequently, Laskell no longer sees the ineptness of the design but only what "it suddenly and darkly spoke of" (*MJ*, p. 325). Trilling would have his reader also see this in *The Middle of the Journey*. For such vision would mean, parodoxically enough, that the reader, following Laskell's lead, now takes "pleasure in the objects" the artist creates, however commonplace they may seem, "and sees life in them" (*MJ*, p. 104), an individualizing life that is the representative fate death ensures humankind. The sacrifice of a particular future grants one the presence of the past as an authoritative universal force:

> he had a strong emotion about the life in objects, the shapes that people made and admire, the life in the pauses in activity in which nothing is said but in which the commonplace speaks out with a mild, reassuring force. . . . an attitude come down the ages, fresh and pure from the distance it had blown, almost fragrant with its simplicity and its long history. (*MJ*, pp. 104, 108)

Trilling, like a latter-day Tacitus in his *Annals*, would add *The Middle of the Journey* to the life in objects, thereby investing this novel about the present with all the authority of the commonplace.

More is occurring in *The Middle of the Journey*, however, than its transfiguration of the middle-class world of alienated labor and commodity fetishism into the latest form of a universal aesthetic reality cherished down through the centuries by all peoples and represented best in the great classics of Western culture. This is so even though the famous essays on the novel of the time, "Manners, Morals, and the Novel" (1948) and "Art and Fortune" (1949) do appear at first to argue simply that the genre, now that the lessons of modernism and its radical experiments with symbolism and point of view have been assimilated, needs just such a neo-realist program if it is to remain a vital production of the liberal imagination capable of reminding us of life's energy, complexity, variety, and ironies as we impose the sterile structures of the modern nation-state upon the world. For one thing, these essays, like the novel they seek to justify, develop the idea of the cultural unconscious in ways that not only anticipate similar developments in recent novel theory but disclose the essentially ascetic will informing Trilling's career. Finally, I would suggest that these essays, like Trilling's fictions, grant the normal glory of bourgeois reality the authority of the commonplace in order to displace modernist and Marxist revolutionary agendas and so complete the dialectic of revisionism that returns the repressed to ideological power, often despite the evident political valencies and alignments of interest. Whether the writer champions as the "real" reality traditional bric-à-brac and transcendent gossip or the historical victimage and subversive reactions of former colonial peoples matters less in professional debate than the fact that such positioning one way or another may grant for the moment greater strategic advantage in one of the many cultural wars going on at any particular time within the literary institution.

For Trilling, the novel searches out from the cultural archive, from "letters and diaries" and "the remote, unconscious corners of the great works," the "unuttered" system of aesthetic quality and moral evaluation of a people, that "sound of the multifarious implication" which constitutes "manners" in the largest sense and which, Trilling claims, only the novelist can articulate in a representative worldly fashion (*MJ*, p. 206). Of special significance now, after the horrors of war abroad and the radical evil of Stalinism at home, is the genre's power to save the human will, "everywhere dying of its own excess" (*MJ*, p. 266). The novel achieves this effect by its refusal to envision those apocalyptic renovations of humankind that always end in disaster and by its heroic acceptance of the conditions of human existence as the best means to school a soul and form a mature individual on the model of the "old novelistic character"—the divinely loving author himself:

> The novel has had a long dream of virtue in which the will, while never abating its strength and activity, learns to refuse to exercise itself upon the unworthy objects with which the social world would tempt it, and either conceives its own right objects or becomes content with its own sense of its potential force—which is why so many novels give us, before their end, some representation, often crude enough, of the will unbroken but in stasis. Surely what we need is the opportunity to identify with a mind that willingly admits that it is a mind and does not pretend that it is History or events or the World but only a mind thinking and planning—possibly planning our escape . . . [by means of] a straightforward prose, rapid, masculine, and committed to events, making its effects not by the single word or by the phrase but by words properly and naturally massed. I conceive that the creation of such a prose should be one of the conscious intentions of any novelist. . . . The novelist could once speak of the beautiful circuit of thought and desire [what James calls "romance"], which exists beside the daily reality but the question is now whether thought and desire have any longer a field of possibility [for] the old novelistic character. . . . The phrase suggest[s] both the fortuitous and the gratuitous nature of art, how it exists beyond the reach of the will alone, how it is freely given and not always for good reason and for as little reason taken away. It is not to be demanded

or prescribed or provided for. The understanding of this cannot of itself assure the existence of the novel but it helps toward establishing the state of the soul in which the novel becomes possible. (*IL*, pp. 269, 270, 279–280)

The author, in other words, embodies this "old novelistic character" in his text, and the reader assimilates its spirit from studying the noble responses of the protagonist to the action, as well as those judgments of the author reflected in the stylish amassing of living detail, that celebrated creation of so-called masculine prose. Although Trilling's examples in these essays include Stendhal's Julien Sorel from *The Red and the Black*, James's Hyacinth Robinson from *The Princess Casamassima*, Proust's Swann—and to his regret and Delmore Schwartz's malicious delight—Duchess de Guermantes from *The Remembrance of Things Past*, the perfect example of what Trilling means by the phrase "the old novelistic character" must await, ironically enough, his suggestive discussion of James Joyce's *Ulysses* a few years later in, of all things, "Wordsworth and the Iron Time" (1950). I think enough has already been cited from these essays, however, to see that Trilling, in a move characteristic of critical humanism, transfers to a literary genre, its authors, and its readers the priestly program of spiritual education assigned in the Judeo-Christian tradition to its sacred texts, divine figures, and holy people. Such displacement preserves the structural centrality of the priest-critic as herald of reality (however envisioned), even as it now would process secular materials in changed circumstances according to earlier timeworn patterns. Trilling's career thus climaxes appropriately in his "realistic" portrayal and critical promotion of the authority of the commonplace. Paradoxical as it may sound, elitistic status is never more firmly based in our time than when it depends on a populist ideology.

As an account of cultural history since the Renaissance, the secularization thesis has been advanced by many thinkers such as Hegel, Nietzsche, and Benjamin in a variety of ways and applications. It has been most effectively popularized in literary studies by Arnold and more recently M. H. Abrams and his critical disciples. It is attractive because it permits the critic to explain historical ruptures as surface phenomena, while thus preserving cultural continuity at the depths. Despite the suspicions it arouses concerning its reductive simplicity and reactionary ideological utility—one thinks of William Bennett's political work or E. D. Hirsch's new idea of "cultural literacy"—I invoke it with respect to Trilling's view of the novel for a reason other than nostalgia or expediency. It puts most tellingly a truth of the human mind discovered by Wordsworth and Freud but often obscured by their speculative assertions and theories, namely, that the mind seems inevitably to recur to the earliest forms of pleasure it has known regardless of the "perverse" nature of that original pleasure or the current obstacles to its reinstitution. What Thomas Mann in *Doctor Faustus* and Theodor Adorno in *The Philosophy of Modern Music* depict as the demonic repetition compulsions of psychic regression and cultural barbarism function not only in the obvious case of Trilling's ironic revival of the liberal patriarchy of middle-class "reality" but in the more complex cases of those critical theorists of today who would challenge the tradition of humanism and its accompanying canon of classic masterpieces in the name of previously excluded peoples, cultures, texts, or more general "oppositional" positions they now claim as their great originals. To recognize this admittedly "romantic" fate of pleasure, however, does not entail a refusal to take a position of one's own on pain of committing the critical equivalent of bad faith; nor does it imply the denial of significant historically conditional differences between Trilling and, say, Fredric Jameson or Edward W. Said. But it does suggest the idea that both humanists and antihumanists may be caught up in conventions of response larger than those of their institutionalized debates.

What I have called the authority of the commonplace refers to the power of the mind's first idea of pleasure. As experience varies from individual to individual and culture to culture, so the nature of this authoritative pleasure varies as well. It is commonplace in the sense that it is always the earliest, most primitive form of pleasure and it is authoritative in that it struggles for recurrence and representation regardless of the present circumstances. The form of pleasure for which Trilling scapegoats others (his fictional and critical "heroes") and sacrifices himself (his "life") is the pleasure of impersonating the first, the earliest, the prophetic prototype itself:

> Between Mrs. Folger and her husband an attitude came down the ages, fresh and pure from the distance it had blown, almost fragrant with its simplicity and its long history. Montaigne's neighbors had talked so; Pascal had overheard such views in the salons of Paris. And back beyond, in Rome and before that Sumer, men and women had [thus] judged each other. (*MJ*, p. 108)

In short, before Moses and Ezekiel I am . . .

Trilling's espousal of what in "The State of American Writing" (1948) he terms the "permanent experiment" in English, that "effort to get the language . . . back to a certain hard, immediate actuality, . . . the tone of highly charged plain speech,"[25] as if one were the first speaker on the subject, the creative voice itself, clearly follows from his espousal of the authority of the commonplace. Similarly, his radical ambivalence toward American literature arises from his recognition that he is in the great tradition of second-comers who through their own fictions of the end would be seen by later generations as a new beginning: "The clue to the nature and power of American literature," Trilling claims in "An American View of English Literature" (1951), is contained in the titles of two American works of fiction which have established themselves in the American mind in a more than literary way—*The Last of the Mohicans* and "The Fall of the House of Usher"—"the image of the solitary man who survives his social group, and the image of the decay and collapse of the social fabric itself" (*SLS*, p. 262). Informed by D. H. Lawrence's view in *Studies in Classic American Literature*, Trilling's position here and throughout his work aspires to be the first systematic critique of his revisionary impulse, and so ironically replicates it in a finer tone. The danger of Trilling's game is that he may fall victim to the fate that ruined Sinclair Lewis who, by opposing personality with society and society with personality, ended up negating both in a manner far from original with him: "What he was interested in was a single human situation whose intended outcome was the denial of society, and also of personality—the situation in which an individual undertakes to be free from and dominant over society, only to submit as fully as possible and to sink prostrated into an abstract anonymity" (*SLS*, p. 269). The dread that pervades this description of Lewis' fatal fall speaks volumes concerning Trilling's own aspirations to glory, his "insatiable desire for praise and notice," as a notebook entry of the time puts it, which "nothing satisfied" so that the more he received the more he required—"grew by what it fed on" ("Notebooks," pp. 24–25), especially during the composition of his novel.

Consequently, Trilling must perfect his oppositional mode of essayistic criticism which freely adopts one position or another, even their antitheses, like trying on new attire, in the name of imaginative resiliency and an admittedly perverse form of intellectual pleasure. Consider, for example, his 1949 contribution to a symposium entitled "The Jewish Writer and the English Literary Tradition":

> I have therefore never felt the necessity of defining my relation to the tradition. For me to do so would be not unlike a tailor's son undertaking in 19th century England to examine the state of his feelings

before writing novels because tailors were traditionally mocked in English literature. A literary tradition is after all remarkably unlike a club or "community" in which one proposes oneself for membership. . . . I even get a kind of intellectual pleasure from maintaining an attitude of ambivalence towards writers who interest me [despite their anti-Semitism].[26]

Although Trilling says what tradition is not, he never says what he thinks it is. This ironic silence frees him to enact what he thinks it is via his "tailor" trope which at once alludes to Carlyle's hero in *Sartor Resartus*, and to the dandy Disraeli, even as it openly envelopes the secret of his own origins as the son of an immigrant Jew who was at first a tailor before moving up to becoming a bankrupt furrier. As Trilling's response in "The Liberal Mind: Two Communications and A Reply" suggests, being an "empirical," "naturalistic," and "pragmatic" critic of the liberal American scene frees him for a covertly knowing fixation on literary origins dressed up in a more-progressive-than-thou gear:

I believe that liberalism has debased its whole intellectual heritage. It is precisely because I am myself a liberal, and a pragmatist and naturalist, that I am depressed by the obvious fact—I have so often pointed to it that it and I have become tiresome—that liberalism has not been able to produce a literature which can strongly engage our emotions, nor a body of thought which can win our happy assent. [This is tragic, for] literature is one of the cultural agents that form the attitudes, even the categories, by which at least some part of life is apprehended.[27]

Trilling habitually criticizes the liberal mind from within its reigning framework of assumptions, with its central belief in the power of education to free the mind from reliance on any firm beliefs. This ironic strategy enables him to indulge in even as he laments what in "The Repressive Impulse" (1948) he describes as the "characteristic attachment" of intellectuals in "our culture today" to "explicit ideas," to ideologies that transcend established structures of class and family to form "new class-structures and new sub-cultures," on the basis solely of "some vision they have of their total being, some fantasy of self which their ideology embodies."[28] With the examples of Hitler and Stalin and their disciples fresh in his readers' minds, Trilling's subtle assumption of worldly messiah status in *The Middle of the Journey* and the major performances of *The Liberal Imagination* could well have been overlooked at the time.

Ironically enough, however, Trilling does take his role as the conscience of liberal culture with evident seriousness in his biting defense of Alma Venus and a genuinely spontaneous nature in his review of *The Kinsey Report* (1947). Trilling rightly fears that the methods of scientific study when applied to human behavior will level every qualitative distinction between individuals, even to the experience of their sexual relationships, in a kind of demonic parody of the naturalism he himself professes. Unable to speak the literary language of such essentially aesthetic distinctions as love and sex, science must take as its model of normality not the mature and integrated self of Freud and heroic culture but simply the average subject that responds immediately and as often as possible to external stimuli produced and manipulated by the environment. Science thereby makes mass consumer society the sole form of human organization conceivable. "But by such reasoning," Trilling observes apropos the report's celebration of immediate sexual responsiveness, "the human male who is quick and intense in his leap to the life boat is natural and superior, however inconvenient and unfortunate his speed and intensity may be to the wife he leaves standing on the deck [of the sinking ship]" (*LI*, p. 236). This "democratic pluralism of sexuality," which does not take into its account of things the emotional quality of the experience it studies, impoverishes life by robbing it of the effort to envision and realize a hierarchy of possible responses from the least to the most lovingly human. Trilling concludes that for this "major cultural document," "quality is not integral to what [its authors] mean by experience" (*LI*, p. 231). It is clear why Trilling must oppose *The Kinsey Report* beyond his nostalgia for the Lawrentian love ethic. For as long as literary culture, particularly that portion of it which flows from the romantics and the nineteenth-century novelists into Freudian psychoanalysis and the great modernists, can determine the nature of the commonplace, of the original pleasure which acts as the mind's measure of authority, then Trilling and his kind can play the high priests of truly liberal education, for they know how to capitalize on and administer the treasure house of "ideas" modern Western culture has continued to amass—like that impervious masculine style of prose, which amasses experience, that Trilling praises as the unique creative achievement of the novel.

In 1950 Lionel Trilling collected most of the essays written over the previous decade in *The Liberal Imagination: Essays on Literature and Society*. This volume made his name, soon becoming a critical best-seller. (The second edition in 1953 alone sold over seventy thousand copies.)[29]

The essays were arranged not really according to original chronology but under such topic headings as "art and society" and "writers and artists." (These vague headings were dropped in subsequent editions.)[30] The arrangement of the essays does make a readily perceptible argument of its own, however, suggesting the movement of its author from "Reality in America" through Freud and our impoverished literary culture to "the meaning of a literary idea" for the truly encompassing mind that the liberal imagination should but has failed to foster owing to its inadequate un-novelistic conception of reality. Thus, like one of the literary works it praises, Trilling's collection classically returns to its point of departure, dialectically renewing itself in the process of demonstrating the authority of the commonplace in its culture's own case.

The final essay in the volume, "The Meaning of a Literary Idea," brings together and systematically elaborates all the themes sounded in the other essays, and subsumes them under Trilling's general polemic for the tragic irony of life and against what the preface describes as the "dull, repressive tendency of [liberal] opinion" (*LI*, p. vi) In the name of ideological writing or social relevance the liberal imagination in America during the 1930s and 1940s according to Trilling devalues "all the gratuitous manifestations of feeling, of thought, and art, all such energies of the human spirit as are marked by spontaneity, complexity, and variety," a claustrophobic situation which only the novel, "the human activity which takes the fullest and most precise account of variousness, complexity, difficulty—and possibility" (*LI*, p. viii) can even hope to remediate. The progressive democratic ideas of American liberalism, although fine in theory, have a tendency, as *The Kinsey Report* makes clear, to be realized in modern mass societies in the most sterile scientistic and bureaucratic forms of expression which blunt, simplify, make rigid and doctrinaire these otherwise essential ideas. One consequence of this paradoxical development is the fact that American liberalism is incapable of producing a literature that can rival in imaginative power and cogency the work of European artists over the previous century, the vast majority of whom were motivated by ideas whose social and moral consequences were horribly tested out in the Second World War.

"The Meaning of a Literary Idea" divides into two parts. The first part discusses the theoretical problem of the relation of ideas to literature, while the second part discusses the specific problem of the lack of viable ideas in American literary culture at mid-century. Trilling begins by noting some of the ways literature, despite the counterclaims of the New Critical formalists, "is involved with ideas" necessarily (*LI*,

p. 282). Since the content of literature, Trilling assumes, is always the same—"man in society" (*LI*, p. 282), or, more precisely, the self-conscious pursuit of pleasure by representative individual figures whose fates inspire our "tears and laughter" (*LI*, p. 282)—literature must portray in some fashion and to some degree minds in thought, if only in calculation of their self-interests. In the process of such portrayal, moreover, emotions are brought into conflict, and "whenever we put two emotions into juxtaposition we have what we can properly call an idea," as when, Trilling goes on to illustrate, "Keats brings together, as he so often does" (*LI*, p. 283), his emotions about love and death, a powerful juxtaposition that usually produces in his case a great stream of associated ideas. Finally, Trilling concludes his theoretical remarks by observing that, depending on how forcefully such ideas are represented and such confrontations contrived or staged, we may be justified in taking the very form of the work itself as an idea, as a dialectic or "developing series of statements" or of images that imply statements (*LI*, p. 283). Consequently, Trilling adds, "the modern feeling" that welcomes literature's aesthetic alienation from ideas, as represented in two classic statements by T. S. Eliot—about the lack of original thought in Dante and Shakespeare and Henry James's possession of a mind so fine no idea could violate it—is dead wrong, as Eliot's later revised positions on this topic concede.

Trilling thus opposes the main current of modern opinion on this subject of literature's relation to ideas, and harkens back to Carlyle, Coleridge, and Aristotle even as he goes on to blast Wellek and Warren's *Theory of Literature* for following myopically the young Eliot's lead into the impasse of aesthetic purity. Yet, he does so understanding all too well the real situation that has given rise to this self-defeating critical reaction:

> A specter haunts our culture—it is that people will eventually be unable to say, "They fell in love and married," let alone understand the language of *Romeo and Juliet*, but will as a matter of course say, "Their libidinal impulses being reciprocal, they activated their individual erotic drives and integrated them within the same frame of reference." . . . There can be no doubt whatever that [such language] constitutes a threat to the emotions and thus to life itself. . . . [As] the people of the idea, . . . we rightly fear that the intellect will dry up the blood in our veins and wholly check the emotional and creative part of the mind. . . . But to call ourselves the people of the idea is to flatter ourselves. We are rather the people of ideology, which is a very different thing. Ideology is not the product of thought, it is the

habit or the ritual of showing respect for certain formulas to which, for various reasons having to do with emotional safety, we have very strong ties but of whose meaning and consequences in activity we have no clear understanding. The nature of ideology may in part be understood from its tendency to develop the sort of language I parodied, and scarcely parodied, a moment ago. (*LI*, pp. 285–85)

It is this ritualized and repressive hegemony of liberal ideology which causes the reaction of aesthetic purity in post-Enlightenment society. But by reducing itself to studious images and lamely avoiding all direct statement of ideas in an effort to evade its abstract enemy, literature actually abandons the field of cultural debate and struggle altogether to take up residence in the academy. Since "the exercise of religion" no longer provides a haven for contemplation in a world of unremitting action, contemplation has become exclusively associated with "the experiences of art" within the university-sanctioned "modern" culture.

Trilling's solution to this general dilemma is to propose that literature recognize, as Hegel and Aristotle both advise, its indebtedness to rhetoric and grammar, to the syntax of the mind in the creation of thought. Literature, even the poetry of *symboliste* indirection, may then begin to re-possess that "aesthetic effect of intellectual cogency" (*LI*, p. 291) which Trilling claims gives "the authority," "the completeness, the brilliance, the *hardness* of systematic thought" (*LI*, p. 290) to literature generally and which in isolated cases he can still find, as in Yeats's "Meditations in Time of Civil War" and Freud's final work, *An Outline of Psychoanalysis*:

> The aesthetic effect of intellectual cogency, I am convinced, is not to be slighted. Let me give an example for what it is worth. Of recent weeks my mind has been much engaged by two statements, disparate in length and in genre, although as it happens they have related themes. One is a couplet of Yeats:
> > We had fed the heart on fantasies,
> > The heart's grown brutal from the fare.
> I am hard put to account for the force of the statement. It certainly does not lie in any metaphor, for only the dimmest sort of metaphor is to be detected. Nor does it lie in any special power of the verse. The statement has for me the pleasure of relevance and cogency, in part conveyed to me by the content, in part by the rhetoric. The other statement is Freud's short book, his last, *An Outline of Psychoanalysis*, which gives me a pleasure which is no doubt different from that given by Yeats's couplet but which is also similar: *it is the pleasure of*

listening to a strong decisive self-limiting voice uttering statements to which
I can give assent. (LI, p. 291; my emphasis)

Trilling adds, tellingly, that he finds it "very difficult to distinguish the
pleasure he has in responding to Freud" from "the pleasure which is
involved in responding to a satisfactory work of art" (*LI*, p. 291). Trilling
then concludes the first part of this argument on a note of qualification
that is also highly revelatory of the rhetorical nature of intellectual
assent in a world of ideological warfare and formalist retreat:

> Intellectual assent in literature is not quite the same thing as agree-
> ment. We can take pleasure in literature where we do not agree,
> responding to the power or grace of a mind without admitting the
> rightness of its intention or conclusion—we can take our pleasure
> from an intellect's *cogency*, without making a formal judgment on the
> correctness or adaptability of what it says. (*LI*, p. 291)

In these elaborate passages, far more of significance occurs than the
clever updating of Coleridge's principle of the willing suspension of
disbelief or of Arnold's critical prophecy that literature, replacing religion, must save us from the mad abstract dark of modern life by producing the "intellectual deliverance" of a new mythic synthesis. Before
going on to examine the rest of "The Meaning of a Literary Idea," I
want to say what this "more" may be.

For Trilling, I believe, the primary aim of critical discourse is to foster
works in the classic tradition of humanism which will inspire the reader
to respond with pleasure to the realistic portrayal of the mind as an
individualized voice narrating the tragic fate of imaginative expression
in the modern world. Trilling's ultimate theoretical position thus resembles what Derrida has stigmatized as that metaphysics of presence
which dreams perpetually of the apocalyptic resolution of all painful
differences in the specular image of the divinely creative word or its
more obviously narcissistic surrogates such as reason, will, and being.
Yet what distinguishes Trilling's critical humanism from this deconstructive bogeyman of "phallologocentrism" is its relentlessly sacrifical
cast. Its emblem, however, is not so much the Yeats who proclaims,
"We had fed the heart on fantasies, / The heart's grown brutal from
the fare," as the Celtic Bard of "Easter, 1916" who is reduced to murmuring name upon name, as "a terrible beauty is born" on the streets
of Dublin. Or, even more aptly, the emblem of Trilling's ironic work of
maturity is, perhaps, a romantic variant after all: the image of a mind
that feeds upon the disasters of human finitude. The chronic aesthetics

of apocalyptic consumption (and not resolution) would thus displace all metaphysics and their deconstructions.

The second section of "The Meaning of a Literary Idea" expresses Trilling's more particular and quite familiar concern with the relation of contemporary American literature to ideas. Since the ascendancy of liberal culture, American intellectuals tend to view literature as an object rather than a subject of study, that is, according to Trilling, as the uniform expression of approved attitudes that engage our progressive hearts even as they pacify our disengaged minds. We have forgotten, Trilling argues, that the great issues most relevant to the literary use of ideas are fundamentally *"primitive"* in nature (*LI*, p. 193; Trilling's emphasis). Such ideas are "love, parenthood, incest, patricide" (*LI*, p. 293), or what can be called the social pieties of the traditional religious culture. Of all the routinely celebrated authors in the modern American canon—O'Neill, Dos Passos, Wolfe, et al.—only Hemingway and Faulkner are able, without self-deception, to represent the "encompassing mind" of the artist as it attempts to transform the recalcitrant materials of life into classic texts (*LI*, p. 297). Such novelists, like the great European modernists in the reactionary tradition, are able to give us the "sense of largeness, of cogency, of the transcendence" of style which reaches us "in our secret and primitive minds" and which "we virtually never get from the writers of the liberal democratic tradition at the present time" (*LI*, p. 301). They can do so because they possess Keats's negative capability and are willing "to remain in uncertainties, mysteries, and doubts," as an index of their strict intelligence, of their "seeing the full force and complexity of their subject matter" (*LI*, p. 299).

It is not so much that these modern authors—Hemingway, Faulkner, Eliot, Yeats, Flaubert—are precisely "religious" in their writings, as that they, like Shakespeare, are in possession of the "detritus" of belief, those "strong assumptions" and pieties about love, parenthood, incest, and the like (*LI*, p. 300) which, when challenged by modern developments, grant their works the true vision of a greater if desolating reality. For minds under such pressure refuse to experience ideas as liberal intellectuals usually do, as "pellets of intellection or crystallizations of thought, precise and completed, and defined by their coherence and their procedural recommendations" (*LI*, p. 302). Instead, these thought-tormented minds must experience ideas "as living things, inescapably connected with our wills and desires, as susceptible of growth and development by their very nature, as showing their life by their tendency to change, as being liable, by this very tendency, to deteriorate and become corrupt and to work harm" (*LI*, p. 303). Until we too emulate what appears to be their exemplary visionary madness, Trilling concludes, we shall lack the strength to stand in "a relation to ideas which makes an active literature possible" (*LI*, p. 303). We, too, must have the courage of our phantasmagoria.

"The Meaning of a Literary Idea" closes *The Liberal Imagination* celebrating an image of the mind in extremis, holding down *hysterica passio*, even as it substitutes its own tragic story for that of a vanished faith. Trilling borrows the pathos of earlier moments in modern cultural history to glorify his own representative disillusionment with the revolutionary god that failed. The essay's epigraph from Keats's "Sleep and Poetry" tells the whole sad story of how this worldly messiah, under the oedipal banner of his chosen "father," Freud, repeatedly sacrifices the liberal imagination and revises his oppositional position, in order to better lead his tragic generation into the academic fold. All this is done of course in accordance with the priestly logic of what I have called the religious unconscious and the authority of the spectral commonplaces it fosters:

> Though no great ministering reason sorts
> Out the dark mysteries of human souls
> To clear conceiving: yet there ever rolls
> A vast idea before me, and I glean
> Therefrom my liberty . . .

The work of maturity thus ever depends on the myth of individual freedom in style, just as the critical impersonation of a culture's characteristic manner requires the convenient reality of a scapegoat-muse. "[In] any culture there are likely to be certain artists who contain a large part of the dialectic within themselves, their meaning and power lying in their contradictions; they contain within themselves, it may be said, the very essence of the culture, and the sign of this is that they do not submit to serve the ends of any one ideological group or tendency." And so, it would seem, all these sublime geniuses come to express, thanks to the work of Lionel Trilling, their critical heir, nothing in particular at all, but "a vast idea" nonetheless.

Chapter Four

Subversive Patriarchy: The Judgment of the World

Ancient Innocence: The Authority of the Commonplace

Although Lionel Trilling did achieve widespread recognition in America and England with the publication of *The Liberal Imagination* in 1950—our belated answer to the literary and cultural essays of Eliot and Leavis—it was not without prompting a considerable amount of penetrating criticism. His position on the novel and his self-styled critique of liberalism from within provoked the most adverse comment. Delmore Schwartz, in a famous attack, "The Duchess' Red Shoes," and Irving Howe, in the first of several reviews and essays, fathered between them the standard critical view of Trilling which later critics adopted to different degrees at different times.[1] These critics defined Trilling's position as stylish opposition for its own sake. For these critics, Trilling, lacking either an intimate knowledge of the modernist authors he cavalierly celebrates or a historical justification for the opposition he strategically espouses, simply generalizes American liberal culture into a monolithic monster suspicious of all imagination and ironic complexity, in order to achieve a purely self-interested aesthetic effect: the dramatization of his self–defining role as the humanistic prophet of ambivalence, the secular priest of the Freudian sacrifice.[2] As we shall see in increasing detail, this critical chorus accusing Trilling's "cultural politics" of being essentially aesthetic, antihistorical, and reactionary would continue to grow steadily until by career's end it threatened to drown out the master's cultivated voice. The major irony of this situation is that the American profession of criticism that emerged in the late 1960s and early 1970s became guilty of the very willful irrelevance of which Trilling stood accused and which, in many ways, he does foreshadow, even as, in his final essays and symposia, he also recognizes and laments it.[3]

Of the many valid explanations than one can adduce for this ironic development (from the farcical cunning of historical conditions to absurdly evident professional bad faith), two loom larger in Trilling's case than all the rest: the traditionally embattled isolation of academic life in America and the highly conventionalized form of the modern writer's revisionary career.[4]

For Trilling, as we see in his fiction especially, the academy stands for more than either the institutionalized expertise of monopolistic professions and service disciplines, or the visible confirmation and seal of the American dream of social mobility. For the academy, in Trilling's eyes, embodies a whole way of life, both formally social and monkishly solitary, a haven of contemplation and free enquiry in a hyperactive practical world. It is *the* critical site in American culture where within more "liberal" limits than available elsewhere the mind may perform in public its spontaneous act of creative thought encompassing ever larger reaches of cognitive space.

The vision in the Dean's committee room from "Of This Time, Of That Place," you recall, precipitates Joseph Howe's spontaneous sacrifice of his mad student Tertan and inspires the former's growing recognition of the tragic dimensions of civilized life. In essence, Trilling views what Gerald Graff calls the "patterned isolation" of the American tradition of academic life as the last vestige of a highly prized and highly costly aristocratic hierarchy and privilege amidst the relentlessly leveling tendencies of modern liberal democracy.

As soon as Trilling perceives, however, that the systematic university study of modern literature replicates in new orthodox formulas the ideological wars of the larger culture and so is undermining from within the already embattled isolation of academic life, he begins slowly, reluctantly, ambivalently, to turn against modernism and toward earlier literature, to ideas of nature and biological determinism, and finally to other, non-Western cultures in a desperate quest for an authoritative principle of order and freedom that could restore the conditions of academic life for posterity's sake.

The traditionally embattled isolation of American academic life; the social mirror of the textual indeterminacy the critical humanist exploits for his own purposes; and the threat to this humanism's authority mounted from within by the adversary culture of modernism: all three forces combine to compel Trilling to the cultivated oppositional stance of the later career.

Even more coercively, if possible, the conventional shape of the modern writer's career determines Trilling's restless revisionism. The career of every post-Enlightenment author of major status consists of three stages: initiation, self-definition, and systematic self-revision (it is this last phase that marks the distinctively modern master). Consider, for example, the career of Wallace Stevens. With *Harmonium* Stevens initiates, belatedly, his poetic career as comic virtuoso of *symboliste* and *imagiste* manners. Then in "The Man with the Blue Guitar" and "Notes Toward a Supreme Fiction," he defines himself as the ironic epic singer of the heroic soldier of the mind, in a modern revision of the Whitman tradition. Finally, however, in the later poetry of *The Auroras of Autumn* and *The Rock*, the Emersonian figure of the poet as spectral scholar returns repeatedly as the last imagined reality in a world without imagination. That is, Stevens himself returns as if after his own death, as a ghostly presence in the minds of his disciple–readers. Similarly, Trilling's career would appear to fall into this pattern of initiation (via the "spectral politics" of Jewish self-hatred and literary ethics), self-definition (as the worldly messiah of tragic maturity), and systematic self-revision (in repeatedly projecting the reflexive fiction of the opposing self beyond culture).

Of course, the well-made drama of this revisionary dialectic, like that of the embattled isolation of American academic life, must appear to be a suspiciously literary constraint on the conditions and forms of the modern writer's imaginative career in our postmodern age of neo-pragmatism and deconstructive realpolitik. Yet, as the institution of English studies reminds us, literature and humane letters generally compose a powerful ideological apparatus, semi-autonomous in its structural effects, that is as representative of the reality of the culture as discursive practices and disciplines more obviously central and authoritative, such as medicine or the social sciences. My point, quite simply, is that especially for Trilling in his time,[5] these two "tropes"— the career of the master and the institution of academic life—constitute literary conventions with developmental patterns or discursive "lives" of their own that materially circumscribe the possible modes of self-expression in such ways as to promote (if not prescribe) the endless revisionism of Trilling and his generation of writers. These conventions coincide with and are reinforced by what Irving Howe characterizes as the "sharp turn" taken by the New York Intellectuals after the Second World War, from a shared liberal orthodoxy to independent hectic quests for the ever new and more comprehensive, an ultimate position "beyond ideology." These quests are all sparked by "[the] desire to capture a bitch goddess whose first name is Novelty."[6] That such celebrity-seeking revisionism should recently recur for the subsequent generation of literary figures at roughly the same place in their careers but under the drastically different historical circumstances of the post-Vietnam-Watergate epoch testifies to the persistence of the literary institution and its ideological forms despite more general historical transformations.

It also testifies to the authority of the commonplace, that wish of the mind to replicate amidst changed circumstances the first form of its pleasure, the original constellation of its self-recognition, which in the case of writers is of course primarily verbal in nature. This psycho-rhetorical *cogito* corresponds not so much to the institution of the symbolic dimension in human discourses, what Lacan poetically designates as "the name of the father"; nor so much to what Freud outlines as the surpassing of the Oedipus complex in the formation of the superego. Rather, it recalls the universal repetition compulsion of the species, representative, for Freud, of the rule of the destructive instinct in the psyche, a going beyond the pleasure principle that, in transcending, ironically fulfills it. Despite Freud's insistence, however, that desire and the death instinct can be kept actually (as well as analytically) distinct, so that Eros can become the builder of cities and Thanatos the solitary destroyer, thereby giving us some reason to hope for civilization's future, the authority of the commonplace, as I see it, unites desire and destructiveness in a passion of self-destruction that promises the ultimate pleasure, the discovery of that previously unspoken formula which, once pronounced, would precipitate a perfect psychic disintegration. For Trilling, as his fiction once again suggests best, the authority of the commonplace takes the form of an ancient innocence.

> She . . . took a handkerchief from her short sleeve and wiped his cheeks vigorously. She did it without any hesitation or sorrow. And he understood that she felt she had a right to do so because they had been lovers. He had the full conception of her spirit when he understood that she had no desire to blot out that incident on the river bank. Her grief did not destroy her moment of passion. . . . She did not have to make believe that her relationship to Laskell, short as it was, had never existed. She scrubbed once more at his face and smiled to him wanly. "There!" she said.
>
> Then she said, "You have been very good." . . . She leaned toward him, touched with the tips of her fingers one of the cheeks she had just scrubbed of tears and put her lips lightly to the other cheek. He closed his eyes against what she was doing. . . . He did not know why her word "good" struck him like an accusation. (*MJ*, 328–329).

This scene of climactic allusion from *The Middle of the Journey* clearly if symbolically dramatizes oedipal transgressions and Christian absolution. The irony is that John Laskell, Trilling's liberal critic-protagonist and spokesman, shares his assimilated author's secret guilty desire to be pronounced what one subtle strain of anti-Semitism considers all members of the Jewish race to be: like women and children, essentially "good" originally and ever after, and thus disqualified by definition from the higher, more heroic moral life of mankind no matter what crime they may commit.[7] Ever more directly to pronounce himself "good" in this radically ambivalent sense is the repressed self-destructive desire that animates Trilling's career of sublime evasion. Trilling's creation of revisionary name upon name for the strange disease of modernity ("the liberal imagination," "the opposing self," the idea of being "beyond culture," "the disintegrated consciousness") thus fulfills primarily this productively defensive intention, rather than being simply a disillusioned leftist's status quest for that cold-war bitch goddess "Novelty." Trilling must pursue and yet avoid the definitive annunciation of his own *grand récit* in the playful series of symbolic displacements that his later career systematically stages and revises.

A question thus resonates throughout the later representative career of Lionel Trilling as modern revisionist: What does the writer who "makes it" do next? Within the professional and cultural contexts of his time—and I think this is still so even for critics who "make it" in the simpler sense of possessing professional visibility in their specialty—the critic, especially the cold-war liberal man of letters—is permitted, often encouraged, to become even more himself, to play out in ever more direct forms whatever happens to be his or her *grand récit*, that is, the authority of the commonplace in this critic's particular case. Hence, Trilling now and until his death in 1975 plays out in every possible variation his dream of ancient innocence, as can be perceived in the following generally uncollected pieces from the 1950s.

A notebook entry from winter 1950–1951 sounds the starkly emblematic theme:

> A catbird on the woodpile, grey on grey wood, its breast distended, the feathers ruffled and sick, a wing out of joint, the head thrown back and the eyes rolled back, white, looked so sick I thought of killing it, when another bird appeared, looked at it, took a position behind it and assumed virtually the same attitude, although not so extremely.
>
> To distract me? This it did once more, although with rather less conviction the second time, then flew away. Suddenly the first bird pulled itself together, flew to a tree above, sat there for a moment seeming to adjust its wing, or exercise it, then flew away. ("Notebooks," p. 32)

The sick catbird and its healthier counterpart enact a ritual of defensive mimicry and therapeutic rivalry that distracts the sympathetic observer from his intended liberal act of euthanasia long enough for both the birds to flee and the scene to be read as a blatant parable of his own critical relationship to the public mind he would represent and correct. But a more pointed and less evident lesson reverberates here as well. This innocent little passage allegorizes the painful situation of what one recent critic calls "the two Trillings" and what I have traced as his "spectral politics." The healthier bird plays the part of "chameleon" savior to the sick victim's "pariah" role, in what looks like a natural work of ironic self-sacrifice in the moral theater of our modern waste-land. Thus, Trilling would redeem the wounded authority figure that can pronounce him "good." The ultimate irony of the passage, how-ever, arises from the final flight of both birds. Success, disgust, salva-tion, coincidence, spring, death? The absence of any definitive answer fosters the repetition of this "innocent" scene of "ancient" instruction in a variety of commonplace settings, all of which assume the academy is the place where such "visions" are fully cultivated if not fully understood.

Also in 1951, Trilling contributes to another symposium, "Seven Professors Look at the Jewish Student."[8] After suggesting that the Jewish student today is less fiercely competitive than before, and that the American intellectual generally is less competent, more bureau-cratically oriented than the heroic European intellectual in the tradition of a Max Weber, Trilling discredits completely the personal or political motives of prestige and social advancement for aspiring to the academic life. Instead, he concludes by solemnly warning that the "academic community must always be on guard against using any other criterion than intellectual power as demonstrated in intellectual accomplish-ment" ("Seven Professors," p. 529). Trilling wants to preserve what he sees as the intellectual integrity of the academy against the encroach-ments of the disintegrating forces of modern liberal culture, precisely because, as he puts it in "Art and Morals" (1953), it is in the academy, however flawed, that we can see "the will" express itself as "grace."[9] As a Schiller or a Schopenhauer would advise, the study of literature especially promotes this spectacle of the reunion of aesthetics and ethics, since it is literature, particularly classic modern literature for Trilling, that, when read correctly, preserves the moral value of signif-icant form in our lives: "We want," Trilling climactically intones, "to keep an area of life in which we can be sure of the existence of the spontaneous, in which we can feel that effect does not only follow upon sufficient cause, in which there is a large element of the gratui-tous and the fortuitous, in which conditions and circumstances and law do not make up the sum of existence" ("Art and Morals," p. 20).

In short, the academy becomes for Trilling the perfect Kantian play-ground of critical mind, because it remains urbanely if duplicitously tied to the American institutions of the larger, solider world of universal struggle for active self-determination. That is, it is in the academy that one can still spontaneously impersonate in his or her gratuitous work the animating *grand récit* and pronounce it good, by "discovering" and revising it in other writers, thereby determining for oneself the self one wants to be. It is no wonder then that, as Grant Webster has shown, the New York Intellectuals, what he aptly calls the bourgeois avant-garde, willingly follow Trilling's lead into the academy.[10]

After the role of our "best and brightest" in the debacles of Vietnam and Watergate, and now after William Bennett and Jeane Kirkpatrick, not to mention Kissinger, Zbigniew Brezinski, and George Will, our generation of critics may not be able fully to appreciate Trilling's liberal vision of academic life. And that the profession of literary study may actually work to preserve grace, spontaneity, and freedom of mind—such naïveté would have to be felt as insulting, a shower of visionary salt for the wound of professional self-hatred endemic in the land. Yet, despite misgivings that would grow throughout the rest of his career, Trilling would continue to hold fast to the liberating potential of the academy. A close look at "the cultural episode" caused by Trilling's speech on the occasion of Robert Frost's eighty-fifth birthday celebration at the Waldorf-Astoria in New York City highlights not only the critical difference a couple of decades may make in the intellectual scene but also the genuinely revisionary function the modern academic critic may indeed serve at certain opportune moments in American cultural history.

On March 26, 1959, Frost's publishers, Henry Holt and Company, gave him a birthday dinner at which Trilling delivered his address delineating "the two Frosts." These are, of course, the amiable Yankee pork-barrel philosopher and the terrifying tragic visionary. In sum, these are the Frost of popular legend and the real poet, author of "Design" and many other masterpieces of mordant irony and macabre wit worthy of strong comparison with the works of the great moderns and even with the classic texts of Sophocles. The "rural" Frost, as the urban critic ruefully admits in his speech, had never been important to him until in rereading the poetry for this occasion Trilling suddenly was struck by its chilling uncanny power. Not surprisingly, given Frost's unofficial poet laureate status in 1959, the resulting éclat was considerable, culminating in a *Newsweek* report with accompanying photos equally chiaroscuro, of the poor old poet and his terrible critic.[11]

Although Trilling is right to say here that Frost as poet never meant too much to him before, Frost as figure did mean quite a lot, as a notebook entry from 1946 demonstrates:

> At Kenyon: Frost's strange speech—apparently of a kind that he often gives—he makes himself the buffoon—goes into a trance of aged childishness—he is the child who is rebelling against all the serious who are trying to *organize* him—take away his will and individuality. . . . But also the horror of the old man—fine looking old man—having to dance and clown to escape (also for his supper)— American, American in that deadly intimacy, that throwing away of dignity—"Drop that dignity! Hands up" we say—in order to come into anything like contact and to make anything like a point. ("Notebooks," pp. 25–26)

Frost, for Trilling at mid-career, represents that defensive mimicry and ironic rivalry and spectral opposition that I have been calling the dream of ancient innocence. The distracting play of public mask and private sensibility permits the pleasure of self-realization in writing to continue without being organized out of existence by the values and institutions of modern American life, by that "deadly intimacy" of the liberal reader which destroys what it seeks to possess by "professionalizing" it in abstract formulas. Thus, Trilling reads Frost as a public figure of resistance to the same professionalism critical humanists would resist from within the academy. No doubt Trilling's resistance to the systematic study of literature is why he gives up teaching American literature in 1951 and, with the exception of this 1959 speech and a 1963 essay, "Hawthorne in Our Time," refuses to write on American authors, especially on contemporary figures.[12] As much as graduate programs in English literature, American studies have usurped the field from public critics and men of letters.

The Frost speech mimics Trilling's sense of the old poet's defensive clowning in a long opening section replete with "clownish humor" and rueful "self-analysis." The critic plays anthropologist of the future speculating on the origins of the cultural rites that serve to honor a demigod named Frost at the onset of spring, before then separating the popular figure of myth from the poet of terrifying lyrics. In the lengthy "self-analysis" that follows, Trilling explains his change in taste by citing D. H. Lawrence from *Studies in Classic American Literature*. Lawrence's "Never trust the teller, trust the tale" becomes Trilling's implicit rule of thumb, Don't trust the popular reader, trust the poetry's hidden power. Trilling then characterizes that power in radically psychological (and not social) terms. Just as Lawrence discovers "an alien quality" in the old American literature originally thought fit only for children and adolescents, so Trilling discovers a terrifying tragic effect in the pastorals of the Yankee sage. Lawrence's "alien quality" is the new experience for which American writers try to invent a new language, the experience of sloughing off the old repressive ego of the Judeo-Christian-humanist tradition and giving painful birth to the new American passion of endless self-revision.

For Lawrence, this new self, paradoxically enough, is more primordially human and native to this continent than the moral self of European consciousness being shed in such works as Poe's tales, Whitman's poetry, or Melville's novels. Similarly, Frost's best poetry for Trilling bears witness to this terrifying process of disintegration:

> I conceive that Robert Frost is doing in his poems what Lawrence says the great writers of the classic American tradition did. That enterprise of theirs was of an ultimate radicalism. It consisted, Lawrence says, of two things; a disintegration and sloughing off of the old consciousness, by which Lawrence means the old European consciousness, and the forming of a new underneath.
>
> So radical a work, I need scarcely say, is not carried out by reassurance, nor by the affirmation of old virtues and pieties. It is carried out by the representation of the terrible actualities of life in a new way. I think of Robert Frost as a terrifying poet. Call him, if it makes things any easier, a tragic poet, but it might be useful every now and then to come out from under the shelter of that literary word. The universe that he conceives is a terrifying universe. Read the poem called "Design" and see if you sleep the better for it. Read "Neither Out Far Nor In Deep," which often seems to me the most perfect poem over time, and see if you are warmed by anything in it except the energy with which emptiness is perceived. ("Frost," p. 451)

Even "the curious tenderness" with which Frost treats his ordinary people in our extraordinary universe arises from this novel terror and not from some traditional notion of poetic justice. For "when ever have people been so isolated," Trilling concludes, "so lightning-blasted, so tied down and calcined by life, so reduced, each in his own way, to some last irreducible core of being. ("Frost," p. 457). Frost's people, like his pastoral world, have realized Lawrence's vision of disintegration and sloughing off of the old consciousness "with a vengeance," according to Trilling, discovering what we may call the beauty of the end, of what is left, after the ultimate radicalism of pure reduction has run its course.

What is most significant in this revisionary reading of Frost is not Trilling's provocation of a literary scandal by equating Frost's public image with that of the bald eagle (the appropriateness of which equation Trilling and his critics seriously debate in detail). Rather, it is Trilling's climactic admission that he feels so "preoccupied with" the sublime spectacle of disintegration unconsciously uncovered in Frost's poetry that he cannot know "what new consciousness is forming underneath." Frost is a Sophoclean "poet who terrifies" because he possesses, Trilling now belatedly sees, "the voice that makes . . . new" all "the terrible things of human life," and as in the case of Sophocles and the Greeks, only a poet who can "make plain the terrible things" can also possibly give comfort ("Frost," p. 412). Trilling in opposing the popular conventional view of Frost as America's New England grandfather would likewise articulate this revisionary creative voice—not for Frost's benefit so much as for the benefit of the academic appropriation of the authority to see things steadily, whole, and anew, in a fashion that would preserve "unorganized" modes of imaginative perception and critical response within a broadly traditional humanistic culture. Hence the authority of the commonplace promotes, for him, critical revisionism. That is, Trilling's practice of the function of criticism in modern American culture corresponds to Lawrence's paradoxical theory of American literary genius as simultaneously "new" and "primordal," as the demonic return of ancient innocence.

The work of Lionel Trilling in the 1950s and thereafter, in opposition to established liberal pieties that would reform all aspects of human life by bringing them progressively under the enlightened rule of law, projects a subversive image of the patriarchal tradition of romantic individualists in modern literature. He creates thereby a canon of subversive patriarchy to mirror ironically the absurd orthodoxy of the dominant culture of enlightened permissiveness. This heroic canon, as we shall see in some detail, consists of figures who, like his Frost, transgress and transcend the revolutionary convention of popular expectation by embodying, in Trilling's critical eyes, a self-conscious and tragic prefiguration of this contradictory situation. In this complex manner, Trilling returns symbolically to all the fathers he once denied in order to pass in liberal circles. Trilling returns to these figures in order to unsay such ultimately debilitating repression without reducing himself in the process to the fatal pleasure of endlessly antithetical refinements of earlier positions. The self-canceling career of the willing victim of ironic repetition thus haunts the rest of Trilling's work. The specter of Isaac Nathan, friend of Byron and betrayer of both original and foster culture, dogs Lionel Trilling's every belated step.[13]

At first sight, however, the "scene" Trilling creates in redeeming Frost's reputation for a new generation of literary intellectuals, and the scene from *The Middle of the Journey* in which John Laskell receives forgiveness for his role in a child's tragic death, would scarcely seem to resemble each other as exemplifications of the authority of the commonplace. In fact, if anything, they appear to be more each other's Other, as it were. In the Frost scene, the critical son rescues the poetic father from his public persona, whereas in the absolution scene, the Muse-Mother publicly forgives the critical son for helping to father an abomination. Yet, as Trilling's structural reliance on the outlines of the Freudian family romance suggests, both these scenes of instruction function to publicly rehabilitate the patriarchal image by dramatizing the sublime power of fatherhood as an institution that takes a variety of forms (literal and symbolic) in modern America, some of which when fully expressed may often prove inimical to, even destructive of, that very culture. If the self-consuming formula that would unstring Trilling's psychic bow is his secret guilty wish to pronounce himself "good" as the god of Genesis does the creation or as the God of St. John's Gospel does his baptized son; then the equivalent apocalyptic trope for America at large would seem to be the vision of a subversive patriarchy. All the primal fathers, long repressed in the interest of assimilation and social mobility, in the name of progressive versions of the American dream, return to wreak havoc and bring down the Liberal House of Culture. Most often these fathers return as fictions of a great force of nature, whether Melville's White Whale, Stevens' Auroras, Pynchon's rainbow spirit of gravity, or what Trilling terms "the morality of inertia."

The Morality of Inertia: Opposing Culture

"The slow smokeless burning of decay," from Frost's poem "The Woodpile," encapsulates almost perfectly what Trilling intends by this phrase "the morality of inertia." In a 1955 essay of this title (written originally for a Union Theological Seminary volume *Great Moral Dilemmas* published the next year and then collected in his own book *A Gathering of Fugitives* [1956]), Trilling uses Edith Wharton's once "classic" liberal critique of the genteel tradition, *Ethan Frome*, as a vehicle for discussing what he ultimately finds more successfully realized in Wordsworth's poetry: that is, what he characterizes as "the morality imposed by brute circumstance, by biology, by habit, by the unspoken social demand that we have not the strength to refuse, or, often, to imagine refusing."[14] Although Trilling claims he does not mean to praise this categorical morality of unthinking duty (*GF*, p. 43)—he even indicts this attitude of unconscious acceptance as being complicitous in the recent Holocaust—his symbolic choice of example from Wordsworth, "To a Celandine," recalls John Laskell's spectral love affair with a rose from the opening chapter of *The Middle of the Journey*, even as it also echoes Trilling's fierce recognition of the mysterious fact of identity in "A Sermon on a Text by Whitman." In each of these instances, what matters to Trilling is this inexorable discovery of worldly identity, a crisis experience of neither "courage" nor "choice" "but necessity" (*GF*, p. 43). Trilling is increasingly to rely on this idea of "biological fact," as a possible theoretical foundation for his oppositions to the pervasive superficiality and "weightlessness" of the "second environment" formed by our modern adversary culture of critical professions.

However noble the ends, this suspicious critical instrument of "biological intelligence" leaves Trilling open to the accusation, most elegantly and consistently argued by Joseph Frank over the years, that in the guise of modern literary ethics our cold-war liberal proposes an essentially conservative aesthetic of acceptance that is, perhaps unwittingly, ideologically motivated. For it is so undiscriminating in its quietistic acceptance of things as they are that it in principle must embrace all established institutions and values as if they were not human creations subject to conscious alteration but facts of nature to be masterfully suffered in virtually sublime silence.

"The Situation of the American Intellectual," Trilling's contribution to a famous 1952 *Partisan Review* symposium, "Our Country and Our Culture," appears at first glance to confirm the substance of Frank's critique, especially when seen in the ravaging context of McCarthyism and the rise to power of Eisenhower and Nixon. This little essay briefly traces the modern history of "mind" in American society. The intellectual class or "mind" initially takes its identity from a now-ritual alienation from its bourgeois origins. In the postwar climate of affluence and anticommunism, however, this class is experiencing, Trilling believes, "a diminution in its sense of alienation" (*GF*, p. 65), especially since its most prominent members are acquiring those leadership positions in government, the professions, education, and, to some extent, even in industry to which they have long aspired. The lessening of alienation, Trilling finds, does threaten to become dangerous by taking the edge off the critical spirit of this class, and yet, in the accompanying diminution of the bad faith that motivates the sentimental tendency of American intellectuals to see alien cultures as superior in every way to our own, such a development is to be welcomed as a positive good, a necessary if temporary corrective to earlier excesses.

As in his contemporaneous celebrations of the sociological works of David Riesman and Erving Goffman,[15] Trilling reads this new accept-ance of our country and our culture as a somewhat mixed blessing. It is to be appreciated insofar as it makes for the acknowledgment of the conditioned nature of the human spirit. It is to be deplored, however, insofar as this new attention to society may promote conformity. On the whole, at this time, Trilling reads this acceptance, however, as providing "the right ground on which to approach" more "transcen-dental things" such as questions of personal authenticity and social justice. Even more to the point for Trilling, this new attitude of the American intellectual class may also provide "the right ground for the literary art to grow in—the right ground for satire, for humor, for irony, for tragedy, for the personal vision affirming itself against the institu-tional with the peculiar passionateness of art." For, as Trilling wryly concludes, "As strange and sad as it may be to have to say it again, literature really is the criticism of life" (*GF*, p. 84).

And yet, just as clearly, the discovery by the formerly disaffected intellectual class of "innocence," "simplicity," and "integrity of life" in cold-war America can express itself unwittingly in a manner that re-calls the aesthetics of betrayal and self-betrayal found in Joseph Howe's academic vision of orderly perfection from Trilling's celebrated novella "Of This Time, Of That Place" of nearly a decade earlier.

> there also comes a moment when the faces, the gait, the love, the manner and manners of one's own people become just what one needs, and the whole look and style of one's culture seems appro-priate, seems perhaps not good but intensely *possible*. What your compatriots are silently saying about the future, about life and death, may seem suddenly very accessible to you, and not wrong. You are at a gathering of people, or you are in a classroom, and, being the kind of unpleasant person you are, you know that you might take one individual after another and make yourself fully aware of his foolishness or awkwardness and that you might say, "And this is my country! And this is my culture!" But instead of doing that, you let yourself become aware of something that is really in the room, some common intention of the spirit which, although it may be checked and impeded, is not foolish or awkward but rather graceful, and not wrong. (*GF*, p. 84)

Thus our American Socrates may become for a moment Sophocles if not Oedipus at Colonus after all. In doing so, however, the intellectual runs the risk, as Trilling recognizes, of espousing "the false language of at-homeness" enshrined in the productions of Stephen Vincent Benét, Thomas Wolfe, and American advertising (*GF*, pp. 84–85).

As we shall see in examining the essays collected in *The Opposing Self* and *Beyond Culture*, Trilling's critical use of the theory of "biological intelligence," which informs the aesthetic of acceptance he propounds there, does indeed invoke the wisdom of nearly mute, insensate things, that "morality of inertia" which Wordsworth celebrates. Yet Trilling is not primarily projecting a more stylish myth of ideological conformity than that pervading the dominant culture during the cold-war era. Rather, he creates in these essays a reflexive fiction standing in consistent opposition to the rule of modernity in all its political and aesthetic forms. Trilling presses into service against the triumph of modern culture (as ersatz custom and artistic innovation) a concept of nature as the authority of the commonplace, what he will call "the fate of pleasure," and resists every attempt—short of final annihilation—to transform all of existence into effective techniques for conscious exploitation.[16] The literary "fathers" that return thus return like Frost, as Father Nature. This critical fiction in Trilling's later work inverts what Adorno in *Aesthetic Theory* describes as the dialectic of domination in which "art stands in for nature by abolishing the latter in effigy."[17] Trilling instead would have nature represent art by liberating the latter via his critical fiction of going beyond culture. Modern art for Adorno, according to one of his better commentators, "represents both the attempt to dominate nature and the attempt to recall what resists domination."[18] As the essays in *The Opposing Self* especially make clear, Trilling recalls what resists domination in order to suspend—at least momentarily—the actual attempts to dominate nature that define our historical epoch as quite likely the last. Trilling performs this genuinely critical function, this work of liberation from the habit of domination, for an entire generation of American intellectuals. Opposing the apocalyptic culture of the more established avant-garde with a radically anti-apocalyptic vision of cosmic stasis and decay may be bad critical strategy on Trilling's part, especially in hindsight, but it is not simply ideological capitulation. It is instead an apocalypse of irony—a questioning of all not with a heroic bang but with a stoic snicker—which completes that return of authority (and authorizing figures) that marks Trilling's revisionary career as a truly representative one.

In 1955 *The Opposing Self* collected occasional essays written over the previous half-decade. This collection, unlike the others, arranges its parts on a subtly dialectical and not generally chronological basis.

Despite this suggestive innovation, about which more later, the best approach to this volume remains primarily via the place each essay occupies in the emerging work of the career as a whole. Before beginning this discussion, however, I want to examine briefly a piece on Arthur Mizener's *The Far Side of Paradise* that Trilling wrote for the February 3, 1951, issue of the *New Yorker*. "Fitzgerald Plain," as he ironically entitled the review, reveals the essential themes and strategies of Trilling's criticism at the time, even as it recalls his earlier, similarly sympathetic treatment of Fitzgerald in *The Liberal Imagination* and as well begins to bid a fond farewell to further extensive involvement with modern American writers. Trilling will focus now increasingly on the history and fate of English literature and culture, with rare exceptions, two of which appear in *The Opposing Self*. This review also suggests the reason for such a development.

Although Mizener betrays Fitzgerald's "fatal submission to the sanctions of social prestige," this submission marks the novelist as a hero in Trilling's eyes. For Fitzgerald's life and work, the career of his spirit, however tragic, disclose a useful moral for naive liberals concerning the rigorousness of "the systems of prestige that lie beneath the American social fluidity" (*SLS*, p. 251). Fitzgerald's snobbery, perhaps like Trilling's own, recalls the "magical importance" that children playing among themselves innocently invest in questions of status and priority. In any event, such "social submissiveness" is not really snobbery or submissiveness at all, for the social image in Fitzgerald, Trilling claims, actually stands for a utopian ideal of the self (*SLS*, p. 258).

Fitzgerald himself suggests as much in a famous letter about being overwhelmed by society "even in Podunk." What really counts for Fitzgerald in this experience is the necessity of having "to start over from scratch" to fashion a self that would measure up to and perhaps triumph over all such circumstances. "He exaggerated the idea of society," Trilling comments, "and his dependence upon it in order, we may say, to provide a field for the activity of his conscience, for the trial of his self" (*SLS*, p. 258). A true son of Puritan America despite himself, Fitzgerald in this light "begins to seem an anachronistic figure . . . legendary in the sense of being a figure of the past" (*SLS*, p. 259).

Yet the figures among whom Fitzgerald fits best are not James and Proust, or Emerson and Milton. Rather, it is the great romantic poets, particularly Keats and Wordsworth. (Ironically enough, Fitzgerald's wake was held in "the Wordsworth Room.") The critical reason for Trilling's conjuction of Wordsworth and Fitzgerald is their celebration of ecstatic boyhood and youth and their painful recognition of a depleting fund of imaginative energies. (Fitzgerald's connection with

Keats, of course, arises from the similarity between the former's trial of the self and the latter's vale of soul making as images for life.)

Finally, Trilling's conclusion summarizes the legendary quality of Fitzgerald in terms that are crucial for understanding the essays in *The Opposing Self*:

> He thought of himself in this way; his notion of America involved the idea of deterioration, of old virtue coming to an end. He set great store by the "belief in good manners and right instincts" he had learned from his father, but he spoke of his father as the debilitated representative of an old idealism, "of the generation of the colonies and the revolution," snubbed and put down by "the new young peasant stock coming up every ten years." It was not only the old virtues that he saw doomed but also the energy of will and imagination. Gatsby, for all that he represents the raw energies of the Twenties, is as anachronistic as his author, for Fitzgerald makes him the symbol of a desire that modern life must deny, the wish to come face to face with "something commensurate to his capacity for wonder." Without the help of that phrase, "the capacity for wonder," no college textbook could hope to deal with the Romantic poets. What they wondered at was, above all, the self, and as our epoch more and more denies the value and even the possiblity of the self, Fitzgerald seems to have ended what they began, to be as far off as they, and to shine with their light. (*SLS*, p. 259)

"Fitzgerald Plain," first of all, would answer Trilling's critics—particularly Robert Warshaw and Delmore Schwartz—who indict his focus on manners in the novel for being thinly veiled snobbery. If it is snobbery, it is sublime snobbery involving a dialectical understanding of self-making in an ever modernizing world. In addition, this little review rehearses a familiar position on American culture developed out of Lawrence that Trilling will perfect in "An American View of English Literature" (*Reporter*, November 13, 1951). As the titles of *The Last of the Mohicans* and "The Fall of the House of Usher" suggest to Trilling, Americans love to produce and consume fictions of the end, about the death of the old personality and the collapse of its accompanying social order, in hopes of entertaining the vision of a new self in a better world of some utopian sort or other. Moreover, Trilling addresses here—obliquely through his virtual apotheosis of Fitzgerald—the subject of "making it" in America and shows his complex attitude toward it. Trilling both recognizes and reasonably laments the endless revisionary displacements that define the modern world. Furthermore, he also

projects back, beyond the ever-present scene of steady decline, a more
sublime realm of legendary figures, whose heroic resistance to modernity stands in judgment of all, even the critic himself who reflexively
repeats the characteristic American convention of the end in his identification with the figure of Fitzgerald he himself creates and then
places among the other Last Romantic Fathers. Finally, then, this review also demonstrates the radically revisionary dialectic that informs
Trilling's increasingly un–American work during the cold war. The universal deterioration ever afflicting the present scene continues to testify
to the sublime power of the subversive patriarchy whose critical judgment alone can provide that "something commensurate to his capacity
for wonder" which Fitzgerald and Trilling so badly need as provocation
for "their" different aspirations to complete the literary tradition. The
morality of inertia, the ancient innocence of Trilling's authoritative
commonplaces, thus would oppose all modern culture in the name of
a sublime principle whose nature paradoxically reveals itself as the idea
of "pastness" itself—an undisplaceable aristocracy of style: "Fitzgerald
seems to have ended what they began, to be *as far off as they*, and *to shine
with their light*" (*SLS*, p. 259; my emphasis).

We have seen this curious side of Trilling's critical humanism before,
of course, in "The Genius of O'Neill" and "Tacitus Now," in "The
Sense of the Past" and, as well, in the strange fondness he expresses
in the fiction for teacups and for the academy. The first written of the
major essays to be collected in *The Opposing Self*, "Wordsworth and the
Rabbis," reveals the underlying motive for this self-opposing principle
of taste that prefers, apparently, whatever possesses the aura of the
dead as more vitalizing than the living art of the present moment.

In April 1950 Trilling attended a conference at Princeton University
commemorating the centennial of a poet's death. The point of his talk
(originally entitled "Wordsworth and the Iron Time" in honor of his
critical mentor Arnold in whose view Wordsworth was the great com-
forter in our bad times) is openly polemical if still delicately put. Trilling
argues that the great works of literary modernism, the ironic masterpieces of Lawrence, Faulkner, Yeats, Conrad, Gide, Mann, and especially Joyce, envision an elemental form of awareness that has
increasingly become unavailable in the modern world. Trilling identifies this endangered innocence with the religious impulse in traditional
Christianity, with "the sentiment of being" in Wordsworth and Rousseau, and, as well, with the image of the ideal "other culture" to be
found in Freud's celebration of England and its literature. Trilling discovers traces of this more primitive but no less thoughtful mode of
mental functioning in the serious play of argument and figure in the

classic style of critical humanism since the Renaissance. For Trilling, this oppositional and elemental knowledge of existence, imaginatively abstracted from these sources and from everyday life by modern authors, passes an adverse judgment upon our rationalized world by virtue of its very simplicity, integrity, and openness to experience. As such, the classic works of modernism have more in common with the characteristic achievements of Wordsworth and the other romantic writers than we usually suspect when we consider only the elaborate defensive artifice of a *Ulysses* or a *Lord Jim*. Finally, and most provocatively, Trilling concludes by claiming that this adversarial judgment, nobly embodied in the vision of nature and the creative person's survival instinct to be found in Wordsworth and his unlikely precursors and heirs, also has strong if latent affinities, despite obvious differences, with that endless proverbial wisdom of the *Pirké Aboth* or *Sayings of the Fathers* in ancient Jewish tradition which Trilling read first as a boy.

> The character of Leopold Bloom, who figures in the life of Joyce's Poet much as the old men in Wordsworth figure in his life—met by chance and giving help of some transcendent yet essentially human kind—is conceived in Wordsworthian terms: in terms, that is, of his humbleness of spirit. If we speak of Wordsworth in reference to the Rabbis and their non-militancy, their indifference to the idea of evil, their acceptance of cosmic contradiction, are we not to say that Bloom is a Rabbinical character? It is exactly his non-militancy that makes him the object of general contempt and, on one occasion, of rage. It is just this that has captivated his author, as the contrast with the armed pride, the jealousy and desire for prestige, the bitter militancy of Stephen Dedalus. Leopold Bloom is deprived of every shred of dignity except the dignity of that innocence which for Joyce, as for Wordsworth, goes with the "sentiment of Being."
>
> Again and again in our literature, at its most apocalyptic and intense, we find the impulse to create figures who are intended to suggest that life is justified in its elemental biological simplicity, and, in the manner of Wordsworth, these figures are conceived of as being of humble status and humble heart: Lawrence's simpler people or primitive people whose pride is only that of plants or animals; Dreiser's Jennie Gerhardt and Mrs. Griffiths, who stand as oases in the wide waste of their creator's dull representation of energy; Hemingway's waiters with their curious silent dignity; Faulkner's Negroes, of whom it is said, as so often it is said in effect of Wordsworth's people, *they endured*; and Faulkner's idiot boys, of whom it is said, *they are*—the list could be extended to suggest how great is the affin-

ity of our literature with Wordsworth. And these figures express an intention which is to be discerned through all our literature—the intention to imagine, and to reach, a condition of the soul in which the will is freed from "particular aims," in which it is "strong in itself and in beatitude." At least as early as Balzac our literature has shown the will seeking its own negation—or, rather, seeking its own affirmation by its rejection of the aims which the world sets before it and by turning its energies upon itself in self-realization. Of this particular affirmation of the will Wordsworth is the proponent and the poet. (*OS*, pp. 131–132)

Quite simply, under the ironic banners of Wordsworth's "suspended will" and the "normal mysticism" of the Rabbis, Trilling is here making respectable for the middle-class academic critics of modern culture he now represents both the rediscovery of romanticism and the study of their own origins. To do so in the age of Eliot, Pound, Leavis, and the Holocaust is no mean feat, especially when one remembers that the site of this performance, Princeton University, was in 1950 and for a long time thereafter a bastion of the Anglo-Saxon "genteel" mind.

As we shall see, this aesthetic vision of nature opposes culture from within by means of its spontaneous transcendental resistance. It essentially defines the argument of the other essays in *The Opposing Self*, even as it informs that of "Fitzgerald Plain." It also fulfills the spectral politics of the earlier career by providing a genuine reason for playing the worldly messiah role for his generation of critics. Trilling, before Hartman and Bloom, before Abrams even, and to all their different benefits, stages in "Wordsworth and the Rabbis" the exemplary recovery of his repressed tradition via the speculative argument for the romantic origins of our latest modernity.

Contemporary historians of literary culture, either in its philosophical/anthropological or cold-war liberal modes, could easily claim that Trilling in *The Opposing Self* and really throughout his career repeats the conventional moves and mystifications of the tradition of critical humanism from Montaigne to—alas!—William Bennett. After all, Trilling does cast a cold eye on all the partisans of the present moment regardless of significant differences in their positions on the intellectual spectrum. And he does then project a vision of the heroic past sublimely subversive of all but its selective representatives from Wordsworth to Joyce. Whether we say that this ironic critical strategy receives its definitive ideological formation and counterrevolutionary edge in Kant's *Anthropology*, George Kennan's policy of containment, or Nietzsche's critique of monumental history in the first of his *Untimely*

Meditations matters less than if we realize what Trilling suggests here and what Max Weber's social psychology of the Prophets in *Ancient Judaism* confirms: viz., the religious nature, the inescapably mythic dimension, of cultural (as of all) criticism.

As his conclusions to "Fitzgerald Plain" and "Wordsworth and the Rabbis," and indeed his conclusions generally attest, both Trilling's style and his mode of argument are realizations of this necessary myth. He abstracts from the particulars of the work or career under discussion a few general ideas that retain the aura of their literary origins. He deploys these general ideas dialectically to represent the tragic complexities of the writer in the context of his time and to contain prophetically the pressing concerns of the present scene of cultural struggle and debate. Except in this purely formal sense, his arguments within an essay and between essays in the same volume, as in *The Opposing Self*, thus never seek final resolution. His arguments instead resolve themselves in resonant images and phrases, revisionary names and formulations that suggest much but remain forever suspended in indeterminacy with respect to definite forecasts or prescriptions for what will or should come next in cultural history. I call this kind of "free" critical writing the style of sublime evasion.

I do not mean to imply by this allusive phrase of my own invention that Trilling employs his style simply to avoid facing or to mystify reality. Rather, I mean that Trilling creates, as generally do critical humanists (and their antagonists), mythic-sounding entities, what Wallace Stevens calls the creations of sound, that contain—by allusion—as many realities as possible: personal, political, epochal. This aspiration to a pregnant allusiveness in fact ensures semantic indeterminacy, even outright contradiction, to some degree or other. In this respect, Trilling's critical writing is not essentially any different from that of Henry James or William Blake, or, for that matter, Harold Bloom, Jacques Derrida, Michel Foucault, or Freud. The features that distinguish Trilling's style from any other are the solemn classical pretense of its pacing, as if Marcus Aurelius were alive and well on Morningside Heights; its ironic reflexiveness, as if a great mind were thinking out loud and the reader were naturally anxious to overhear its intricate intonations; and, at its best, its aristocratic plainness and perspicacity, as if the story the style tells could very well account for the reader's own mode of imaginative existence. Whatever else reading Trilling does, it certainly does give one the sense of an enlarged if sacrificial world.

The rest of *The Opposing Self* makes a fine case in pointed counterpoint. In the most famous and perhaps best essay that he ever wrote, "The Poet as Hero: Keats in His Letters" (1951), for instance, Trilling, thanks to Keats's ironic doctrine of negative capability, makes the consumptive unrealized genius of the legend over into the priest of "tragic salvation" (*OS*, p. 42). Keats appears to be a kind of muscular aesthete of the mind and the perfect exemplar of "mature masculinity" (*OS*, p. 22), who "stands as the last image of health when the sickness of Europe [change for change's sake] began to be apparent" (*OS*, p. 43). "He believed that life was given for him to find the right use of it, that it was the kind of continuous magical confrontation requiring to be met with the right answer" (*OS*, p. 4). After the debased reality and barbarous rhetoric of Hitler and Stalin, appreciation for the definitive poetic expression of passionate irresolution becomes a redeeming virtue in any authentic man of this world.

This theme of what it means to be a man in but not of the modern world, and particularly what it means to be a father (literally or symbolically), is taken up again by the essays "Anna Karenina" (1951) and "William Dean Howells and the Roots of Modern Taste" (1951). In the former, Trilling claims for Tolstoi a superiority of "moral imagination" in envisioning the human spirit amidst life's "inescapable conditions" and vicissitudes, especially as compared with what "the characteristic criticism of our time," "the psychological analysis of language," can reveal about this great novel of tragic romantic passion. (Trilling is taking aim here at both the New Critics and Philip Rahv's earlier essay on Tolstoi.) To illustrate his case Trilling adduces a series of sublime examples of "the moral imagination" at work in literature.

> there are moments in literature which do not yield the secret of their power to any study of language, because the power does not depend on language but on the moral imagination. When we read how Hector in his farewell to Andromache picks up his infant son and the baby is frightened by the horsehair crest of his father's helmet and Hector takes it off and laughs and puts it on the ground, or how Priam goes to the tent of Achilles to beg back from the slayer the body of his son, and the old man and the young man, both bereaved and both under the shadow of death, talk about death and fate, nothing can explain the power of such moments over us—or nothing short of a recapitulation of the moral history of the race. And even when the charge of emotion is carried by our sense of the perfect appropriateness of the words that are used—Cordelia's "No cause. No cause"; or Ophelia's "I was the more deceived"; or Hamlet's "The rest is silence"—we are unable to deal analytically with the language, for it is not psychologically pregnant but only morally right; exactly in this way, we feel, should this person in this situation speak, and

only our whole sense of life will explain our gratitude for the words being these and not some others.

In short, there are times when the literary critic can do nothing more than point, and *Anna Karenina* presents him with an occasion when his critical function is reduced to this primitive activity. (*OS*, pp. 63–64)

These Arnoldian touchstones not only define by association Tolstoi's similar genius but also, placed all together like this, compose a virtual Mosaic anatomy of fatherhood, and its attendant phallologocentric metaphysics.

The Howells essay, one of the least persuasive in Trilling's canon, develops this patriarchal undercurrent into a full-blown if fairly undialectical opposition between the bourgeois "daddy" of letters and avant-garde orthodoxy. For most of the essay Trilling elaborates this simple contrast between a confessed middle-class editor of *Atlantic Monthly* and author of *A Hazard of New Fortunes*, who saw "the smiling aspects" of American family life and wrote in balanced if not greatly distinguished praise of them, and a more abstract, reified modern taste which would rather succumb imaginatively to what Hannah Arendt in her analysis of totalitarianism calls "the godhead of disintegration" at large in our world than read about the plight of literary mediocrities hunting for a room during the Gilded Age for fifty or more pages of merely competent realistic prose:

> When we are so eager to say how wrong Howells was to invite the novelist to deal with the smiling aspects of life, we have to ask ourselves whether our quick antagonism to this mild recognition of pleasure does not imply an impatience with the self, a degree of yielding to what Hannah Arendt calls the irresistible temptation of disintegration, of identification by submission to the grandeur of historical necessity which is so much more powerful than the self. (*OS*, pp. 89–90)

Trilling rereads into Howells and his poor reputation the origins of his own critical opposition to contemporary liberal culture, so prey to the fascination of the abomination that is Stalinism. Trilling accomplishes this revisionary feat by adducing Arendt's formula for totalitarianism but in a form that alludes to Arnold's more general definition of tragedy as the sublime acquiescence to an inevitable fate. Trilling thereby subsumes Arendt's subversive conception of "the godhead of disintegration" from *The Origins of Totalitarianism* under his already established system of self-reference. The aim is, explicitly, to make use of Howells to reveal a not "very intense kind of pleasure" that "will at least serve, in Keats's phrase, to bind us to the earth, to prevent our being seduced by the godhead of disintegration" (*OS*, p. 90), that is, to prevent our being seduced by a purely radical, unbourgeois way of life which envisions the total remaking of humankind as we have known it through aesthetic and/or political means of a violently revolutionary nature.

This line of argument, echoing obliquely Lawrence again on American literature, in turn inspires (among others) Trilling's colleagues Richard Chase and Quentin Anderson to develop their immensely influential critiques of our tradition of apocalyptic novels and imperial selves. And yet, so far in this essay, Trilling does not account for the authority of the commonplace, its peculiar affectivity, which resides normally in its complicity with the godhead of disintegration, especially now but not only in our age. Trilling's conclusion suddenly raises this awful prospect and proposes a most disturbing solution for it—silence:

> The dying anguish of Roland or the distress of a Lear stripped of power moves us by its exceptional quality but loses its special eloquence when reproduced simultaneously in several thousand copies: the extreme has become the commonplace of our day. This is not a situation that can be legislated or criticized out of existence, but while it endures we are not in a position to make a proper judgment on Howells, a man of moderate sentiments. It is a disqualification that we cannot regard with complacency, for Andre Girle suggests it implies that we are in a fair way of being disqualified from making any literary judgments at all. (*OS*, p. 90)

In this shocking conclusion to an otherwise blandly discursive essay, Trilling tips his doubly ironic hand via that conditional invocation of Gide's authority. Not only does Trilling stand in opposition to the radical politics that would automatically dismiss such a middle-class patriarch of nineteenth-century American letters as William Dean Howells, but he also clearly opposes that debased aestheticism celebrated as tragic gaiety by Yeats in "Lapis Lazuli" which, as the first few lines here suggest, welcomes every and any passionate intensity in experience, even the calculated brutality of modern war, as sublime inspiration for its heroic play. Trilling's perfection of the Forsterian comic manner that casts ironic aspersions on both sides in cultural debates reminds us that in an age of universal mechanical replication even our once-individualizing deaths have become carbon copies of each other.

As a result of this ubiquitous destruction, all of us, Trilling included, are no longer able to pass judgment—one way or another—on anything, least of all the traditional ethic of the truly magnanimous man, the Aristotelian incarnation of the golden mean. In our age, the return of such an ethos is the most radical prospect of all—an actual realization of Trilling's sublime catachresis of the commonplace extreme. In the name of his simple contrast between Howells and modern taste, therefore, Trilling demonstrates the ironic and effective complicity of the commonplace with the godhead of disintegration, not so much in his explicit statements as in the argument his stylistic practices implicate.

In a time that defines itself as essentially and ever modern, perpetually suffering burnout and always already starting afresh, what more appropriate master trope could a critic propose for serious consideration than the figure of opposition to end all opposition, the opposing self par excellence that stands radically—because traditionally and commonly—opposed to that very habit of revisionary displacement, performed by a vanguard elite of one stripe or other, which appears to make our culture repeatedly *happen*. The slow, conditional, ironic return of the Fathers, that is, would thus cure their hectic heirs of the modern disease of apocalyptic thinking with a real vengeance. The perverse pleasure in sublime disintegration that Lawrence sees in Poe and Trilling sees in Frost, for instance, is heralding the ultimate apocalypse: William Dean Howells as the debilitating god of domestic joys, whose utter blandness and banality paralyze, Gorgon-like, the latest batch of wholly academic revisionists.

In the later career this patriarchal counterrevolution of spectral masters would repeatedly subvert modernity (identified with radical politics and visionary aesthetics from the romantics on) by transforming all that is modern into the scapegoat-muse, the inspiring provocation of the fathers' return to titular power in Trilling's text. This revisionary pattern thus resembles the specular play of narcissistic desire and deconstructive irony variously characterized by contemporary theorists as a compensatory romance of interpretation; a textual logic that has served since Longinus as effective therapy for cases of male hysteria in changing times; an ascetic discipline of abjection; and, most comprehensively, one of the purely gratuitous effects of the formal materialism of the duplicitous sign.[19] The resemblance ends, however, when one recognizes the mock-sublime nature of this rhetorical economy in Trilling's hands. Whose interests could one imagine this apocalyptic apoth-

eosis of the commonplace Howells actually hurting? Like Lawrence in
Etruscan Places when he realizes that the grand burial mound at Vulci,
a sunken ruin now, was once topped by its phallic sculpture and so
composed a gigantic visionary breast, the later Trilling's casual reader
can appreciate the curious view and move on to the next occasion for
imaginative response. But to do so would be to overlook too much in
Trilling's critical career and especially the exemplary manner through
which he works everything out.

Putting my case for the later Trilling in this way sounds more than a
bit like that form of special pleading for which critical humanists from
Sam Johnson to Wayne Booth are infamous. The individuality of an
author's style—whatever that may mean—justifies all and cannot itself
become successfully subject to systematic analysis for the purpose of
discovering the general law of representaion at work in (or as) this
specific style. The inexhaustible particularity of the object—or subject—of humanistic study is often alleged but rarely defined, except as
some variant of the genius trope in suspicious contrast to the common-
ality of the rule and its interchangeable instances. This contrast between the organic monad and the mechanical effigy underlies all notions of self-versus-other modes of determination in aesthetics, ethics,
and political theory. Of course, the perfectly unique instance, like the
absolutely original commonplace, are mythical constructions, regulative fictions, what Kenneth Burke calls god–terms, that found and
delimit the field of humanistic representation, even as they function as
the ultimate sources for all subsequent genealogical derivation. In
short, any appeal, even my own above, to the particular manner via
which an author can be said to realize his vision, whatever the latter's
content, presumes, wittingly or not, the classic bourgeois ideology of
the individual in its myriad forms, that has given rise in modern times
to all the things which Trilling for one both opposes and finds apparently inescapable.

Fatal Pleasure: The Unforming Word

Certainly, the essays on Dickens and Orwell in *The Opposing Self* that
Trilling composes next do indeed paint modern culture in the bleakest,
most claustrophobic colors possible. It is as if Trilling were now succumbing to that extremist habit of writing which in "Wordsworth and
the Rabbis" he laments and resists as a communal failure of the imagination he wants no parts of, and which he says T. S. Eliot, as the
leading literary intellectual of his generation, unwittingly celebrates in
The Cocktail Party:

> We imagine, with nothing in between, the dull not-being of life, the
> intense not-being of death; but we do not imagine being—we do not
> imagine that it can be a joy. We are in love, at least in our literature,
> with the fantasy of death. Death and suffering, when we read, are
> our only means of conceiving the actuality of life. (*OS*, p. 129)

Yet, ironically enough, in his introduction to *Little Dorrit* (1953) and in
"George Orwell and the Politics of Truth" (1952), Trilling seems as
much an extremist of the modern imagination as Eliot. From the perpetual displacement that is modernity and that is most often envisioned as imprisonment or self-exile, there seems no escape, except an
attenuated aesthetic vision of negative transcendence that derives from
the religious ideal of self-abnegation which Trilling praises in Hegel
even as he condemns its more severe and explicitly ascetic manifestations in Eliot and modern literature generally:

> Hegel defines his faculty of Gemüt as expressing itself as a desire, a
> will, which has "no particular aims, such as riches, honors, and the
> like; in fact, it does not concern itself with any worldly condition of
> wealth, prestige, etc. but with the entire condition of the soul—a
> general sense of enjoyment." (*OS*, p. 127)

Like "the sentiment of Being" in Rousseau and Wordsworth or the
discovery of identity in the self's encounter with death in Whitman,
Hegelian *Gemüt* represents the systematic denial of every specific object of desire as a general sense of pleasure in oneself. The resem-
blances of this romantic vision to Schopenhauer's conception of genius
(informing *Matthew Arnold*) and to Freud's speculations on primal narcissism (informing "Art and Neurosis" in *The Liberal Imagination*) are
rather evident. What may not be so evident is that the romantic vision
of pleasure and the modern vision of critical negation (in Eliot and
others) are equally religious in nature, if not both obviously ascetic.
The negative transcendence of the world, what Walter Pater in *Marius
the Epicurean* terms "the will as vision," can manifest itself either as a
generalized sense of enjoyment in being a self abstracted from any
particular object of pleasure, or as a painful internal exile of total
alienation.

The above passage is especially characteristic of the later Trilling.
For he repeatedly portrays the return from modern developments to
romantic and earlier origins as an emotional and cultural advance. It is
not so much that Trilling sees modern culture as a fall from original

glory as that he regards it as an occasion for this free movement of the mind between alternative imaginative possibilities and all the different gradations in between. The power of criticism to articulate the revisionary analysis, the liberating word, which can unform our attachments to this or that aspect of modernity and so launch the prodigal's return, will become Trilling's favorite pastime, the fatal pleasure of his final years.

Trilling reads *Little Dorrit* as Dickens' demonic allegory of the diseased social will which only a Dantesque final vision can somewhat mitigate. As a revisionary gloss upon Wordsworth's image of modern life from his great ode ("Shades of the prison-house begin to close upon the growing boy"), the image of the prison, so central to the novel, demonstrates for Trilling how Dickens anticipates the Freudian conception of the mind as a juridical function:

> One way of describing Freud's conception of the mind is to say that it is based upon the primacy of the will, and that the organization of the internal life is in the form, often fantastically parodic, of a criminal process in which the mind is at once the criminal, the victim, the police, the judge and the executioner. And this is a fair description of Dickens' own view of the mind, for, having received the social impress, it becomes in turn the matrix of society. (*OS*, p. 48)

As his notebook entries in the 1940s predict, the mind, at the opening of the Age of Conformity in fortress America fittingly envisions itself in terms of this official figure of incarceration, in an ironically poignant reversal of the modern symbol of revolutionary hopes, the fallen Bastille.

The familiar complex of radical evil and masculine protest returns here in Trilling's readings of Blandois as arch rebellious son and Iago-like principle of negation in human nature upon which all such revolutionary hopes founder, and of John Jarndyce as the hollow image of beneficent paternity whose symbolic, Samson-like castration at Mr. Pocks's hands is, despite its oddity, entirely appropriate in the symbolic context. Yet the use to which Trilling puts the autobiographical element in *Little Dorrit* is of far more puzzling significance than this psychologizing of social meaning. Trilling contends that Arthur Clennam's Flora Finching was based on Maria Beadnell, the "one friend and companion" of Dickens' youth whose return to him after her marriage to another revealed the inevitable anticlimax of the years. For Trilling, the final schematic, even forced vision of the novel's conclusion, in which Little Dorrit appears as a latter-day Beatrice and "Paraclete in female form" (*OS*, p. 57), nevertheless represents Dickens' heroic negation of the unmitigated social will, a negation that we should emulate:

> the last infirmity of noble mind may lead to the first infirmity of noble will. Dickens, to be sure, never lost his love of form, or of whatever of life's goods his miraculous powers might bring him, but there came a moment when the old primitive motive could no longer serve, when the joy of impressing his power on the world no longer seemed delightful in itself, and when the first, simple, honest, vulgar energy of desire no longer seemed appropriate to his idea of himself. . . . the whole energy of the imagination of *Little Dorrit* is directed to the transcending of the personal will [and] the negation of the social will, to the search for the will in which shall be our peace. (*OS*, pp. 55, 56, 57)

In an allusive critical imitation of the Circumlocution Office, Trilling concludes his reading of *Little Dorrit* on a highly suggestive if still indeterminately religious note reminiscent of the conclusion of *The Waste Land* or of *Ash Wednesday*:

> This novel at its best is only incidentally realistic; its finest power of imagination appears in the great general images whose abstractness is their actuality, like Mr. Merdle's dinner parties, or the Circumlocution Office itself, and in such a context we understand Little Dorrit to be the Beatrice of the *Comedy*, the Paraclete in female form. Even the physical littleness of this grown woman, an attribute which is insisted on and which seems likely to repel us, does not do so, for we perceive it to be the sign that she is not only the Child of the Marshalsea, as she is called, but also the Child of the Parable, the negation of the social will. (*OS*, p. 57)

What are we to make of this nuptial-sounding allegory of reading, that in its last lines also recalls Eliot's *Burnt Norton*?

At the heart of Trilling's vision of subversive patriarchy, that return of all the repressed fathers which *The Opposing Self* stages, lies this spiritual rebirth of the female will as a symbolic representation of Trilling's own renewed creative receptivity to "the great general images" of the Western tradition, "whose abstractness" comprises "their actuality." Like the fierce lineaments of an abstract expressionist canvas intended to demonstrate the formal energies of the medium itself, the "fathers" in Trilling thus appear fundamentally as the aesthetic principles and archetypes that animate the careers of imaginative artists and the cultural life of a people. As we shall see, this avowedly "masculine" conception of style serves to cultivate and protect the subversive vision of innocence and spontaneous receptivity to life that Trilling, following the lead of Wordsworth and Joyce, characterizes as "poetic materialism" (*OS*, p. 131), a mythical state of nature which Freudian psychoanalysis permits Trilling to posit as being beyond culture. To anticipate a bit, the presiding genius of this reflexive critical fiction of a transcendent supernature, however, turns out to be not the commonplace Howells but the savagely ironic Jane Austen.

The three remaining "sires" of this curious development, Orwell, James, and Flaubert, complete Trilling's personal canon of subversive patriarchs, each representing another of "the great general images" from the modern antimodern tradition "whose abstractness is their reality," and another aspect of Trilling's style of critical judgment as well.

Against, for example, the incessant displacement that characterizes modernity and that generally makes a genuine collective memory increasingly impossible in the Soviet bloc and the liberal democracies alike, Trilling in the Orwell essay (1952) projects the "truth-telling" chronicler of the Spanish Civil War from *Homage to Catalonia* as an "archaic figure" of "the virtuous man," the plain-speaking man of Wordsworthian duty. Orwell's importance to the present moment is inestimable precisely because his life and work form a coherent career that stands for a single idea, that old-fashioned English idea of "not being a genius" (*OS*, p. 136). "If we ask what it is [Orwell] stands for, what he is the figure of," Trilling claims, the answer is "the virtue of not being a genius, of fronting the world with nothing more than one's simple, direct, undeceived intelligence, and a respect for the powers one does have, and the work one undertakes to do" (*OS*, pp. 137–138).

Despite himself and his secular, anti-establishment sentiments, Trilling represents Orwell the way Walter Bagehot would have, as exemplifying the old Anglican virtue of being true to one's station in life, of espousing the gods and the golden rule of the copybook maxims (*OS*, p. 138). In celebrating the clear-eyed liberal Orwell, Trilling outflanks Eliot's High Church influence by assimilating it and going it one better and giving it an ironic twist of his own. In addition, he makes Orwell conform (as do all Trilling's heroes) to the model for the most genuinely interesting and seminal literary minds, a model celebrated in "The Meaning of a Literary Idea" and borrowed from Allen Tate's essay on Emily Dickinson. Such minds, like Shakespeare or Dante, are the refined and hardy products of a decaying religious tradition that resist the final disintegration by repeatedly returning to the imaginative inspiration of the old virtues, even as they refuse to compromise their contemporary worldly insights.

Trilling realizes that this "conservative" reading of Orwell courts intellectual disaster by invoking snobbery, hypocrisy, and even that most ignominious idol of the cave, stupidity, as domestic bulwarks in support of "the crumbling ramparts of the moral life" (*OS*, p. 140). Yet he feels that ultimately the use of Orwell to sanction a Charlie Marlowe-like belief in "the strong feeling for the commonplace" (*OS*, p. 140) so scarce now can only help, ironically enough, to promote "the democracy of mind" (*OS*, p. 139).

> He is not a genius—what a relief! What an encouragement. For he communicates to us the sense that what he has done any one of us could do.
>
> Or could do if we but made up our mind to do it, if we but surrendered a little of the cant that comforts us, if for a few weeks we paid no attention to the little group with which we habitually exchange opinions, if we took our chance of being wrong or inadequate, if we looked at things simply and directly, having in mind only our intention of finding out what they really are, not the prestige of our great intellectual act of looking at them. He liberates us. He tells us that we can understand our political and social life merely by looking around us; he frees us from the need for the inside dope. He implies that our job is not to be intellectual, certainly not to be intellectual in this fashion or that, but merely to be intelligent according to our lights—he restores the old sense of the democracy of the mind, releasing us from the belief that the mind can work only in a technical, professional way and that it must work competitively. He has the effect of making us believe that we may become full members of the society of thinking men. That is why he is a figure for us.
>
> In speaking thus of Orwell, I do not mean to imply that his birth was presided over only by the Gods of the Copybook Maxims and not at all by the good fairies, or that he had no daimon. The good fairies gave him very fine free gifts indeed. And he had a strong daimon, but it was of an old-fashioned kind and it constrained him to the paradox—for such it is in our time—of taking seriously the Gods of the Copybook Maxims and putting his gifts at their service.
> (*OS*, pp. 138–139)

To counter the self-deception of decent liberals who have no doubts about the causes they quickly embrace and discard, Trilling proposes Orwell, the genius of not being a genius, who even in *Keep the Aspidistra*

Flying, *"summa* of all the criticisms of a commercial civilization that
have ever been made" (*OS*, p. 143), "insists that to live" even amidst
the plagues of the Depression and the rise of totalitarianism "is not
without its stubborn side" (*OS*, p. 143). For Orwell never believed that
"political life could be an intellectual idyll." Rather, he realized from
the first the vicissitudes of being an intellectual in a bourgeois democracy who must tell the truth—one man's truth—in an exemplary way.
"And what matters most of all" in our mendacious modern world,
Trilling concludes, is exactly "our sense of the man who tells the truth"
(*OS*, p. 151).

Clearly, Trilling's "Orwell" is a mythic figure of liberal contradiction
and heroic antiheroic proportions. Like the Burmese ex-policeman narrator in "Shooting an Elephant" who tells how it really feels to be
caught between British imperialism and the alien codes of colonial
peoples, Orwell is for Trilling the ordinary man whose genius for the
truthful telling of the ironic commonplaces of modernity constitutes
him as supreme critic of our culture, which just happens also to be the
object of his commentator's own aspiration. Yet what's crucial to the
formal literary coherence of this "Orwell" as an inspiring figure for
liberal academics in post-World War II America is "the stubborn joy"
he takes, Trilling reassures us, in resisting the mindless economy of
revisionary displacement operating in modern culture as its dominant
system of representation. It is Orwell's "biological social heroism" in
standing for an outmoded style of intellectual life that recommends
him, in Trilling's opinion, to our sustained attention.

Unlike the sacrificial theory of genius in *The Liberal Imagination*,
which, as we have seen, celebrates the ironic neutrality—and so neu-
tering—of the supposedly representative author, Trilling's sacrifice of
the idea of genius itself here is not in the perversely consistent interest
of a higher disinterestedness. Just the opposite: it is in the service of a
staunchly personal appropriation and expression of social reality that
"the stubborn joy" of the oppositional critic like Orwell sustains. While
one could read this stance as sanctioning the absurd bad faith of academic intellectuals who self-deceptively like to believe they are systematically antisystematic and rigorously antiprofessional, such a
reading—intentionally or not—overlooks the whole point of the essay,
which is to suggest that the critic can repeatedly choose to resist the
dominant modes of representation in the culture even if his or her
resistance must inevitably suffer defeat now. This position has something of a quixotic aura about it, perhaps, but more to the point is what
it says about Trilling's solution to the problem of what the critic who
makes it in our time can do with the rest of his or her career. For

Trilling, the answer is to project continually, in active and intelligent response to changing circumstances, the opposing principle of authority subversive of the currently reigning orthodoxy of modern culture.

In support of this oppostional strategy, Trilling adduces, as his enthusiastic reviews collected in *A Gathering of Fugitives* and *Speaking of Literature and Society* attest, David Riesman's sociological analysis of American culture in *The Lonely Crowd* and *Individualism Reconsidered*. All that Trilling takes from Riesman is the antithesis between the inner-directed traditional character of the Puritans and their secular heirs and the outer-directed conforming personality of the organizational man and his cipherlike governmental and academic fellow travelers. This simple oppostion—soon to become the opposition between sincerity and authenticity—is the substance of Trilling's appropriation of Riesman's influence in the early 1950s. While this may look like critical opportunism and opposition for opposition's sake, it really is not. What it is, however, is homage to the ancestors. For Trilling enshrines in the figure of the opposing self the memory of the fathers in principle, particularly the memory of his Jewish origins. Understanding this meaning of Trilling's oppositional stance enables us to appreciate the introduction to *The Bostonians* (1953) collected in *The Opposing Self*, which otherwise would simply be a disappointing performance, especially when compared with the earlier essay in *The Liberal Imagination* on this novel's companion piece in the James canon, *The Princess Casamassima*.

The story of the novel is elementally romantic. In the America of the Gilded Age, Basil Ransom, a displaced and disaffected Southern aristocrat, rescues Verena Tarrant, a freethinking Northern democrat, from the destructive influences of Olive Chancellor's unnaturally rigid feminism. The primitive generality of the tale empowers Trilling to make his introduction the occasion for discussing James's "dialectic," his defense of the masculine character, and his anxiety over the future of American family life. In discussing these Jamesian distinctions, of course, Trilling also betrays his own preoccupations.

Take, for example, Trilling's gloss on the characteristic form of James's fiction:

> It may be said of James—with, of course, some risk of excessive simplification—that virtually all his fiction represents the conflict of two principles, of which one is radical, the other conservative. The two principles are constant, although circumstances change their particular manifestations and the relative values which they are to be judged to have. They may be thought of as energy and inertia; or

spirit and matter; or spirit and letter; or force and form; or creation and possession; or libido and thanatos. In their simpler manifestations the first term of the grandiose duality is generally regarded with unqualified sympathy and is identified with the ideality of youth, or with truth, or with art, or with America; the second term is regarded with hostility and represented as being one with age, or convention, or philistinism, or decadent Europe. But James's mind is nothing if not "dialectical"—the values assigned to each of the two opposing principles are not permitted to be fixed and constant. . . . Life [for example] may be seen to express itself in death and through death. . . . The nature of the terms of James's dialectic suggests why his fiction is always momentous. And it is quite within the scope of his genius to infer the political macrocosm from the personal microcosm, to write large and public the disorder of the personal life. (*OS*, p. 96)

I have cited this passage at length because, whether or not it clarifies James's fiction, it certainly illuminates Trilling's criticism. With this difference: while he summons the other great minds of the past that contain a similar grand opposition of order and disintegration, Trilling, unlike the young James anyway, usually endorses the second term in the dialectic, under the aegis of a decidedly masculine figure, in order to subvert established orthodoxies and in the name of a returning force of renewed imaginative repression. Yet as he says of James, so may we say of Trilling: his mind is "nothing if not 'dialectical'—the values assigned to each of the two opposing principles are not permitted to be fixed and constant." In short, Trilling speaks sometimes on behalf of the living and sometimes of the dead.

Or, at least, the dying. Trilling sees the militant feminism in *The Bostonians* as a more direct and profound threat to civilized life than the revolutionary anarchism in *The Princess Casamassima*. Following James's lead, Trilling claims that in a country like America where the domestic norm has been "a bitter total war between the sexes" (*OS*, p. 98), to question the last principle of coherence, the masculine character, is to undermine society completely, as the women take over the culture and the men "lite out for the territories," to their mutual destruction. This is why Trilling reads what Basil Ransom says about "the masculine character" under siege not only as true to James's own beliefs but also as prophetic of the saving heroic grace of the otherwise unacceptable Southern Agrarians, the Fugitives of *I'll Take My Stand* and *Understanding Poetry* fame.

"The whole generation is womanised," [Ransom] says, "the masculine tone is passing out of the world; it's a feminine, a nervous,

hysterical, chattering, canting age, an age of hollow phrases and false
delicacy and exaggerated solicitudes and coddled sensibilities,
which, if we don't look out, will usher in the reign of mediocrity, of
the feeblest and flattest and the most pretentious that has ever been.
The masculine character, the ability to dare and endure, to know and
yet not to fear reality, to look the world in the face and take it for
what it is—a very queer and partly very base mixture—this is what I
want to preserve, or, rather, as I may say, to recover; and I must say
that I don't in the least care what becomes of you ladies while I make
the attempt." (*OS*, p. 100)

While Ransom's speech may uncomfortably remind us of his later
avatar, Rhett Butler from *Gone with the Wind*, Trilling's use and endorsement of it would seem to confirm Neil Hertz's analysis in "Medusa's
Head: Male Hysteria under Political Pressure." Whenever a general
challenge to ruling-class power is made, women, in texts and in history,
are more often than not likely to become the particular scapegoats for
working out the worst anxieties of that class's male members. There is
indeed in all this bother about the masculine character something a bit
adolescent and reactionary, even protofascist in a dangerously juvenile
way, as Trilling's sentimental appeal to James's famous formal tribute
to his mother after her death also testifies. And the essay concludes on
an apocalyptic if not hysterically regressive note, with the future spectacle of "the sacred mothers refusing their commission and the sacred
fathers endangered" (*OS*, p. 103), as the keystone in the arch of the
American family crumbles and the arch falls to pieces. Yet the important thing here as throughout *The Opposing Self* is Trilling's attempt to
base a moral principle—resistance to domination in any form—upon a
biological foundation, symbolized in James's novel by the triumph of
love over "the bitter total war of the sexes." One may quarrel with the
specific expressions of the attempt, as in this case, or even with the
risks inherent in making it—one thinks of Lawrence's failures in this
regard—but I think we can still appreciate the general reasons for it, if
we remember that Trilling writes amidst the cold war, at the opening
of the Age of Conformity in American society, and as *The Middle of the
Journey* makes clear, in a state, common at the time, of complete disillusionment with the programmatic solutions of both the Christian-
humanist revivalists and Communist or even socialist sympathizers
among the American intellectuals.

If Orwell stands for truth telling and James for the imagination
capable of the masculine tone that rings true to personal form—unlike
the castrated bell from his 1929 letter for Elliot Cohen—then the Flaub-

ert of *Bouvard and Pécuchet* for Trilling represents what it may mean to be beyond culture and still remain human. "Flaubert's Last Testament" (1953) opens with Trilling agreeing with those critics who, like Pound and Hugh Kenner, place *Bouvard and Pécuchet* in the genre of intellectual satire, to which, he reminds us, belong *Gulliver's Travels, Candide, Rameau's Nephew*, and, to a lesser, more qualified extent, Joyce's *Ulysses*. Trilling's main emphasis here and throughout the essay, however, is to argue that while "ideas are life and death" to Flaubert's title characters, and they are indeed poor man's Fausts who run through all the collected knowledge of the race in an encyclopedic display of their own inexhaustible superficiality and inner emptiness, the book is really not a nihilistic condemnation of bourgeois society, nor a misanthropic curse cast upon the species at large. Rather, it is, first of all, a masterful comic portrayal of that common mechanism of the human mind which, at a certain point in the development of an individual or a civilization, rejects completely the great wealth of cultural productions as inessential, as degrading forms of mere distraction for the distraction's sake: the open secret of ineluctable hypocrisy.

> The human mind experiences the massed accumulation of its own works, those that are traditionally held to be its greatest glories as well as those that are obviously of a contemptible sort, and arrives at the understanding that none will serve its purpose, that all are weariness and vanity, that the whole vast structure of human thought and creation are alien from the human person. (*OS*, p. 171)

This ascetic attitude is of course familiar to us from Trilling's valorization of Hegelian *Gemüt* and the vision of genius in Schopenhauer. It suggests a radical withdrawal from the world: an intellectual form of "lite-ing out for the territories."

Flaubert's novel, for Trilling, is not however a last testament in praise of Bartleby the Scrivener-like total alienation. For one thing, Bouvard and Pécuchet compose "a sort of bachelor Baucis and Philemon" and so a minimal society of sorts, "rustling their leaves at each other with a sweet papery sound" (*OS*, p. 172). Similarly, although the novel celebrates the rejection of culture, albeit in the comic mode, it is significant to Trilling that, as originally planned, "something was to follow" as an appendix to this novel. The "Dictionary of Accepted Ideas" was to be the great achievement of these intellectual clowns. This suggests to Trilling "that reduced as the two friends are, they have not lost their love of mind, to which they testify by recording the mind's failures" (*OS*, p. 173). Their being able to continue to work together, Trilling finds, especially *sans raisonner*, redeems Flaubert's intellectual clowns from pure absurdity, as they constitute the resistent nucleus of a human order beyond the known conventions of society. Far from suffering from a Swiftian madness at the reality of mankind, they manage to live out their lives, in their funny, prototypically scholarly manner, confirming Henry James's obervation that life is nothing if not sacrificial. The sacrifice of the self in the name of a higher principle, life's finest achievement, is theirs, therefore, as it is their creator's, not only in the disciplined creation of his art but in his often self-destructively misguided pedagogic devotion to his niece, Caroline Commanville, who in her later aesthetic effect upon society seems like the relic of a natural aristocracy, thus justifying all of Flaubert's earlier sacrifices for her— Caroline being, in Trilling's eyes, perhaps Flaubert's crowning achievement as an artist:

> Flaubert spent thirteen years on Caro's education, and the goal of his affectionate efforts was like that of Nature in Wordsworth's poem ["The White Doe"]:
> This Child I to myself shall take;
> She shall be mine, and I shall make
> A Lady of my own
> —a Lady who in her own person should be the answer to the vulgarity and stupidity of the time. (*OS*, p. 175)

Rather than the degraded form of the Pygmalion myth in such commercial entertainments as *My Fair Lady* and *The Bride of Frankenstein*, we would be better off recalling Yeats's great wish in "A Prayer for My Daughter" for the renewal in our time of the ceremony of innocence. At least we might get the high poetic tone of Trilling's romantic allusions right.

Trilling concludes the essay by using *Trois Contes* ("A Simple Heart," "The Legend of Julian the Hospitaler," "Herodias") to exemplify that extreme nihilism natural to the mind when it considers the human condition clearly, a nihilism which Flaubert in his last testament truly perfects and comically transcends:

> In each of the stories the protagonist exists beyond the life in culture and stands divested of every garment that culture weaves. Julian [for instance] passes beyond parental love, beyond social rank, beyond heroism and fame, beyond the domestic affections, beyond all the things, persons, and institutions that bind us to the earth, and he reaches that moment of charity which is the surrender of what Flaub-

ert believed to be the richest luxury of culture, the self in the sepa-
rateness of sensibility and pride that define it. . . . The *Tales*, that is,
continue Flaubert's old despair of culture, which was, we may say,
the prime condition of his art; it was a despair which was the more
profound, we need scarcely say, because it was the issue of so great
a hope. Emma Bovary had tried to live by the promises of selfhood
which culture had seemed to make, and culture had destroyed her.
Frédéric Moreau had ruined himself by never quite believing in the
selfhood which culture cherishes as its dearest gift. Now Flaubert
considers the condition of the spirit which puts itself as far as possible
beyond the promises, the consolations, and the demands of culture;
in each of the *Three Tales* he asks what remains when culture is
rejected and transcended. The answer, given with a notable firmness
and simplicity, is that something of highest value does remain—it is
the self affirmed in self-denial; life is nothing unless sacrificial. And
Bouvard and Pécuchet, sitting at their double copying desk, having
a work and each other, stripped of every idea, every theory, every
shred of culture beyond what is necessary to keep men alive and still
human, are, in their own mild negation of self, intended by Flaubert
to be among the company of his saints. (*OS*, pp. 179–180)

In other words, amidst the sublime intimations of a nuclear holocaust
for all peoples, and as his own stories would predict, Trilling discovers
in Flaubert's unfinished modern masterpiece of intellectual satire: Paradise—academic style. Or are Bouvard and Pécuchet in germ the Robinson Crusoe and Friday of the modern university?

"Having a work" (even if it is *trouvailler sans raisonner*—copying the
human archive) and having "each other" (even if it is as burnt-out
comedians of the Enlightenment ideal, "rustling their leaves at each
other, with a sweet papery sound")—such are the minimum social
conditions, as Trilling projects them out of Flaubert's last testament,
for human life in the modern world. This life is indeed beyond culture
in the double sense of the word as his 1955 preface to the entire volume
of *The Opposing Self* makes clear: beyond the unconsciously accepted
conventions that appear thereby to be natural laws; and, as well, beyond the orthodox styles of conscious rebellion against those conventions (*OS*, p. 11). In criticism of culture (both as social convention and
as artful opposition), Trilling envisions this paradise—of eunuchs!

The modern opposing self, with "its intense and adverse imagination of the culture in which it has its being" (*OS*, p. i) and its "powers
of indignant perception" (*OS*, p. ii), repeatedly discovers in the course
of the past two centuries its enemy in the very culture that fosters it,

which it denounces as "its oppressor" (*OS*, p. ii). Trilling cites Hegel as being the first thinker to appreciate fully how the modern self conceives of this "alienation" as the means for "the fulfillment of its destiny" (*OS*, p. iii). Such "alienation" is "the terrible principle of culture" (*OS*, p. iii) itself. The source of this principle, as Hegel also understood, lies in what Trilling calls "a kind of cultural mutation" (*OS*, p. iii), by which he means the addition to the mind's faculties of "a new category of judgment," that of "quality" (*OS*, p. iii).

> Not merely the deed itself, [Hegel] said, is now submitted to judgment, but also the personal quality of the doer of the deed. It has become not merely a question of whether the action conforms to the appropriate principle or maxim of morality, but also of the manner in which it is performed, of what it implies about the entire nature, the being of the agent. (*OS*, p. iii).

What inspires the opposing self's critique of culture is modern culture's institution of this new mode of judgment based upon an essentially aesthetic perception of a quality this culture can envision in art but cannot foster among its people generally as a form of life. The aesthetic foundation of moral judgment requires that spirit appear not only as utility or law but as grace, as manner and style. Whatever inhibits or supresses this development of the spirit, the self must oppose. And what generally acts as the agency of repression is culture itself.

Consequently, the episodes from the modern history of literature that Trilling discusses in the *The Opposing Self* confirm Arnold's belief that literature is a radical criticism of life. As Trilling's discovery of a positive utopian virtue in Flaubert's last testament demonstrates, however, such criticism generally takes the form of an endangered or lost— an assumed—innocence. The literary work recalls this vision of innocence and in recalling it condemns the culture for which it must remain lost.

> [Arnold] meant, in short, that poetry is a criticism of life in the same way that the Scholar Gypsy was a criticism of life of an inspector of elementary schools. . . . It is the despair of those who, having committed themselves to culture, have surrendered the life of surprise and elevation, of impulse, pleasure, and imagination. The Scholar Gypsy is poetry—he is imagination, impulse, and pleasure: he is what virtually every writer of the modern period conceives, the experience of art projected into the actuality and totality of life as the

ideal form of the moral life. His existence is intended to disturb us
and make us dissatisfied with our habitual life in culture, whose
nature his existence defines. (*OS*, p. v).

For Trilling, the careers of Wordsworth and Yeats define the field of
play for the opposing self in the English tradition as a "long quarrel
with the culture," a quarrel over how the self should realize its energies
in terms of grace, manner, style, and imagination. "Such quarrels,"
Trilling adds, "we recognize as the necessity not only of the self but of
culture" (*OS*, p. vi). The pleasure taken in the life of the imagination,
of autonomy, of surprise and elevation, can arise for us only in the
imagination of "selves conceived in opposition to the general culture"
(*OS*, p. vi). In short, this adversarial imagination making for "a new
idea in the world," and whose vicissitudes, modulations, and negations" (*OS*, p. vi) make the thematic unity of Trilling's volume, confirms
for Trilling that ours is an intellectual gadfly or Socratic culture whose
latest romantic academic hero-figure is, appropriately enough, the
Scholar Gypsy and his avatars, the traveling theorists of the conference
roadshows.

Thus, the essays of *The Opposing Self*, taken in the order of their original publication, very clearly trace the history of the literary intellectual
in modern humanistic culture as the figure for a disintegrating dialectic
of romantic acquisitiveness and pseudoreligious askesis that concludes
with the vision of an ironic apocalypse to end all such visionary acts: a
literal consumption of the entire world of knowledge in the writing of
our eunuch fathers, those ur-academics Bouvard and Pécuchet. So
forbidding a vision does surely criticize, as do any of Beckett's chillingly
funnier ones, the culture that fosters it. In their collected form, however, these essays compose a somewhat different story.

The first three essays, for example, on Keats, Dickens, and Tolstoy,
tell the story of a fall from glory, from the last image of mental health,
into the prison/madhouse of the social will, from which the only escape
is a loving vision of the ordinary, especially of domestic, familial relations, those between fathers and sons being the most significant. Similarly, the next three essays, on Howells, James, and Wordsworth,
represent a progressive movement toward this goal for Trilling himself.
First comes his homage to the genius of the commonplace, to be followed next by his rediscovery of the masculine tone, the masculine
character of the critic, who then can recover in displaced allegorical
form, at a Princeton conference of international Wordsworth scholars,
his origins in all the Sayings of the Fathers—origins which are also
representative, it so happens, for the culture of opposition this secular

Jewish critic also ironically opposes. Finally, the essays on Orwell and Flaubert project the ideal of the truth-telling critic of that culture who is quite willing to envision living beyond all culture in heroically self-destructive emulation of the idea of the intellectual as ascetic comedian.

Whatever complex of professional motives and autobiographical circumstances may operate here, one thing appears certain. Trilling in collecting these essays for *The Opposing Self* arranges them to stage his criticism of culture as the self-education of an aspiring subversive patriarch, of a would-be member of the canon of authors he sublimely projects as his raison d'être, those masterful authors who, each in his own manner, transcend the culture they both espouse and oppose in their self-overcoming, containing styles of mind. Trilling thus subverts the most forbidding implications of his own insights by succumbing to the spectacle he creates from his essays. He is the victim of the fatal pleasure of the unforming word, that revisionary critical power which disconnects the critic from the immediate forms of his cultural concern and launches him on *the specular quest for inclusion in a subversive patriarchy of his own making*.

Put in this way, Trilling's later career especially would be open to the charge not of acquiescing in the cynical conformity of the Eisenhower years but of ironically anticipating the worst, narcissistic excesses of the counterculture he loathed, and, especially, the revisionary madness of all those performing selves in contemporary theory. Just imagine it: Lionel Trilling as Harold Bloom's great original. Although Trilling does make much of cultural despair for self-promotion purposes, as the final essay in *The Opposing Self* on *Mansfield Park*, demonstrates, he, unlike his ironic heirs, never fully gives in to it, and that makes all the difference in the world.

This 1954 essay opens with a discussion of Austen's irony, for Trilling writes in the general context of the modern rediscovery of the ironic mode of saying the opposite of what one means and of comprehending more of life's essence by way of paradoxes, anomalies, and absurdities than is available to the resolutely literal-minded. In addition, he writes in the more specific context of Marvin Mudrick's pathbreaking study of the same year, *Jane Austen: Irony as Defense*, which rediscovers her powerful prominence in this modern way of judgment.

Before discussing the novel, however, Trilling makes it clear that Austen's irony, while malicious to the closed-minded who expect life to conform to their statements about it, partakes of nothing of that supposed moral superiority and aesthetic detachment that in *Pride and Prejudice* define Mr. Bennett as a moral nonentity and a helpless prig. And while critics who protest that her irony is merely the glamorized mask of feminine coercion or social constraint include Mark Twain and Albert Gërrod, such attacks on Austen's perverse repression of animality and vital spirits are not exclusively a masculine province, as the similar criticisms of Charlotte Brontë and Waldo Emerson testify. Rather, what all these critics betray is the modern "fear of imposed constraint" (*OS*, p. 184), which Austen, like Freud, and unlike her critics, recognizes as the cost one must pay for the civilizing play of irony, wit, and imagination in all their spontaneous forms of stubborn joy. For without such imposed constraint, such power of repression, we would not have any culture to speak of at all.

Mansfield Park, for Trilling, thus directs irony against all those who use irony to hide the fact of necessary repression of the severest kind; it offends every one of "our modern pieties" about liberation from every form of repression. Consequently, this novel of all Jane Austen's novels has been the least well received. But in Trilling's eyes, its greatness is "commensurate with its power to offend" (*OS*, p. 185). For *Mansfield Park* envisions a condition of active withdrawal from the world as the ideal of the opposing self, a vision that prefigures that which informs Trilling's reading of Flaubert's final masterpiece:

> To deal with the world by condemning it, by withdrawing from it and shutting it out, by making oneself and one's mode and principles of life the very center of existence and to live the round of one's days in the stasis and peace thus contrived—this, in an earlier age, was one of the recognized strategies of life, but to use it seems not merely impracticable but almost wicked. (*OS*, p. 185)

In a time of reflexive social awareness and overt sexuality, Trilling finds Austen's ascetic irony temptingly compelling. This is clever critical strategy for insinuating a subliminal comparison between the helter-skelter "patterned isolation" of American subcultures with an earlier way of life once chosen out of religious conviction by an entire pilgrim people whose English vestiges *Mansfield Park* provocatively celebrates.

Unlike the divine enlargements of life that the comic mode in *Pride and Prejudice* affords, *Mansfield Park* displays that anti-vital element that T. E. Hulme identifies as the essence of religion. This anti-vital element not only informs the irony of the plot which betrays Thomas Bertram's daughters of the blood in behalf of the spiritual foundling Fanny Price, that terrified little creature who finds a home in Mansfield Park and becomes its mistress. It also shapes the contrast between characters on the basis of their attitude toward selecting a vocation or profession, what in the old sense was termed one's calling in life. While Mary

Crawford cultivates the style of sensibility as brilliantly as Elizabeth Bennett, she suffers at her author's hands for her failure to distinguish between the permanent commitment to a social role and the power to play any role, as the novel's central debate over the influence of amateur theatricals represents most vividly. The impersonation of passion is a dangerous thing, and contrasts unfavorably with the discipline of a calling, especially that of the ministry. Stoic apatheia, as Wordsworth in "Resolution and Independence" argues, must be the lot of the self that would survive its own excessively imaginative power:

> That the self may destroy the self by the very energies that define its being, that the self may be preserved by the negation of its own energies—this, whether or not we agree, makes an irony that catches our imagination. . . . [For] it is an irony directed against irony itself. (*OS*, pp. 191, 196)

Trilling's perception here is of a piece with Nietzsche's conception (in the *Genealogy of Morals*) of the ascetic ideal and the function of the priest in regulating this ideal for the benefit of any social group or "herd" (Nietzsche's word). Trilling, in recommending *Mansfield Park* to his readers' attention, is performing precisely this function, as he attempts to govern the amount and the direction of their resentful will-to-power over this most offensive text. To understand how Trilling performs this same service for himself in *The Opposing Self* we must turn to his extravagant conclusion.

The essay's conclusion first rehearses Trilling's argument that, as Hegel, Nietzsche, and Dewey all saw, the modern way of judgment (or literary ethics), which evaluates every action in terms of the quality of style that an action may impute to its agent, is a secularized form of spirituality which constitutes a new internalized reign of terror every bit as sublimely repressive as Madame Guillotine. As a result, Trilling offers the extravagant surmise that in her loving attitude toward the stupid vulgarian Lady Bertram, whose only thought is for the preservation of her easeful inertia, Jane Austen is "teasing herself, that she is turning her irony upon her own fantasy of ideal existence as it presented itself to her at this time." That is, "Lady Bertram is her mocking representation of her wish to escape" (*OS*, p. 200) from the harsh refinements of personality and secularized spirituality. Austen's severe irony thus encompasses its own opposing ideal of selfhood.

Trilling then closes *The Opposing Self* with a climactic pronouncement disclosing his own (more than Austen's) critical motives—and the causes of "the disgust which is endemic to our culture":

She is the first to be aware of the Terror which rules our moral
situations, the ubiquitous anonymous judgment to which we respond, the necessity we feel to demonstrate the purity of our secular
spirituality, whose dark and dubious places are more numerous and
obscure than those of religious spirituality, to put our lives and styles
to question, making sure that not only in deeds but in décor they
exhibit the signs of our belonging to the number of the secular-
spiritual elect. . . . She herself is an agent of the Terror—our mistress
in these matters. . . . [*Mansfield Park*] imagines the self safe from the
Terror of secularized spirituality. In the person of Lady Bertram it
affirms, with all due irony, the bliss of being able to remain unconscious of the demands of personality (it is a bliss which is a kind of
virtue, for one way of being solid, simple, and sincere is to be a
vegetable). It shuts out the world and the Judgment of the World.
The sanctions upon which it relies are not those of culture, of quality,
of being, of personality, but precisely those which the new conception of the moral life minimizes, the sanctions of principle, and it
discovers in principle the path to the wholeness of self which is peace.
When we have exhausted our anger at the offense which *Mansfield
Park* offers to our conscious pieties, we find it possible to perceive
how intimately it speaks to our secret inexpressible hopes. (*OS*, p.
201)

In the absence of the divine absolute, the rule of aesthetics, of style,
of pleasure in its humanly sanctioned forms becomes in our secular
culture all in all. This is spectral politics with an incisive vengeance.
And Trilling in the passage plays to the hilt the role of worldly messiah,
for he would mediate between the values and assumptions of our time
and the anti-vital principles (the subversive patriarchy in the abstract)
that ironically animate this novel Trilling insists is so offensive to modern taste. Managing his own ambivalent moments of resentful rage
and secret nostalgia for stasis with consummate grace and tact, Trilling
thus helps to manage therapeutically, cathartically, his audience's similar affective complexities which few could ever express with as much
dialectical suggestiveness. Moreover, Trilling subtly derives modern
culture from the spirit of his own displaced origins, via the profoundly
repressed ghetto imagery which haunts the margins of all those "dark
and dubious places" of our secularized spirituality. And, thanks to that
transumptive trope for the Longinian sublime par excellence, "the
Judgment of the World," Trilling subsumes every element in the passage to his critical revision of Arnoldian humanism, in which our modern world reevaluates itself out of willful existence. Finally, in the comic

enlargement of Lady Bertram, Trilling projects the vision of mythical wholeness—indistinguishable from pure inertia—that supplements and completes his own ironic perception of the paradoxes, anomalies, and cosmic disjunctions of life. This supreme passage therefore is the satyr play to the tragedy of renunciation enacted in the rest of the essay; a similar relation holds between this essay and the entire volume, with Austen's relation to Lady Bertram being mirrored (and measured) by Trilling's relation to Austen—or, as Yeats says in his "High Talk," "mirror on mirror all's the show."

Whether or not one reads the essays of *The Opposing Self* in the original order of their composition, then, Trilling's essay on *Mansfield Park*—the last written for the volume except for the preface—when viewed in the perspective of absolute irony, transforms Austen and her teasing alter ego, Lady Bertram, into the daughters of the patriarchal memory. It is as if behind all the sayings of the fathers that Trilling recalls in the decade of the 1950s, the time of his greatest influence, there stands the archetypal muse-mother of his morality of inertia: Nature in her most princess-like mood, America on enforced vacation under Eisenhower. This mythical return to the Mother, following the revival of the patriarchal specters, fits the model of regression developed by the recent theorists of narcissism. Julia Kristeva's "The Abject of Love," for example, is particularly apropos in this respect. Kristeva argues, on the basis of her clinical experience and the latest deconstructive readings of Freud, that preceding the emergence of object relations with the initial formation of the oedipal triangle in the nascent ego there is a recognizable blank, corresponding to the linguistic bar dividing the sign from itself, beyond which the narcissistic fantasies of the mother flourish in all their awful fascination.[19] The difference in Trilling, however, as his stress on the anti-vital or mortifying elements in Austen's judgment of the world strongly suggests, is that beyond the first oedipal relation, beyond the repressive cipher of Kristeva, and so even beyond the narcissistic mother, there remains a more original force—and fate: the pleasure of the self-fathering voice. What Trilling says of Flaubert's devotion to his niece Caroline could very well be said of his own desire in *The Opposing Self*, as represented most fully in his Austen essay:

> the goal of his affectionate efforts was like that of Nature in Wordsworth's poem:
>> This Child I to myself shall take;
>> She shall be mine, and I shall make
>> A Lady of my own

—a Lady who in her own person should be the answer to the vulgarity and stupidity of the time.

A Lady, that is, who contains the gentleman within, as Leopold Bloom,
that truly unmanly man, contains the imprint of "his" author, or as
pastoral America contains now and ever, it seems, the chilling designs
of Trilling's Frost:

> The sound was behind me instead of before,
> A sleepy sound, but mocking half,
> As of one who utterly couldn't care.
> The Demon arose from his wallow to laugh,
> Brushing the dirt from his eye as he went;
> And well I knew what the Demon meant.[20]

So Death *is* counterrevolutionary after all . . .

Chapter Five
Normal Mysticism: Varieties of Transcendent Experience in the Late Work

Savage Civility: The Spirit of Gravity

This inner history of Lionel Trilling's career comes to a close amidst the cold-war consensus and countercultural rebellions of the 1950s and 1960s, whose legacies of neo-conservatism and neo-Marxism are still very much with us. Richard M. Pells in *The Liberal Mind in a Conservative Age* and Morris Dickstein in *The Gates of Eden* have written the most useful popular studies of these dialectially interrelated decades.[1] And Donald Pease in "*Moby Dick* and the Cold War" and in his forthcoming book, *Cold War Texts*, provides the most acute and comprehensive analysis of the ideological constraints on American culture during this entire period.[2] My subject, however, is now not so much Trilling's dissent from the orthodoxies of dissent—whether those of Marxism, modernism, or the counterculture. Rather, it is the imaginative dynamic of his representative career in criticism which makes all his dissent possible by projecting a positive purpose for the critic to perform in his work, a purpose that is positive in the most fundamental way: *to give the critic pleasure.*

Clearly, what gives Trilling pleasure is struggle—struggle against a structure of beliefs and styles of living, against a culture, that is itself sublimely self-divided between centripetal and centrifugal forces variously identified at different times. The first model of such an opposing culture, as we saw in "Notes of a Departure," is America itself. This is succeeded in later years by the liberal or Stalinist imagination, the cold-war polar world, and finally by the academic modernism of the adversarial culture Trilling helped to promote. In all these instances and their variants, the basic dynamic resembles that of the Jew in the world of the goyim. Such a world both attracts by virtue of its cultural affluence and intellectual opportunity and repels because of its threatening

power of physical persecution and of persecution in its most seductively demonic psychological mode, the promise of perfect assimilation. Struggle for and against assimilation to the larger opposing Other,
whether called liberalism, modernism, or, most primitively and inescapably, America, creates and defines Trilling's character. And the creation of character in such a sense is what gives this critic pleasure.
Transcending the opposing culture by an opposing style of his own—
such is Trilling's stubborn joy. Naturally, Trilling must always assume
a ground for this joyful dance of transcendence, some foundation,
some form of necessary opposition to be overcome by the spontaneous,
gratuitous imagination of the critic. Otherwise, there could not be any
motive for his chosen metamorphosis.

It is no wonder, then, that Trilling feels at his career's end that he
faces his greatest challenge, in the emergence of a counterculture
which not only opposes particular positions he may have espoused but
which, more radically, opposes the kind of self he has created over the
years: a self that can choose to espouse this or that position at one time
or another, according to its estimate of the conditions affecting its
powers of choice. This conditional self of Trilling's confronts in the final
analysis a postmodern culture of the disintegrated self. Such a culture
would abolish, in the service of liberation movements (racial, feminist,
and antiwar), the ideological justifications for the liberal dialectic of
freedom and necessity which fosters the repressive or ascetic character
formation of the modern Western intellectual, as most fully defended
by Freud and most fully exposed by his revisionary critics.

As we shall see, Trilling responds to this emerging counterculture
by analyzing its salient absurdity (the celebration of madness) and by
proposing a more radical alternative both to the counterculture and to
the bourgeois Protestant ethos it hopes to displace. For Trilling would
found the dialectic of freedom and necessity that informs the conditional self on a provocatively revisionary basis, with a more sublimely
repressive horizon of opposition: that of the great dead. Trilling, in
other words, for the last third of his career especially, lives among the
imposing dead, as if already dead himself. And through his exemplary
if often misread works of this final phase he beckons us to come and
follow him.

This formulation sounds, I admit, like a weird mixture of traditional
humanism and perverse ancestor worship. Its latent necrophilia
couldn't possibly appeal to Lionel Trilling, the latter-day prophet of the
rational intellect. Yet, for his kind of critic, the one necessary condition
inspiring the antithetical quest is the inescapable recognition of another
writer doing better in language what one would do oneself if one had

the opportunity. Before this recognition of genius, of the verbal power Trilling wants for himself, every ideological and individual defense must crumble, if the agonist is to pursue his pleasure in overcoming the resentful other in himself once again. Nietzsche has best characterized this pleasurable agony by christening it in *Thus Spoke Zarathustra* as "the spirit of gravity." Suffice to say, Trilling has his own joyful name for it, and it is Freud.

Although *Civilization and Its Discontents* and *Beyond the Pleasure Principle* clearly shape his corrective stress, for his quixotic liberal audience, on the tragic vision reality, it is, as "The Meaning of a Literary Idea," strongly suggests, *An Outline of Psychoanalysis*, Freud's posthumously published and unfinished intellectual testament, that gives Trilling one of his greatest aesthetic experiences that rivals, he claims, the appreciation inspired by the heroic spectacle of his master's life.[3] The 1949 review prompting Trilling's favorable comparison of Yeats and Freud in the former essay is "Freud's Last Book" (collection in *A Gathering of Fugitives* in 1956). And this little review for the *New York Times* not only looks back to Trilling's famous essays on Freud and related topics in *The Liberal Imagination*, it also anticipates his later uses of Freud in *Beyond Culture* (1965) and *Sincerity and Authenticity* (1971) to create a power of repression, essentially religious (and not rational) in nature, against which it would mean something to strive in order to remain, unlike his postmodern heirs and opponents, civilized and rational, even if fiercely, savagely so.

Trilling begins his review with a necessarily sketchy account of the original conditions of composition—Freud's London exile from his Nazi-occupied homeland—and of the original pedagogical intention of the *Outline*: "to bring together the doctrines of psychoanalysis," as Freud himself puts it, "and to state them, as it were, dogmatically," and he adds, "in the most concise form and in the most positive terms." Three things strike Trilling about this book: what it reveals about Freud's personal "life-style"; what light that revelation sheds on the relationship between literature, especially Shakespearean drama, and Freud's creation, the new discipline of psychoanalysis; and what it suggests about the traditional intellectual orientation toward mind, nature, and truth that underlies all these matters and, until recently, has defined the modern West as a tragic culture.

Unlike pseudoscientific, self-negating modern intellectuals, Freud is heroically self-assertive. What he knows, he knows, and if any of his theories are proven wrong, he will be the first Freudian to admit it. Similarly, his invention, psychoanalysis, like literature, especially Shakespearean tragedy, is devoted to the truth of the human condition—man's sublime finitude amidst a nonhuman cosmic order. Finally, as his questionable theory of the death instinct testifies, Freud, the last and perhaps the greatest spokesman for Western culture, envisions an "ultimate tragic courage in acquiescence to fate," whose "grandeur" cannot be missed (*GF, p.* 64)

While his earlier essays "Art and Neurosis" and "Freud and Literature" were, as we have seen, more critical in their thrust, at least at first, they, like this review, also conclude by celebrating Freud as the last representative of the tragic view endemic to the Western tradition in its classical, religious, and humanistic incarnations. Unlike these essays, however, and like his later work on Freud, especially *Freud and the Crisis of Our Culture*[4] and "The Authentic Unconscious" (in *Sincerity and Authenticity*), the review spells out the reason why this vision is so important:

> The tragic vision requires the full awareness of the limits which necessity imposes. But it deteriorates if it does not match this awareness with an idea of freedom. Freud undertook to provide such an idea—it was his life-work and if in an *Outline of Psychoanalysis* he insists on the limiting conditions of man's biological and social heritage, yet one of the last sentences of the book is an instigation to the mastery of the hard inheritance. It is a sentence from Goethe: "What you have inherited from your fathers truly possess it so as to make it your very own." (*GF,* p. 65)

The language of possession and appropriation may obscure the main point here: that the tragic vision of existence promotes a full awareness of human finitude and so provokes the projection of an idea of freedom in heroic opposition. It is like Yeats's definition of the demonic imagination as that prospect, uniquely one's own, which of all those prospects not impossible is the most difficult to bear. Moreover, what such a prospect entails is the quest to master one's cultural inheritance— that portion of the past which, as Trilling notes, generally constitutes the ethical norms of conscience, or what contemporary moral theorists would term the axiological conventions one assumes for action. (Nietzsche, of course, characterized this ethical motive as the ascetic will of priests and their religions.) What Goethe, after Milton, envisions as God the Father, and Hegel, in *The Philosophy of Right*, refers to as the Penates (the Roman household gods),[5] Freud christens the superego, that internalized antithetical successor to the Oedipus complex.[6] All these analogues of one another—and no doubt one could adduce more[7]—circumscribe by overdetermination the same cultural phenomenon: How in the Western tradition fate is repeatedly said to father the preferred kind of subjectivity. For Trilling, only the insistence upon the severity of reality in its natural and social manifestations, only such repeated avowals of the spirit of gravity, can instigate the creation of the personal and cultural forms of grace and style, of spontaneous and gratuitous acts of imaginative identification and transference, that make existence authentically human. Whether or not this emphasis on reality's severity applies any longer now to things as they are doesn't really matter for Trilling, since as a characterization of the traditional conditions of intellectual production, of reading and writing, it still rings true. In any event, the final sentence of *An Outline of Psychoanalysis* crystallizes Freud's and his disciple's ultimately mortifying intent: "In the establishment of the super-ego we have before us, as it were, an example of the way in which the present is changed into the past" (*GF*, p. 64).

So, according to Trilling's reading of Freud, the function of the critic is to make what's present part of the past, to extend the empire of the dead by building up the superego, the conscience, of the intellectual and in so doing constituting the voice of conscience for the culture as a whole. The critic of culture is therefore the secular form of the prophet in this profound sense.

At first glance, such a critical ideology sounds horribly ascetic and elitist. And certainly, with few exceptions, Trilling's often minor pieces written at the height of the cold war abroad and Eisenhower's alienating consensus at home confirm this impression. Although in a 1952 review of Edmund Wilson's *The Shores of Light: A Literary Chronicle of the Twenties and Thirties*, Trilling appears to pay more than lip service to what he terms "the democracy of letters," it turns out, however, that he is actually referring to the multitudes of dead authors the reader may freely encounter in aspiring to the civilized life, much as Wilson has already done. Similarly, in a 1956 introduction to a selection of John O'Hara's short stories, Trilling affirms "the imagination of society" found there in terms that suggest a Kafkaesque recognition:

> It is the imagination of society as some strange sentient organism which acts by laws of its own being which are not to be understood; one does not know what will set into motion its dull implacable hostility, some small thing, not very wrong, not wrong at all; once it begins to move, no one can stand against it. It is this terrible imagination of society [that O'Hara reveals]. (*SLS*, p. 283)

Like the imposing "democracy" of dead authors, "this terrible imagination of society" inspires a sense of intimidation, to which it appears that the most fitting response, as "The Smile of Parmenides Makes One Think" (a 1956 review of Irwin Edman's *The Philosophy of George Santayana*) suggests, is the frozen visage of Mona Lisa.[8]

While an introduction to *The Broken Mirror: A Collection of Writings from Contemporary Poland* (1958), in contrasting the benign humanistic intentions of American "pragmatism or instrumentalism" with "Stalinist Marxism" and its "own single-mindedness" to "subvert or conquer the world" (*SLS*, pp. 308–309), does argue for the grip the cold-war framework had on even as subtle and flexible a mind as Trilling's, another essay of the time, "Reflections on a Lost Cause: English Literature and American Education," offers a more compelling cause for his increasing sepulchral aesthetics. Thanks both to the decline of England as a political power and the rise of alternative forms of critical study (comparative or world literature, modernist literature, New Criticism, American studies), Trilling argues, there is less and less "prestige" (*SLS*, p. 355) attached to "English studies" with its traditional, Arnoldian mission of representing for modern literary intellectuals the ideal image of the other culture, that secret bastion of values critical humanism must discover as still alive somewhere and so still relevant to our circumstances. Only thus may humanism continue to dominate the cultural scene with authoritative visions of a better world. In short, the grounds for the profession of English studies are, especially in America, now disintegrating. Consequently, Trilling, loyal to his intellectual origins in Arnold and the Anglo-American tradition in criticism, has no choice in such an alien world but to espouse the dead and seek to impose the standards of the past upon the present in as severely ascetic a form as possible.

Yet every critic, insofar as he finds worth (of whatever sort) in past figures, works, and cultures, becomes the potential understudy to Nietzsche's gleeful gravedigger scholar of the present from "The Use and Disadvantage of History for Life." In the name of what greater power, beyond the virtue of professional coherence, does Trilling sacrifice modernity? The outlines of an answer emerge from a series of other minor pieces scattered throughout the decade (1956–1965), which, in appraising Joyce's *Letters* (*SLS*, pp. 285–294), Freud's final years (*SLS*, pp. 295–299), Proust's criticism of Sainte-Beuve (*SLS*, pp. 310–321), Nabokov's *Lolita* (*SLS*, pp. 322–342), or Norman O. Brown's *Life against Death* (*SLS*, pp. 361–366), all celebrate the writer as a heroic character whose resistance to modernity takes the form of a passionate devotion to the memory and possible utopian return of what Trilling citing Yeats once called the "ancient grace that has been lost" (*SLS*, p. 384) in our time. Trilling glosses this Yeatsian sentiment as follows:

> Yeats's complaint against the imposed necessity of [writing] criticism serves to identify the one element of modern literature which, more than any other, defines its difference from all earlier literature—the writer's intense consciousness of the circumstances in which he exists and carries on his work, his unremitting and troubled and bitter awareness of his culture. . . . Poems and essays are at one [however] in affirming the necessity of restoring to Western man some earlier instinctual way of being and the mental powers and the joy that are assumed to go with it. (*SLS*, pp. 383, 385)

Another little review essay, "A Comedy of Evil," also from 1961, can serve to gloss Trilling here on Yeats with Trilling on Dostoyevsky via Nietzsche's Zarathustra. This is revisionary intertextuality with a vengeance. "The Laughter [in Dostoyevsky's short novels] is ultimate, absolute, and terrible. Like Zarathustra's it declares the nothingness of human life—and by that declaration requires that the void be made into a cosmos" (*SLS*, p. 391).

Here, then, is the final cause—beyond the cold-war framework of polar oppositions (Us vs. Them), beyond the professional politics of English studies versus every other competing discipline—of the growing ascetic ideology in Trilling's later career. Origins ever determine all: for the imposing examples of the great dead from the traditional canon that the critic internalizes can obliterate from his mind the mind's modern degradation in endless displacements long enough to enable him to envision the dead again in their worlds, as if it is only by means of such traumatic identifications and apocalyptic transference that he can, for a few brief moments anyway, transcend the grinding routine of the present age in the pleasure of vision. While there are as many means available to achieve this effect as there are forms of such transcendent experience, what Trilling declares Zarathustra's divinely demonic laughter to be—"ultimate, absolute and terrible"—encapsulates the dialectic of necessity and freedom, now based on the intercession of the sacred dead, in a nutshell, as it were. "Like Zarathustra's [laughter,] it declares the nothingness of human life—and by that declaration requires that the void be made into a cosmos."

Trilling's major essays of the second half of the decade, "Freud: Within and Beyond Culture" and "Isaac Babel," both from 1955 and collected in *Beyond Culture* (1965), rehearse this romantic dialectic of creative desire, elaborating and refining it in significant ways. These essays make it clear how the world of necessity repressing the self must itself be repressed, avoided via its mocking representation, if the self's resentment of existence, its demonic rage against its own historical degradation and mortality, is to become a mode of aesthetic transcendence. This sublime method of new-world-making is both a personal style and a form of cultural politics subsuming self and other in visions of nature and her imaginative interpreters. Unlike the originals in Wordsworth and Emerson of this revisionary psychology of the modern writer, Trilling's nature is a self-conscious fiction, a semantically indeterminate commonplace. It is an authoritative cipher like the dominant blank of reality in Stephens, which constitutes the voiding of the modern world. Similarly, Trilling's imaginative interpreters (the Great Dead) do not function as specular surrogates for himself as much as they designate the position of judgment, the space of sublime measure, occupied by any of the worldly messiahs who aspire to the tragic condition of the great dead. The development of Trilling's career, from politics to literary ethics and modernist aesthetics, thus culminates in a speculative metaphysics of the creative mind. This "vision" testifies not only to his underlying religious sensibility but to the mythic function that since Blake and Shelley defines the role of the writer in modern culture as critic of his or her time.

The Freud essay was originally the fifth anniversary lecture given to the New York Psychoanalytic Institute and Society, to mark the day of the founder's birth. It was then "somewhat" revised and expanded, as Trilling notes, and later the same year published as the monograph *Freud and the Crisis of Our Culture*. As incorporated in *Beyond Culture* ten years later, it was revised again, primarily cut, especially its opening remarks on the universal cause of alienation and its universal remedy: the sublime works of human genius. These omitted remarks, despite their note of formal homage, to Freud and the other great dead, are important not only for sounding the modernity theme of Trilling's final years but also for revealing the ironic position he occupies in relation to this theme.

Trilling begins the essay by casually making a few general points: that what alienates one generation from another is their different ideas of the past; that this kind of alienation, more fundamental than any other, is especially acute now in our time owing to the tremendously accelerated rate of historical change; but that, for a teacher of modern literature, this alienation is less painful, in fact can be overcome, while rereading, for example, the classic modern works of Joyce, Lawrence, Eliot, Proust, or even Kafka. The reason that literature can effect this cure is that its power of aesthetic illusion can re-envision the past, represent it. Finally, Trilling closes his prelude by claiming a similar status for Freud's works and ideas, now "the slang of our cultural life" (*FCOC*, p. 12), which nonetheless make the past, individual and communal, return to life again. The "peculiar intimacy" (*FCOC*, p. 13) between psychoanalysis and literature, a familiar Trilling topic, lies, however, not so much in any parallel mimesis of reality as in a shared mythic expressionism, a similar will to summon the memories of our first loves, an imagined invocation that constitutes the singular, obsessive continuity of the self. For Freud and Trilling after him, this return of our first loves in analysis and our return to our first loves in literary study equally disclose the shape of our individual critical identities. Thus, for Trilling, psychoanalysis and literature also equally guarantee the reality or weight of the self amidst the many distinctive ideological determinations and diffusions of modern existence. Freud said we are all ill; Trilling says we all *need* to be ill.

As the essay asserts in conclusion, the idea of the biological foundation of the self in the will, which Freud and post-Enlightenment philosophy and literature both hypothesize, ironically becomes "a liberating idea" in the context of the totalitarian impetus of all modern ideologies. For, to Trilling, it "suggests that there is a residue of human quality beyond the reach of cultural control and that this residue of human quality, elemental as it may be, serves to bring culture itself under criticism and keep it from being absolute" (*BC*, p. 98). Joseph Frank in his famous attack, "Lionel Trilling and the Conservative Imagination," raises a serious objection to this formulation. Frank wants to know how, logically, a form of biological determinism can be the basis of a liberating idea of resistance to social determination. The following passage from Trilling's essay appears most questionable in this regard:

> We reflect that somewhere in the child, somewhere in the adult, there is a hard, irreducible, stubborn core of biological urgency, and biological necessity, and biological reason, that culture cannot reach and that reserves the right, which sooner or later it will express, to judge the culture and resist and revise it. (*BC*, p. 99)

The answer to Frank's question, however, is given symbolically, in Trilling's subsequent allusion to those "martyrs of the intellect," "Giordano Bruno and Socrates" (*BC*, p. 101), and, more explicitly, in what he has to say about the role of the superego in leading us "beyond culture."

As the surrogate of society, of culture, the superego extends the communal domain inward to the deepest recesses of the mind. But one of its major functions nevertheless "seems to be" Trilling claims, "to lead us to imagine that there is a sanction beyond the culture, that there is a place from which the culture may be judged and rejected" (*BC*, p. 101). The critics of culture, those "martyrs of the intellect" like Socrates and Bruno, therefore, perform for the public mind by means of their tragic fates this same impressive revisionary function which the superego performs in each individual psyche. That is, they, like the superego they incarnate, envision the place of judgment, and for Trilling, following Freud and other great modern writers, this place is named, in one of culture's most magnanimous acts, nature: "This intense conviction of the existence of the self apart from culture is, as culture well knows, its noblest and most generous achievement" (*BC*, p. 102). That is, as if in anticipation of Frank, Trilling admits that logic has nothing to do with it. The critical function of an individual in a culture is founded upon the will, the desire to transcend culture and the social role of the self, by means of this fiction of nature as the place of sublime judgment. Social determination and biological determinism first balance and then cancel out each other, producing an intellectual void that fictions of the opposing self would fill.

The personification in Trilling's language betrays the purely rhetorical basis of his claim. That culture as a whole acts just as an individual acts happens only in myth or poetry. Earlier in the essay, for example, he notes that the moral life assumes each person's power to suspend disbelief in another's existence, in an act of imaginative sympathy that transcends our innate narcissism (*BC*, pp. 81–82). Trilling goes further, in reminding us, via examples from Keats's life and work, how the self also finds "a gratification in regarding its own extinction" (*BC*, p. 85). "For literature," Trilling reminds us, "has always recorded an impulse of the self to find affirmation even in its own extinction, even by its own extinction" (*BC*, p. 85). Tragedy in particular envisions this form of self-transcendence as an "assertion of the death-instinct," that "effort of finely tempered minds," like those of Keats or Oedipus, "to affirm the self in an ultimate confrontation of reality" (*BC*, p. 86). Finally, even the poet's own love of fame—which must supplant all other loves, as both the otherwise very different careers of Milton and Flaubert attest—ultimately expresses the same mechanism of self-overcoming, of radical askesis and self-sacrifice, even of demonic self-destruction. For "the poet's idea of fame," according to Trilling, is the "intense expression of the sense of the self as the self." This sense is lost in the creation of "the thing" that now forever defines it, a creation "which is conceived to be everlasting precisely because it was once a new thing, a thing added to the spirit of man" (*BC*, p. 88). In short, then, death of self as the final form of transcendence becomes the new "criticism of life" (*BC*, p. 86). And culture, in critically projecting a state of nature beyond itself as the place of its own self-judgment, thereby imagines, heroically, tragically, and freely, its memorable negation as its climactic magnanimous act of mourning for the crime of its own perpetuation. Thus, Trilling would revise Freud's own myth of the death instinct by applying it to the history of culture, four years before the publication of Norman O. Brown's *Life against Death.*

The kind of culture Trilling presumes here is not, primarily, the culture to be found in modern democracies, which, despite occasional outbreaks of hysterical forms of repression, like McCarthyism in America, are not fundamentally and consistently repressive enough. (The case of totalitarian societies Trilling conveniently never addresses.) Instead, he argues from the example of Freud and Austria that heroic individual resistance to severe social repression can provoke the discovery of the self as a "biological fact," much as Whitman in *Democratic Vistas*, confronting his own death, discovers the mysterious fact of identity. And this discovery can free the individual from the pressures of conformity and consensus formation, regardless of whether he or she also belongs to a dissenting group as Freud himself did.

Whether Trilling is correct about Freud and Vienna, his point about America appears cogent, viz., that here the imaginative dialectic of freedom and necessity can scarcely function since we no longer possess the spirit of gravity in any form to instigate productive imaginative resistance. Consequently, we need the literary critic, our worldly messiah, to make death the new criterion of life by adding to the human spirit the spectral prosthesis of the traditional canon of authors, that subversive patriarchy, as Trilling himself does here and in related essays of the time. Against this sublime if mournful standard, we may measure and so discover ourselves.

The idea of the self that Trilling finds in psychoanalysis and literature is a freely chosen fiction as much as the idea of nature beyond culture is culture's finest achievement. Both fictions preserve a degree of noble passion amidst ruthless modernities in the figure of the creative genius, and so allegorize covertly the memory of European Jewry whose destruction almost sealed the fate of its hero, Sigmund Freud, as well.

All of this stress on the strength of resistance with which the individual mind meets repression (its own as well as society's) does remind one of what Christopher Isherwood in *Lions and Shadows* describes as the neurosis of the truly strong (really weak) man, the macho posturing of the not too secret victim of male hysteria. And Trilling's desire, following the example of James and Freud, to defend the masculine character (it comes up again in the essay), as well as the senior Trilling's lifelong impersonation of the hysterical father, raises the suspicion that our critical Jay Gatsby doth protest too much. The essay on Issac Babel (1955) also conjures the specter of *hysterica passio*—at first.

Issac Babel, author of *Red Cavalry*, a series of short stories about a Cossack regiment in the Soviet army, is the subject of Trilling's most revealing autobiographical reflections. When Trilling claims, for example, that the aggression of Babel's style—its "ruthless speed," "significant distortion," "rigid foreshortening" (*BC*, p. 108), and real poignancy in describing the many beauties of "male grace"—gradually is replaced under the growing Stalinist repression by a studied laconic litotes, until Babel, ironically enough, becomes "a master of the genre of silence" (*BC*, p. 106), clearly Babel now represents Trilling's latest ideal image of the modern writer:

> A good many years ago, in 1929, I chanced to read a book which disturbed me in a way I can still remember. The book was called *Red Cavalry*, it was a collection of stories about Soviet regiments of horse operating in Poland. I had never heard of the author Issac Babel—or I. Babel as he signed himself—and nobody had anything to tell me about him, and part of my disturbance was the natural shock we feel when, suddenly and without warning, we confront a new talent of great energy and boldness. But the book was disturbing for other reasons as well. (*BC*, p. 103)

There is nothing more powerful than a dead ideal.

Not only did *Red Cavalry* cast doubt on the great Russian Experiment by its superb depiction of the brutal repression of the Polish Jews by the now "progressive" Cossack regiments, it also touched a deeply rooted and disturbing sense of identity in Trilling himself that he had repressed, perhaps as ruthlessly in a psychological sense. A cento of passages about Babel and his father speaks volumes about Trilling's own sense of the real motive for the family romance and for writing:

> The Jew conceived his own ideal character to consist in his being intellectual, pacific, humane. . . . We might put it that Babel rode with a Cossack regiment because, when he was nine years old, he had seen his father kneeling before a Cossack captain who wore lemon-colored chamois gloves and looked ahead with the gaze of one who rides through a mountain pass. . . . Such an experience, or even a far milder analogue of it [such as the young Freud witnessing his father have his fur hat knocked off into a Vienna gutter], is determinative in the life of a boy. . . . But Babel's father [unlike Yefim Nikitich

Smolich, his "adopted" father, a real man and proofreader who taught the boy to swim] did not think about vodka, and smashing somebody in the face, and horses; [Babel's father instead] thought about large and serious things, among them respectability and fame. He was a shopkeeper, not well to do, a serious man, a failure. The sons of such men have much to prove, much to test themselves for; if they are Jewish, their Jewishness is ineluctably involved in the test. (*BC*, pp. 108, 112, 114)

The writer, at least the alienated Jewish writer, identifies with his "ideal" antithesis in order to incorporate all that he lacks and could not receive from his literal great original. In revisionary reaction to the fate of having a weak, hysterical father, Babel "carries as far as he can his sympathy with the fantasy that an ultimate psychic freedom is to be won through cruelty conceived of as a spiritual exercise" (*BC*, p. 119). Both the macho posturings of Norman Mailer and the ambivalent desire for assimilation of Lionel Trilling are thereby explained by I. Babel's prior example. The difference between Mailer and Trilling, of course, resides in the latter's severe internalization and redirection of such aggressive impulses within his own psyche.

What Trilling does not fully explain, however, is the elaborate celebration of the male body, as well as the masculine character, in both Babel and his clearly sympathetic commentator:

[Babel] was drawn by what the violence [of the Cossacks] goes along with, the boldness, the passionateness, the simplicity and directness—and the grace. Thus the story "My First Goose" opens with a description of the masculine charm of the brigade commander Savitsky. His male grace is celebrated in a shower of tropes—the "beauty of his giant's body" is fully particularized: we hear of the decorated chest "cleaving the hut as a standard cleaves the sky," of "the iron and flower of that youthfulness," of the long legs, which were "like girls sheathed to the neck in shining riding boots." Only the openness of the admiration and envy—which constitutes, also, a qualifying irony—keeps the description from seeming sexually perverse. It is remarkably *not* perverse; it is as "healthy" as a boy's love of his hero of the moment. And Savitsky's grace is a real thing. Babel has no wish to destroy it by any of the means which are so ready to the intellectual confronted by this kind of power and charm; he does not diminish the glory he perceives by confronting it with the pathos of human creatures less glorious physically, having more, or a higher, moral appeal because they are weaker and because they suffer. (*BC*, pp. 118–119)

The obvious analogue for this vision of male glory is Lawrence's unconscious love of his father's form as it is displaced into his later fiction, even as he often self-consciously loathes—in the earlier works especially—what his father or his substitutes represent intellectually. And Trilling notes the Lawrentian analogue, as well as those to Yeats and Forster:

> The grace that Babel saw and envied in the Cossacks is much the same thing that D. H. Lawrence was drawn to in his imagination of archaic cultures and personalities and of the ruthlessness, even the cruelty that attended their grace. It is what Yeats had in mind in his love of "the old disturbed exalted life, the old splendour." It is what even the gentle Forster represents in the brilliant scene in *Where Angels Fear to Tread* in which Gino, the embodiment of male grace, tortures Stephen by twisting his broken arm. (*BC*, p. 119)

How to account for Trilling's investment here?

Similarly, how should we explain his investment in Babel's discovery, in the passive, persecuted Jew of the Polish provinces, of a counterimage both to his Cossacks and to the Odessa Jews of his youth, with their impudent messianic delusions. For this is an image with an orthodox religious aura that Babel and Trilling after him strangely approve as well:

> Yet the Jews of Poland are more than a stick with which Babel beats his own Jewish past. They come to exist for him as a spiritual fact of consummate value. . . . the play of Babel's irony permits him to respond in a positive way to the aura of religion. "The breath of an invisible order of things," he says in one story, "glumness beneath the crumbling ruin of the priest's house, and its soothing seduction unmanned me." . . . Yet it is chiefly the Jews who speak to him of the life beyond violence. (*BC*, p. 124)

Trilling's own explanation is that if "Babel's experience with the Cossacks may be understood as having reference to the boy's relation to his father" (*BC*, p. 125), then "his experience of the Jews of Poland has, we cannot but feel, a maternal reference" (*BC*, p. 125), and that, finally, this oedipal opposition of violence and victimage, of adopted father and actual mother, that makes Babel's art was not "a dialectic that his Russia could not permit" (*BC*, p. 125).

Trilling's reading of Babel could be explained away, of course, as expressing merely the masochistic envy of the victim for the victimizer's sadistic power or even as a classic instance of Jewish self-hatred. Such explanations would make this essay into the spectral reenactment of the Freudian movement from primal sadism to primal masochism which accompanies the child's narcissistic choice of himself as love object once the ideal maternal breast has been lost. And the passage from the story "Gedali" that Trilling cites in closing does appear to confirm the correctness of this severe reduction of the essay's field of meaning.

> In the story "Gedali" [Babel] speaks with open sentimentality of his melancholy on the eve of Sabbath—"On those evenings my child's heart was rocked like a little ship upon enchanted waves. O the rotted Talmud of my childhood! O the dense melancholy of memories." When he has found a Jew, it is one who speaks to him in this fashion: ". . . All is mortal. Only the mother is destined to immortality. And when the mother is no longer living, she leaves a memory which none yet dared to sully. The memory of the mother nourishes in us a compassion that is like the ocean, and the measureless ocean feeds the rivers that dissect the universe." (*BC*, p. 125)

My preferred reading of this essay is more perverse, and less sentimental, than Trilling's words would seem to warrant, and yet I think it accounts for more of its representative aspects and representative power.

In Babel Trilling does read the classic story of the Jew in a gentile world. The structures and values of the larger society unman the fathers of the alienated sons, displacing them with more attractive images of power and achievement, to which the sons guiltily wish to assimilate. In the ambivalent process of aspiring to the greater culture, the sons discover that their growing power then permits them to rescue the repressed images of their real fathers in the work of liberation their textual memories perform, to varying degrees of explicitness and according to the dictates of individual awareness and social circumstances. The sons, in this symbolic fashion, can stage their "dead" fathers' return, can remember them anew, can mother them into existence again, as it were, within the systems of representations in which they now exercise some influence.

This may be the rival dialectic that the Mother Russia of Uncle Joe

Stalin could not permit Babel. It is certainly one that, as we have seen repeatedly, liberal America has ever encouraged the author of *The Opposing Self* to create by means of his savagely transcendent, subversively allusive, and sublimely ironic patriarchy. The perverse majesty of necessary repression and the heroic reality of self-sacrifice, even to the point of willing self-destruction, the cultivated eye for the niceties of personal style, the critical reduction of the novel and the culture it represents to the morality of manners, and, of course, the stately sinuosities of his own prose—as if a finely tempered mind were thinking out loud—all these major topoi of Trilling's representative modern career in criticism have as their driving intention this return in glory of the spectral father. The creative motive for modern revisionism is ever sublime enmity and the sweet rage of a perfect revenge. The wish to be a son in whom the father is well pleased follows as the original reaction formation for desiring a different father who could please the son: It is no wonder then that Trilling asserts Babel's captivation in *Red Cavalry* by the ecclesiastical painter Pan Apolek, "who created ecclesiastical scandals by using the publicans and sinners of the little towns as the models for his saints and Virgins" and whose masterpiece, the Christ of the Berestechko Church, reveals "the most extraordinary image of God" Babel has even seen in his life (*BC*, p. 124). Significantly, Trilling himself now completes the highly modulated hymn of praise for this Christ figure in his own voice: "a curly-headed Jew, a bearded figure in a Polish great coat of orange, barefoot, with torn and bleeding mouth, running from an angry mob with a hand raised to ward off a blow" (*BC*, p. 124). In Babel's captivation by his own character's subversive masterpiece of sublime revisionism, we can see as well Trilling's similar self-betraying fascination, and an ideal portrayal of his critical imagination at work liberating his dead godhead—of disintegration.

If Trilling's "Freud: Within and Beyond Culture" ironically constitutes the place of judgment beyond culture out of the authoritative indetermination of the natural, then the Babel essay stages the act of judgment as a religious allegory of reading. The cultural effect of such reading is to release the radical subversive potentials of sublimely repressed origins. By enlarging the spaces within the systems of representation in society, Trilling incorporates as prophetic figures not only the previously excluded patriarchs, Freud and Babel, but, as well, all Jewish fathers. In other words, Trilling's critical style of sublime irony makes his Jewish precursors more publicly acceptable in American culture as alternative origins useful to subsequent generations of readers for purposes of discursive legitimation. One could imagine a similar project, for different political ends, being performed on an entire discipline or historical archive.

Trilling thus invokes the great dead as a repressive standard of judgment in a chaotic permissive society, as a veritable new criterion of life, not in order to rule out of court all attempts at liberation and revision of the cultural heritage but rather to govern the various kinds of subjects (or "selves") being created and the manners of their expression in the process of critical reading. The desired subjects are to be savagely civil, empowered and constrained by the spirit of gravity, normally mystical and romantically rational; they are to achieve an essentially negative transcendence of the present moment by exploring the semantic indeterminacies of classic works with a severely ascetic discipline of (self-)irony. The semantic indeterminacies of canonical texts are to be hosts to the projected "god-terms" of Trilling's attentive readers. The pedagogical intention, always important in Trilling's work, now becomes all in all.

The other essays collected in *Beyond Culture* test the effectiveness of this revisionary critical practice in a variety of ways. "*Emma* and the Legend of Jane Austen" (1957) disputes the old myth of the gentle Jane and the new myth of the mere ironist by arguing, among other things, that in *Emma* Austen employs the genre of intellectual idyll, which Schiller first defined for critics of culture, in order to examine the limits of intelligent love, of the pedagogical conception of human relationships based on the model of Socrates and Plato and celebrated in *The Symposium* by the daemonic myth of Eros that Diotima recounts. The "legendary" atmosphere of the idyll form pervades the novel, according to Trilling, and so allows us to become Emma's sympathetic confidants and conscience-stricken critics, as this artist of another's subjectivity would shape Harriet to her will. As ironic readers of this obviously reflexive reading, then, we become somewhat "unconditioned," as if occupying the position, along with our author, of the great dead who are judging the success or failure of Emma's experiement in self-fashioning and, of course, of Austen's and that of her latest auditor. When the mind becomes "a battlefield" of "private judgments of reality," as in the relativistic modern world, "the unconditioned freedom that the idyll hypothecates," Trilling concludes, "is shown [by the novel finally] to be impossible, yet in the demonstration a measure of freedom is gained" (*BC*, p. 47). Emma and we now know what Austen knows about intelligent love: it must involve the sacrifice that real love or critical intelligence always entails. So, we may suppose, Trilling's sublime fiction of judgment would function as Austen's intellectual idyll does in the novel: Trilling sacrifices his position by exposing its once secret basis of power.

"On the Teaching of Modern Literature" (1961), invoking the ghost of Arnold's first lecture as professor of poetry at Oxford a century ago, was occasioned by the institution of a course in modern literature in the Columbia College English curriculum. The essay examines the specific form of intelligent love, the specific pedagogical intention, informing the profession of literary study in America. Like Nietzsche, Freud, and the great masters in the canon of modern writers, literary intellectuals have assumed "that life was justified by our heroic response to its challenge" (*BC*, p. 21). We therefore have taught the literature of authenticity and aesthetic rebellion which questions all the bourgeois assumptions about existence, in the belief that the works of Joyce, Mann, Kafka, Lawrence, Gide, and the rest could save us all from the death-in-life of an overly rationalized everday world. "The stern pleasure of masculine moral character," in other words, would come to all from the systematic university study of the recent past, an imaginative activity that would bring order and passion to us. In this light, the writer would become the sublime critic of culture, and his heirs would follow his monumental example.

What has happened, however, is nothing of this sort. Instead, the critic, "who writes for an ideal, uncircumscribed reader" (*BC*, p. 26), has as a teacher in the classroom made his students over into "ideal, uncircumscribed" consumers of the dark truths of the Abyss. Owing to our mode of instruction—the institutionalized disciplining and socialization of the undisciplined, antisocial energies of the modern psyche—our students cannot appreciate how truly threatening modernism is. Just imagine a "pop" quiz on *Notes from the Underground*, and Trilling's despair becomes our own. Just as Austen's Emma does in her own way, here a celebrant of the radical potentials of modernism suffers a perversion of the loftiest pedagogical intentions.

Ultimately, Trilling's objection to the professionalization of modernism must be seen in light of larger developments in literary culture than the institution of a new course in the Columbia College curriculum. The leading critic always requires an oppositional base outside the academic apparatus of representation if he or she is to exercise a credible avant-garde role in appropriating the opposition for his or her own revisionary purposes. The animus to established culture on the part of the literature and criticism the leading critic espouses or examines is thus essential to the entire operation, as Trilling's famous description of his dialetic makes clear:

> and since my own interests lead me to see literary situations as
> cultural situations, and cultural situations as great elaborate fights
> about moral issues, and moral issues as having something to do with
> gratuitously chosen images of personal being, and images of per-

sonal being as having something to do with literary style, I felt free to begin [teaching the new course in modern literature] with what for me was a first concern, the animus of the author, the objects of his will, the things he wants or wants to have happen. (*BC*, p. 12)

"Gratuitously chosen images of personal being"—that selection of the objects of the critical will is a key to understanding Trilling's dialectic of opposition and appropriation and his representative antiprofessional stance. Although allusively resonant to the point of studied evasiveness, the formula becomes accurate enough with further thought. The oppositional critic freely, arbitrarily, and even excessively or spontaneously selects from among currently unsanctioned or neglected images of the avant-garde or of the traditional canon those which he wishes to stand for the type of subjectivity he needs to sponsor in the culture if he is to see himself replicated for posterity's sake. That is, critical revisionism is the "moral" equivalent of war—a total war for imaginative survival. If there is no pool of currently unsanctioned images or no avant-garde, if everything is sanctioned within the established systems of representation in the academy and the culture generally, then anything goes and so nothing has value, especially the value of distinction.

Trilling's "solution" to this crisis of the opposing teacher in an established adversarial culture is not, however, to embrace "postmodernism." He rightly suspects that much contemporary literature is just disintegrated modernism. Rather, it is to theorize, in a revisionary manner, the original radical impulses of modernism, recalling to our minds its productively self-destructive impetus and so suffering the shock of the new once again in the hopes of redeeming modernism from its academic degradation:

> I venture to say that the idea of losing oneself up to the point of self-destruction, or surrendering oneself to experience without regard to self-interest or conventional morality, of escaping wholly from the societal bonds, is an "element" somewhere in the mind of every modern person who has to think of what Arnold in his unaffected Victorian way called "the fullness of spiritual perfection." But the teacher who undertakes to present modern literature to his students may not allow that idea to remain in the *somewhere* of his mind; he must take it from the place where it exists habitual and unrealized and put it in the conscious forefront of his thought. And if he is committed to an admiration of modern literature, he must also be committed to this chief idea of modern literature. I press the logic of

the situation not in order to question the legitimacy of the commitment, or even the propriety of expressing the commitment in the
college classroom (although it does seem odd), but to confront those
of us who do teach modern literature with the striking actuality of
our enterprise. (*BC*, pp. 20–27)

Trilling thus remakes the entire movement of modern culture over the
past century or so, from Frazer and Nietzsche to Dostoyevsky, Freud,
Conrad, Eliot, and the rest, into a single sublime figure, one of Arnold's
tragic heroes who confronts fate with heroic resistance. One wonders
whether or not Trilling is aware of how much his palinode for high
modernism echoes the self-destructive aesthetics of experience to be
found in the lives as well as the works of America's leading poets at
the time, Lowell, Ginsberg, Berryman, Roethke, . . . Similarly, one
wonders how these words sung in ironic yet intended praise of the
heroic ideal could inspire and did inspire "the modernism in the
streets" of the counterculture he so loathed.

    A couple of essays in the volume, "The Leavis-Snow Controversy"
(1962) and "The Two Environments: Reflections on The Study of English" (1965), give us some idea of how Trilling increasingly felt, I think,
as the decade of the 1960s marched on. Essentially, Trilling responds
to the famous "two-cultures" debate between Lord Snow and critic
Leavis, in which the latter rather hysterically attacks the former for
noting and endorsing the decline of humanistic study from, and the
rise of scientific study to, a position of centrality in the university and
in modern society generally, by in effect intoning sotto voce, "a plague
on both your houses." Leavis especially raises Trilling's hackles for
giving all literary critics a bad name thanks to his scandalously tasteless
performance. Invoking Arnold's guiding maxims for educators—that
education should "supply the means for a criticism of life and teach
the student to try to see the object as in itself it really is" (*BC*, p. 139)—
Trilling decides that neither Snow nor Leavis is a good educator and so
we are really in sad shape when the best of the two cultures are clearly
so bad.

    Similarly, as both "On the Teaching of Modern Literature" and "The
Leavis-Snow Controversy" would lead us to expect, Trilling's reflections on the fate of literary study in "The Two Environments" concludes somberly. He contrasts the high idealism of the profession's
original educational mission to create a new class of free-floating general intellectuals, critical of culture and of themselves when need be,
with the acutal results of a literary education, namely, the institution
of a second environment of "transcendent gossip" beyond conventional
bourgeois culture in which the terror of avant-garde style reigns:

> The criterion of style, the examination of life by aesthetic categories, yields judgments of a subtle and profound kind, of compelling force. Such judgments are the stuff of the great classic literature of the modern period. Yeats and Eliot, Lawrence and Joyce, each in his own way, have instructed us how to make these judgments for ourselves, teaching us that there can be nothing within that passeth show, that whatever is within of grace or lack of grace will manifest itself in the timbre of the voice, the rhythm of the speech, in how the foot meets the ground, in the feel of the chosen cloth, in the fashion of the house inhabited. By such things we learn to know our neighbors; they yield a knowledge that transcends the knowledge of mere actions. They make the ground for a kind of judgment more searching and exigent than that of the old morality of the deed, a judgment that is rather cruel, really, but fascinating; it promises not only a new kind of truth but a new kind of power, very exciting. (*BC*, p. 193)

Around what Trilling sincerely believes is "the great classic literature of modern times" has grown up "a cultural environment which might well lead serious teachers to think twice before undertaking to prepare their students to enter it" (*BC*, p. 198). As if in prophecy of the performing selves of the countercultural revolutions to come, Trilling decries the mass indoctrination of an entire generation in the passive consumption of modern literature's beneficent aggression. In dark speculation, Trilling concludes that modern literature, which the theory of literary education originally supposed was "a suitable means for developing and refining the intelligence" (*BC*, p. 201), for carrying the self beyond culture and all its hollow idols, has instead been inverted by the development of this second environment into an institutionalized adversarial culture that sets up "the old idols in new forms of its own contrivance" (*BC*, p. 202). Such a culture would never suppose that an individual, when confronted by the necessary angel of modern literature, is to wrestle with him rather than ask who clips his wings so stylishly.

The deterioration of high modernism into cultural fashion and a new orthodoxy of style so appalls Trilling that in "Hawthorne in Our Time" (1964) the critic is driven to agree precipitously with Henry James's mistaken estimate of his famous precursor as a genial allegorist of the spirit who contrasts, in Trilling's distorted view, most favorably with that modern celebrant of the tyrant dream of society and the absurdly autonomous imagination, Franz Kafka (see especially *BC*, pp. 174–180). In what is clearly a self-criticism as well as a criticism of "our time," Trilling impotently concludes: "Our judgment of Hawthorne may have to be that he is not for us today, and perhaps not even tomorrow." He is, in Nietzsche's phrase, Trilling pointedly adds, "one of the spirits of yesterday—and the day after tomorrow" (*BC*, p. 180). In the final analysis Trilling is asserting that his subversive patriarch Nathaniel Hawthorne is so subversive he cannot even be heard now. Instead, as Nietzsche contends about himself in *Ecce Homo*, this Hawthorne must be born posthumously, in the mind of some ideal reader of the utopian future, which the untimely critic of the present desperately projects as his specular supplement. This ideal reader is the reflective offspring of the disintegrating mirror-stage of his latest critical essay in cultural despair.

As a valedictory address to the 1964 graduating class of Northwestern University suggests (*SLS*, pp. 398–466), and the addendum on irony to the preface in the 1968 reprint of *Beyond Culture* demonstrates by its very necessity, Trilling feels he must tell his reader where and how he is being ironical. Trilling thus recognizes that the literary-humanistic consensus that had supported the public realm of cultural debate in liberal America for half a century or more is currently in the process of breaking up (*SLS*, pp. 407–410). This is the case even before the civil rights, black power, antiwar, and radical feminist movements and their right-wing antagonists take to the streets and try to take over the classrooms and the bureaucratic offices in the late sixties and throughout the seventies. The ideal of the refined and educated mind, whose refinement and education stand as ironic witness to the barbarous crudities of established power, regardless of its official orientation "left or right"—this ideal of aesthetic humanism from Schiller and Arnold to Richards and Trilling does not seem so much reactionary or even quaint as a sublime blank in the cultural memory. Nowhere does Trilling better dramatize this ironic development and his terrible recognition of the critical role he has played in unwittingly promoting it than in the great essay of *Beyond Culture*, and indeed of the entire decade, "The Fate of Pleasure" (1963).

Spiritual Psychoanalysis: Immortal Passions, Mortal Ecstasy

"The Fate of Pleasure" is one of the first and still one of the finest essays in critical theory by an American literary intellectual. Its argument traces the changed conception of and response to pleasure by leading post-Enlightenment intellectuals from Wordsworth and Keats, through Carlyle, Bentham, Nietzsche (one of Trilling's heroes here), and Dostoyevsky (his Underground Man is Trilling's villain), to the great modernists (Yeats, Joyce, Lawrence, and Kafka) and the Freud of *Beyond the Pleasure Principle* (whom Trilling revises in a devastating manner).

Once, from the Renaissance through the eighteenth century, as Werner Sombart in *Luxury and Capitalism* maintains, the pursuit of pleasure in the forms of luxury and refinement was considered a legitimate quest for power and the signs of power. Pleasure after the French Revolution, the Romantic reaction, and the Victorian repression, however, rapidly becomes one of two unattractive things: either the primitive dynamic force driving the pleasure-pain calculating machine of the mind hypothesized by the utilitarians, positivists and their radical opponents and modern scientific and literary heirs; or the vulgar degrading representation of an individual's spiritual enslavement to a materialistic social order, whether democratic or totalitarian in structure. The poet, who according to Wordsworth brings relationship and love, now brings visions of the death of spirit ("Mistah Kurtz—he dead") and the fate of pleasure ("I can connect nothing with nothing"), in the culture of specious goods. Consequently, for modern literary intellectuals, their academic fellow travelers, and their masses of students, the condemnation and rejection of the specious good of pleasure has become what Lawrence in *Women in Love* calls the "last distinction," separating high cultural life from its dreaded and disdained popular antagonist.

In thus tracing this curious development of pleasure, Trilling is aware that the historical method inevitably entails an implicit critical irony subversive of the acceptance of the phenomenon under discussion as natural and necessary and not subject to fundamental change. And Trilling wants to take an adversarial position on this development because it has led, he believes, to the equally specious opposition between politics and art institutionalized by the academy in our time. For it is Trilling's view that, just as in the life of the individual there comes a climactic moment when the destructive instincts become dominant that make for the ego's self-definition at the expense of the object (which the ego ever would consume), so there arises in the life of a culture a similar developmental crisis moment, which now we are experiencing in modern literature and art, and which sanctions a gratification of the death instincts by an entire class of intellectuals as their last desperate distinction from the mass. The pursuit by a ruling class of gratification in unpleasure, in aggression and destruction, is a political phenomenon, one that must eventually take an even more virulent form as a self-destructive politics of death in which the offspring of this intellectual class turn against their great originals in a cultural equivalent of Armageddon. Obviously influenced by his reading of Norman O. Brown's *Life against Death* (1959), Trilling in 1963 nevertheless creates a unique version of such neo-Freudian revisions prophetic of one influential way of looking at what is to come by decade's end. Modern art and politics are thus of a piece in their opposition to life itself, in Trilling's view.

Clearly, as his final discussion indicates, Trilling intends "The Fate of Pleasure" to be a theoretical revision, as well as cultural/historical application, of Freud's most speculative essay in metapsychology, *Beyond the Pleasure Principle*. For there Freud does not, as Trilling will do, definitively identify ego and death instincts in a neat formula that equates self-preservation and object destruction. Nor does Freud there suggest, as Trilling does, that in some dire circumstances actual self-destruction equals symbolic self-preservation. And in *An Outline of Psychoanalysis*, Freud's last book, which Trilling knew well and admired greatly, Freud explicitly denies the possibility—that Trilling proposes— of such an identification of ego and death instincts. For there Freud sees in the development of the ego primarily the work of the other great metapsychological divinity, Eros. Yet in concluding his *Outline* as he does, by describing the operation of the superego, that psychic institution of ethical norms, as the major means by which the individual and the group transform the present into the past, actually making the present past,[9] Freud himself does provide some basis for Trilling's radical revision. In addition, in "Mourning and Melancholia" (1917), another Trilling favorite, Freud permits himself to speculate that in cases of suicide the ego, having internalized the lost or rejecting love object, seeks to master the masterful other in every way possible, including its own pathetic death. Here, again, Freud himself has given Trilling the opening he needs to mount his revisionary elaboration of Freudian ideas which would assimilate psychoanalysis to his own Arnoldian version of personal and now communal tragedy, that sublime acquiescence to fate ever in the back of Trilling's mind which defines the essence of his critical humanism.

Just as clearly, Trilling intends "The Fate of Pleasure" to be a revision of Wordsworth's famous preface to *Lyrical Ballads*, as the essay's magisterial opening paragraph suggests:

Of all critical essays in the English language, there is none that has established itself so firmly in our minds as Wordsworth's Preface to *Lyrical Ballads*. Indeed, certain of the statements that the Preface makes about the nature of poetry have come to exist for us as something like proverbs of criticism. This is deplorable, for the famous utterances, in the form in which we hold them in memory, can only darken counsel. A large part of the literate world believes that Wordsworth defines poetry as the spontaneous overflow of powerful feelings. With such a definition we shall not get very far in our efforts to think about poetry, and in point of fact Wordsworth makes no such definition. Much less does he say, as many find it convenient to recall, that poetry is emotion recollected in tranquillity. Yet the tenacity with which we hold in mind our distortions of what Wordsworth actually does say suggests the peculiar power of the essay as a whole, its unique existence as a work of criticism. Its cogency in argument is notable, even if intermittent, but the Preface is not regarded by its readers only as an argument. By reason of its eloquence, and because of the impetuous spirit with which it engages the great questions of the nature and function of poetry, it presents itself to us not chiefly as a discourse, but rather as a dramatic action, and we are prepared to respond to its utterances less for their truth than for their happy boldness.

This being so, it should be a matter for surprise that one especially bold utterance of the Preface has not engaged us at all and is scarcely ever cited. I refer to the sentence in which Wordsworth speaks of what he calls "the grand elementary principle of pleasure," and says of it that it constitutes "the naked and native dignity of man," that it is the principle by which man "knows, and feels, and lives, and moves." (BC, pp. 50–51)

As Trilling notes, Wordsworth here is echoing and controverting "St. Paul's sentence which tells us that 'we live, and move, and have our being in God' (Acts 17:28)" (BC, p. 61).

Moreover, however, I think that by claiming for Wordsworth's preface a poetic status as "dramatic action" superior to its conceptual status as critical argument, Trilling is not only implicitly making a similar claim for his own work, particularly the rest of the essay to follow, but also attempting to ward off some possible attacks on his own "impetuous spirit" for giving way to "eloquence" at the expense of cogent reasoning. Once we grant Trilling his quantum of bad faith here, however, I also think that reading his essay as a dramatic action reveals much of his hidden motivation, not to mention fulfilling the contemporary dictum, manufactured out of Kenneth Burke, J. L. Austin, and French deconstruction, which enjoins us to read every piece of writing as at least potentially a performance of the figures it produces.

In any event, if we do read Trilling as he wants here to be read, what do we discover? Another quotation from late in the essay gives us a clue:

> We instinctively resent questions which suggest that there is fault to
> be found with the one saving force in our moral situation—that
> extruded "high" segment of our general culture which, with its
> exigent, violently subversive spirituality, has the power of arming us
> against, and setting us apart from, all in the general culture that we
> hate and fear.
>
> Then what justification can there be for describing with any de-
> gree of adversary purpose the diminished status of the principle of
> pleasure which characterizes this segment of our culture? (*BC*, p. 70)

In entertaining the prospect of finding fault with what is "surely one
of the chief literary enterprises of our age," what Trilling carefully
terms "the destruction of what is considered the specious good" (*BC*,
p. 67), our critical educator is restraining, curtailing, severely disciplining "that extruded 'high' segment of our general culture" which makes
for "the last distinction" between modern intellectuals and the masses,
in emulation of Moses when he saw his people worshiping the golden
calf, or, better yet, of Jesus when he scoured the Temple clean of money
changers and the other merchants of sacrifice. Since Trilling, unlike C.
Wright Mills, is no prophet of participatory democracy, there really is
something perverse and self-negating in the spectacle of his turning
against the literary life in our time. It reminds one of what Trilling says
earlier in the essay about Keats's dialectic of erotic pleasure which may
begin in every form of sensual delight no matter how vulgar but ever
concludes in a sublime negation of all the beauties of pleasure, a heroic
renunciation of Shakespearean fruit in favor of Milton's epic gloom,
that leaves the poet and his reader in "the country of La Belle Dame
Sans Merci." That poem's scene of "erotic fulfillment which leads to
devastation, to an erotic fulfillment which implies castration" (*BC*, p.
56), is a characteristic Keatsian fate which explains perfectly well, with
only a few minor alterations, the scene of askesis enacted in this passage and in the essay as a whole. Trilling, in short, by means of his
prophetic theory of the fate of pleasure in the emerging postmodern
era, is here symbolically castrating himself and the class of literary
intellectuals he has always sought to represent and guide. He correctly
foresaw that the postmodern era can no longer recognize a viable
distinction between popular and high cultural forms and values, because the postmodern really bears ironic testimony to the success of
the adversary culture as a modernism for the masses.

If this reading of the essay's dramatic action is correct, two further
questions arise, for both of which another later passage from the essay
supplies the answers. The questions, quite simply, are: why does Trill-

ing perform his particular critical play, and where does it leave him, what position is left for him to occupy? In his discussion of a famous scene in the *Confessions* in which Saint Augustine reflects on the motive informing his boyhood theft of some pears from a neighboring orchard, we discover Trilling's own motive and his place:

> Of all the acts of his unregenerate days which he calls sinful and examines in his grim, brilliant way, there is none that he nags so persistently, none that seems to lie so far beyond the reach of his ready comprehension of sin. He did not steal the pears because he was hungry. He did not steal them because they were delicious— they were pears of rather poor quality, he had better at home. He did not steal them to win the admiration of the friends who were with him, although this comes close, for, as he says, he would not have stolen them if he had been alone. In all sin, he says, there is a patent motivating desire, some good to be gained, some pleasure for the sake of which the act was committed. But this sin of the stolen pears is, as it were, pure—he can discover no human reason for it. He speaks again of the presence of the companions, but although their being with him was a necessary condition of the act, it cannot be said to have motivated it. To the mature Augustine, the petty theft of his youth is horrifying not only because it seems to have been a sin committed solely for the sake of sinning, but because, in having no conceivable pleasure in view, it was a sort of negative transcendence—in effect, a negation—of his humanity. This is not strange to us—what I have called the extruded high segment of our general culture has for some time been engaged in an experiment in the negative transcendence of the human, a condition which is to be achieved by freeing the self from its thralldom to pleasure. Augustine's puzzling sin is the paradigm of the modern spiritual enterprise, and in his reprobation of it is to be found the reason why Dostoevski condemned and hated the Christianity of the West, which he denounced as, in effect, a vulgar humanism.

To be aware of this undertaking of negative transcendence is, surely, to admire the energy of its desperateness. And we can comprehend how, for the consumer of literature, for that highly developed person who must perforce live the bourgeois life in an affluent society, an aesthetic ethos based on the devaluation of pleasure can serve, and seem to save, one of the two souls which inhabit his breast. Nearly overcome as we are by the specious good, insulted as we are by being forced to acquire it, we claim the right of the Underground Man to address the "gentlemen" with our assertion, "I have

more life in me than you have," which consorts better with the refinement of our sensibility than other brags that men have made,
such as, "I am stronger than you," or "I am holier than thou." Our
high culture invites us to transfer our energies from the bourgeois
competition to the spiritual competition. We find our "distinction"—
last or penultimate—in our triumph over the miserable "gentlemen,"
whether they are others or ourselves, whether our cry be, "I have
more life in me than you have" or "I have more life in me than I
have."

   Now and then it must occur to us that the life of competition for
spiritual status is not without its own peculiar sordidness and absurdity. But this is a matter for the novelist—for that novelist we do
not yet have but must surely have one day, who will take into serious
and comic account the actualities of the spiritual career of our time.
(*BC,* pp. 70–71)

In other words, the modern undertaking of negative transcendence
inspired by our dread of Eden, and to be achieved by gratuitous symbolic acts that condemn the gratifications of mere pleasure, is the equivalent, the modern analogue, of Augustine's sin in its "pure" form, and
Trilling's critique of it all is akin to Augustine's Christian (self-)
condemnation.

   To assume that such perverse acts of pure style as those which
Dostoyevsky's Underground Man performs prove one has more life in
oneself than pleasure-seeking counterparts is to transfer illegitimately
"our energies from the bourgeois competition" of everyday life to "the
spiritual competition" for perfection, which the extraordinary moments of negative transcendence in classic modernist works would
seem to endorse as the model of human existence. Echoing Emerson
in "The Poet," ironically enough, Trilling wryly remarks, apropos this
inverted fate of pleasure, that "the life of competition for spiritual
status is not without its own peculiar sordidness and absurdity." This
situation indeed is, as Trilling adds, one for "the novelist—for that
novelist we do not yet have but must surely have one day, who will take
into serious and comic account the actualities of the spiritual career of
our time." For the novelist, that is, whom Trilling hopes to become on
publication of his second but—alas!—never to be completed novel.
(That such a prophesized novelist does nevertheless arise is clear from
Trilling's endorsement, two years later in "The Two Environments"
essay collected here, of Saul Bellow's trenchant critique of modernism's
spiritual squalor on his reception of the Pulitizer Prize for *Herzog.*)

   "The Fate of Pleasure" thus joins Trilling's other great essays in creative criticism such as "Reality in America," "Princess Casamassima," "The Poet as Hero: Keats in His Letters," "Mansfield Park," and "Wordsworth and the Rabbis"—but with this significant difference: in the deployment of his own revisionary theory Trilling uses the theoretical and rhetorical revisions of his major precursors, Freud and Wordsworth, to define himself as the self-confessed former sinner of pure style turned Saint Judas who now eschews what "On the Teachings of Modern Literature" describes as "gratuitously chosen images of personal being"; in the process, he also hopes to prepare the taste to come by which his later work, especially his masterful *Prefaces to the Experience of Literature*, will be judged. Trilling's later works are intended to be taken as the spiritual form of psychoanalysis which would cure by a severe self-discipline the cultural superego, all the dead and subversive fathers of the intellectual class, for which the absurd and sordid competition for spiritual status has become the latest mode of self-enslavement, what Régis Debray (among others) has taught us to see as celebrity culture. The work of liberation Trilling would perform in "The Fate of Pleasure" and in all his final essays, then, is meant to save us from (among other things) the intellectual decadence that manifests itself in literary study these days as revisionary madness, or professionalism unbound, that rampant careerism which is threatening to destroy imaginative culture in America totally, all in the name of the highest values of one sort or another, of course, but actually, as Tocqueville foresaw, really out of the sublime enmity endemic to democratic societies.

The essays collected in *Beyond Culture* thus have, as the preface notes generally about modern intellectual production, "the clear purpose of detaching the reader from the habits of thought and feeling that the larger culture imposes, of giving him a ground and a vantage point from which to judge and condemn, and perhaps revise, the culture that produced him" (*BC*, p. iv). And the particular habit of thought and feeling Trilling seeks to judge and condemn, and perhaps to revise, is this very revisionary practice of critical writing itself. Trilling, therefore, does not propose here the impossible project of entirely transcending culture in the sense of a total human environment. Rather he proposes the idea of going beyond this conventional adversarial piety of high culture inherited from the classic modern intellectuals from Mann and Nietzsche to Freud and Lawrence and all the others. "To stand beyond culture" by way of an original "autonomy of perception and judgment," to "liberate" oneself from "the tyranny" of received ideas—this is the latest myopic orthodoxy, the newest received idea, which Trilling would attempt to transcend from the neo-Augustinian

210   *Normal Mysticism*

vantage point that the dramatic action of his revisionary theory of the fate of pleasure in our post-Enlightenment world appears to afford him:

> And around the adversary culture there has formed what I have called a class. If I am right in identifying it in this way, then we can say of it, as we say of any other class, that it has developed characteristic habitual responses to the stimuli of its environment. It is not without power, and we can say of it, as we can say of any other class with a degree of power, that it seeks to aggrandize and perpetuate itself. And, as with any other class, the relation it has to the autonomy of its members makes a relevant question, and the more, of course, by reason of the part that is played in the history of its ideology by the ideal of autonomy. There is reason to believe that the relation is ambiguous. (*BC*, p. vii)

Trilling is truly uneasy in making this point, as the concluding paragraph of the preface makes all too clear:

> Most of the essays in this volume were written out of an awareness of ambiguity. Some of them propose the thought that we cannot count upon the adversary culture to sustain us in such efforts toward autonomy of perception and judgment as we might be impelled to make, that an adversary culture of art and thought, when it becomes well established, shares something of the character of the larger culture to which it was—to which it still is—adversary, and that it generates its own assumptions and preconceptions, and contrives its own sanctions to protect them. The early adversary movement of European art and thought, it has been said, based itself on the question, "Is it true? Is it true for me?" The characteristic question of our adversary culture is, "Is it true? Is it true for us?" This is a good question too, it has its particular social virtues, but it does not yield the same results as the first question, and it may even make it harder for anyone to ask the first question. The difference between the force of the two questions is suggested by the latter part of my essay on Freud. The second question is asked by the group of psychiatrists to whom I refer; it serves an unquestionably useful purpose. The first question was asked by Freud himself.
>
> Several of the essays touch on the special difficulty of making oneself aware of the assumptions and preconceptions of the adversary culture by reason of the dominant part that is played in it by art. My sense of this difficulty leads me to approach a view which will

seem disastrous to many readers and which, indeed, rather surprises me. This is the view that art does not always tell the truth or the best kind of truth and does not always point out the right way, that it can even generate falsehood and habituate us to it, and that, on frequent occasions, it might well be subject, in the interests of autonomy, to the scrutiny of the rational intellect. The history of this faculty scarcely assures us that it is exempt from the influences of the cultures in which it has sought its development, but at the present juncture its informing purpose of standing beyond any culture, even an adversary one, may be of use. (*BC*, pp. vii–viii)

Like Plato or Augustine or Rousseau, Trilling sanctions the play of the rational intellect in service of a normal mysticism, which takes the form of an aesthetics of experience. By containing the excesses of the adversary culture, the rational intellect can once again make possible, Trilling believes, the single individual's creative appropriation of original experiences, the only authentic incentive to imaginative inspiration.

Talk about your exploitation of cultural despair! For what else is Trilling doing in "The Fate of Pleasure" and indeed in all the essays collected in *Beyond Culture* but inducing a fundamental despair over the "progress" of American higher education and then recommending by his example the therapeutic remedy for it? "What was once [among modern artists] a mode of experience of a few has now become [among members of the adversary culture] an ideal of experience of many" (*BC*, p. 74). In fact, too many. Yet Trilling is not simply berating mass culture as if he were an adjunct of the Frankfurt school of criticism. Rather, like the classic Freudian analyst, only operating not with an individual client but with an entire segment of the intellectual culture, Trilling would use his criticism as a means to effect the transference of authority from the mortal and mortifying ideal of aristocratic modernism to his own belated liberal criticism of that ideal as it has declined within the democratic context of the permissive society. In tracing the history of pleasure, the first and ultimate category of all aesthetics, from its direct pursuit and relation to power to the pursuit of its demonic impotent opposite, Trilling's paradoxical and literally "utopian" criticism functions like a high-class fun-house mirror, focusing and distorting this fatal development just enough to dramatize the dead end that lies in wait for the American intellectual class of his generation and their many diverse heirs if they remain, as they have, wedded to the high-modernist aesthetic ideology. (One thinks of Hilton Kramer's influential work, especially his recent book *The Revenge of the Philistines* and of his even more influential journal, the *New Criterion*.) Trilling's function of criticism, however, is not a neo-conservative polemic but a form of spiritual psychoanalysis. In the ironic recognition of the mortal ecstasy, the imaginative self-destruction at least, to be suffered by anyone who continues to espouse an outmoded ideal, Trilling would bring to sublime completion the immortal passion of the great dead as they constitute the cultural superego of this class.

> It is impossible to say that—whether for good or for bad—we are seeing a mutation in culture by which an old established proportion between the pleasure-seeking instincts and the ego instincts is being altered in favor of the latter. If we follow Freud through the awesome paradoxes of *Beyond the Pleasure Principle*, we may understand why the indications of this change should present themselves as perverse and morbid, for the other name that Freud uses for the ego instincts is the death instincts. Freud's having made the ego instincts synonymous with the death instincts accounts, more than anything else in his dark and difficult essay, for the cloud of misunderstanding in which it exists. But before we conclude that *Beyond the Pleasure Principle* issues, as many believe, in an ultimate pessimism or "negation," and before we conclude that the tendencies in our literature which we have remarked on are nothing but perverse and morbid, let us recall that although Freud did indeed say that "the aim of all life is death," the course of his argument leads him to the statement that "the organism wishes to die only in its own fashion," only through the complex fullness of its appropriate life. (*BC*, pp. 75–76)

From now on in his criticism, and especially in his *Prefaces to the Experience of Literature* (1967), Trilling will exorcise the sovereign ghosts of the modernist-shaped canon in this neo-Freudian manner. That is, he will provide his attentive student-readers with the accumulation of anticathexis necessary for them to capitalize on his own and his generation's sobering experience of attempting to form a life based on literary ethics, so that the next generation may invent a radically new psychic economy that may aid them in avoiding the liberal decadence known as postmodern culture. In this light, Trilling's later criticism takes the form of a series of encounters, like that which occurs between Wordsworth and the ancient leech gatherer in "Resolution and Independence," all of which have as their aim the transmission to us of his knowledge of how to combat the cycle of high spirits and despondency and madness, once the characteristic affliction of the poets only but now the tragic model of the good life for millions—in part, of course, thanks to Trilling's own earlier work and that of his circle.

Trilling in his late work would thus undo the lingering effects of what his first work had helped to promote. Trilling's invocation of Augustine or Rousseau or Freud in their final years of self-revision as the ascetic models for his own final essays is, therefore, not inappropriate if still somewhat—charmingly—immodest. The intention Trilling in a 1966 essay attributes to Tess Slesinger, author of *The Unpossessed* (1935), a first (and only) novel about being young in the 1930s in America, that "in one especially vivacious and articulate moment she took notice" not only of "the scrawls" made on the human soul's dirty slate "by family, class, ethnic, or cultural groups, the society in general" but also of what "she had not expected to see" there, "the scribble . . . made by the spiritual intellect itself" (*LD*, p. 24)—what Trilling here attributes to a long-dead radical feminist woman author he once knew and loved in his strange way, he clearly prescribes now for himself in the last phase of his career, as his conspicuous allusion to Yeats's finest poem of approaching death, "Man and Echo," aptly underscores. But with this real distinction from the projected aim for Slesinger, Trilling, like Yeats at the end, would also scrub clean the slate of the literary life, wiping away all its amassed wealth of sublime graffiti, especially his own more questionable contributions to the soul's history in the modern American world.

The Great Vision: A Typology of Transcendent Modesty

The Experience of Literature (1967) was once a standard anthology of classic works in the three traditional literary genres of drama, fiction, and poetry. (I myself drew considerable sustenance from its original pages.) The huge volume—also available in a three-volume paperback edition—ranges over the entire history of Western literature from the Greeks to the then-present moment of the middle 1960s, even including in the fiction department its editor's own generally recognized novella masterpiece, "Of This Time, Of That Place." Formed according to "no special theory" (*PEL*, p. iv), deploying in its individual prefaces to every included text a wide variety of critical methods—literary history, cultural criticism, New Critical close readings of significant forms, psychological analysis, and philosophical speculation—the anthology, in acknowledging that "the making and the experience of literature is what the zoologists call a species-characteristic trait of mankind" (*PEL*, p. ii), also acknowledges its function as Trilling's "zoo" for new readers of great literature, or at least as his elegant guidebook to the imaginary museum of established masterpieces. The anthology also clearly displays its liberal orthodoxy in this benign naturalistic orientation toward the conventional staples of the introductory sophomore survey. It also reflects the elitist intentions that work against so-called minor authors and "minority" or "marginal" literature of women, persons of color, and other writers not already canonized by the institution of English studies. For Trilling, as for his generation, what finally counts the most remains the gratuitously chosen images of personal being, the truly (in this sense) "memorable" scene or sublime phrase or figure, what here he terms, perhaps in conscious remembrance of his first "master-piece," the 1936 essay on Eugene O'Neill, "the force of style" (*PEL*, p. v) that comes across even the vast gulfs of time.

While not representative of today's interests or tastes, perhaps, *The Experience of Literature* is still a generous-looking anthology for its time. And its prefaces, especially those on drama and fiction, are by its own preferred standard "memorable" for their "force of style." As a body they constitute an original if at points also a misleading appropriation, "a new experience" as Lawrence would have it, of the primary ele-ments of the modern literary life. These little prefaces, which Diana Trilling in her preface to the volume reports cost her husband great pains in composing, are models of critical response of a kind obviously no longer available to us in this age of habitual systematic suspicion of all forms of sensibility and sentiment. Moreover, I think, the consistent argument that runs through the volume like a ground theme subject to many subtle modulations and often considerable ironic variation makes these prefaces the critical substitute for that autobiographical-sounding comic novel about the absurd, sordid, and quite serious "actualities of the spiritual career of our time" (*BC*, p. 75) which Trilling could never finish. As such, and in their informing pragmatist conception of Aris-totle's original aesthetics of experience, the prefaces function as John Dewey in *Art as Experience* claims poetry, the first of the arts, paradig-matically functions: viz., as the ideal imaginative completion of the formative energies of human experience ever cut short by life's una-voidable exigencies.[10]

Certainly, the recurrent patterns of argument in the prefaces do lend a lot of credence to my point. Trilling always manages to home in on that aspect in each work under discussion which, when all the prefaces are read together, helps to comprise the features of the literary life in modern America, a single fatal portrait of the God of critical humanism that has now failed, too. Trilling's implicit (and, therefore, more effec-tively influential) *grand récit* tells the tale of the Young Man from the Provinces—which in America often means from an excluded social group—who would transcend his origins by aspiring to the condition of literary genius as represented by the exemplary career of the great modern masters of aesthetic opposition, and who comes at last to realize not only his own painful lack of genius but, as well, the generally pernicious effects of the ideology of genius, pervaded by the critical institutions to which he now ambivalently belongs. For these effects are currently undermining, in the name of every radical form of self-determination imaginable, the last vestiges of the liberal bourgeois public sphere and so are preparing the way for the massive cultural regression that must surely follow in its wake, and has, of course, now come to pass for us. If all this makes Trilling's *Prefaces* sound like his critical version of Yeats's classic prophetic vision in "The Second Coming," it is only a partially appropriate echo. The other Yeatsian vision to which Trilling himself tellingly alludes, and which he self-consciously analyzes and so implicitly compares to his own late meditations, is that vision of savage refinement contained in *Purgatory*.

This overview of Trilling's *Prefaces* may sound forced to some, and far too overdetermined or obsessively constraining to correspond to Trilling's intention for what are, after all, a set of anthology introductions to classic texts. And yet, I do not mean to suggest that Trilling here rides a proto-theoretical or polemical hobbyhorse. His mind is far too severely graceful, his method far too politely casual, for anything resembling critical pathology. Nonetheless, even in prefaces that rightly do not make the failed spiritual career of the young aspirant from the provinces the chief focus of their discussions, the reader who has been schooled by this very curriculum of master works that Trilling has selected cannot fail to hear, amidst other sometimes admittedly discordant notes, the underlying theme being repeatedly if softly struck.

Consider, for example, how five of Trilling's more "impersonal" dramatic prefaces—to *Oedipus Rex*, *King Lear*, *The Doctor's Dilemma*, *Six Characters in Search of an Author*, and *Galileo*—just happen to project the spectral outlines of a story that could plausibly be taken as the literary representation of the life of the critic. For the critic must always proceed to produce meaning—like the Oedipus who amidst the wealth of human evil presses on to the conclusion that destroys him—"if he is still to compel respect" (*PEL*, p. 6) in our Lear-like nihilistic world where even great art often fails to provide the "final music that summons" into being, out of the contradictory norms of nature, "the future" (*PEL*, p. 13). Such an impossible challenge to discover meaning for the experience of literature may induce in part the ironic reaction of "the conscious pathetic eloquence" of a Dubedat in Shaw's unlikely comedy of mistaken respect and certain self-deceit, which appears "to mock itself, at least a little" (*PEL*, p. 43). Such self-born mockery in Shaw's character reminds us, I think, of that which ironically haunts Trilling's own perfected solemnities habitually now. For he, like Shaw, discloses "the theatricality" of the verbal medium in his reflexive uses of it, much as Pirandello's absurdist masterpiece stages "the elements of theater itself" (*PEL*, p. 48) as the dramatis personae in a potentially endless "repetition" which makes up the purgatorial life of all imagined characters (*PEL*, p. 50), especially the character which the critic creates for himself. For such a passionate life of pure style has become Trilling's public fate as Edmund Wilson's heir to the title of America's last man of letters. The remaining possible escape from such a fate, as Brecht's perverse revision of *Galileo* suggests to its critic, can only be the transcendent postulate of the ever "protean mind," the sheer genius of revisionism for revisionism's sake (*PEL*, p. 66).

It may seem that I am teasing an autobiographical fiction of the critic as critic out of these prefaces that is at best only latently there, embedded in yet best left to stay under their general surface meanings as a resonant penumbra of sensibility. After all, Trilling's ever universalizing diction and emphasis upon "ideas" does create a considerable degree of semantic play that often amounts to an inviting semantic indeterminacy. Yet even in his less clearly interested prefaces, where Trilling does not obviously engage matters of direct formal or thematic consequence to him, there emerges a similar spectral allegory.

In recounting the Maupassant tale "Duchoux," for instance, Trilling puts the ultimate stress not on the deficient father's "unnatural" rejection of his recently discovered son but on the son's even greater if still clearly mirroring deficiencies. No human father, Trilling assumed, could ever be well pleased to see any resemblance, however remote, in such a son (*PEL*, p. 95). The motivational parallel with Trilling's own rejections of the emerging counterculture as early as the essays "On the Teaching of Modern Literature" (in 1961) and "The Fate of Pleasure" (in 1963) is quite evident. Similarly, as he reads Chekhov's "Enemies," the story becomes for Trilling a poignant vignette about the competition for spiritual status, as Aboguin, a deceived husband, and Dr. Kirilov, a bereaved father, both haunted by the absence of all heroic possibilities in pre-Revolutionary Russia, engage in a sordid, absurd skirmish for superiority in grief (*PEL*, p. 99), in a game of one-upmanship played as if over the graves of their lost loves. All this is in contrast to, Trilling assures us, Chekhov's own exemplary authorial modesty, a modesty so sublimely ironic—and, apparently, contagious—that Trilling designates it "transcendent" (*PEL*, p. 96). So much for Trilling's transcendently immodest heirs such as Norman Podhoretz of *Making It* and *Commentary* fame, as well as the poet David Shapiro who on being arrested for "rioting" at Columbia used his one phone call to proclaim to his old teacher, "Lionel, your tradition has failed me."[11] (Of course, such ironic eloquence demonstrates just the opposite.)

As if in deliberate counterpoint to these gestures of critical self-alienation, Trilling understands the very next story in the volume, "The Pupil" of Henry James, as an ultimately devastating critique of the tutor-narrator, Pemberton, whose climactic evasion of all real commitment to his brilliant devoted student, Morgan Moreen, occasions the latter's death. Trilling bitterly concludes, in a manner that cannot help but recall the plot of his novella "Of This Time, Of That Place," that "there are occasions when, if a man is not a saint" or "a genius of morality," he is "nothing at all" (*PEL*, p. 106). In something like the rites of passage that transform an adolescent into an adult that both Dinesen's "The Sailor-Boy's Tale" and Lawrence's "Tickets, Please" ruefully celebrate, Trilling here would seem to be initiating himself into the final phases of his career in self-revision. Even the heavy stress he places on the sterility of the modern Waste Land in Hemingway's "Hills like White Elephants," or the compensatory imaginative joy he takes in seeing Faulkner in "Barn Burning" ape a Keatsian cameleon poet by taking a Shakespeare-like pleasure in creating both a Colonel Sartoris and an Abner Snopes, compose a reflexive gesture that fits the developing picture of the critic as a radical self-revisionist that all these prefaces finally print.

Although like Sarty Snopes, for example, Trilling believes that every aspiring young man from the provinces must finally break the tie with the father who is "a ruin of a man," Trilling also clearly feels, like Sarty again or Faulkner himself, a strong attraction for the "metallic integration" of the father, for his bitter hostility to society, and for his sense of outraged social status (*PEL*, p. 154). Trilling's remarks about being a son of a ruined father in his essay on Isaac Babel in *Beyond Culture* come to mind in this connection. In any event, guilty shades of the family romance of cultural aspiration close round the aging critic as Trilling in reading "Barn Burning" hovers sublimely over and ironically between approving Major de Spain's justified rage at Abner Snopes's destruction of his expensive rug and this villain's "passion for independence" at all costs even when it may become, as here, "virtually an insanity" (*PEL*, p. 154).

I suppose all this self-reference I am uncovering in Trilling's *Prefaces* could still be seen as my own succumbing to what in his introduction to Maugham's "The Treasure" he calls the childlike "pleasure of storying" (*PEL*, p. 91), by which Trilling means the delight one takes in simply telling or seeing simply told an ingenious story for its own sake.

But the selection and arrangement of the anthology's contents, often unusual and not always chronological, are entirely Trilling's own doing, and so suggest this reflexive intention at some level of his mind.

In addition, the prefaces to John O'Hara's "Summer's Day" and Camus's "The Guest" belie my facile exercise in self-suspicion. The former story, as Trilling claims, contrives a poignant contradiction between the snobbery of inherited social status and the reality of procreative power, as Mr. Attrell, the social lion, must recognize at last that Mr. O'Donnell, the frustrated social climber he deeply insulted, is indeed his superior in a most important respect (*PEL*, p. 159). That is, Mr. O'Donnell, unlike Mr. Attrell, still has sons and heirs to carry on the name (Mr. Attrell's only son, we are told early on, committed suicide). For a critic who repeatedly and with increasing vehemence writes off his own professional heirs as the decade of the 1960s hurtles on, such a concern for posterity must be confronted at least on a symbolic level, as I submit it is here. Consider, as well, the ominous conclusion of "The Guest" where Camus's Algerian antihero and lover of the desert discovers how a "single involvement of feeling will implicate" one in "a future of human involvements" that ever threaten to destroy one's independence: "Daru has learned," Trilling says, "that an instinctive impulse of compassion for a fellow-being will lead to his expulsion from the austere Eden of his solitude" (*PEL*, p. 169). Or, as the priest of savage civility already knows, every immortal passion recovered from the great dead entails a mortifying if not mortal ecstasy of the critical reader. Consequently, perhaps it would be better to remain in "the austere Eden" of scholarly solitude than to achieve a literary value in the world by plying the trade among students and colleagues who can see only the mythic husk of one's reputation and not the person it masks.

It is, however, the introductions to poems that he has rarely if ever previously invoked in his long career which provide the most cogent evidence, I think, for the autobiographical allegory I find ironically pervading Trilling's *Prefaces to the Experience of Literature*. In opening the poetry section with "Edward," a fifteenth-century anonymous ballad about a patricide undertaken at a mother's behest, Trilling not only parallels but "tops" his openings for the earlier fiction and drama segments or transgresses his own transgressive code. For these other sections begin respectively with Hawthorne's "My Kinsman, Major Molineux," and, of course, Sophocles' *Oedipus Rex*. The autobiographical oedipal dimension of this selection and arrangement thus extends beyond self-conscious allusion to Trilling's Freudian origins as a major literary critic, down to the present act of the critic in the process of composing these prefaces in this way.

Similarly, other of these poetic prefaces reflect equally on Trilling's career-long as well as present concerns. This is why, for Trilling, Wyatt's "They Flee Me" and Dickinson's "Go Tell It!—What a Message" have as much to do with the decline of the masculine ideal in the postclassical, postmedieval world as with their ostensible subjects of lost love (*PEL*, p. 187) and the heroic sacrifice of the Spartans at "Sweet Thermopylae" (*PEL*, p. 268). In this same fashion Donne's "Valediction Forbidding Mourning" and Milton's *Lycidas* are praised by Trilling for the self-consciously strong effects of their masculine styles. Despite Dr. Johnson's pointed critiques of both poets, Donne pleases his reader, Trilling counters, precisely because he takes one aback with that coldly geometric conceit for passionate devotion (*PEL*, p. 193) which has encompassed so much critical history within its span; and Milton, for Trilling, triumphs over his lack of genuine grief for Edward King, by means of his imperious mastering of all the stops he plays, subsuming all beneath the invulnerable weight of his own immaculate conception of himself as poet (*PEL*, p. 208). In this self-ruthless fashion, Trilling's poetic heroes achieve their sublime status as classics of our literature by defeating their own "feminine" gift for pathos.

The chief engine of such empowering self-defeats is, not surprisingly, the great poet's ironic dialectic of sublime and realistic effects: what the preface to Marvell's "To His Coy Mistress," on the one hand, calls "the force of a metaphor" which "does not depend on its visual explicitness" but on "the awesomeness of the great vague trope" that the poet invokes (*PEL*, p. 205); and, on the other hand, what the preface to the *Essay on Man* celebrates as the antithetical virtues of "precision," "regularity," "uniformity," and "balance" (*PEL*, p. 207) which the virtuoso performer can put to good use in developing a rational theodicy of Father, Judge, and King. That is, as the preface to Hopkin's "The Leaden Echo and the Golden Echo" spells out, Trilling sees the poet's function to be the creation of "a religious conceit" (*PEL*, p. 264)—and not a religious idea—of God the Father. For such a patriarchal conceit can help to subdue *hysterica passio*, and grant even opium-eating Coleridge enough "transcendent strength" to take pleasure, for "a climactic moment in 'Kubla Khan'" (*PEL*, p. 231), in all of life including the prospect of madness or death.

The point of Trilling's aversion to the passive and allegedly feminine aspects of the imagination becomes, paradoxically enough, more manifest in his later discussions of negative capability, that passive attending upon the event of poetic inspiration, which resists the hysterical route out of the emotional impasses that chronically accompany all anxiously imposed constraints. According to Trilling, for instance, such a strong or wise passiveness informs Yeats's successful attempt, beginning in "Sailing to Byzantium," "to make his own [tragic] representation of himself as an aging man a chief element of his creation." For Yeats thereby "added a whole stage of life to man's existence." In "his passionate resentment" of old age, he made the world feel its "resinous power" (*PEL*, p. 269). Trilling's curious celebration of the tired universalized diction that ironically animates Frost's "Neither Out Far nor In Deep" (*PEL*, p. 284) explains this emphasis on Yeats's singular achievement. Trilling is reading his own characteristic later style and his own highest hope for that style into these discussions of Frost and Yeats. He would like nothing better than to use his generalizing allusive style of allegorical self-reference to add his own patriarchal representations of himself to the canon of great critics. I submit that his elaborate conclusion to the e.e. cummings preface champions the poet's power "to startle us," "to make the old words . . . shed their commonplaces" and "shine with the freshness of invention" (*PEL*, p. 290), because this power, "analogous with the beneficent workings of Nature," which cummings attributes to his own father, virtually transforming him into "some pagan fertility god"—this poetic power of Father Nature betrays Trilling's own secret desire for himself as much as it alludes to "My Father Moved through Dooms of Love" (*PEL*, p. 290), about which I have already spoken at some length in the first chapter.

The central motive for critical work in the humanist tradition has never been more clearly or succinctly exposed as in Trilling's preface to e. e. cummings' poem "My Father Moved through Dooms of Love." The poem itself is most memorable insofar as it occasions the revelation. For this motive, despite the modern displacements of the Judeo-Christian mythos, remains religious through and through. As in Isaac Babel's story of the painter Pan Apolek who portrays Christ in the scandalous image of a persecuted Polish Jew—Trilling's ruined father, one recalls, came from Bialystok on the ever-shifting Polish border—the critical humanist in his sublimely ironic writing envisions (in symbolic form) the resurrection of the great dead, both personal and cultural, the personal via the cultural, and thereby also creates for himself the public identity of secular savior whose imaginative career is necessarily one of redemptive sacrifice for and magnanimous celebration of the Other still alive in the critical subject. Jesus Christ took on the form of a servant, and in this form brought a new kingdom to the earth. The critical humanist would do likewise, aesthetically, and so usher in a cultural renaissance. This is one of the things Trilling means by the phrase from the Babel essay "a new species of reality."

As we saw in "The Fate of Pleasure" and the other essays collected in *Beyond Culture*, Trilling and his generation come at the end of this tradition of critical humanism in America, during a time when its very success as an institution, a discipline, a way of life—as an adversary culture—is threatening to bring about its catastrophic defeat. As we will see, Trilling increasingly identifies the culprits in this fatal development as the counterculture and its academic prophets and fellow travelers. Self-indictment is an easy thing for a critical cold warrior to do who comes to imaginative maturity during the McCarthy era, but does not really make for accurate judgments. Rather what Trilling has to say in "The Fate of Pleasure" and elsewhere about the systematic transfer of competitive energies from the bourgeois world to the "spiritual" or intellectual sphere of academic life does bear on this matter. For Trilling a generation ago was already discerning in the professional institutionalization of international modernism the wholesale destruction and replacement of Renaissance humanism as an effective ideology and as a possible way of life. (In America, of course, it barely took hold anyway, and then, in this century, only among ever smaller enclaves of critics who continued to look to Europe for their intellectual orientation and inspiration.) That the high-modernist writers, thinkers, and artists would be appalled by this development of their culture into the aesthetic ideology of the imperial multinational corporation goes without saying. If the prefaces to *The Experience of Literature* so far discussed constitute an autobiographical allegory of Lionel Trilling, our last critical humanist, a kind of critical novel, ironic typology, and comic anatomy of the spirtual career of our time, the rest of them both complete the story and serve as Trilling's rueful celebration of the great modernist dead amidst a savage critique of the tragic historical fate they have suffered and inspired. In this radically ambivalent manner, Trilling finally does become like one of Arnold's sublime heroes, finely resisting to the end the end that cannot be finally resisted.

Trilling celebrates the dark society of the great modern dead for their apparently inexhaustible power of self-revision which ever added new stages to their developments and to their representations of human existence. They possessed, in other words, the ability to turn not only against the internalized perceptions and judgments of their changing milieu but also against their own oppositional positions before they could become a personal form of intellectual orthodoxy, that is, before they could harden into academic formulas useful for ideological exploitation. Like Babel's, their ironic work, in short, remains primarily a work of individual liberation in behalf of their "fathers." Such work would construct "a new species of reality."

This does not mean, however, that Trilling suddenly resolves his radical ambivalence toward the moderns or toward modernism. Trilling has special scorn for the aesthetic ideology of the critical institution that has been called into existence by the bewilderment of the would-be "progressive" middle class before the avant-garde masterpieces. In this sense, Trilling emulates his ideal of the self-made modern revisionist who turns against his own earlier positions when the need arises to do so: when they are no longer really *his* positions, whether they have also been adopted now by others or not. Yet in another sense, Trilling, as we have seen, has always had reservations about the effects of the great modern classics, reservations inseparable from his admiration for them, even as they are quite separable from the disdain he directs at modernism's academic institutionalization, with its own demonically parodic effect on America's literary intellectuals.

In part, of course, this is just a matter of resenting the metamorphosis of the cult classics of one's youth into the fodder of the undergraduate curriculum. Yet Trilling has a larger point to make as well. In so far as the great modern works of Yeats, Eliot, Joyce, Lawrence, Proust, James, Mann, and Kafka, in their formally subversive negations of the established social order, challenge the reader to think critically, passionately, about this order and the works that so challenge its authority, Trilling then can continue to admire the moderns. But, increasingly, for his students and for him, these modernist classics evoke nothing more than a perfunctory response of familiar recognition and hollow-sounding praise. The acceptance of the unacceptable, the socialization of the antisocial, has led to the degradation of the great modern dead, and insofar as they have come to stand for the tradition, this decadent development is rapidly incorporating the entire realm of the past. It is this academic emasculation of modernism, of high culture generally, as well as the spectacle of modernism in the streets during the student and antiwar rebellions of 1968, that lead Trilling himself to cast an increasingly cold eye on the traditional Western notion, so influential in transforming the world since the Renaissance and the Enlightenment, that the pursuit of knowledge will bring about fundamental communal and/or individual changes for the ultimate good of all. In other words, the opposition between modernism and the liberal imagination, as well as its grand ancestor that Freud best contains, the opposition between romanticism and rationalism, becomes more and more for Trilling now a single monumental identity so terribly threatening to life itself he must even turn in the end against higher education. The growing, apparently conservative cast to Trilling's thought (as represented, for example, by "Mind in the Modern World") can be explained in this context. The work of liberation that Trilling would ever perform in his career is, to the extent that any one person can do so, to mediate the conflict between the revolutionary principle and the conservative instinct within himself and within that admittedly limited portion of society which his writings and teaching can in fact affect. The aim, as always, is to become ennobled by wrestling with the angel in the work, and in return giving thanks for one's blessed wounds. "Our typical experience of a work, which will eventually have an authority with us," Trilling observes in "The Fate of Pleasure," "is to begin our relation to it at a conscious disadvantage, and to wrestle with it until it consents to bless us. We express our high esteem for such a work by supposing that it judges us" (*BC*, p. 62). And just as certainly, Trilling clearly adds, we dread the moment "when it no longer does seem to judge us, or when it no longer baffles and resists, when we begin to feel that we possess it, we discover that its power is diminished" (*BC*, p. 62). That is, it is not only our "fathers" who move through dooms of love, we "heirs" do so, too. The work of liberation Trilling would perform is to discover ways in which we and our students can continue to wrestle with the great dead by resurrecting new reasons for our love even if it means perversely arguing against education itself.

Of the twenty-odd prefaces to *The Experience of Literature* that remain, approximately half bear most immediately and powerfully on this theme, so ironic for a critical humanist to sound, especially in an anthology intended for undergraduate use. Three dramatic prefaces— to *The Wild Duck*, *The Three Sisters*, and *Purgatory*—movingly celebrate the magnanimity of mind that Ibsen, Chekhov, and unlikeliest of all, late Yeats each display by recognizing that the disease of modernity is the desire to impose upon life, or even, in the Yeatsian instance, upon the afterlife, a single rule of one's own invention which we christen the truth.

The secularized, postromantic form of spirituality, as Trilling after Hegel in *The Philosophy of History* characterizes it, invests the demystification of reality and the discovery of truth—in the sense of what underlies all illusions of personal distinction and social piety—with the moral prestige and authority once reserved to the church and expected solely of leading members of the ruling classes. The rest of society was, of course, to live unselfconsciously by habit, custom, and convention. Since the Enlightenment, however, the revolutionary principle of modernity in intellectual life has taken the form of a quest for truth, even the truth that there is no truth, no matter what the personal or communal costs. In place of the church and religion as the custodians of ethical norms, intellectuals—"playwrights, novelists, poets, and philosophers" (*PEL*, p. 36)—and their subversive creations and the ideologies of their disciples have come to dominate our lives in the form of the monumental influences of our sublime educators.

One consequence of this modern development, Trilling adds, has been the aspiration of ever larger numbers of people to the unconventional life of artistic genius, moral authority, and intellectual autonomy. The materials for tragic and comic irony thus abound given the rise of the intelligentsia to power in this sense. As little Father Time's suicide note in Hardy's *Jude the Obscure* puts it, "Alas, we were too menny."

Ibsen and Yeats choose to dramatize the tragic and Chekhov the comic pathos of this development. The plots of the plays are familiar. Gregers Werle in *The Wild Duck*, demonic educator made in the Ibsenite image, decides to take Hjalmar Ekdele at his word, that he is a wronged man of unfulfilled genius. Werle tells Ekdele finally that his wife and daughter are not originally his own but, respectively, the former mistress and actual offspring of Werle's own father. Now that Ekdele knows the truth, Werle feels, he is free to confront reality and demonstrate his true status as one of the unsung heroes of the modern spirit. Like the tragic wild duck in the artificial forest that Ekdele's father keeps in the garret for the pleasure of the avowed illusion, however, the would-be heroic son cannot stand very much reality. Similarly, Yeats's protagonist, incorporating demonic seducer and tragic victim in one character, decides that, to liberate his mother's ghost from the purgatorial remembering of her living passions, he must put an end to the crime of generation by reenacting the previous murder of his own father in the present killing of his own son. The result of this violent imposition of one old man's deranged will upon the living and the dead is the perpetuation of his mother's and now his own agony. Finally, while Chekhov exploits the pre-Revolutionary pathos of the Russian provincial intelligentsia for all it's worth, the vivacity of his style and the final heroic affirmation of life by his female protagonists does indeed make *The Three Sisters* into a comedy. More important, in the dark light of his own imminent death Chekhov in so contriving this climax exemplifies most successfully of these three modern playwrights the shocking celebration of the magnanimous mind. Such a mind, as Trilling explains, would live life as "the speeches at the end of *The Three Sisters* suggest it must be lived: without the expectation of joy, yet in full attachment, and cherishing what may be cherished, even if that is nothing more than the idea of life itself" (*PEL*, p. 36). One detects in these words, and even more in those that immediately follow, Trilling's own quiet avowal to make his soul, as Yeats would say, before the end comes. "A man of affectionate disposition upon whom death had had its hand would probably not be concerned with making a rational or prudential judgment upon life: more likely he would be moved to wonder if a transcendent judgment might not be made" (*PEL*, p. 36).

In order to understand what Trilling means by "a transcendent judgment" of life as opposed to "a rational or prudential" one, I think we must examine his insistence in the preface to *Purgatory* that Yeats sincerely believed in the reality of the afterlife as dramatized there and expounded in *A Vision*. Once Trilling accepted Yeats's occult conviction, he admits, he saw this otherwise merely violent and presumptuous play as being, "like *Oedipus Rex* and *King Lear*, a tragic confrontation of destiny, less grand than its predecessors but not less intense" (*PEL*, p. 53). In fact, Trilling also admits to a fascination with Yeats's account of the soul in judgment:

> According to *A Vision*, the career of the soul after death is complex, but to understand *Purgatory* it is enough to know that after the soul is separated from the body at death it is not separated from its passions, its pains, and—this is of particular importance to the play—from the consequences of its actions during life. In order to achieve freedom, the soul must purge away these elements of its fleshly existence that still remain in its imagination. It accomplishes this by returning to its fleshly experiences, seeking to understand them and to disengage itself from them. The process—it has something of the aspect of a spiritual psychoanalysis—can, Yeats tells us, go on for a very long time. He says that where the soul has great intensity and where the consequences of its passions have affected great numbers of people, the process of purging its passion and its experience "may last with diminishing pain and joy for centuries." But in the work of liberation, the dead can be aided by the living, who are able, Yeats says, "to assist the imaginations of the dead." (*PEL*, p. 54)

As Helen Vendler demonstrates in her early book on Yeats's *A Vision* and the later poetry written in its occult shadow, one can discover there amidst its esoteric theories of historical change and personality development the makings of a visionary poetics. So, too, I want to suggest that in Trilling's positive formulation of Yeats's beliefs here we can discover the final form of the allegory of reading sustaining his entire critical career.

The mind of the critic in encountering the continuing force of style in past works of genius assists the imaginations of the dead in a kind of spiritual psychoanalysis, a work of liberation. By completing their passions in his later understanding of them, the critic frees his mind from its merely rational or prudential concerns and thus is able to identify with their transcendent judgments, such as Chekhov's sublime acceptance of the idea of life in all its complex unruly fullness, or Yeats's at the conclusion of "A Dialogue of Self and Soul," or, for that matter, like its model, Neitzsche's repeated *amor fati* in *The Gay Science* and his later texts.

I know some of the major objections to this view. It makes Trilling, of all modern critics the least likely, into a epigone of Yeats. It contradicts his later praise of the rational intellect as a corrective to the excesses of the literary imagination. It represents him as a pseudoreligious figure, prototype of the New Right. Or, worse yet, it exposes all too clearly the pernicious ideological silliness of critical humanism that would recommend that we waste time on such projects as understanding dead authors when we have a living world to save (or at least our portion of it) from the hegemonic clutches of the powers that be. The most immediately potent objection, however, because it would subvert the project of critical humanism no matter how conceived, is that raised by the recent debates over the canon and the politics of interpretation.[12]

The arguments against the traditional canon of authors and masterpieces in modern literary study are as persuasive as they are self-evident. The works we study have been selected by the profession over the years because they either reflect or at least don't seriously challenge the self-interests of the professionals concerned and the larger culture which supports them and supports their institutions and publications for its own seductively coercive purposes of eliciting the consent of the diverse peoples—both here and abroad—it would govern and the minds it would colonize. Consequently, members of previously excluded and, to varying degrees, still excluded or marginalized groups cannot see themselves represented in the works the academy privileges for study and replication or in those the larger culture promotes among the masses. That is, the canon does not represent excluded or marginalized peoples in the ways they would wish to see themselves and their chosen if neglected precursors represented. Finally, this hegemony of the canon, reinforced by an equally repressive metaphysics of presence, the phallologocentric philosophical ideology of Western culture, must and is already being fundamentally, deconstructively, and historically subverted by critical argument, the growing weight of numbers, and an institutional reformation that will make possible, it is presumed, an authentic and sustained tradition of radical critique that can help to lead one day to the revolutionary transformation of American society for the ultimate benefit of all the world's people. In short, the old gang will be gone sooner or later.

If this argument, which sounds to me as visionary as Yeats's poetics of the dead, is taken seriously, Trilling's entire career, indeed the entire project of critical humanism, whether conceived along the lines I suggested or according to an even more questionable notion of "cultural literacy,"[13] makes no sense at all. Indeed, Trilling's representative work of liberation would appear to be thoroughly obscurantist, repressive, and destructive of life—one's own and the lives of untold many.

This argument against the kind of critical humanism Trilling supposedly embodies in his career is not, however, as strong or subtle as one of its most recent ironic variants. In its strong form, this revisionary argument claims that from Immanuel Kant to Edward Said the rhetoric and institution of critical humanism, in both its conservative and its oppositional manifestations, enshrine the figure of the leading intellectual in an arrogant position as the sublime educator of the species. Such an egregious act of political self-interest and professional self-promotion, which obviously obscures the facts of power and how it actually operates in modern society, stands as much in the way of the possibilities of genuine progress toward increased self-determination for people in this country and its "colonies" as does the traditional politics of canon formation or the superannuated "man-of-letters" ethos to which Trilling, among others, subscribes.[14]

Like the arguments of purely deconstructive critics, of sixties counterculturalists, or of the intellectual grandfathers of us all—the left-wing radicals of the 1930s of Trilling's generation who later became cold-war liberal anti-Communists and apologists for America during the Age of Conformity and the blacklist—all these latest arguments against the canon magnify the significance of an academic matter (what is taught in the classroom) to world-historical status. They also repress the most painfully intense reality that any of us must repeatedly face: the recognition that we are not geniuses.

It doesn't take a latter-day Tocqueville, or even a Harold Bloom, to demonstrate to us how compulsive enmity and resentment inspire the American dream. Our success in our chosen field of endeavor is often purchased at the expense of all other considerations and regardless of all personal or public costs. Yet, it will be argued, this underside of the American dream, like the traditional notion of genius to which our popular press and middlebrow journals still pay lip service, is an ideological derivative of the more fundamental hegemonic construct of the self, of the bourgeois subject, whose now self-conscious and so postmodern sense of fictional individuality ensures the defeat of long-term collective action and of the pursuit of merely individual happiness as well. If each of us feels that, as Emerson in "Experience" exults, he or she is an infinitely repellent orb touching another at one point only and that only passingly in a lifetime of otherwise solitary splendor, then to "fictionalize" this ideology of individualism and disperse it into various networks of discursive practices diminishes rather than increases the possibilities for an effective public sphere, subsuming the latter in a fatalistic vision of linguistic and institutional power.[15]

Of course, none of us can live like Emerson, not even Emerson did. Nor do any of us live as if that French import, the critique of the subject, makes the reality of our selves on a daily basis any less real, even as it indeed makes the discussion of the self in contemporary intellectual circles much more problematic and abstract.[16] In fact, this ideology of the purely positional subject, whose identity is entirely the function of its position at the moment in the overlapping networks of language, desire, ideology, and the conditions of economic production, fulfills Trilling's most dreaded prophecies in his late work, that the disintegration of self facilitates the manufacture of interchangeable psyches or social roles, a development that is all too appropriate for the media society of the spectacle. The transformation of the monumental conception of genius into the freely circulating images of celebrity, of tradition versus fashion, is only one case in point.[17]

Regardless of these important complications, I think the experience of reading still can disclose the reality of the self, and not solely in a negative way. Informing the reading experience, at first naively and later with greater professional discipline and sophistication, is a horizon of interest (among other interests) that takes as its object of concern how well or how badly the author performs or simply is "the function of articulation" we are experiencing. (I would say "the mind" we are encountering but that would be too provocative.) As in our reactions of pleasure to the lovers we select, the latent genealogical dimensions of the experience—the questions of who formed, and to what end, "our" norms of judgment, and such like questions—are foregrounded, become significant, only when we feel so overwhelmed and threatened by an activity we originally chose to engage in that we need analytic distance to preserve our "selves." The creation of this analytic distance permits the release of all our pent-up resentment over the freedom we have "willingly" surrendered until now. This emotional dynamic of domination and resentment underwrites the reading experience known as the sublime, and speculatively theorized in a variety of ways.[18]

My little phenomenological sketch of the reading experience is intended to highlight antithetically the originary phase of this experience of being uniquely imposed upon, of having just our sense of self delightfully usurped in just this manner for the time we choose to read, so that we appreciate this particular force of style we would like for our own, and would emulate it where we can or mock and subvert it where we can't. For Trilling throughout his career, as we have seen, and particularly here in the *Prefaces*, it is the first appreciative sense of the force of style that dominates the dialectic of response, making the image of the magnanimous mind of the critic his primary source of pleasure. Trilling's "fate of pleasure," the pleasure that singles him out and judges him, whose normative power has all but disappeared in intellectual life, is thus this magnanimous vision of the mind that overcomes its own resistances, its disbelief in the reality and individuality of the Other, even to the point of willing self-sacrifice.

Since the 1960s especially, I would submit, we have now had several generations of academic readers who resist this central experience of reading by repressing their recognition of genius, of the usurping power in the text they espouse, solely to further this or that professional end or "political" goal. The "greater" the goal, of course, the more excusable the means, no matter how mean-spirited the latter may be. No longer able really to love what they now merely use and once wanted to devote their lives to studying, they make a living out of destroying the intellectual sources of joy in others, specifically their student-disciples, all in the exalted name of more power of self-determination for the people. In essence, the demonic educator in Ibsen's *Wild Duck* is the great-grandfather, in Trilling's view, of the increasingly prevalent character type of the postmodern critic, what I would call the "genius" of resentment.

I use Trilling here to summon this genius of resentment, however, not to blame the marked decline in the public tone of American intellectual life upon certain "spirits of revenge."[19] I don't doubt that the poor in spirit we will ever have with us. Rather, I hope that Trilling's lifelong devotion to an imaginative career as a critical humanist that has as its regulative ideal the magnanimous vision of mind can serve as stark contrast to the contemporary scene where, as I have already suggested, the possibility of even envisioning what he may mean by his praise of Ibsen's "magnanimous mind" has virtually disappeared.[20] For this contrast highlights the deteriorating conditions of intellectual production, as academic life since the "liberation" of the 1960s, ironically enough, has increasingly come under the rule of the bottom line.

What we have been remarking in Trilling's *Prefaces*, then, and what explicitly emerges as the systematic argument in those remaining, is actually the guiding quality of his career. Trilling always attempts (if sometimes fails) to discover under the impetus of the force of style that gives him pleasure in reading a work whether or not, or the degree to which, an author's mind as apparently expressed there is able to transcend not the human condition or historical circumstances—the apocalyptic illusion of imperial selves—but its own beliefs, so as to recognize the cogency, the beautiful necessity, even the real genius, of another mind and its beliefs. As Hegel argues in *The Phenomenology of Mind*, and Arnold in "The Function of Criticism" observes in Edmund Burke's admission of the desirability (as well as inevitability) of liberation, the drive to achieve a mutual recognition of this kind, however deferred and mediated by discourse, can be a world-historical phenomenon of revolutionary impact.[21] While the Aristotelian vision of the golden mean between excess and privation is the obvious classical source for this ethic of magnanimity, the immediate influence upon Trilling for his conception of the liberal imagination's quest for true nobility of mind is, as I have earlier argued, the Judeo-Christian tradition of ascetic self-denial and sacrifice—of "kenosis"—as translated and moderated by Freud and the doctrines of psychoanalysis.[22]

Magnanimous Mind: The End of Reading

One could construct an ethical typology of the magnanimous mind from the remaining prefaces, with examples drawn from various authors whose works represent the tragic excess or absence of self-sacrifice in their protagonists. Hawthorne's "My Kinsman, Major Molineux" demonstrates the ambivalent necessity to sacrifice, according to Trilling, our familial ties, at least until we can establish a sense of identity, otherwise we remain forever dependent or forever rebellious (*PEL*, p. 72). (The prodigal son motif seems decisive here.) If Hawthorne's tale establishes a mean, however disquieting, then Melville's "Bartleby the Scrivener" represents for Trilling the fatal excess of self-sacrifice, as both Marx's theory of alienating reification and Freud's theory of suicidal depression help him to see. As we have seen, Bartleby has radically internalized the social world he is radically alienated from. The social world is now the specter of his abandoned-object identifications. This specter defines a major portion of his psychic life. His decision "to prefer not to," even to the point of death, therefore, would sacrifice his actual life so as to cast off this symbolic demon that has been possessing him. Bartleby's ultimate destruction, then, is also ironically his triumphant liberation (*PEL*, pp. 76–77).

Antithetical to both this mean and this excess of noble mind, "The Grand Inquisitor" section from Dostoyevsky's *Brothers Karamazov* represents perfectly, Trilling finds, Kant's sense of "Radical Evil," in which we aspire to do good in order really to rule others. This fable demonstrates not only the title character's generous lack of authentic magnanimity, despite his "humane" avowals, but, as well, the radical absence of magnanimity in the Christian messiah as imagined by the creator of that Underground Man who has become a legendary character in modern society precisely because he is totally devoid of the magnanimous vision of others (*PEL*, p. 83). We can see Trilling moving throughout his *Prefaces* along the imaginary graph of possible responses that these three stories plot and making the necessary discriminations and judgments among characters, authors, and texts according to the standard of noble self-sacrifice and what it may require to live by its imperatives. Let me be clear about this: the typology of the literary mind in Trilling's *Prefaces* does not take the form of a systematic, logically articulated treatise in value theory but appears in the implicit comparisons that pragmatically arise as Trilling makes his major distinctions between the kind of mind that would impose its vision on others for their own good (Kant's Radical Evil) and the kind embodied in the works of artists whose imaginative generosity of feeling may be read from the freedom of response their works grant the reader. Such artists may inspire emulation but if so it is their ability to see things in more than one way that is emulated. Conrad's "Secret Sharer," for example, a natural for the master of spectral politics, tests the limits of imaginative sympathy with another mind even as it darkly suggests, as Trilling explains, that "Leggatt's fatal violence . . . constitutes the ideality" (*PEL*, p. 169) to which the protagonist aspires. The reason Conrad's young sea captain recognizes in the murderous other captain a kindred spirit for whose escape he risks his crew's safety and his own life and reputation is that they share a secret: mastery of the ultimately coercive force of psychical violence is "the disconcerting secret that the young captain undertakes to hide from the crew" (*PEL*, p. 111), for it is the secret "concealed at the heart of all authority" (*PEL*, p. 111). That is, nobility of mind arises in part from an intimate awareness of destructive repression.

"The Secret Sharer" suggests how far one must go by way of imaginative sympathy if one is to perfect a self. On the other hand, Forster's "The Road from Colonus," with its echoes of Sophocles' late play *Oedipus at Colonus*, laments the intervention of well-intentioned others in the chosen course of one's life. Mr. Lucas is one for whom the prospect of death beneath the "tree-shine," in "a moment of transcendence," possesses a curious healing power. He would in fact have suffered the ultimate panacea when the central tree of the village square is struck by lightning and falls, if his imperviously devoted daughter, Ethel, had not whisked him away before the sweet disaster could occur. "When Mr. Lucas is led down the road" from Colonus, Trilling observes, "we know that he has been deprived of his salvation" (*PEL*, p. 130). Mr. Lucas may be no belatedly vulnerable Oedipus but his daughter is certainly no greatly devoted Antigone.

The idea of death, one can see, affords Mr. Lucas a momentary sense of transcendence that rises in its intensity to a loving acceptance of life without his presence. The mortal ecstasy, expressive of an immortal passion, bears a strong family resemblance to the aesthetic attitude of Professor Cornelius, the protagonist of Mann's "Disorder and Early Sorrow." The difference between those two aesthetic responses, however, is more significant than any perceived similarity. For Professor Cornelius, a scholar of history, cannot accept the present as it is, nor the future of passion and rebellion that is emerging for his beloved young daughter. Rather than embrace, as Mr. Lucas would do, the idea of his own passing, Professor Cornelius would instead supress time itself, freezing the present moment, if he could, seeing it forever in its arrested development as a Keatsian vision of marmoreal perfection. Professor Cornelius himself recognizes at last how severely neurotic this response is, as he rightly associates it with no longer quite re-pressed incestuous feelings for his own daughter. If Gregers Werle from Ibsen's *Wild Duck* represents for Trilling the demonic intellectual mode of the revolutionary principle, then Professor Cornelius embod-ies the perversely life-denying love of the dead past that Trilling iden-tifies as the decadent form of "the conservative instinct" (*PEL*, p. 135). Whenever, as here, he employs naturalistic rhetoric for a social phe-nomenon, Trilling is alluding to Freud's idea from *Beyond the Pleasure Principle* that all living forms seek death, each in its own way, striving to restore an earlier state of existence, that of inorganic matter. Profes-sor Cornelius possesses too much of this conservative instinct. This psychoanalytic translation of a social reality does not try to explain the immediate interests of the conservative mind-set in general, only the original genesis (self-love) and the ultimate goal (nonlife), which on a powerful mythic level serves as a supremely cautionary tale, I think, for all concerned.

The literary ethics of the magnanimous mind in these prefaces con-stitutes Trilling's vision of what an effective moral agent would have to be like if the paralyzing modern impasse between the revolutionary principle and the conservative instinct in all their diverse conflicting manifestations might become an empowering dialectic of imaginative development toward an exemplary achievement of nobility in personal style. This is the work of liberation that he attempts to perform throughout his career. That Trilling fails often enough in the attempt I have shown; that this vision of the magnanimous mind has its severe limitations and self-deceptions should be by now evident. Nonetheless I find it a desirable aim for the intellectual life that should not be lost sight of or mocked in our struggle to carve out a career and make the world ready for revolution.

It is of special significance, I think, that it is the aesthetic view of life, so much maligned these days for its alleged necessary complicity with the status quo in the profession or in the culture at large, that enables Trilling to imagine for himself a mode of moral agency that, ever mindful of the claims of past and future, nevertheless makes room for the selective appreciation of the present moment. Trilling's desire is thus not really for what Stevens self-mockingly calls utopia, a perpetual "holiday in reality." And the critical commentaries to two later fiction entries, Isaac Babel's "Di Grasso: A Tale of Odessa" and Bernard Malamud's "The Magic Barrel," offer strong testimony in support of this contention, counterpointing perfectly the incestuous aesthetics of the conservative instinct in its fatal decline that pervade the Mann tale.

"Di Grasso," a thinly veiled autobiographical story from *Red Cavalry*, dramatizes how, in Trilling's view, the "disciplined violence" of art can grant even to the least likely person an aesthetic experience which, in inspiring an act of moral decency, leads to another person's transcendent, virtually mystical vision. In a performance of an otherwise crude popular melodrama, Di Grasso, the leading figure in an itinerant troupe of actors and once famed for his Shakespearean impersonations, suddenly gives a smile, soars into the air, sails across the entire stage, brings down the villain "having bitten through the latter's throat," amidst growls and grimaces begins "to suck blood from the wound" (*PEL*, p. 138). This "great murderous leap," which with its extraordinary "power of levitation" Trilling likens to one of Nijinski's, represents in its most primitive form the saving spectacle of "noble passion," of great impulse, overriding mere convention. One heroic leap of a provincial virtuoso thus suggests the idea of liberation from the weight of social circumstances, even from the human condition itself. Aesthetic illusion, recognized as such, still gives pleasure.

For Di Grasso's climactic leap, Trilling shows, unexpectedly occasions in the grotesque wife of the ticket speculator a recognition of "all large-minded emotions" that her husband lacks. On learning that he has spitefully been keeping a pocket watch that belongs to the father of his assistant who narrates the story, the now enraged wife in an act of moral decency forces its return. The final result of this sequence, however, comes after the narrator-assistant feels released from his adolescent anguish over the fate of his father's watch. He experiences a transcendent vision of his hometown, "for the first time" seen with "a distinctiveness such as he had never before experienced," with all the things appearing around him "as they really were: frozen in silence and ineffably beautiful" (*PEL*, p. 140).

Thus, as Trilling formulates the action of the story, an "aesthetic experience has produced an act of moral decency, the act of moral decency becomes the cause of a transcendent experience." And, as Trilling also concludes, this action that leads to "the pure and peaceful contemplation" in the last paragraph of the story originates in "the violence of the actor's leap" (*PEL*, p. 140).

One can read in Trilling's preface to Babel's "Di Grasso" the modern ideology of critical humanism. Art can redeem life thanks to the subtle subversive influences of its liberal imagination of noble or grand passion. And the literary critic is the one, of course, who best can mediate these influences by showing us what works of art generally mean. Yet this is only one level of the critical allegory at work in Trilling's preface. It matters, for instance, that it is a persecuted Jewish writer of Stalin's Russia whose story represents in an exemplary manner the humanistic vision of the critic; it also matters that Trilling discovers this vision here in the first place. More significantly, besides this aspect of sotto voce polemic, the preface also possesses an intimate personal dimension. It is not only that Trilling here rehearses once again his belief that "the act of creation is bound up with the aggressive impulses" (*PEL*, p. 137) and so reminds us that these prefaces compose the critical version of that novel about "the spiritual career of our time" he envisioned in "The Fate of Pleasure" for the novelist that is to come. It is also that what Trilling carefully reinscribes, in full awareness of all the ironies involved, and thereby brings back in displaced allegorical form, is "the sense of his and his people's origins" (*PEL*, p. 140).

Trilling's liberal acceptance of the idea of transcendent experience in its great variety is thus both a revelation about the latent "metaphysical" or religious foundations of his thinking and, more interestingly, the vehicle for insinuating a little more of the tragic history of his people into the experience of literature, of the canon. Finally, in stressing Babel's graphic depiction of the actor's "great murderous leap," Trilling permits the figure to suggest not merely the idea of liberation but that of a nursing vampire "sucking blood from the wound." He thereby prophetically represents the worst thing that critics of his practice and of humanism generally could ever say.

Trilling's *Prefaces*, as in this case, disclose why the rhetoric of the sublime master, of the magisterial intellect, serves a useful critical purpose. Especially in the humanities, recognition as such a figure can empower the critic to create opportunities for the representation of formerly excluded peoples.[23]

The preface to Malamud's "The Magic Barrel" tells why this function of the humanist deserves a measure of appreciation, not simply wholesale condemnation. The story describes the rendezvous of Leo Finkle and Stella Salzman that occurs finally over the vehement objections of the girl's orthodox father. The latter is a refugee from the Nazi destruction of European Jewry who would preserve the old strict ways in a strange new land where girls are not reproved as whorish for dressing in style and youthful passion is not automatically thought wrong. The story then follows Leo's mind as he awaits Stella, believing that their imminent transgression of the patriarchal code will mean his salvation as a man. The final scene of the story, another transcendent moment, imports the favorite imagery of Marc Chagal into the Riverside Drive scene to charmingly ironic effect, as "violins and lit candles [are] revolved in the sky" (*PEL*, p. 171).

"The Magic Barrel" thus allows Trilling not only to recall for his American student-readers Chagall's Jewish mysticism and the fates of the Holocaust victims but, as well, to identify the religious cultures and theocratic communities of Puritan New England and Eastern Europe. Such a critical strategy naturally suggests that Trilling himself is a belated, secular Jewish analogue of the current deracinated heirs of our original Founding Fathers. Beyond this symbolic act of self-legitimation, Trilling also provides some literary basis for America's identification with the Jewish people in exile and their permanent need for an "original" homeland.

Typically, however, Trilling subsumes these levels of professional, ethnic, religious, and historico-political allegory in the containing transcendent vision of the mind's magnanimous passion for "life." Although Trilling cites the Blake of *Innocence and Experience* as his traditional analogue, I am reminded in the following passages, especially in his imagination of the lovers becoming images, and every beloved image becoming body, more of Yeats from "The Phases of the Moon," the prefatory poem to his own *Vision* (1937):

> Much of the curious power and charm of "The Magic Barrel" is surely to be accounted for by the extraordinary visual intensity of a single paragraph, the last but one, which describes the rendezvous of Leo Finkle and Stella Salzman. The glare of the street lamp under which Stella stands, her white dress and red shoes, and also the red dress and white shoes that Leo had expected her to wear (for this too is envisioned), the bouquet of violets and rosebuds that Leo carries as

he runs toward her—these elements of light and color make a scene which is pictorial rather than (in the literal sense of the word) dramatic. Nothing is *said* by the lovers, the whole meaning of the moment lies in what is *seen*. Indeed, had a single word been uttered, the effect of the strange and touching tableau would have been much diminished. In their silence, the lovers exist only in the instant of their first sight of each other, without past or future, unhampered by those inner conditions which we call personality. They transcend personality, they exist in their essence as lovers, as images of loving. And our sense of their transcendence is strengthened by those "violins and lit candles" that revolve in the sky, as if the rendezvous were taking place not in the ordinary world but in a world of emblems, of metaphors made actual. . . .

For that Stella is sinful, that she is sin itself, is the judgment passed upon her by her father's tradition. Her father curses her, although he loves her, and he mourns her as dead because she is unchaste. He speaks of her as "wild," "without shame," "like an animal," even "like a god." And the young man, bred to the old tradition, is no less ready to recognize her sinfulness, although his image of sin is not repellent but attractive: he eagerly anticipates Stella's appearance in a red dress, red being the color of an open and shameless avowal of sexuality. Red may be the color of sin in general, as when the prophet Isaiah says, "Though your sins be scarlet, they shall be white as snow," but more commonly it represents sexual sin in particular—one of the synonyms the dictionary gives for *scarlet* is *whorish*.

The reader, of course, is not under the necessity of believing that Stella is what her father makes her out to be—possibly her sexual life is marked merely by a freedom of the kind that now morality scarcely reproves. Her dress is in fact not red but white, the virginal color; only her shoes are red. And in her eyes, we are told, there is a "desperate innocence." We see her not as Sin but as what William Blake called Experience, by which he meant the moral state of those who have known the passions and have been marked, and beautified, by the pain which that knowledge inflicts. This is the condition to which Leo Finkle aspires and which he calls his redemption. His meeting is with life itself, and the moment of the encounter achieves an ultimate rapture because of the awareness it brings him, like an illumination, that the joy and pain he had longed to embrace, and had been willing to embrace as sin, need not be condemned. (*PEL,* pp. 170; 173–174)

Trilling's appreciation for literary representations of so-called transcendent experiences can be explained away as the "naturally" sensitive response of an aging scholar to the prospect of his own demise. Yet the Wordsworthian resonance of these visions for Trilling, in which mind and nature reciprocally interact rather than apocalyptically war with each other, suggests that now as much as earlier in his career, Trilling imagines the intensities of aesthetic experience as occasions for passionate self-overcoming and not solely for the will's vain triumph. If the phrase "liberal imagination" means anything for Trilling more than the ironic lack of imagination on the part of the American left wing, it must mean this generous openness to the force of style already in our worldly surroundings, rather than a formal openness to some utopian future.

Trilling's *Prefaces* dramatize the possibilities of worldly response for the aspiring mind as it would work to achieve—for itself and for those others who find its influence beneficial—the liberation we all quest for both from the self-destructive form of resistance to the specious good that really serves no one's interests, and from the radical evil. As we have seen, the commentaries to "The Grand Inquisitor" and "Bartleby the Scrivener" illustrate these contrasting extremes in the Grand Inquisitor's total lack of self-sacrifice that sacrifices others in the name of the specious good and in Bartleby's excessive sacrifice that, however noble its intentions, clearly cannot be taken as a life model. As we have also seen, the vision of the magnanimous mind does entail a price for its realization. Hawthorne's "My Kinsman, Major Molineux" shows that severing the ties with family, and here symbolically with the father, is painful for all concerned, but the stylish moderation of the demonic laughter in Hawthorne's tale suggests the possibility for a further refinement into the purely comic mode. Similarly, although "The Secret Sharer" commentary argues that at the heart of authority over others lies the latent power to kill, it also suggests by the success of the Young Captain's quest that sympathetic identification with the feelings of others—those of Leggatt, of course, and of the crew as well—must also function if there are to be any successful communal ventures. "The Road to Colonus," however, shows how the excess of such identification can deny in the name of rational concern and filial piety the consummation for which another so devoutly wishes. Even more painfully, Trilling's comments on the fate of the conservative instinct in "Disorder and Early Sorrow" disclose how the quest for magnanimity can so easily become a tragic example of love of another based wholly on narcissistic impulses (and so not love at all), that would vainly seek to espouse and preserve what nothing can prevent from passing away: viz., all the images of assumed innocence. And finally, as Trilling's prefaces to Babel's "Di Grasso" and Malamud's "The Magic Barrel" argue, the type of transcendence, of self-overcoming, most noble and moving is that afforded by the disciplined violence of art as it gratuitously commemorates the complex spontaneous influences of human passion upon the world of everday life.

This celebratory contemplative mode of art that Trilling champions thus stands opposed to the exploitation of art in the modern competition for spiritual status that "The Fate of Pleasure" prophetically laments. It defines what Trilling means by the phrase in "Wordsworth and the Rabbis" he borrows from modern Jewish theology, "normal mysticism," by which he refers to Wordsworth's "conception of the world being semantic" and to the poet's "capacity for" taking "intense pleasure" in such a world of preestablished orders not of human making (*OS*, p. 126). Although the phrase comes to mean, as we shall see, something a little different in Trilling's final years—less the pleasure felt in contemplating the artistic representation of the nonhuman orders of the world and more the desperate faith in the power of such orders to resist the tyrannical will of modern civilization—it nevertheless helps to establish now the fullest context for understanding the complex irony of the finest single preface, that to Joyce's "The Dead." In Trilling's eyes, "The Dead" depicts the last nineteenth-century titan's climactic, magnanimous identification with his own creation, Gabriel Conroy, that prototypical modern intellectual, as the latter surrenders to the vision of the annihilating snow.

Trilling opens his preface with the final scene of "The Dead." Gabriel Conroy learns from his tearful wife, Gretta, that before coming to Dublin from the west of Ireland she had had the great tragic love affair of her life. The seventeen-year-old Michael Furey stood in the rain to sing for his beloved the ballad of "The Lass of Aughrim." This romantic act precipitates his final bout of consumption. "He died for the love of me," Gretta cries, and Gabriel realizes how all his married life he has been judged and rightly found wanting by a sublime standard embodied in this triumphant specter of heroic passion. Unable to love a woman so radically, incapable of the transcendent sacrifice of self required, Gabriel cries generous tears at last for his wife as she sleeps. As he now sees an apocalyptic snow fall faintly through the universe, "like the descent of their last end," he cries, too, for all the living and the dead.

Gabriel Conroy represents for Trilling one of those "creatures of modernity" (see the preface to Ibsen's *Wild Duck*, *PEL*, p. 26) for whom daily existence feels like a state of "death-in-life." Not content "to live by habit and routine and by the unquestioning acceptance of the circumstances into which they have been born" (*PEL*, p. 113), such people "believe they have the right to claim for themselves pleasure, or power, or dignity, or fullness of experience" (*PEL*, p. 113) once considered the sole prerogative of select members of the privileged classes. The psychological dilemma posed by this new situation of ever-rising expectations is acute. Insofar as we moderns feel "free to assert the personal claims which are the expression of a heightened sense of individuality" (*PEL*, p. 113), Trilling observes, we fall prey to a radical uncertainty about and a greatly diminished sense of personal identity. Increasingly, as Gabriel Conroy finds, only the "imagination of death" can provide "the image of life" (*PEL*, p. 114). The work of liberation necessitates a chronic work of mourning that few people at any time could bear, a mourning for the inevitable and perhaps desirable passing of all the works of the species.

Joyce's "The Dead" thus prophesizes the bitter development of the adversarial culture that is examined in *Beyond Culture* from the equally fictional standpoint of an internalized vestigial fragment of original nature not assimilated to or contaminated by social orthodoxies of one sort or another. Such "nature"—inseparable from "death"—individualizes one by the standard of the type and fate of pleasure that a person pursues as his or her highest value. In short, by the measure of each modern individual's characteristic way of dying. This prospect is chilling, to say the least, a kind of visionary or poetic anthropology of our Western death culture. Just imagine: an entire class of intellectuals, educators of the future, who aspire to the condition of that "old and rare species of man" (*PEL*, p. 114), the genius that, for example, animates a James Joyce, only to discover, if they are honest with themselves, that the best they can ever hope to become are avatars of Gabriel Conroy at the end. As Trilling classically phrases this emotional dilemma apropos Conroy: "he has the knowledge of excellence but cannot achieve it for himself; he admires distinction and cannot obtain it" (*PEL*, p. 114). The reason for his (and our) awful fate is that we belong to a new class, based on mental not economic capital, whose "large demand upon life," fostered originally by the revolutionary principle of modernity, is supported "neither by native gift nor moral energy" (*PEL*, p. 114). For a lifelong partisan of the aspiring mind ever resistant to the temptations to apocalyptic passions or totalitarian thinking, whose greatest desire was for recognition as a novelist of moral realism, this reading of "The Dead" sounds like his and his generation's tragic anagnorisis.

In claiming that Joyce spares his Conroy nothing of the knowledge of his own representative mediocrity, Trilling, we feel, is sparing himself (and us) nothing as well. Yet, as he brilliantly argues, the final vision of "The Dead," while relieving none of the pain of all these ironic resignations, also represents one of the greatest acts of self-overcoming imaginable: Joyce identifies with his prototypically "academic" protagonist and, through this generous act of genius, we do likewise, identifying with both sublime creator and his sad creation:

> This sudden identification of the author with his character is one of the most striking and effective elements of the story. Joyce feels exactly what Conroy feels about the sadness of human life, its terrible nearness to death, and the *waste* that every life is; he directs no irony upon Conroy's grief, but makes Conroy's suffering his own, with no reservations whatever. At several points in the story he has clearly regarded Conroy's language, or the tone of his thoughts, as banal, or vulgar, or sentimental. But as the story approaches its conclusion, it becomes impossible for us to know whose language we are hearing, Conroy's or the author's, or to whose tone of desperate sorrow we are responding. It is as if Joyce, secure in his genius and identity, were saying that under the aspect of the imagination of death and death-in-life there is no difference between him and the mediocre, sentimental man of whom he has been writing. (*PEL*, p. 117)

And so, through Joyce, does Trilling make Gabriel Conroy the great original of the modern American intellectual class.[24]

The spiritual competition between Michael Furey and Gabriel Conroy, however, can be thought to complicate this picture of sweet pathos. It could even be seen to extend to a mock singing contest between them—"The Lass of Aughrim" versus "The snow was general over Ireland." In this colder revisionary light, a cogent case could also be made for seeing in the figure of Michael Furey a demonic emblem of Yeats's Celtic Twilight gothic romanticism that succumbs finally to the cosmic poignancy of this poor-man's Jimmy Joyce. Yet even such an ingenious antithetical reading remains within Trilling's more general (and really Emersonian) terms of original genius and (self-)critical imitation. And even if one wishes to question the precision of these terms, particularly that of genius, I think the force of Trilling's argument still largely holds. Practically speaking, after all, it does not matter that the idea of original genius may be nothing more than a mythic trope. It does matter in our society of the spectacle, however, not to be recognized in any degree as the figure of one's greatest wish. The net effect of Trilling's original reading of this classic experiment in ironic point of view is thus to stage the epiphany of the indifferent god of creation as the snowy Lamb of the World. Such spectral scapegoating is a critical achievement of considerable imaginative magnitude.

From the essays collected in *Beyond Culture* celebrating Freud's critical nature or Babel's fierce style of lamenting "the fate of pleasure" in various ways, to the ethical typology of the aspiring mind found in *Prefaces to the Experience of Literature*, Trilling has been steadily turning away from modernism in its institutionalized academic form of the adversarial culture. He has increasingly found solace and challenge in the dark society, as Pater called it, of the great dead masters of Arnold's grand style, particularly as he observes the discipline of English studies in America surrender its intellectual coherence to the wide-ranging interests of its consumer-oriented students, and its code of civility to the purely theatrical effect of such spectacular intellectual "events" as the Leavis-Snow debates over "the two cultures." Ever alert to the seductive allure of apocalyptic thinking that underlies the plague-on-both-your-houses gesture of the Forsterian comic mode, Trilling continues to work to represent the public mind of the American intellectual class to itself, in order to rouse it from the sleep of its latest obsession or orthodoxy. Ironically enough, however, as we have seen, the public sphere of the liberal imagination (of de facto Gabriel Conroys) started to disintegrate even before the Armies of the Night, the tribal heirs apparent, started to march on the Pentagon to perform its ritual exorcism. Meanwhile, of course, the momentum of his career as a critic who has made it leads Trilling to allegorize his own origins, all his "fathers," *into* the traditional canon in the form of a subversive super-patriarchy of magnanimous Jewish minds—Shylockian *Übermenschen* who really are content because greatly dead. The ideological constraints of his displaced messiah complex requires as a penultimate career move this celebration of transcendent sacrifice as a sort of critical equivalent to the mythical harrowing of hell. Yet informing the "conservative instinct" of "normal mysticism," which takes pleasure in reading the semantic indeterminacies of classic texts for the revisionary opportunity they provide the critic to continuously work his and his "fathers' " liberation, appears to be a residual strain of virulent irony that would turn nihilistically against the very idea of higher education itself, as if in grotesque fulfillment of the suggestion in the earlier story "A Light to Nations" that education only leads many, all to many, to professionalize their resentful rage against the gifts of others and so against life itself.

> for I saw how she lived: she fastened hard to some superior and took on that person's color all her day until she thought she was

being shaken off, and then she would snap hard in revenge, perhaps at the other person, more likely at herself. ("Nations," p. 404)

A specter appears to be haunting the end of Trilling's career, and it bears an uncanny resemblance to his own creation, Joseph Howe, the poet-critic-educator in "Of This Time, Of That Place," who in 1943, well before it became de rigueur, named names and had the perverse majesty of his "mad" student genius Tertan-Ginsberg hustled off the campus. Only this time Trilling doesn't so much snitch as call names, and would if he could have packed off to the asylum the better part of an entire society. For rather than benefiting from the humanistic instruction and imaginative example of America's critic, the adversarial culture is more and more whoring after strange gods, such as Norman O. Brown, David Cooper, R. D. Laing, and Michel Foucault. Consequently, the figure that Trilling most strongly resembles at the end is not the sublime model of self-transcendence, the God of Blake's "Tyger," the law of whose nature is to overcome his nature (*PEL*, p. 217), but that "unreceived" messiah and jackdaw of despair, "The Hunter Gracchus" of Kafka (*PEL*, p. 120). As his 1929 letter in support of Elliot Cohen's stewardship of the *Menorah Journal* makes clear, there are some fates worse than death, and one of these is for a critic to suffer the symbolic castration of not being heard.[25] And while in his preface to "Resolution and Independence" he endorses Wordsworth's stoic cure for the manic-depressive fate of poets, suffering in silence when so threatened is not Trilling's way of making "the anti-vital element" a source of stability in his life (*PEL*, p. 224). Eloquent apathy is more like it.

Actually, Trilling at the end does what he has done repeatedly in his career, and that is to project the end generally. His remarks in the preface to "Out of the Cradle Endlessly Rocking" on that poem and on Whitman's *Democratic Vistas* demonstrate this traditional strategy of criticism humanism in its peculiarly American variant. Trilling notes that on one matter at least Whitman and James were as one. Poets and writers "immenser far" must and would arise to compose "the great poem of death" and so check the power of American vulgarity by bringing "faith and large-mindness." With "the anchor" of this chronic death consciousness (like that of Joyce in "The Dead"?), Americans especially will be able to resist the weightlessness of modernity "and make great poems of death" (as Whitman puts it). "The poems of life are great" Trilling also cites Whitman as saying, "but there must be poems of the purports of life; not only in itself but beyond itself." For only in this way, our critic concludes, may we "confront Nature." By projecting this chronic death consciousness, Trilling would raise the level of cultural debate to ultimate concerns, and thus sublimely evade the specific crises of the moment. To confront nature sure beats in sublimity confronting a university provost.

Trilling, in short, would ever have us all be like his idol Henry James at death who, as Edith Wharton reports, "in the very act of falling . . . heard a voice which was distinctly, it seemed, not his own, saying, 'So here it is at last, the distinguished thing!'" (*PEL*, p. 260). What "weight-less" postmodern America therefore needs, in Trilling's view, is more not less of "the spirit of gravity."

Chapter Six

Infectious Apocalypse: The Revisionary Madness of Postmodern Culture

Striking through the Masks: The Ethics of Impersonation

Our pleasures identify if not define us. And their patterns of interaction, development, repression, or renunciation condition if not determine the shapes our lives take. According to Wordsworth in his preface to *Lyrical Ballads*, Freud in *Beyond the Pleasure Principle*, and Trilling, their critical heir, in "The Fate of Pleasure," pleasure and its pursuit, although mediated by the available resources and values of society, tend nevertheless to establish a natural-seeming hierarchy among persons, a rough division at least into those for whom direct, frequent, and readily accessible forms of external stimulation become a way of life, and those few others—Arnold's "humane aliens," Nietzsche's "antithetical men," Kant's "ill-natured men,"[1] Freud's "normal neurotics," David Riesman's "inner-directed individuals"—for whom pleasure takes a more "spiritual" or antithetical turn in which the overcoming of resistances in the mind by the mind's own primarily cognitive efforts, an elusive, rare, and difficult experience to have and cultivate, marks them as contemplative types. For such "mental travellers" the hostility of the established order is a *desired* given, the more hostile the better, since it permits them to focus exclusively on themselves, without arousing too much distracting guilt, against the dramatic background of a generally adverse imagination of society.

To envision and then to work toward the apocalyptic liberation of all peoples from the repression of society is thus not simply a silly utopian project. It is also a serious threat to the critical character structure of the individuated intellectual. Without the opposition between a hostile external environment and a self-transcending subject, such intellectuals schooled by critical humanism might be denied their greatest pleasure, that of "the sentiment of being" as Rousseau calls it in the famous fifth excursion from *Reveries of the Solitary Walker*.[2] The mind, progressively emptied of all definite expectations and regrets, focuses entirely upon the present moment of steady rhythmical motion of some kind (water lapping rocks, a boat knocking, verses chiming, figures resonating, concepts unfolding), until such proto-musical images of the acquiescent will, this irrational fact of our own existence, fills the mind, making us feel for as long as the experience lasts "self-sufficient like God" (*RSW*, p. 89).

The pursuit of this ultimate, singular, and individuating pleasure or god-effect (for each person, the condition of its occurrence will be different) also identifies the individual generally as a contemplative type. In place of the Cartesian cogito, Rousseau thus puts the sentiment of being. The belief in the educational value of the pursuit of this "highest" pleasure—that as many people as possible ought to seek this spectral peak experience in self-reading—defines the contemplative as a modern oppositional intellectual devoted to the work of liberation as informed by the experience of literature and the discipline of literary study. (Today, of course, "the sentiment of being" goes by other names, such as "play" and "power.")[3]

Thus, what may be described as a genuine form of selfhood for a marginal few becomes the norm of behavior for many through the system of modern education. Rousseau himself, of course, explicitly warns against this development (see *RSW*, p. 91). While this fiercely privatized pleasure serves the immediate interests of liberal capitalism by making collective action less palatable, the production of a large class of individuals seeking such pleasure helps to disintegrate the public sphere of culture minimally necessary for the maintenance of any recognizable civilized order. And, as we saw in the previous chapter, this ideology of liberation fosters the development of a new, larger class of habitually oppositional intellectuals for whom a transcendent judgment passed upon the world, whether from an aesthetic or a political angle, is sweetly de rigueur. An entire class of would-be Hjalmar Werles and Gabriel Conroys and Isabel Archers and Maggie Tullivers, as the sublime educators of future generations, promotes the imaginative efficacy of the pleasure of apotheosis—such a prospect makes Pope's *Dunciad* by comparison appear liberal, humane, and tolerable. But, as Trilling now discovers, such a class is in a constant state of self-revision, so that the models of selfhood best suited to realize this pleasure repeatedly change like other fashions in society, creating an infectious form of intellectual apocalypse that even Trilling cannot finally resist. Just imagine it: styles of the last judgment now define the manufacture of modern intellectual history. Yet another stimulated demand to be satisfied. Intellectual forms of revolution purely for the consummate spectacle's sake.

As Trilling notes in a 1971 autobiographical essay, "unmasking" social conventions has itself become the pleasurable norm of modern intellectual work (whose motivation, as I have suggested, is the experience of apotheosis), so that, from the beginning of his career, he has proposed a reflective ironic valuation on this critical mode of being oppositional: viz. "unmasking the unmaskers" (*LD*, p. 240) currently in power within the culture. To do so successfully, Trilling has had to make his own mask, perfecting it as an instrument for "striking through the mask" (*LD*, p. 240) of others even as, when occasion warranted, he has struck through his own chosen self-image as subversive patriarch.

In Trilling's fiction for the *Menorah Journal*, such as "Notes of a Departure" (1929), "A Light to Nations" (1928), and "Impediments" (1925), he is already exploring the romantic mask of the wandering sage that the history of anti-Semitism assigns to Jews as one of their possible roles to play in gentile society. (See, as well, "The Changing Myth of the Jew.") Trilling makes this image his self-image by deploying it subversively, by playing ironic variations upon it: liberal critic within liberalism, the opposing self within the culture of the opposing self, the modern adversary of adversarial modernism. In each instance the social conditions of American culture are provisionally accepted as givens, in order to develop the appropriately oppositional response and vision that would ensure amidst the resulting dramatic social background the staged discovery of the sentiment of being, the mysterious fact of identity, once again.

Thus, Trilling makes use of the idea of society to impersonate an oppositional critic in the mode of the subversive patriarch, to turn himself into the intellectual equivalent of Wordsworth's Old Men or the critical avatar of Joyce's Leopold Bloom. By saying this, I mean that the presiding genius of his rhetorical strategies and conceptual energies, the desired specter that haunts his modulated critical style and ambivalent tone, is consistently that of a subversive patriarch, a New York Intellectual version—within the domain of academic culture—of Forster, Frost, and Freud, that familiar compound ghost whose ironic commitment to the commonplace is ever positioned to be destructive of the latest orthodoxy. From the slow smokeless burning of universal decay arises this specter of liberal decadence.

For such a critic, the adoption of a role proves to be "an iterated impersonation,"[4] an act of overwriting with personal and public effects, created by one's works. Such an ethic of "sincere" impersonation both makes possible and must ever remain alienated from the radical revisionary mode of authentic impersonation, so prevalent in postmodern culture for which there is no "real" self but only this process of playing and surpassing "selves" itself. It is one thing for a few deracinated intellectuals to emulate Rousseau and envision the apotheosis of their quiescent wills in a figure of divine self-sufficiency. It is for Trilling quite another thing for an entire generation of students to demand that society and indeed the world be completely reconstructed according to their desire for a perfected autonomy. Yet, while he was intellectually opposed to this imperialistic utopian anarchy, Trilling's very opposition becomes contaminated by it, as if he took on the major features of his opponent in the very act of opposition. The words from his 1949 introduction to *The Portable Arnold*, originally made with the totalitarian sublime in mind, sound now fatally prophetic for Trilling and our time: "The extremity of our condition makes us value extremity in ourselves, for men adopt as their own the nature of whatever overawes and oppresses them" (*PA*, p. 10). These two ethics, of "sincere" and "authentic" impersonation, thus correspond to the imagined conditions of the great modernist authors and their critical heirs respectively. The latter, of course, resemble more the fictional surrogates of these authors than they do the authors themselves—Gabriel Conroy rather than Joyce.

Sincerity and Authenticity (1972) collects in revised form the Charles Eliot Norton Lectures that Trilling gave at Harvard University in the spring of 1970. It represents not only Trilling's response to the student and other rebellions of the late 1960s; it stands as well as the summary statement of his career on the topic of literary ethics. Like Arnold but with less certainty of expression, Trilling had believed that literature could provide us with an "intellectual deliverance" (Arnold's phrase from the 1859 inaugural lecture at Oxford as professor of poetry, "On the Modern Element in Literature"). But for Trilling what this meant is, of course, not a new mythos to replace that of the old religion but a newly revised ethos of the noble mind. That is, the study of literature, particularly modern literature and, for Trilling, particularly the novel, would train the judgment of an ever-growing class of enlightened readers in the complexities and disciplined glories of the moral life. Because, as "The America of John Dos Passos" (1938) puts it, the modern novelist goes beyond the law of social convention and sees into the hearts of men and women, the sensitive experienced reader can learn and evaluate the possible modes of human agency appropriate to the moral life of the present moment.

Trilling's invocation, frequent in his career, of John Dewey's position says it most succinctly. Dewey observes in his *Ethics* that in an epoch of many competing ethical imperatives and no dominant norm of behavior, people begin to base their moral judgments not so much upon the supposed good or evil nature of the action to be performed as upon the "quality" of being or "style" of personhood they think the action necessarily (i.e., conventionally) attributes to any agent that performs it. Not the imperative "Thou shalt not do certain things" but the imperative "Thou might not want to appear to be like a certain kind of character" now rules the moral life. Ethical essentialism or absolutism gives way to a more relative, situational, and less imperative morality. Pragmatically speaking, that is, morality for Trilling (as for his mentor Dewey) comes down to a matter of "style" or "taste," of the educated imagination as modern literature directly discloses it. Aesthetic judgment is thus the comparative, problematic foundation of practical reason. In other words, Trilling's literary ethics is an aesthetic categorical imperative in a world without categories or imperatives.

In Trilling's always ambivalent mind, he hoped that the study of modern literature, in light of the great classics and the latest developments in such social sciences as cultural history and psychology, would produce an archive of instructive ethical performances that in turn could lead to the development of the magnanimous or truly liberal imagination. The dialectic of the individual in society should result, then, in the ever-approximating realization of this ideal of self-sufficient godlike understanding. The sublime spectacle of the mind's apotheosis, Trilling's highest vision of pleasure, always centers on the idea of a mortal god. In educating themselves through the traditional examples of large-minded genius, the aesthetic elite (Trilling's elect) will approach the only form of divinity possible for humankind: noble sacrifice of self. All of Trilling's heroes are "saints" of this sort. Even Joyce, as we have seen in the previous chapter, appears in Trilling's eyes as a self-overcoming figure of great understanding.

As we have also seen, Trilling has become increasingly appalled by what modern American higher education based centrally on the humanistic study of literature had in fact produced: a class not of genial Joyces but—at best—would-be Gabriel Conroys and at worst a resentful host of "unreceived" messiahs like Kafka's Hunter Gracchus. What Trilling has fully realized now is that the critical imitations of literary figures—characters or authors—is necessarily a counterproductive form of impersonation. For it requires the painful reshaping of the self according to the highest designs provided by external authorities, in order to achieve as its end result an ideal congruence between avowal and actual feeling. Such sincere impersonation, in other words, assumes that a measure of hypocrisy must inform society, and hypocrisy assumes a radical insincerity between the avowal of a role and actual feeling. The emerging desire for the free expression of actual feeling characterizes the ethic of authenticity. But insofar as this ethic, too, has been established as a canonical form of the moral life, taught and assimilated, it necessarily becomes a more severely contradictory ethic of impersonation than that of sincerity. Instead of taking as a role model the humane Forster of the novels, a new rebellious generation of American intellectuals have arisen to cultivate as their savage god the Underground Man of Dostoyevsky. In short, the fierce spectral politics of Trilling's first published work, "Impediments," has come back to haunt the entire culture of liberal humanism. In thus successfully educating America in the wisdom of literary ethics, Trilling and his brethren have prepared the ground for their own undoing. If the moral life has come down to gratuitously chosen images of personal being, then who is to say that your gratuitous symbolic act of choice is any better than mine just because yours is consistently avowed and informed by a more genteel taste. Mine, in fact, may be madly made and likewise revised but precisely for that reason it may have more "life" in it than your classical mask. Just as the advancement of the capitalist economy undermines the work ethic of the bourgeois, so, too, the advancement of higher education in America has undermined the culture of the intellectuals.

Because the study of these "cognate ideals" of sincerity and authenticity is "virtually co-extensive with the culture of four centuries" (*SA*, p. i), Trilling's little book is necessarily less a comprehensive history than a critical theory of ethics, or what he terms "the rhetoric of avowal" (*SA*, p. 70). In the first chapter, "Sincerity: Its Origins and Rise," Trilling ironically disavows any Woolfian certainly about what a change in "moral idioms" (*SA*, p. 2) may imply about a change in human nature. Instead, he simply notes that beginning in the sixteenth century in England, the moral life appears to have added to itself a new required element, sincerity. Yet in Shakespeare's *Hamlet* even a Polonius can transcend his radical limitations when he eloquently advises his son, Laertes, to be ever true to himself so that he thus may never be false to any man. For Trilling, to speak of the sincerity of Ulysses or of Abraham is to speak nonsensically, anachronistically. Similarly, Shakespeare's villains—Edmund and Iago especially—portray what is for the first time so greatly and realistically feared: the perfected hypocrisy of a class of villanous overreaching Machiavels.

One reason for this sudden privileging of sincerity, according to Trilling, is the spectacular rise of the middle class and the greater social mobility an increasingly urban and money-based economy makes possible. For the more feasible it becomes for more people to aspire successfully to positions superior in wealth and prominence to those of their origins, the greater the possibility of conscious hypocrisy and thus the greater the danger to the social fabric. But, in Trilling's view, the tradition of Renaissance humanism provided a corrective for this development, by means of its belief, best phrased by Schiller in his *Letters on Aesthetic Education*, that within each person there is stamped an archetype of an ideal human being to which, amidst all the changing circumstances of life, one aspires to remain true (*SA*, p. 5). If one is sincere, then, one is "clean, or sound, or pure" (*SA*, p. 12), a perfect echo of that human ideal and not a mere embodied dissonance, a sincere impersonation of one and the same sane ideal.

Yet as the fate of Alceste, the hero of Molière's *Misanthrope*, drama-tizes, uncertainty over whether being true to this ideal or "best" self represents being also true to one's own actual self can lead not simply to disillusionment with this or that aspiring hypocrite but to the uni-versal nihilistic judgment "that the life of man in a developed com-munity must inevitably be a corruption of truth" (*SA*, p. 18). In terms of Trilling's historical allegory, this development can be read as a shift from the noble ideal of self-fashioning to be found in Castiglione's perfect courtier to the prophetic politics of plain speaking as practiced by the Puritan divines, who are the original instance of advanced intellectuals in a realm first thought to be "society," that is, a human domain capable of being revised. Trilling cites Michael Walzer's 1967 book *The Revolution of the Saints: A Study in the Origins of Radical Politics* as his authority on this matter, noting that the Puritans were the first social activists with "a formulated conception of what society is and a prophecy of what it is to be" (*SA*, p. 121).

The basis for the intellectual's authority to direct the future, as the example of Rousseau in his *Confessions* most fully testifies, is the sincere expression of his personal vision, the truthfulness of the individual's word. The rise of sincerity as a new moral idiom thus reveals a mutated cultural life that proposes for bourgeois modernity this ideal of the autonomous individual. This development ironically corresponds, Trilling adds, with the increased popularity of autobiography, the new fascination with divided interior spaces in homes, and the growing demand for better mirrors.[5]

> At a certain point in history men became individuals. . . . And [the individual] begins to use the word "self" not as a mere reflexive or intensive, but as an autonomous noun referring, the O.E.D. tells us, to "that . . . in a person [which] is really and intrinsically *he* (in contra-distinction to what is adventitious)," as that which he must cherish for its own sake and show to the world for the sake of good

faith. The [modern] subject . . . is just such a self, bent on revealing himself in all his truth, bent, that is to say, on demonstrating his sincerity. His conception of his private and uniquely interesting individuality, together with his impulse to reveal his self, to demonstrate that in it which is to be admired and trusted, is, we may believe, his response to the newly available sense of an audience of that public [to be educated] which [the invention of] society [has now] created. (*SA*, pp. 24–25)

I think it is only fair to say at the outset of this analysis that Trilling's story of the origins and rise of sincerity as a new or newly foregrounded element in the moral life of nations is as much an explantory myth of modernity as are Eliot's "dissociation of sensibility," Nietzsche's critique of historical consciousness, Foucault's epistemic disjunctions, or Bloom's post-Miltonic revisionary anxiety. Given his career-long stress on the ethical effects of cultural forms upon individuals in society, it is inevitable that Trilling formulate the argument here in terms of the models of selfhood that the early sincere and later authentic cultures of modernity produce and promote. As we shall see, Trilling makes this mythic intention increasingly evident in succeeding chapters through comparisons of the theory of sincerity and authenticity with Hegel's dialectic of master and slave, Nietzsche's tragic aesthetics of Apollo and Dionysus, and Freud's cosmic war of Eros and the death instinct. Of course, the great original of Trilling's opposition of sincerity and authenticity is the Arnoldian conflict of the conservative instinct and the revolutionary principle, which in turn derives not simply from Edmund Burke's *Reflections on the Revolution in France* but as well from Burke's earlier treatise on the beautiful and the sublime. Although Trilling often sides unexpectedly with the disintegrative forces, however named, his "dialectic" generally if ironically privileges the forces of humane order by portraying the quest for order as a heroic lost cause in the modern world. The pathos of this strategy empowers his critical project subversive of liberal pieties. The ultimate form that this dialectic of sincerity and authenticity takes is the bitterly resentful combat between Trilling (as representative of his cold-war liberal brethren) and all their rebellious postmodern offspring.

Trilling's second chapter, "The Honest Soul and the Disintegrated Consciousness," consists of readings of Diderot's *Le Neveu de Rameau*, Hegel's *Phenomenology of Mind* and Goethe's *Sorrows of the Young Werther*. The major point of these readings is to argue that the ethic of authenticity emerges from and is a more radical version of the ethic of sincerity. The authentic individual realizes the hypocritical project of impersonation informing both modern ethics, and in an apocalyptic rage of absolute cynicism, resentment, and nihilistic self-hatred condemns civilization as a pure sham and often destroys himself or goes mad to escape the universal corruption. (Hence, Trilling's "playful" etymology of authenticity from the Greek *authento*, meaning "not only a master and a doer, but also a perpetrator, a murderer, even a self-murderer, a suicide," as these "ancient and forgotten denotations bear upon the nature and intention of the artistic culture of the period we call Modern" [*SA*, p. 131].) For informing the protean quest for the authentic or true self is the dreaded recognition that, authentically speaking, there is no self to be discovered at all, no basic unique disposition and certainly no "genius" in the loosely exalted sense of the word. In essence, Trilling is demonstrating the total, inescapable failure of the humanistic program for higher education in modern democracy. But Trilling's position possesses a greater subversive potential than this proto-neo-conservative-sounding polemic against democratic institutions. (Trilling has no illusions about the rise of a new aristocracy, for instance.) To anticipate a bit, Trilling in this volume bears climactic witness to the underlying will to holocaust shaping the very idea of education, of culture, from the beginning.

To begin with, however, I must admit that Trilling's reading of *Rameau's Nephew* is an obvious misreading. For one thing, he argues that the text, as the forefather of Dostoyevsky's *Notes from the Underground*, represents a seriously divided intention. It both disapproves of the Nephew's resentful cynicism and secretly admires his energetic if comic virtuosity, even as it formally endorses the Diderot speaker's urbane acceptance of social hypocrisy and yet forcefully inspires our sympathy for the Nephew. I can see no evidence in the text for this reading. In fact, as I read the climactic scene of the dialogue, the text endorses Diderot's celebration of Diogenes the Cynic, "the philosopher who has nothing and asks for nothing" and who nevertheless receives everything he needs including the services of the most sought-after courtesan in Athens.[6] The point of this last "fact" is that the Nephew earlier in the dialogue had shamelessly confessed his shame at playing pimp for a rich Jew with an eye for gentile girls, and Diderot had been disgusted by the Nephew's crude bigotry as well as by this prostitution of his talents and those of the beautiful virgin. That Trilling misreads the text results in part, I think, from his studious "genteel" omission of this and related scenes, of the Nephew's fierce anti-Semitism. In any event, the text presents the philosopher as the singular type of the happy man, a figure that in the guise of Diogenes the Cynic ever in quest of an honest man, and ever ready to retire self-sufficiently to his classic tub when disappointed, incorporates dialectically the major features of both dialogue participants: the Nephew's authentic universal cynicism and Diderot's comic representation of sincere disillusionment.

If we grant Trilling's blindness, the question I must ask is: Why this bias in favor of the Nephew? Trilling faithfully recognizes the Nephew's mean-spiritedness, his being "tortured by envy of his famous uncle and bitter at having to live in his shadow." But, like Harold Bloom a few years later in *The Anxiety of Influence*, Trilling here is also sensitive to what he feels is representative in the Nephew's fate of resentful belatedness: "Despite his native abilities and the cruel self-discipline to which he has subjected himself, he must endure the peculiar bitterness of modern man, the knowledge that he is not a genius" (*SA*, p. 29). That is, the Nephew is the great original of the Underground Man in us all.

That Trilling himself sees in the Nephew the spectral protrait of his own alter ego or "Secret Sharer" is a plausible inference. It would explain the awe and exalted hyperbole in his reading of the Nephew's climactic impersonation of the whole art of opera, as the latter commends the latest forms:

> The episode issues in his most elaborate mimetic display, for he proceeds to *be* opera, to impersonate the whole art—this musical Proteus, or perhaps he is to be *called* Panurge, sounds all the instruments, enacts all the roles, portraying all the emotions in *all* voices and all works. The astonishing performance proposes the idea which Nietzsche was to articulate a century later, that man's true metaphysical destiny expresses itself not in morality but in art. (*SA*, pp. 32–33)

By misreading Diderot's intention, therefore, Trilling can rationalize this appreciation of the Nephew's great power of impersonation, a style of critical performance that he himself has sacrificed in order to maintain the iterated impersonation in his career as a moral realist more than half in love with a transcendent aestheticism beyond good and evil, whose other name is death.

Trilling even records in an ironic allegorical mode the perfect explanation for his own practice of outrageous misreading. It reflects his own propensity for symbolic self-destruction, his own cultivated perversity:

> [The Nephew] is the victim of an irresistible impulse to offend those with whom he seeks to ingratiate himself. And stronger than his

desire for respect is his appetite for demonstrative self-abasement;
his ego, betraying its proper function, turns on itself and finds
expression in a compulsive buffoonery, at once inviting shame and
achieving shamelessness in a fashion that Dostoevsky was to make
familiar. (*SA*, p. 29)

For the critic who even now finds it hard to recognize himself as such,
who still thinks of himself as primarily a novelist, and who suffers from
Jewish self-hatred, the motive for such self-conscious misreadings
could not be put more classically.

A more strategic reason for Trilling's misreading of *Rameau's Nephew*
appears in his account of the section in Hegel's *Phenomenology* entitled
"Der sich entfremdete Geist; Die Bildung," which J. B. Baillie renders
in the original English translation as "Spirit in Self-Estrangement—The
Discipline of Culture." Hegel's argument is that in order to advance in
the historical process of increasing self-determination, the human
spirit must free itself from the "noble" ethos of dutiful heroic support
of external authority and deliberately become "base," resentfully
scornful of all inhibitions and constraints upon the power of self-
expression, even to the point of universal rebellion. Thus, the "base"
spirit ironically becomes the dialectical basis of a new and higher nobility, that of the free spirit.

Trilling, given his own earlier misreading, is able to accuse Hegel of
wrongfully attributing to Diderot both a simple endorsement of the
sincere noble ethos, which Trilling associates with "the old visionary
norm" of the good life in Shakespeare's final romances and Jane Austen's major novels, and an equally simple condemnation of the emerging modern ethos, which, as we have seen, Trilling associates with the
fierce authenticity of the Underground Man (*SA*, pp. 43–44). Trilling
can thereby appear more complex and profound than the notorious
wizard of dialectical transgression, since his own reading of Diderot,
however wrong, is at least not as simple as Hegel's sounds in Trilling's
opportunistic and distorted formulation.

In this self-revealing way, Trilling can appropriate Hegel's view of
the Nephew's representative "baseness" for his own argument and as
the expression of his highest desire for liberal culture:

> It is therefore not Diderot-*Moi*, not the *philosophe* with his archaic love
> of simple truth and morality, with his clearly defined self and his
> commitment to sincerity, who, for Hegel, commands esteem. Rather,
> it is Rameau, the buffoon, the flattering parasite, the compulsive
> mimic, without a self to be true to, it is he who represents spirit

> moving to its next stage of development. . . . [a] momentous aban-
> donment of individuated selfhood to become all the voices of human
> existence, of all existence. (*SA*, p. 44)

Not only is this Diderot-*Moi* Lionel Trilling writ large, and Rameau's
Nephew the original Performing Self, but Hegel is the unsuperseded
precursor of the racial evil in Trilling's book, which appears in the final
chapter under the forms of Norman O. Brown, R. D. Laing, David
Cooper, and Michel Foucault. Underground Men all, given their argument, as Trilling reads it, for the radical truth of madness (and of
society's total unauthenticity).

Ironically enough, however, in a footnote to his argument here,
Trilling recalls the incident in which the Nephew displays his "true"
baseness by telling how he had seduced "a bourgeois girl on behalf of
a wealthy patron" (*SA*, p. 45). What Trilling omits to say is that the
patron in question was a Jew, and that the Nephew is a resentful anti-
Semite forced to play the pimp by his lack of wealth and of honor. I cite
this textual "fact" not only as evidence of Diderot's strong critique of
the Nephew and all that he represents (it is clear from the text that the
author's good taste alone excludes prejudice from the mind of Diderot-
Moi). It also confirms Hegel's reading of the central intention of *Rameau's Nephew* which, as already noted, is to propose for the reader's
emulation neither Rameau-*Lui* nor Diderot-*Moi* as the ideal figure of
understanding but rather Diogenes the Cynic. Nietzsche, of course,
accepts this proposal in his parable of "The Madman" from *The Gay
Science*, in which the only rational man among the truly mad vainly
searches with a lantern at midday for an honest man, in order to bring
him the good news of God's demise. Thus, Trilling's omission of the
wealthy patron's identity and what it entails sincerely testifies to the
impossibility of the critical desire to be authentically representative, to
express all the voices of human existence in a universal conversation,
especially when, as here, even to attempt to represent fairly what the
text says would compromise the argument the critic needs to make in
order to maintain his own authority as the wiser if sadder latecomer.

Trilling concludes his analysis of the Honest Soul and the Disintegrated Consciousness by circling back from Hegel's 1807 *Phenomenology*
to Goethe's early romantic classic of 1774, *The Sorrows of the Young
Werther*. This work is roughly contemporaneous with the composition
of *Rameau's Nephew*, which first appeared in Goethe's German translation of 1805, before going on to influence formatively, according to
Trilling, the thinking of both Marx and Freud on the matter of modernity's self-alienation. In the novel's first part Werther, having already

suffered the trauma of love betrayed, immerses himself in the protective noble simplicity of the ordinary round of pastoral life, much as Wordsworth was also to do and much as did the royal figures of Shakespeare's final comic romances. The disintegrative forces of modern love destroy Werther's bucolic paradise, and lead him to commit suicide, a fate almost as widely emulated in Europe at the time among sensitive young men as Werther's habitual style of dress.

Trilling's reading of the novel, his best critical performance in the second chapter, brings together his earlier, clearly distorted views on Diderot and Hegel, in an act of interpretation that, although also an act of self-interpretation, nevertheless illuminates rather than obscures the text:

> If we try to explain his [Werther's] failure in the terms of Hegel's celebration of Rameau, we can say that his alienation did not proceed far enough: he was not able to achieve that detachment from himself which for Hegel constitutes Rameau's triumph and significance. The Nephew deserves admiration, Hegel says, because through him Spirit is able to pour "scornful laughter on existence, on the confusion pervading the whole and on itself as well." Spirit is expressed as *esprit*, *Geist* becomes *geistreich*. Werther is incapable of embodying this desperate cosmic wit; irony is beyond his comprehension. He is in all things the sincere man; even in his disintegration he struggles to be true to the self he must still believe is his own. It is much to the point, especially in the light of Rameau's willful impersonations and role-playings, that Werther expressed his sincerity by a singular and apparently unchanging mode of dress—everyone in Europe knew, and many imitated, Werther's costume of dark blue coat, yellow waistcoat, and boots, and Goethe is at pains to mention that it was in this costume that Werther died. To the end and even in his defeat he held fast to the image of a one true self. This tenacity was what had destroyed him. *A disintegrated consciousness, he had persisted in clinging to the simplicity of the honest soul*. (*SA*, p. 52, my emphasis)

This conclusion does not merely demonstrate Paul de Man's theoretical understanding of reading, that our best insights into texts often arise out of a systematic blindness to their avowed intentions. For this conclusion also functions as a reading of the position that Trilling has adopted throughout his career. He is the author of a critical character who is ever on the verge of embracing yet always already resisting the godhead of disintegration. A disintegrated consciousness, Trilling has persisted in clinging to the assumed innocence of his gratuitously chosen self-image—that of the subversive patriarch of liberal culture.

The third chapter, "The Sentiment of Being and the Sentiments of Art," directly addresses the conflict of discovering versus making a self in terms of the Augustinian hostility of Rousseau and his unlikely offspring, Robespierre and Jane Austen, toward the infectious influences of society upon the individual, especially in the form of the dramatic impersonations of the theater. That the preferred arts of the first two members of this latter-day Puritan troika are oratory and the novel (Rousseau admired *Clarissa*) is an irony that Trilling scarcely presses at all in his discussion of Rousseau's *Letter to M. d'Alembert on the Theatre*. Given an audience schooled in the remorseless demystification of society by Flaubert and Joyce, taking advantage of Rousseau in this way would have seemed just too unfairly easy. Trilling does press the point rather more, however, with Robespierrre and his Festival of the Supreme Being of June 8, 1793. The reason is not to expose the bad faith of the revolutionary principle. Instead, it is to dramatize how in the name of a more radical mode of personal sincerity, in the name of the authentic self, Robespierre, as every modern must, has to establish "a self of his own devising made up of elements derived from various personages who had figured, to popular acclaim, on the stage of History" (*SA*, p. 70). At a certain phase in the history of the self, in other words, the singular self—Trilling uses Wylie Sypher's phrase—no longer serves as an ultimate foundation of individual identity, and so disappears.

Although Trilling is the first to admit that "to trace the history of the self" is to deal "with shadows in a dark land," to be confined at best to "diffident" predications and "speculative" conclusions (*SA*, p. 54), he nonetheless attempts to correlate the emergence of the self as a cultural idea subject to these peculiar vicissitudes with the growing fear of the "new circumstance" of infectious influence that a modern urban, mass society creates. Packed into cities, increasingly reduced to lives of dull routine punctuated by sensationalistic debauches, these new individuals are both being made by and being subjected to "the constant influence, the literal *in-flowing*, of the mental processes of others" which "in the degree that they stimulate or enlarge" our minds, make our minds less our own (*SA*, p. 61). A person can no longer know what it may mean to be sincere, to be true to oneself, since he is more and more the collective production of ideological contagion (*SA*, p. 61). At best, one can aspire to simulate sincerity, approximate the noble ethos, by becoming "a reiterated impersonation" (*SA*, p. 66). The alternative is to be the professional plaything of the winds of intellectual fashion. Trilling himself has chosen the former course in his career, even as he has repeatedly stood against change for change's sake in this latter sense.

These opposing sentiments of art—Rameau's authentic disintegration and Diderot's sincere impersonation—equally entail the "negation of self through role-playing" (*SA*, p. 76), which the commitment to an artistic culture, however conceived, requires. Alienation from the traditional ethos of the noble self cannot finally be overcome through art or the high culture it legitimates. This is so for Trilling because he takes as his exemplars of the sentiment of being, of what Whitman calls the mysterious fact of identity, Rousseau, Wordsworth, and Jane Austen.

Although he discusses briefly the passages from Rousseau's *Reveries of a Solitary Walker* I have previously discussed and refers in passing to Wordsworth's emblems of authentic being such as the Leech-Gatherer and Michael, figures who simply are all that they feel at the moment and nothing else, Trilling reserves the greatest portion of his chapter for a rehearsal of his reading of *Mansfield Park*. Of all Austen's novels, you will recall, Trilling finds this one the most hostile to modernity. Recognizing only good-versus-evil and not good-and-evil, the novel imposes a categorical rather than a dialectical mode of judgment in its condemnation of every form of impersonation and not simply those of the amateur theatricals performed at Sir Thomas Bertram's estate. *Mansfield Park*, according to Trilling, thus affronts modern aesthetic preferences not least in its giving the estate to Bertram's mousy ward, Fanny Price, the embodiment of an inflexible moral rectitude. In support of a traditional, virtually Augustinian morality and in the name of the "vocations" or "callings" of old-fashioned professional duty or domestic service, "pandemic impersonation" is savagely opposed and the sense of self as the original role one is born into or cut out for is no less savagely privileged.

Even in this strong form of his argument, using Austen against the sentiments of art and for the sentiment of being, Trilling cannot entirely evade the idea of role-playing that must inform a sense of identity related to a social function. The way he recognizes this contamination of his argument by that which it opposes is in his original observation concerning the typical action of Austen's novels in which "the archaic ethos is in love with the consciousness that seeks to subvert it" (*SA*, pp. 76–77). Like his formula for Goethe's *Sorrows of the Young Werther*, this remark indirectly illuminates the texts under consideration even as it directly sheds more light on the critic considering them.

Yet Trilling does not really intend wholly to evade the necessary hypocrisy of society. What he wants is to be able in good faith to focus on the essential feature of the sentiment of being as he understands it to appear in Austen's least characteristic novel. And as the central scenes in Trilling's only novel would lead us to expect, this feature is the "archaic" attitude toward time that *Mansfield Park* permits him to celebrate, ironically, and with all due respect to the proliferating complications:

> *Mansfield Park* discriminates between right and wrong. This discon-
> certs and discomfits us. It induces in us a species of anxiety. As how
> should it not? A work of art, notable for its complexity, devotes its
> energies, which we cannot doubt are of a very brilliant kind, to doing
> exactly the opposite of what we have learned to believe art ideally
> does and what we most love it for doing, which is to confirm the
> dialectical mode and mitigate the constraints of the categorical. *Mans-*
> *field Park* ruthlessly rejects the dialectical mode and seeks to impose
> the categorical constraints the more firmly upon us. It does not con-
> firm our characteristic modern intuition that the enlightened and
> generous mind can discern right and wrong and good and bad only
> under the aspect of process and development, of futurity and the
> interplay and resolution of contradictions. It does not invite us to any
> of the pleasures which are to be derived from the transcendance of
> immediate and pragmatic judgements, such as grave, large-minded
> detachment, or irony, or confidence in the unfolding future. It is
> antipathetic to the temporality of the dialectical mode; the only mo-
> ment of judgement it acknowledges is *now*: it is in the exigent present
> that things are what they really are, not in the unfolding future. A
> work of art informed by so claustral a view might well distress our
> minds, might well give rise to anxiety. And not least because we
> understand it to be saying that even the reality of the reader himself
> is not, as he might wish to think, what it may become, but ineluctably
> what it is now. This is a dark thought, an archaic thought, one that
> detaches us from the predilections of our culture. But when its first
> unease has been accommodated, it can be seen to have in it a curious
> power of comfort. (*SA*, pp. 29–80)

Trilling thus would discover in Austen a perspective on our Rameau's Nephew culture, a perspective that is akin to the mythic substratum of what Nietzsche calls critical history. Trilling himself, of course, in "Tacitus Now" and "The Sense of the Past" from *The Liberal Imagination*, understands mythic foundationalism as the implicit aesthetic of critical humanism, which recreates the past both to sharpen our experience of the present and to repress momentarily the ever-disintegrating, all-too literally utopian prospects of modernity. Needless to say, to manage such a feat of selective deliberate forgetting necessitates the self-imposition of an imaginary scene of repression wholly at odds with educational practices of the modern academy.

"The Heroic, the Beautiful, the Authentic," the fourth chapter of *Sincerity and Authenticity*, contrasts the classical Aristotelian idea of the large-minded tragic hero and its romantic transformation into the poet aspiring for sublime status as a cultural monument with the traditional Judeo-Christian endorsement of order, moral beauty, and the common good of all, at the center of which stands the noble ideal of "intelligent love." According to this latter, essentially ascetic idea, "the deepest and truest relationship that can exist between human beings is pedagogic" (*SA*, p. 81). Before T. S. Eliot in *The Four Quartets*, therefore, or even Plato in *The Symposium*, Trilling contends, the ancient Jewish rabbis viewed life so: As a quest not for individual apotheosis but for communal wisdom. Life is conceived to be, that is, much as Keats imagined it, a school of identity formation in which individuals form social units under the leadership of loving masters who are usually the truly disinterested dead writers or otherwise fundamentally uncompromised figures. Trilling has in mind, as "Wordsworth and the Rabbis" in *The Opposing Self* suggests, the kind of antiheroic heroism glimpsed in Wordsworth's poetry and fully revealed in Joyce's *Ulysses* by the figure of Leopold Bloom.

Trilling's point in uncovering this antiheroic heroic aesthetic in representative modern authors is to prepare the ground for his objection to the orthodox perception of the post-Enlightenment "aesthetic revolution" that persistently invokes the heroic morality of personal authenticity even at the cost of the very idea of society. As in "The Fate of Pleasure" Trilling here opposes the habitual rejection of aesthetic beauty, of limits, and the equally habitual celebration of the sublime of infinitude. In a footnote (*SA*, p. 98), he makes it clear that it is not solely the habit of authenticity that makes the difference between high modernism and postmodern culture. It is also the fact that contemporary art neither finds nor provokes any significant resistance to its demands from its growing audience. Postmodern culture is modernism for the submissively "radical," intellectual "masses," that is, a more and more mindless sort of modernism. In short, Trilling argues, "the situation no longer obtains in which the experience of a contemporary work begins in resistance and proceeds by relatively slow degrees to a comprehending or submissive admiration" (*SA*, p. 98). Wordsworth's worst fears for the spread of sensationalistic culture have been realized, ironically enough, in large part owing to the educational success of "high" art:

The artist seeks his personal authenticity in his entire autonomous-
ness—his goal is to be as self-defining as the art-object he creates.
As for the audience, its expectation is that through its communication with the work of art, which may be resistant, unpleasant, even
hostile, it acquires the authenticity of which the object itself is the
model and the artist the personal example. (*SA*, p. 100)

Over the past century and a half or so, Trilling notes, the power to
confer the sentiment of being, of being strongly oneself, has been
transferred from every external source of authority—God, nature, society—except one: that of avant-garde art and the culture it authorizes.
In our time, the modern artist must provide his audience with the only
form of the sentiment of being they can receive, and it is defined wholly
in terms of the ideal of personal authenticity. The proposed autonomy
of the object the artist makes, of the new thing that he adds to the
human spirit and that seems ever fresh because it was once original,
carries over to the artist, enabling him to assume a stance of opposition
to established society and its forms and values. As the above quotation
hints, it is this mode of autonomy that his audience would consume
and make its own. The contradiction in this process of exchange becomes glaring as an entire new class and its adversarial culture emerge.
The majority of the audience now becomes the unthinking mass of so-
called critical intellectuals while the thinking few who nevertheless
remain desperately attached to the radical theory of the avant-garde
begin to withdraw their credence even from the last external form of
authority, modern art and its culture. From now on they will discover
their basis of authentic selfhood entirely within themselves, or vainly
self-destruct in this ultimately futile attempt.

Trilling's argument against these dismal developments concludes
with an ill-spiritied but revealing satire of Nathalie Sarraute's reading
of Flaubert's *Madame Bovary*. Just as Austen stood for all Trilling admires, so Mme. Sarraute, as he refers to her, comes to stand for the
now commonplace and unconsciously hypocritical demand of the adversarial culture that unless we renounce every idea, every feeling,
every perception not original with us, we are no better than the creatures of modernity, the ideological fixations of a dominant discourse,
and as such, we do not even deserve to think of ourselves as people.
Rather we are mere figures of speech, absurd fictions of bad faith like
Madame Bovary in her romantic conception of herself that her author
lashes so subtly but no less definitively. (*Tropismes*, as Trilling remarks,
is the apt title for Mme. Sarraute's first book of fictions.)

Would Madame Bovary, we wonder, have lived a more authentic life,
would her sentiment of being have more nearly approached single-

ness and particularity, if at the behest of a more exigent taste she had chosen as the stuff of her dreams the well-made, expensive images of a more creditable form of romanticism? Will not any art—the most certifiedly authentic, the most shaming—provide sustenance for the inauthenticity of those who consciously shape their experience by it? It was the peculiar inauthenticity which comes from basing a life on the very best cultural objects that Nietzsche had in mind when he coined the terrible phrase, "culture Philistine." What he means by this is the inversion of the bourgeois resistance to art which we usually call Philistinism; he means the use of the art and thought of high culture, of the highest culture, for purposes of moral accredi- tation, which in our time announces itself in the facile acceptance of the shame that art imputes and in the registration of oneself in the company of those who, because they see themselves as damned, are saved.

Rousseau is not mocked. The arts no longer seek to "please," but pleasing was never the only technique of seduction, and art can still lead us into making the sentiment of our being dependent upon the opinion of others. The concerted effort of a culture or of a segment of a culture to achieve authenticity generates its own conventions, its generalities, its commonplaces, its maxims, what Sartre, taking the word from Heidegger, calls the "gabble." To the gabble Sartre has himself by now made his contribution. As has Mme. Sarraute; as did Gide; as did Lawrence—as must anyone who undertakes to satisfy our modern demand for reminders of our fallen state and for reasons why we are to be ashamed of our lives. (*SA*, pp. 104–105)

I cite the passage at length because it summarizes Trilling's critique of postmodern culture so clearly. Postmodern culture is the culture of "pandemic impersonations" adopted ironically as part of the doomed quest for an illusive autonomy and authenticity. What the passage thus clarifies as well is how desperate he is. In its accumulating vehemence and straining contradictory allusions, as well as in its histrionic person- ification, self-conscious apostrophes, and apocalyptic tone, this conclu- sion has the primary effect of transfiguring our subversive patriarch into the quixotic defender of the Madame Bovary in us all.

"Society and Authenticity" for a fifth time rings the changes on Trilling's theme. Authenticity, the quest to realize the true self, the Me Myself, develops out of the ethos of sincerity, which had privileged the idea of being true to one's self so as never to be false to any man. This ironic development reaches its decadent apocalyptic climax in the con- temporary orthodoxies of dissent and their celebration of the truth of madness. The quest for a legitimate community has progressively bred the abomination of a universal solipsism embraced—in theory at least—by the advanced segments of the intellectual class. Conrad's *Heart of Darkness* appropriately frames the fifth chapter which also contains a confrontation between the Victorian code of duty and the playful aestheticism of conscious insincerity to be found in Wilde and Nietzsche. In so structuring his argument, Trilling comes as close as he has done so far to the heart of his own radical ambivalence about modern cultural life. For Trilling reads the theory of the mask in Wilde and Nietzsche as providing a philosophical justification for the aesthetic discrimination among imperialisms in *Heart of Darkness*, as well as for the tragic paradoxes of its final vision in which the lie of the ideal—the right English ideal—that Marlow tells to Kurtz's Intended is the paradigm of what separates civilization from savagery. (We recall with a shudder the sublime Kurtz's last "chivalrous" words, "The horror! The horror!" as Marlow assures the Intended that the last words her beloved hero of the ideal pronounced were her name.) Trilling's outrageous act of criticism resembles nothing so much as making Pilate and Judas saints for the crucial part they both played in salvation history, unless it resembles even more the "true" lie of Marlow's he ironically celebrates.

Before drawing out the implications of this chapter for Trilling's larger argument, I want to remark on his conception of and attitude toward what he now calls postmodern (née "adversarial") culture.

The "postmodern," like "modern" or "romantic," is a much disputed term. Some literary scholars, such as Maurice Beebe, argue that it is a new name for an old phenomenon: that of decadence. Since roughly the end of the Second World War, according to Beebe, we have been witnessing the energies and forms of modernism playing themselves out in a parodic and pastichelike imitation of the great original. Other literary critics such as Ihab Hassan, William Spanos, and Alan Wilde argue a counterposition. For they, each in his own way and to a different degree, see postmodernism as representing both a continuation of earlier literary modes and values (modern, romantic, and ancient), and a real break with the immediate modernist past as canonized by the academy according to New Critical standards. Similarly, critical theorists such as Fredric Jameson and Jürgen Habermas also have had their considerable say on the question.[7] The best overview on this extensive debate, however, especially as it is affected by the rise of poststructuralist discourse, can be found in the last chapter of Jonathan Arac's recent book *Critical Genealogies: Historical Situations for Postmodern Literary Studies*.[8]

As Arac observes, postmodernism is a term to conjure with as much in the disciplines of art history, economics, and cultural analysis as in literary studies. It generally represents the partially realized desire to move away from the international imperial style in architecture (Venturi), the overcentralized political and economic system of late capitalism (Bell), and the *grand récits*—"tall tales" as Arac calls them—or great coordinating mythologies that have previously animated society (Lyotard). What exactly postmodernism is moving toward—shopping malls versus skyscrapers as our cathedrals, spreading deregulation and monopolistic takeovers, each intellectual faction its own "playful" ideological fiction of "power"?—is not generally certain.

For me, a remark that Arac cites in his brilliant and surprisingly sympathetic analysis of Daniel Bell functions as an emblem of the postmodern. In "Modernism and Capitalism" (reprinted as the introduction to a 1978 paperback edition of *The Cultural Contradictions of Capitalism*), Bell asserts that he is "a socialist in economics, a liberal in politics, and a conservative in culture" (*CG*, p. 206). Although Arac tactfully does not remind us of the obvious allusion here, for purposes of my argument I must press the point home.

T. S. Eliot in his 1927 introduction to a selection of religious writings by Lancelot Andrewes declared his "faith." Eliot was henceforth to be known as a "classicist" in literature, a "conservative" in politics, and a "Catholic" in religion. Similarly, Northrop Frye in a famous pronouncement in his first book, repeatedly stressed, as Harold Bloom and other critical theorists after him would also do, Blake's vehement prophetic opposition to this triple-headed monster and his own prophetic election of the antithetical tradition of romanticism, revolution, and Protestantism.[9] Clearly, in the culture of modern criticism and theory, the lines have been drawn, and for some time.

Modernist intellectuals, whether founders or academic reformers and opponents, have thus felt the need to define themselves and their positions with a virtually systematic consistency as ultimately "conservative" or "liberal" in orientation. It is the drive for a systematic totality, for the development of one's positions into a world of one's own, into a symbolic heterocosm as internally consistent and as externally oppositional as possible, that defines the modernist impulse in intellectual history. Yeats in *A Vision* is the grand reductio ad absurdum of this belated version of the post-Enlightenment ideal.[10]

Bell's ability to accept the pragmatic pluralism of his own differences, in politics, economics, and cultural matters, testifies to what he sees (and often still laments) as the radical discontinuities and disjunctions of realms (political, economic, and cultural) that characterize the postwar American polity, an institutionalized fragmentation which he suspects only a religious revival could possibly surmount. Here I would part company with Bell, for it is on this issue of ultimately having to surmount disjunctions and discontinuities that he parts company finally with the genuinely postmodern attitude as found best displayed in the late poetry of Wallace Stevens, the major fiction of Donald Barthelme, and the early criticism of Foucault and Derrida.[11] The postmodern, in other words, permits a plurality of mutually exclusive differences, whereas the modern, as the "classical" revision of the romantic, makes imperative the problem of order and its potential solution in the formal enclosures of art or myth.

Trilling's own position, so influential for the work of Bell, Lasch, Jackson Lears, and Gerald Graff (among others), takes issue with the postmodern *not* primarily on this question of total consistency versus pragmatic pluralism. Given his cold-war-liberal suspicion of any manifestation of a totalizing desire as a sign of the totalitarian urge, one would expect that Trilling, if this issue did count the most with him, should side with the champions of the postmodern. Trilling instead opposes the postmodern because of its ease of acceptance, its promotion of a cultivated passivity among its audience, its semi-automatic aesthetic or moral or political "radicalism"—*ever espoused but never lived*. The moderns, however unwittingly inconsistent and imperiously authoritarian or formalistic, at least were *serious* and saw life if not whole then at least as a matter of weight. They tried to live their lives according to their beliefs. That is, it is not the work of this or that artist or author or architect or thinker that Trilling really despises. Rather, it is the conditions of cultural production and of academic life as institutionalized by the American system of higher education that he cannot stomach. And he cannot stomach the flighty, "weightless" new environment not because he is the original antiprofessional critic but because of the kinds of subjectivities (as now we would say after Lacan) it produces.[12] In order to clarify this issue, a return to Trilling's fifth chapter is here in order.

Confronted by the Victorian demand for art to be a morally uplifting (because disciplined) form of *work*, and by the counter-demand of aesthetic radicals like Wilde and Nietzsche for the playful "truth of masks" ("Every profound spirit," Nietzsche recalls in *Beyond Good and Evil*, "likes masks"), modernism originated as an ironic impasse between the cognate ideals of sincerity and authenticity. Against the background of the imperialisms that led to the Great War, modernism would oppose to the weight of this inherited impasse a counterweight of unprecedented violent aesthetic innovation out of the depths of original feeling. Or so Trilling would have the story go:

Surely something not less than violent was needed to startle this
dull pain of the social world and make it move and live, to retrieve
the human spirit from its acquiescence in non-being. It needed the
perpetration of acts of unprecedented power and mastery, such as
the acceleration of the racing car celebrated by Marinetti, whose
"ideal axis passes through the centre of the earth," a new energy, in
immediacy and swiftness more that of the mobile machine than that
of the gradual processes proposed by the organicist ideal. But the
organic might be permitted if it was sufficiently feral, like Nijinsky's
unprecedented levitations, his sudden leaps upward and out of sight
of the audience, or the murderous tiger-leap of the actor Di Grasso
which Isaac Babel made the symbol of all true art. Or like Kurtz's
plunge downward from light into darkness. It was the perpetration
of this terrible deed that gave Kurtz the right to affirm the authenticity of life, which he did by articulating its horror. He spoke it with
his last breath: "The horror! The horror!" (*SA*, pp. 132–133)

In other words, the passionate pursuit of authenticity was *once* historically justified by material circumstances, *once* morally imperative for
the original talents involved, and *once* aesthetically validated in the
fiercely inspiriting works produced.

For all their avowed ironies, the great moderns were sincere artists
who created what their age demanded: its own authentic mask of
purely sacrificial affirmation: "The horror! The horror!" indeed. But,
and this is Trilling's point, we come long after the modernist moment
is over, and live in a time which may demand many things but which
surely doesn't need the absurd academic echoing of modernism in the
streets.

It is easy enough to write Trilling's views off as the resentful grous-
ing of the soon-to-be-displaced critic of American culture who in a last-
ditch effort to save his position hysterically espouses and finally embraces the most reactionary forces in our society. But I think Trilling
does have a cogent case to make against postmodern counterculture as
an academic phenomenon, now perhaps even more than during the
Vietnam debacle since the ethos of that counterculture now clearly
occupies the academy not only in the guises of advanced critical theory
and ideological analysis but in the institutional forms and organization
of the profession of literary study. The annual convention of the Modern Language Association, for example, currently exhibits such a pre-
ponderance of "leftist" sentiment—at the 1985 convention in Chicago
over half the numerous special sessions were avowedly "radical"
(Marxist, third-world, feminist) in orientation—that to be an advocate

merely of avant-garde theory is now to be too embarrassingly middle of the road. The thrust of Trilling's position, formulated at the beginning of their recent development, is that such "liberation movements" rather easily overwhelm opposition in the academy to constitute a new orthodoxy proudly out of touch with the larger realities of American society. Ever since Louis Kampf in his presidential address to the 1971 MLA convention complained of the complicity of critical humanists with the forces of imperialism, racism, and sexism, the profession has progressively transformed itself not into a comprehensive institution of serious critique but into an airy "radical" ghetto in the land of looking-glass wars. All this was done much as Trilling foresaw.

In "The Authentic Unconscious," the sixth and finest chapter of *Sincerity and Authenticity*, Trilling addresses directly and for the first time in this study what he terms "the specific developments in our contemporary arts by which the preoccupation with authenticity expresses itself" (*SA*, p. 134). At the same time he expresses in a quintessential manner his views of "authenticity as a criterion of art and as a quality of the personal life which may be either enhanced or diminshed by art" (*SA*, p. 134). As the literary ethic of contemporary art, authenticity appears formally as "the drastic reduction in the status of narration, of telling stories," and ideologically as an "assent" to "the doctrine that madness is health, that madness is liberation," since "a form of assent," Trilling ironically notes, "does not involve actual credence" (*SA*, p. 171). Trilling thus connects the modern American convention of rejecting or overlooking the past with avant-garde experiments with nonmimetic modes of fiction writing. The coincidence of these developments in the era of the counterculture, Trilling believes, fosters (among other things) the withdrawal of faith in the classical Freudian ethos of tragic renunciation and the simultaneous renewal of utopian hopes for an ultimate liberation from a repressive civilization and its radical discontents. In the process of narrating this critical history, Trilling finally theorizes the act of interpretation he has practiced throughout his career, even as he fundamentally revises Freud's conception of the superego. He thereby leaves his readers the instrument and the regulative ideal by which they can work to recreate the authentic unconscious of the critic even in the worst imaginable of postmodern worlds. The subversive patriarch of the American bourgeois avant-garde, long associated with the Trotskyite mission to promote debate about "Marxism and Modernism," both witnesses the end of the liberal culture of Western imperialism and discovers a new species of personality almost entirely formed in the experience of reading. After Trilling, in other words, to be a critic worthy of the name means ever to embody "a view that proposes an antinomian reversal of all accepted values, of all received realities" (*SA*, pp. 179–171), including, of course, and at times especially, the value and reality of just such a view.

We no longer take pleasure in the act of telling stories with a recognizable hero and a moral lesson to be imparted. Trilling cites Walter Benjamin from his classic essay "The Storyteller" on "the old-fashioned ring" (*SA*, p. 135) of such an idea of realistic narration, in making his larger point that "there is something inauthentic for our time in being held spellbound, momentarily forgetful of oneself, concerned with the fate of a person who is not oneself but who also, by reason of the spell that is being cast, is oneself" (*SA*, p. 135). We no longer cede authority to the narrator of such heroic fiction which proposes itself as an alternate world, both a momentary escape and a moral exemplum for us. We no longer can do so because such fiction has become for us after Beckett and LBJ just too degrading an experience. So the "new novel" of Alain Robbe-Grillet, Nathalie Sarraute, and their American surfictional epigones joins forces with what J. H. Plumb sees as the institutional and social pressures in modern American life for all of us to be future-and-youth-oriented, with the further result that we have engineered, as Plumb's famous book entitles it, "the death of the past." The advanced literary consciousness of the day has thus conspired with established American society to bring about the end of literary culture by progressively eliminating—as irrelevant—"narrative history" from "the curriculum of our schools":

> [This development] bears upon the extreme attenuation of the authority of literary culture, upon the growing indifference to its traditional pedagogy; the hero, the exemplary figure, does not exist without a sharp and positive beginning; the hero is his history from his significant birth to his significant death. (*SA*, p. 139)

That is, the traditional humanistic pedagogy of the culture of the father in all his manifestations has now been superseded, outmoded, in the name of immediate social justice and personal relevance. Consequently, the family itself has been further disintegrating, as has the kind of self shaped by the traditional family: "And perhaps the low status of narration can be thought to have a connection," Trilling adds significantly, "with revisions of the child's relation to the family— traditionally the family has been *a narrative institution*: it was the past and it had a tale to tell of how things began, including the child himself; and it had counsel to give" (*SA*, p. 139). For Trilling, all these interrelated developments—the low status of narration, the death of the past, the breakup of the patriarchal nuclear family—converge in the current debates over the psychoanalytic theories of the mind and those of Freud's postmodern revisionists over the issue of personal authenticity versus social repression. The rest of his chapter thus reads as if it were to be called "Freud and the Armies of the Night."

Trilling reminds us that "psycho-analysis is a science which is based upon narration, upon telling," that its "principle of explanation consists in getting the story told—somehow, anyhow—in order to discover how it begins," and that it "presumes that the tale that is told will yield counsel" (*SA*, p. 140). In essence, then, psychoanalysis for Trilling is the "scientific" theory of the bourgeois family, of the family as represented in the traditional humanistic culture of the realistic novel. Henry James and not Shakespeare or Sophocles is Freud's literary alter ego. So in defending Freud from his errant offspring, Trilling is justifying his own cultural moment and his critical position as subversive patriarch of that moment.

Trilling rehearses the development of Freud's theory of the mind which posits two dynamically opposed mental systems: consciousness striving vainly for an Alceste-like sincerity in a Tartuffian society of institutionalized hypocrisy; and a demonic, Caliban-like unconscious—a divided fate that arises from the founding experience of all human civilization repeated in the case of each individual in every generation: the Oedipus complex. In phrasing Freud's theory this way, Trilling intends not only to stress its literary antecedents. He also means to leave the theory open to its first major critic's basic accusations. In *Being and Nothingness*, in the chapter entitled "Bad Faith," Sartre argues that Freud arbitrarily divides the mind in two and promotes the idea that consciousness should view the unconscious as a *thing*, a *mechanism*, an *alien entity* wholly responsible for acts and thoughts and impulses that to save face the conscious mind wishes to disown. Trilling thus can now refute easily these interrelated charges of gratuitous self-fragmentation and irresponsible self-reification by simply noting that Sartre's 1941 critique somehow fails to take into account the systematic revisions Freud made in his theory of the mind beginning in 1920 with *Beyond the Pleasure Principle*, developing further in 1923 with *The Ego and the Id*, and culminating in 1930 with *Civilization and Its Discontents*. Trilling thus elegantly dismisses the ignorant Sartre.

The primary revision that Freud makes in his theory of the mind concerns the presence in the ego of an agency that, as Trilling says, "produces powerful effects without being itself [always] conscious and which requires special work before it is made conscious" (*SA*, p. 147).

This means "there is something in the ego which is also unconscious, which behaves exactly like the repressed" (*SA*, p. 147). This agency or psychic institution, partly unconscious in operation and yet the source of higher mental functions such as critical judgment, moral idealization, remorse, guilt, and loyalty, is the superego, of course, whose role in the mind far exceeds that of ordinary conscience in any rational prudential sense, as Trilling will shortly detail. The superego complicates Freud's theory, reinforcing the mind's divisions as Sartre would no doubt remark, even as it also reduces the danger noted by Sartre of irresponsible reification—or scapegoating—of one part of the mind by another part. For the superego dramatizes how Freud's mature theory creates, in Trilling's words, "two consciousnesses, one of which is not accessible to the other by intuition" (*SA*, p. 149) but rather inferable by interpretation, and both of which conjoin in the workings of the superego, especially as read by the ego in analysis. Thus, as Trilling concludes his refutation of Sartre, "the good faith of psychoanalysis is not impugned" by "the situation" it "postulates" (*SA*, p. 149), since this situation is one of division and dialectical mediation, of mechanism and intention, and not, as Sartre claims, simply a matter of fetishistic splitting alone. In this eloquent fashion, Trilling also answers Sartre.

When this revision in Freud's theory is combined with his speculative hypothesis of the death instinct, a synthesis that *Civilization and Its Discontents* carries out, the result is disastrous for revolutionary ambitions, according to Trilling. For the mature theory says that the superego draws upon the aggressive energies of the bipolar fund of instincts (eros and death being the two poles), to become in severe cases of neurosis virtually autonomous in its production of unconscious guilt, gratuitously cruel often to the point of inducing the organism's self-destruction. No amount of conceivable social change could eliminate or even greatly mitigate this fateful source of inescapable suffering, although such remedies as therapy, perhaps, can alleviate in some instances the worst effects of the superego's operation. A cento of citations will spell out Trilling's argument completely:

> *Civilization and Its Discontents* . . . stand[s] like a lion in the path of all hopes of achievement of happiness through the radical revision of social life. . . .
>
> As Freud now describes the dynamics of the unconscious, the direct agent of man's unhappiness is an element of the unconscious itself. The requirements of civilization do indeed set in motion an exigent disciplinary process whose locus is the ego, but this process, Freud says in effect, is escalated by the unconscious ego far beyond

the rational demands of the societal situation. The informing doctrine of *Civilization and Its Discontents* is that human mind, in the course of instituting civilization, has so contrived its own nature that it directs against itself an unremitting and largely gratuitous harshness. . . .

[Guilt] takes its rise from an unfulfilled and repressed wish to do wrong, specifically the wrong of directing aggression against a sacrosanct person, originally the father, and it is experienced not as a discrete and explicit emotion but as the negation of emotion, as anxiety and depression, a diminution of the individual's powers and the perversion of the intentions of his conscious ego, as the denial of the possiblity of gratification and delight, even of desire. Guilt is Blake's worm at the root of the rosetree. . . . The terrible paradox [is] that although the superego demands renunciation on the part of the ego, every renunciation which the ego makes at its behest, so far from appeasing it, actually increases its severity. The aggression which the ego surrenders is appropriated by the superego to intensify its own aggression against the ego, an aggression which has no motive save that of its own aggrandizement. The more the ego submits to the superego, the more the superego demands of it in the way of submission. . . . the whole of [Freud's] dark history [of the superego's development], fascinating though it be, is not essential [for our argument]. It will be enough if we understand that although it was to serve the needs of civilization that the superego was installed in its disciplinary office, its actual behaviour was not dictated by those needs; the movement of the superego from rational pragmatic authority to gratuitous cruel tyranny was wholly autonomous. (SA, pp. 151, 152–153, 153–154, 154).

Whatever Freud's reasons may have been, what motive can Trilling have to propose at this time the theory of "the primal No," this "ferocious idol of the psychic cave" (SA, p. 155)?

Trilling himself provides an answer in a digression on Nietzsche's repeated speculation from *The Gay Science* that one effect of the death of God will be the growing weightlessness of existence. Everything is permitted so nothing has value. If under the reign of the Judeo-Christian ethos everything had weight, was so terribly serious—the Spirit of Gravity, after all, is Zarathustra's enemy—now that we have said goodbye to all that, Nietzsche fears everything will become weightless, lightweight, material for the trivial and foolish play of human beings with no sustainable drive for power in any form whatsoever (SA, p. 156). Trilling recalls the philosopher's fear, in order to invoke Nietzsche's principle of reading—look for the underlying will in a text

or author, the latent motive, and articulate that. Applying this meth-
odological principle to Freud, Trilling argues that Freud proposed his
revised theory of the mind to counteract the growing weightlessness
of modern culture, and insofar as his theory has gained assent it has
preserved in "scientific" form the essential ascetic will of the outmoded
Judeo-Christian tradition, and so has fulfilled the wishes of the great
romantic and modern writers and their critical humanistic heirs (*SA*,
p. 156).

Whether Trilling has succeeded in explaining Freud's or his own
motive here is not really a debatable question. For by idealizing Freud's
vision into the modern equivalent of classical theater, the Book of Job,
and Shakespeare's tragedies, Trilling clearly is telling himself one of
those stories of aesthetic transcendence and moral exemplification
whose spell convinces him while the spell lasts that he and his hero,
while different, are also one and the same—capable of casting a Yeatsian "cold eye" on life, on death, and of living "an irony of simultaneous commitment [to] and detachment [from experience] such as is
required by Aristotle's large-souled man" (*SA*, p. 159). In a postmodern age of countercultural passions—for sexual, social, and political
revolutions—"so patrician an ethical posture," Trilling significantly
remarks, "cannot fail to outrage the egalitarian hedonism which is the
educated middle class's characteristic mode of moral judgment" (*SA*,
p. 159). Ironically enough, therefore, the reason that Trilling has been
painting Freud's mature theory of the mind in the most uncompromis-
ing colors possible is not to exorcise this "ferocious idol of the psychic
cave" and so moderate the misery of civilized life (Freud's announced
aim at the end of *Civilization and Its Discontents*).[13] Rather, Trilling wants
to outrage middle-class public opinion in America of the early 1970s by
putting on once again the mask of the subversive patriarch and—
through the heroic example of his Freud—"shaming" us all into seriousness. What magnanimity!

This is a part, of course, that Trilling has played throughout his
career. With Arnold or Forster or James, Keats or Frost or Austen,
Trilling has so contrived his readings that he is able to appear as the
figure authorizing their heroic examples of the magnanimous mind, a
figure strongly subversive of the current liberal pieties in the name of
an archaic noble ethos now all but lost in the modern world. Trilling
has used critical writing—imaginative interpretation—to perform the
special work of therapy necessary to make that portion of the ego that
remains unconscious available to conscious control. Trilling has thus
fulfilled a social function of criticism in articulating and working
through the constituent elements of the superego that has been formed

in him during the experience of reading by the discipline of literary study and that subsequently has been revised according to the gratuitous and autonomous exigencies of his psychic development. His work has shown the public mind of his time its own worst—and best—images. There is considerable historical value in doing so, to say the least.

Trilling's entire career as a representative critical humanist has depended intellectually upon Freud's secularization and internalization of the Judeo-Christian morality—the psychic necessity of suffering, for example, being the equivalent of Adam's curse due to the Fall. But what if the kind of mind Freud's theory presupposes is less and less prevalent owing to changing social and familial circumstances? What if a kind of mind with a radically different structure, or at least radically different afflictions, appears—what then?

Steven Marcus in "The Psychoanalytic Self" notes just such a changed situation as he describes the new kind of patient coming to therapy during the decades of the 1960s and 1970s that led to the development of Hans Kohut's greatly influential revision of Freud's theory of narcissism in *The Analysis of the Self* (1971) and *The Restoration of the Self* (1979). Both *The Culture of Narcissism* and *The Minimal Self* by Christopher Lasch, for example, depend heavily on Kohut's theory of the narcissitic personality disorders.[14] Here is the patient profile by Marcus:

> Such patients lack . . . an adequate foundational or "nuclear super-ego" upon which later structures may be built up. What in their experiences these patients have suffered is, in general, fathers whom they have been unable to idealize, in large measure because, according to Kohut's testimony, the fathers themselves have been disturbed in their own self-esteem so that they have been unable to tolerate the role of idealized figures that children (sons of course in particular) require of their parents if they are in fact to achieve the large-scale internalizations of structure that form a superego. . . . Such persons are, in Kohut's words, "not predominantly swayed by guilt," that is to say, by structural pressures exerted by the superego; on the contrary, their "predominant tendency," in this connection is to be "overwhelmed by shame" . . . [to the point where their psyches always feel on the verge of] disintegrating. (pp. 321–322)

Persons motivated primarily by a sense of shame and not guilt possess an under- rather than overdeveloped superego owing to the absence in their early experiences of a patriarchal figure worthy of and capable of tolerating the child's idealization. While Kohut's theory speculates about a corollary failure on the part of an unemphatic mother, the crucial role in determining the development of these narcissistic personality disorders remains the father's.

Kohut's revisionary theory of narcissism thus underscores the predominance in our time of what David Riesman in *The Lonely Crowd* (1950) originally called the purely "other-directed personality type," which Trilling has always lamented, despite his own social orientation as a literary critic, and has most memorably portrayed in his 1967 preface to Joyce's "The Dead," in his characterization of Gabriel Conroy as one of the new species of men who possess the knowledge of excellence but neither the native gift of talent nor the moral energy to attain excellence for themselves and so, unless redeemed by the experience of literature, are fated to turn in resentful rage against life itself. What Trilling now sees in *Sincerity and Authenticity*, however, is that academic culture fostered by modern literature has not saved us from but only made more certain the smarmy apocalypse of all the Underground Men.

It would be politically expedient for me, in terms of my immediate professional self-interest, to discuss Trilling's position here as merely the predictable climax of the conventional family romance in which, in this case, Freud as the representative of the tragic law of life has replaced David Trilling as the failed would-be rabbinical student and irresponsible father, so that the anxious son, whose identity is ever on the verge of disintegration, may assimilate his adopted precursor's severe strength and project his actual precursor's disabling weakness entirely onto his native culture in the form of a hell of mirrors to which it is completely condemned. For, put in this manner, no one need take Trilling's critique of this new personality type seriously. It could all be seen as just his own psychopathology writ large in the most New York Intellectual of styles. In his "jeremiad" against such neo-Freudian revisionists as Marcuse, Laing, Brown, Cooper, and, by implication, Foucault, however, Trilling's criticism demonstrates an impersonal power that demands we take his argument seriously.

Although Trilling understands all the neo-Freudians he attacks as taking essentially R. D. Laing's position, in *The Divided Self* and *The Politics of Experience*, on the social determination and ideological definition of insanity, he does recognize significant variations, and marks these by the degree of respect he accords their arguments. While Norman O. Brown in *Life against Death* and his Phi Beta Kappa speech at Columbia University gets accused of coming close to intellectual cant for clownishly recommending madness—"holy" madness, of course, and not mere insanity—as the route to apocalyptic thinking and the "liberation" of polymorphous perversity (*SA*, pp. 169–170), Marcuse in *Eros and Civilization* warrants Trilling's most sympathetic critical response for the poignant contradiction between the utopian perspective of his argument which calls for the elimination, through revolution, of the adversity and aggressions of social life and his personal preference for the personality type formed in adversity. A band of genial hedonists in the park is a social vision that gives Marcuse pause, making him more than a bit "apprehensive" (*SA*, pp. 161–165) about the cultural future, even though a society in which the vast majority live and die without genuine pleasure, while the occasional heroic individual like Freud gets the greatest pleasure in taking his own way to death despite the pain, satisfies the Marxist in Marcuse even less. R. D. Laing and his disciple David Cooper (in his introduction to the original English translation of Foucault's *Madness and Civilization*) receive the greatest amount of Trilling's attention, and provoke the climactic prophetic wrath of his critical career.

Laing argues that schizophrenics, the kind of clients psychoanalysis has never claimed to cure, suffer from a fundamental "ontological insecurity" similar to that of Kohut's narcissistic personality disorders only much more severe. Laing's schizophrenics, that is, suffer from a chronic anxiety of engulfment, a dread that their very being is in danger of being overwhelmed. Unlike classical therapists who see this as part of their symptomatology, Laing believes it is precisely due to the actual conditions of their original familial situations that his patients feel and act as they do. Their "madness" is the "sane" or at least understandable response of threatened selves to an "insane" society that would coerce them into its destructive mold (familial or otherwise). Society thus causes their bizarre symptoms as implicit critical reactions, and then defines them as incorrigible in order to get rid of these telling embarrassments. In short, "madness," as Thomas Szaz was the first to announce and Deleuze and Guattari also criticize in *Anti-Oedipus*, is an ideological weapon in the West just as much as it is in the Soviet bloc.[15]

Cooper, following his master's lead and using Foucault's historical analysis of the discursive construction of insanity, draws the inevitable if absurdly reductive conclusion when he proclaims "madness" to be the "lost truth" in "our age," a "way of seizing *in extremis*" the "groundwork" of "what we are about." Much to Trilling's mounting angry incredulity, Cooper continues in this vein:

> "The truth of madness is what madness is. What madness is is a form of vision that destroys itself by its own choice of oblivion in the

face of existing forms of social tactics and strategy. Madness, for instance, is a matter of voicing the realizing that I am (or you are) Christ." (*SA*, p. 170)

Cooper's mentor Laing is a little more careful in the formulation of his claims for madness as "health fully realized at last" (*SA*, p. 170). He claims that it is only *sometimes* that "transcendental experiences . . . break through in psychosis" (*SA*, p. 170) to show their relation to the originary visions of the great religions. But even Laing must succumb at last to the logic of his position and declare that "true sanity entails in one way or another the dissolution of the normal ego, that false self completely adjusted to our alienative social reality" (*SA*, p. 170). The modern quest of Diderot's Nephew has thus led to insanity as our most authentic state.

Despite the differences he duly notes among Freud's revisionary critics, the whole thrust of Trilling's argument in this last chapter of *Sincerity and Authenticity* has been to assimilate them all to Cooper's extreme position, the easier to condemn them all in the end. The question I must raise is why Trilling's rush to judgment here? One part of the answer, of course, concerns the immediate historical circumstances and Trilling's disgust at the "symbolic" and "gratuitous" nature of some student rebellions.[16] But there is a deeper level of disgust, one of self-disgust. Consider Cooper's climactic claim for madness once again: "madness . . . is a form of vision that destroys itself by its own choice of oblivion in the face of existing forms of social tactics and strategy." Consider now Trilling's own climactic claim in *The Liberal Imagination* for Hyacinth Robinson's exemplary tragic fate:

> it would seem that a true knowledge of society comprehends the reality of the social forces it presumes to study and is aware of contradictions and consequences; it knows that sometimes society offers an opposition of motives in which the antagonists are in such a balance of authority and appeal that a man who so wholly perceives them as to embody them in his very being cannot choose between them and is therefore destroyed. This is known as tragedy. . . . Hyacinth's death, then, is not his way of escaping from irresolution. It is truly a sacrifice, an act of heroism. He is a hero of civilization because he dares to do more than civilization does: embodying two ideals at once, he takes upon himself, in full consciousness, the guilt of each. He acknowledges both his parents, as it were. By his death he instructs us in the nature of civilized life and by his consciousness he transcends it. (*LI*, pp. 80, 86)

What Trilling sees in Cooper is the return of his own earlier position cŏme back to haunt him in a more virulent mode. What he could entertain only as an imaginative possibility in the service of civilization and must call heroic self-sacrifice, another generation, trained by his kind of critic, would carry out under the banner of a militant madness radically opposed to all culture. The Tertans have bested the Howes this time round. No wonder Trilling loses his temper—eloquently, of course. He is angry at his own youthful great hopes for the moderating educational influence of literary culture upon the apocalyptic politics of liberal America.

> Who that has had experience of our social reality will doubt its alienated condition? And who that has thought of his experience in the light of certain momentous speculations made over the last two centuries, of which a few have been touched on in these pages, will not be disposed to find some seed of cogency in a view that proposes an antinomian reversal of all accepted values, of all received realities?
>
> But who that has spoken, or tried to speak, with a psychotic friend will consent to betray the masked pain of his bewilderment and solitude by making it the paradigm of liberation from the imprisoning falsehoods of an alienated social reality? Who that finds intelligible the sentences which describe madness (to use the word that cant prefers) in terms of transcendence and charisma will fail to penetrate to the great refusal of human connection that they express, the appalling belief that human existence is made authentic by the possession of a power, or the persuasion of its possession, which is not to be qualified or restricted by the co-ordinate existence of any fellow man?
>
> Yet the doctrine that madness is health, that madness is liberation and authenticity, receives a happy welcome from a consequential part of the educated public. And when we have given due weight to the likelihood that those who respond positively to the doctrine don't have it in mind to go mad, let alone insane—it is characteristic of the intellectual life of our culture that it fosters a form of assent which does not involve actual credence—we must yet take it to be significant of our circumstances that many among us find it gratifying to entertain the thought that alienation is to be overcome only by the completeness of alienation, and that alienation completed is not a deprivation or deficiency but a potency. Perhaps exactly because the thought is assented to so facilely, so without what used to be called seriousness, it might seem that no expression of disaffection from the social existence was ever so desperate as this eagerness to say

that authenticity of personal being is achieved through an ultimate isolatedness and through the power that this is presumed to bring. The falsities of an alienated social reality are rejected in favour of an upward psychopathic mobility to the point of divinity, each one of us a Christ—but with none of the inconveniences of undertaking to intercede, of being a sacrifice, of reasoning with rabbis, of making sermons, of having disciples, of going to weddings and to funerals, of beginning something and at a certain point remarking that it is finished. (*SA*, pp. 170–172)

The subversive patriarch of liberal culture here reveals the purpose for which he has spent a lifetime in assimilating to and ironically opposing himself against modern America: to pronounce his representative knowledge of imaginative excellence in all its minute particulars as good in itself, as if Trilling were suddenly, climactically, transformed into the divinely fathering voice of this beloved Word, in whom the critic at least is well pleased. If each one of us is to envision himself a Christ, in other words, Trilling is the one who sincerely understands what such a role authentically comprises: "the inconveniences of undertaking to intercede, of being a sacrifice, of reasoning with rabbis, of making sermons, of having disciples, of going to weddings and to funerals, of beginning something and at a certain point remarking that it is finished." The apocalyptic tone, at least in our postmodern age, is indeed infectious.

Internal Exile: Final Texts for Pharisees and Radicals

I have been tracing the inner history of the career of modern America's last major literary critic. How the religious unconscious of the secular oppositional critic conditions the development of that career has been my subject. The work of Lionel Trilling, as we have seen, has repeatedly cast him in the role of the subversive patriarch of liberal culture for half a century. With the passing of that culture as an effective national force during the last decade of his career and that following his death, also has passed the possibility for any later critic to adopt an oppositional stance broadly relevant to the intellectual classes in the country. Why this should be so has already been suggested in part by Trilling's own late argument against education. The literary ethics of both sincerity and authenticity have demonstratively failed as universal ideological substitutes for the old religious ethos. And these humanistic replacements based on the experience of reading have not themselves been replaced by anything else in intellectual circles, certainly not by a new literary ethic founded upon a humane study of letters. Nor does Trilling think it necessarily wise or beneficial that we attempt to formulate a new humanism on some other basis, for whether we call that basis "theory" or "pragmatism" or "history" or "pluralism," all such "foundations" still derive their authority from the primary pleasure of impersonation—reading.

In an epoch whose rule is pandemic impersonation for professional gain, everyone becomes either Rameau's Nephew or his demonic offspring, Dostoyevsky's Underground Man. That in the public arena we have only these antithetical alternatives for criticism means that Trilling's role of loyal opposition no longer makes sense, is a dead issue. Loyal opposition to cynical self-advancement or revisionary madness for its own sake? The potential for deception of others and of oneself inherent in the experience of reading, of telling ourselves stories of identification and authority, has been so thoroughly exposed—the Wizard of Oz being our "divinity"—that no one, least of all ourselves, can take what we do seriously no matter how we characterize it. As a perverse sort of exclusive pleasure it is all right—but for us alone. Criticism has been ghettoized in American society and in its universities. Hence, the prevalence of the exile motif in current criticism.[17] As we shall see, Trilling in his last years increasingly felt the relevance of this topos for his entire career. Internal exile in postmodern America becomes his avowed preference over aping either of the awful Normans—Mailer or Podhoretz.[18] Always America's "exile in residence," as it were, Trilling in his last texts now sounds as if he were speaking from "death's dream kingdom."

The Last Decade collects the essays and reviews of this final phase in Trilling's career. With the exception of the appendix, "Some Notes for an Autobiographical Lecture" (1971), the selections have been arranged by Diana Trilling in the original order of publication. Framed by personal reflections on the different novelistic projects of Tess Slesinger and Jane Austen, the volume enacts the withdrawal of criticism from the contemporary world or the fate of internal exile ironically being suffered by America's leading humanist who is increasingly against humanism, or certainly against an educational program for the masses and perhaps for anyone. In the end, the subversive patriarch has turned himself into a travel-wearied, aged Oedipus of revisionism who must be content with a Colonus of the mind.

"A Novel of the Thirties" was originally published as the afterword to the 1966 republication of *The Unpossessed* and as "Young in the Thirties" in *Commentary* (October, 1966). Trilling begins with the early promise of energetic imagination and ambition that marked those writers, including himself, associated orignally with Elliot Cohen's *Menorah Journal* and its project of "normal" or "positive" Jewishness, of promoting among young Jewish intellectuals a more cosmopolitan cultural identity than either their own community or alien America could then afford them. He then contrasts this original spirit with the "desiccation" and "corruption of the spirit," the sense of great hopes greatly betrayed, that the radical decade bequeathed to the tone of intellectual life in modern America. Trilling, following Murray Kempton's lead in *Part of Our Time* (1955), believes that this disillusioning experience created the intellectual class in the country. And the value of Tess Slesinger's novel resides primarily in its passionate representation of the fate of this class. Trilling stresses that the novel's male characters especially suffer from intellectual "desiccation" and "corruption." Their fate derives not from blind faith in an unworthy and offstage ideal (the Communist Party) but from a substantiated lack of imaginative and emotional power to sustain a realistic commitment to any cause outside the self: "The failure of the men to possess the women is consonant with their inability to surrender themselves to the ideals they profess" (*LD*, p. 17). As ever, Trilling's novelist's eye focuses on the social irony: hypocrisy as a failure of romantic illusion.

What he terms the "familiar" dialectic in modern intellectual life is at work in *The Unpossessed*. As self-possessed oppositional intellectuals discover that the principle of corruption that they despised in the old society is reappearing among themselves as they would forge a new society, they simply give up all hope or deny what they know to be true (*LD*, p. 20). Trilling sees this "radical" dialectic to be part of a larger dialectic—that of modern civilization and its discontents. Ever-growing numbers of people, unfitted by birth or personal gift, nevertheless aspire to the intellectual life. Their resentment over what they have to give up increases with their professional advancement and disillusionment over not being geniuses, until they finally "give up" the intellectual life itself for "the blessed stupidity of nature and instinct" in the form of domestic or professional routine (*LD*, p. 24). (After her first marriage to Herbert Solow fails Slesinger remarries, has a child, and goes off to Hollywood to write solely for the movies before dying of cancer at the age of thirty-nine). This "Rimbaud syndrome" (as I call it) clearly affected Tess Slesinger, and as clearly has considerable allure for Trilling himself:

> Tess Slesinger, who might herself have been "that girl standing there" of Yeats's little poem ["Politics"], enrolled herself early among those who [for better or worse] understood to advance the "great work" [of what "Man and the Echo" calls "the spiritual intellect"].

> Like the friends with whom she began her public intellectual life, she
> believed that there was no better occupation than to scrub the (dirty)
> slate [of human history] clean of the scrawls made on it by family,
> class, ethnic or cultural group, the society in general. She did not
> change her judgment of the enterprise, but in one especially viva-
> cious and articulate moment she took notice of the scribble she had
> not expected to see on the slate—the one made by the spiritual
> intellect itself. (*LD*, p. 24)

Even before the popular outbreaks of campus radicalism, Trilling understands one source of its motivation to be the self-destructive development of the diseased superego. As the ego sacrifices more and more
of its pleasures to the drive for intellectual "success," the superego
increases its unrealistic demands until some "ultimate" sacrifice is
made: that of the intellect or of life itself. This "lesson," perhaps more
than any other, Trilling and his class have passed on to the next generation where it is generally automatically presumed, not painfully
earned.

"James Joyce in His Letters," two years later in 1968, makes precisely
this point. Trilling portrays Joyce as the last representative of the Titan-
ism, the heroic will, of the nineteenth-century intellectual. While Joyce
in his work goes on to demonstrate, as Eliot put it, "the futility of all
English styles," and of just about everything else, he begins as a romantic aspirant to "the fair courts of life" (as Stephen Dedalus at the
end of *A Portrait of the Artist* so memorably phrases it). Joyce's Faustian
progress in his career, as his letters tellingly reveal, is like that of a
"sandblast," going through sector after sector of knowledge and showing the beautiful nullity at its heart. Joyce not only personally resists
the nullity so as to write, he also wishes to make it prevail generally so
as to witness the destruction of the merely human. Typically, he depicts
the will in extremis, disintegrating and moving mightily to entropy.
Even the infamous "dirty" letters to Nora can be read as a means for
knowing another soul in ultimate intimacy so as to better prepare for
creating Molly Bloom, the Beautiful Nullity Herself. Gone from Trilling's view of Joyce is any extended or favorable comparison to Wordsworth's stoic humanism. Instead, the later Joyce is praised precisely
for his inhuman capacity for living life as a ghost, in ironic fulfillment
of the visions of James in "A Jolly Corner" and of Yeats in *A Vision*.

A Keats has thus become a Kafka, a Shelley has come to inhabit
Yeats's "mad abstract dark," and this is exactly Trilling's point:

> If this is so, as I think it is, it brings the obscene letters into accord
> with what I have proposed as the controlling tendency of Joyce's

genius—to move through the fullest realization of the human, all-too-human, to that which transcends and denies the human. It was a progress he was committed to make, yet he made it with some degree of reluctance. . . . The ethos and mythos of the nineteenth century could still command from him more than some degree of assent. The merely human still engaged him, he was not wholly ready to go beyond it. The fair courts of life still beckoned invitation and seemed to await his entrance. He was to conclude that their walls and gates enclosed nothing. His genius is defined by his having concluded this rather than taking it for granted, as many of the generation that came after him have found it possible to do. (*LD*, pp. 55–56)

I think what Trilling says of Henry James as a critic in "What Is Criticism" (1970) is most apropos here. "Try as we may, we cannot down our consciousness of Henry James the man, the man-writing," Trilling claims, and I think it is no less true for Trilling now in these final essays. He becomes, as he says James does for us, "part of our experience of his work, which we see not as a collection of particular aesthetic objects but as an intention, the enterprise of a lifetime, which has its own coherence and form and is thus in itself an aesthetic object of a kind" (*LD*, p. 74). As Trilling completes the aesthetic object that his career has become for him and for us, he joins Tess Slesinger and James Joyce in coming to a transcendent judgment upon the intellectual life in the modern world. Trilling's genius is that he, too, has personally reached this conclusion and has never presumed anything simply on another's authority.

One reason why "Mind in the Modern World," the first Thomas Jefferson Lecture of the National Endowment for the Humanities (1972), is such an unsatisfactory, disturbing performance is precisely that it does presume its conclusions rather than reach them. For in it Trilling argues that the ancient authority of mind, newly recognized since the Renaissance as having the natural right to rule society, is resentfully under attack for its undemocratic hierarchical principle of order and for the personal deformation its rational imperative admittedly works upon the lives of intellectuals, and that the leading figures in the attack are such disaffected intellectuals as Louis Kampf (the president of the Modern Language Association of America for 1971), who speak from positions of professional authority against the very institutions that have authorized them. In short, Kampf and Company begin their careers as oppositional critics of culture exactly where Trilling is now concluding his own career. Despite the precedent of the Joyce essay this argument cannot but appear rather self-servingly hypocritical. While it may be true that Kampf and Co., unlike Joyce or Nietzsche, presume their conclusions, Trilling does so here as well, especially where affirmative action programs are concerned. For Trilling, that grand opponent of institutional hypocrisy, opposes affirmative action programs in the academy on the ground that they expose openly what everyone secretly knows about the university's economic and social function: to confer middle-class accreditation on once-excluded groups. Consequently, affirmative action programs are bad for morale within the professions. That is, such government-sponsored programs destroy the hypocritical ideal, the fiction, that objective, disinterested principles of mind determine the nature and structure, "the mystique," of intellectual life in modern America (*LD*, pp. 110–126). Trilling, in short, is arguing for professional hypocrisy and against intellectual honesty. Having presumed his conclusion that Kampf and Co. are totally wrong, Trilling must concoct this unworthy argument in order to prove his point.

Why this presumptuousness? One answer could be that Trilling is in his own way as much at the end of his tether as is the H. G. Wells of *Mind at the End of Its Tether* invoked at the opening—or as Kampf for that matter. Another solution is to say that when Trilling's own self-interest and legitimacy as a leading academic are threatened he will do anything in their support, even embrace hypocrisy. I think the most fruitful path to an answer is to recall Trilling's concern for how an action reflects upon, indeed constitutes, its agent. It is one thing for members of formerly excluded groups, working largely within the established rules of the game and out of a sense of community-inspired ambition and pride, to flood into the universities and professions and gain prominent places there. But for Trilling it is quite another thing to require a government-sponsored program to accomplish this same goal for an entire class in one fell swoop. The discipline of social initiation for select individuals is missing, and therefore the morale for these new members of the intellectual classes will be bad, too. They will feel that they have not earned their positions in any significant way, that they are only being paid off for the great wrongs done in the past to their race or class. In this fashion, as well, their potential radicalism is being bought off. Or so it will appear to all concerned. Consequently, no one in this situation *can look good*. And the mind thus loses its last, purely aesthetic basis for being valued as a model for the ideal polity (the modern reversal of Plato's formula) (*LD*, p. 120).

And finally, with the passing of "mind" as a regulative ideal for modern man, there also passes the humanistic rationale, that one studies the past for its celebrated heroic instances of mind at work:

> The efflorescence of mind in the two centuries before our own seems so closely bound up with the vivid imagination of the past that we are led to conclude that the urgent recollection of what man has already done and undergone in pursuit of his destiny is a necessary condition of comprehending and intending mind. And if now we may be aware of a diminished confidence in mind, of a disposition to withdraw our credence from it, we might conjecture that this is, if not a consequence, then at least a concomitance of our diminished awareness of the past, of our disaffection from history. (*LD*, p. 105)

Without the monumental conception of the past, no present can imagine a standard to measure itself by, and so must become content with a growing sense of universal diminishment, occasionally punctuated by apocalyptic spectacles of one sort or another.

Although Trilling does remind us and himself that "mind does not move toward its ideal purposes over a royal straight road but finds its way through the thicket of its own confusions and contradictions" (*LD*, p. 127), and that the ideal of disinterested objectivity while never absolutely realizable can nevertheless serve the interests of the sympathetic imagination by enforcing the attempt to see things from a different point of view before passing judgment, the ultimate effect of "Mind in the Modern World"—even if one credits fully its climactic heroic endorsement of the mind's freedom "to examine a course it has taken and to correct it" (*LD*, p. 128)—is prophetically chilling:

> We know that when we cast up the fortunes of mind at any given moment in history, what makes the object of our concern is mind as it defines itself by its ideal [i.e., *fictional or ideological*] purposes, by its power to achieve order, inclusiveness, and coherence. It is when we take mind in this [mythic] sense that I believe there is reason for disquietude about its future, discerning as I do within the intellectual life of the nation, and not of our nation alone, a notable retraction of spirit, a falling off in mind's vital confidence in itself. (*LD*, pp. 127–128)

Trilling pauses at this point to remind us all, once again, that the situation he sees emerging has occurred before in "the history of mind." "There have always been periods," he reassures us, "when mind shines forth with a special luminosity," and as many periods if not more, he darkly counsels, when mind "withdraws into the shadows" apparently to trace there its own tragic trajectory. Carrion comfort this. Yet, he concludes, our situation is novel in a fateful sense:

> In the past, when a retraction of mind took place, it might well seem to affect only such specific and discrete intellectual life as a society had developed: what was thought of as an ornament of the general life was no longer there and yet the general life went its traditional way. In our time this cannot be the case. When mind, far from being ornamental, part of the super-structure of society, is the very model of the nation-state, as now it is for us, any falling off of its confidence in itself must be felt as a diminution of national possibility, as a lessening of the social hope. It is out of this belief that I have ventured to urge upon you the awareness that mind at the present time draws back from its own freedom and power, from its own delight in itself.
> (*LD*, p. 128)

Surely, simply because mind ever wishes "to be conscious of itself" (*LD*, p. 128) cannot inspire much hope, otherwise Freud would not have needed to invent the discipline of psychoanalysis, nor Trilling have been required to anatomize for America's "best and brightest" in 1972 what they should have already realized about the failure of the dream of mind in the jungles of Vietnam or Morningside Heights.

In the essays on Slesinger, Joyce, and the fate of mind, Trilling has been withdrawing his credence from the humanistic ideology that has animated his career. He progressively erases mark after mark he himself has made on the dirty slate of the intellectual history of modern America. He is thus left with nothing but a hypocritical creed, the fictional ideal of the mind's freedom, an admittedly outmoded *mystique*, which he bluntly asserts and embraces. The most appropriate emblem for this entire story of mind in the modern world, from Jefferson, Joyce, and Wells to the thirties radicals and Louis Kampf, is the scene from Plato's *Phaedo* of Socrates in prison preparing himself and his disciples for the "suicide" a people's court has ordered for this enemy of the Athenian state. Better internal exile and intellectual suicide (at least) than the public life of postmodern America. Or so "Mind and the Modern World" all but argues in the final analysis.

One explanation for Trilling's doleful position would be to claim that the then-declining force of the cold-war-liberal paradigm of American culture leads to this impasse for him and the other New York Intellectuals. Certainly two other essays of the time, "Art, Will, and Neces-

sity" (1973) and "Aggression and Utopia" (1971, 1973), read contemporary developments in art, literature, and sensibility almost entirely in terms of the earlier struggles against cultural Stalinism. Both
the mindless celebration of the artistic will that Harold Rosenberg in
The De-Definition of Art laments to find among contemporary artists and
the structuralist denial of the individual will that Robert Scholes in
"The Ill-Liberal Imagination" welcomes among recent novelists are,
according to Trilling, the broken fragments of the postwar dialectical
synthesis of the conservative instinct and the revolutionary principle
that equally threaten now to put an end to civilized life as we know it,
for they bring about the formation of a radically new kind of personality
whose utopian prototype William Morris envisioned in *News from Nowhere* in the mistaken belief that the human species would be better off
without the spiritual as well as the material modes of competition and
heroic accomplishment. Whether the artist is thought capable of subsuming reality within his will, or the individual will thought to be
subsumed by some deterministic historical process or structure of culture, the underlying desire or hidden motive in both cases is the apocalyptic urge to put an end both to the incessant conflict of wills that is
society and to the repeated need to overcome personal passivity in the
face of this adverse reality. A final monolithic order or totalitarian scene
of ultimate persuasion with either I or IT as the presiding deity—such
is the "authentic" unconscious Trilling discovers all around him, now
as always, because it is his own. Or, rather, because he is of it.

There is great merit to this critical understanding of Trilling. But
more central than the ideological failure of his historical moment is
Trilling's correct perception of the failure of critical humanism generally. Once religion, then moral convention, and finally good taste provided the legitimate foundations for judging personal conduct and
public policy. Now there are no foundations, literary or otherwise, only
naked self-interest projected as revolutionary "theory" or "practice"
on the part of isolated egos or purely partisan factions and, in the
ultimate analysis, the sheer weight of numbers. Although Trilling did
not live to see it, his worst nightmares foretell the spectacle of Ronald
Reagan as actor-president and Norman Podhoretz, Trilling's least dialectical disciple, as petty sage of the national interest: "When mind . . .
is the very model of the nation-state . . . any falling off . . . must be
felt as a diminution of national possibility, as a lessening of the social
hope."

"The Uncertain Future of the Humanistic Educational Ideal" (*American Scholar*, Winter 1974–1975), unlike "Mind in the Modern World,"
deals directly and honestly with the problem of the disappearance of

an intellectual purpose for higher education in America. Originally a paper delivered at a conference entitled "The Educated Person in the Contemporary World," sponsored by the Aspen Institute for Humanistic Studies, the essay opens with a striking contrast between the Columbia College Great Books tradition of education summarized by the title of John Erskine's famous 1920 essay, "The Moral Obligation to Be Intelligent," and the contemporary attitude that sees education solely as a compensatory ritual of social initiation intended to redress what Richard Sennett and Jonathan Cobb entitle their book—*The Hidden Injuries of Class*. Trilling strikes this contrast not out of resentful nostalgia alone. He also wants to make the point that without the earlier belief of aspiring groups in the ability of education to lead an individual not merely to better paychecks and a house in the suburbs but to magnanimity of mind, the urban working classes of today are reduced to pursuing culture only insofar as it signifies their movement up in class financially. Consequently they can only resent strongly their own class aspirations as a betrayal and disintegration of their original culture (*LD*, pp. 169–170). Without some educational goal beyond the victory of one's class interests, aspiration disintegrates into cynicism and the public sphere into warring factions. That is, we get the spectacle of *our* society.

Traditionally, of course, the humanistic ideal of education had the goal of fashioning a unique self from the conflict between class interests and social conventions under the direction of what has customarily been seen, by partisans as different as William Pitt and William Blake, as (in the inevitable Arnoldian formula) "the best that has been thought and said" in Western culture. Whether one thinks of Castiglione's *The Courtier*, the masks of Wilde and Nietzsche, or Yeats's daemonic soul-making, the humanistic educational ideal had as its goal the discipline of self-culture, as much as the ancient religions once seriously proposed "orders" for life. The ascetic ideal in religious or secular forms has been the only meaning that humankind has devised for itself on this earth, as Nietzsche was the first to insist. Postmodern American society is attempting the experiment of doing without the ascetic ideal. As a result Trilling can envision nothing for the future but an unprecedented, ultimate psychic mobility on a massive scale.

This desire to fashion, to shape, a self and a life has all but gone from a contemporary culture whose emphasis, paradoxically enough, is so much on self. If we ask why this has come about, the answer of course involves us in a giant labor of social history. But there is one

reason which can be readily isolated and which, I think, explains
much. It is this: if you set yourself to shaping a self, a life, you limit
yourself to that self and that life. You preclude any other kind of
selfhood remaining available to you. You close out other options,
other possibilities which might have been yours. Such limitation,
once acceptable, now goes against the cultural grain—it is almost as
if the fluidity of the contemporary world demands an analogous
limitlessness in our personal perspective. Any doctrine, that of the
family, religion, the school, that does not sustain this increasingly
felt need for a multiplication of options and instead offers an ideal of
a shaped self, a formed self, has the sign on it of a retrograde and
depriving authority, which, it is felt, must be resisted. For anyone
concerned with contemporary education at whatever level, the assimilation that contemporary culture has made between social idealism, even political liberalism, and personal fluidity—a self without
the old confinements—is as momentous as it is recalcitrant to correction. Among the factors in the contemporary world which militate
against the formulation of an educational ideal related to the humanistic tradition of the past, this seems to me to be the most decisive.
(*LD*, pp. 175–176)

Trilling's position not only concludes the speculations of his later career
on the ethics of impersonation; it also summarizes the point of his
entire career in a manner that anticipates the work of Christopher
Lasch in *The Culture of Narcissism* and its sequel, *The Minimal Self*.[19] The
desire to be authentically oneself, in opposition to the sincere adoption
of a single role, a reiterated impersonation of a social function, leads in
the end to the apocalypse of the self, the revelation that the truly
authentic self unencumbered by imposed norms of all the ruling
groups or cultures is a loose collection of partial selves fluidly bleeding
one into another as circumstances determine. That is, the authentic
self is the perfect worker/consumer in a postindustrial society that
requires maximum flexibility for the interchangeable deployments of
personnel and maximum fluidity for the transient fixations of stimulated needs. The spectral politics of the shaped self that Trilling practiced for so long have been outmoded by the global economy of the
disintegrated self. Although one can say that the completion of this
modernization process in our postmodern age may herald a truly world
revolution, Trilling's somberer assessment sounds more realistic: a new
order of disintegrated selves for the entire earth.

Trilling's anti-utopian vision does sound somewhat duplicitous. For
the contemporary resistance to any manifestiation of the traditional

authority of the shaped self stems also from a valid sense of social injustices. Even more pointedly perhaps, such resistance assimilates the very virtues of literary culture—multiplicity, variousness, spontaneity, gratuitously chosen images personal being, etc.—that Trilling himself has championed all these many years as corrective measures necessary for the education of the liberal imagination. To envision no future for this humanistic educational ideal—which is really what he does here—marks the cruel beginning of Trilling's final turn against literary culture and against education itself. What goal can the critic have in such a desperate context?

"Why We Read Jane Austen," a paper intended for a Jane Austen conference at the University of Alberta in October 1975, but left incomplete at his death on November 5, 1975, gives Trilling's prophetic answer to this question. The paper begins with Trilling's puzzlement at the tremendous interest of Columbia students in a class on Austen he gave in the fall 1973 semester. He believes that this interest results from Austen's having become as much a *figure* of pure resistance as William Blake was only five years previously. Thanks to the traditional ethos and realistic psychological development of her characters, both of which qualities are quite absent from the contemporary "high" cultural novel, Austen appears now to oppose the established intellectual culture as much as Blake's mythological spectres once opposed his society's political establishment. Ironically enough, of course, Trilling laments this development which his own essays on Austen have helped to foster over the years. And he laments it because he finds that under the stimulus of Clifford Geertz's work in cultural anthropology he can no longer accept the fundamental principle of humanism, that by reading the works of different peoples of the past one can readily understand what principles and values are common to humankind and opportunistically use this universal standard of humanity as an effective weapon against all present threats to the human order in our time. He no longer can believe that the critic ought to be "oppositional" or even can be effectively oppositional, since the humanistic ideal is based on a patent illusion, one that his own many students still avidly cultivate (*LD*, pp. 212–213).

Instead, Trilling proposes for himself alone an ideal of selfhood wholly textual in nature. This ideal is similar to the sense of pastness, arrested by aesthetic form, that Keats's poetry celebrates, that Schopenhauer's philosophy promotes, and that Thomas Mann makes the cornerstone of modern humanism. In the final analysis, however, it is radically other, drawn in fact from Javanese and Balinese cultures, just as Yeats's later occult aesthetic was in part drawn from the Japanese tradition of theater:

> Of the three cultures Mr. Geertz touches on . . . at least two of them,
> the Javanese and the Balinese, may readily be thought of as bringing
> life under the dominion of some form of conceptual or aesthetic
> "death." Javanese culture may indeed verge upon the bizarre in the
> overtness of its intention to control, up to the point of actual negation,
> what we think of as the characteristic processes of life (*LD*, p. 221).

Governed by two dualities, "refined"/"vulgar" and "inside/outside,"
the person in Javanese culture is all externality and performance, so
that one is ever "refined" on the "outside" and never "vulgar" or
"deep," having little or no "interior." One is to achieve this goal, Trilling cites Geertz as saying, by "meditation," which "thins out" the
"emotional life" of "the civilized man" to "a kind of constant hum;
through etiquette, he both shields that life from external disruptions
and regularizes his outer behavior in such a way that it appears to
others as a predictable, undisturbing, elegant, and rather vacant set of
choreographed motions and settled forms of speech" (*LD*, p. 221).

While Trilling admits that by Western standards this mode of selfhood seems to verge on the "state of severe mental pathology" (*LD*, p.
222) that postmodernism celebrates, he also confesses that for him it
possesses "quite considerable charm" (*LD*, p. 222) for its orientation
toward death, something deemphasized in postmodern polemics. Like
great tragic art in the West this aesthetic of death would "transmute
life into art" and thus "put [it] into our [imaginative] possession and
control" (*LD*, p. 223). Even when recognizing the greater limitations of
Balinese culture in this connection, Trilling admires the fact that for
these people, too, it is "dramatis personae, not actors, that in the
proper sense really exist," that populate the world (*LD*, p. 223). And
these "dramatis personae," of course, are the daemonic characters, the
great undying passions, of one's ancestral voices. To become oneself
such an aesthetic object of form, such a text or figure of death, is
paradoxically, "by very reason of the deprived condition" of one's
"existence," to be thought "to celebrate and perpetuate life" (*LD*, p.
225). As an ultimate formulation of the revisionary critical humanist's
avowed "self" and "ideal" of education, Trilling's characterization
rings true.

Disclosed here shortly before his death is the underlying motive and
work of Lionel Trilling's long career. As the appended autobiographical
essay makes clear, Trilling early on saw himself as a critic of critics, of
those who took an oppositional stance—"unmasking the unmaskers"
(*LD*, p. 240) is the way he puts his role. To this end he wrote himself
into modern American culture as its subversive patriarch whose texts

were ironically structured as object lessons, parables for all pharisees and radicals.[20] His dialectical imitations of opponents' positions clarified his own radical ambivalence on every subject and, he hoped, could help others do likewise. What Trilling has discovered and fully recognized at last is the inappropriateness of this personal ideal of critical work for anyone else. Whatever it may have once been for others, it is now his mode of life alone. "In Whittaker Chambers there was much to be faulted," Trilling correctly concludes in the introduction to the 1975 republication of *The Middle of the Journey*, "but nothing I know of him," he gratuitously adds "has ever led me to doubt his magnanimous intention" (*MJ*, p. 203). Who but Trilling could ever believe this of anyone again?

Against Education: "My Father Moved through Dooms of Love"

I conclude this study of Trilling's career with two brief quotations from conference proceedings in March 1974 and September 1974.[21]

> The ability to test by one's own actual experience what one's opinions are seems to me a very hard thing to come by. And it seems to me that so long as we are not able to judge things not only as intellectuals but in our social roles [as householders, parents, spouses, etc.], we are a failed class. I think this is the great sin of the intellectual: that he never tests his ideas by what it would mean to him if he were to undergo the experience that he is recommending. . . .
>
> To define the function of criticism as oppositional seems to me dangerous. . . . this is the first culture that calls itself a culture. . . . This is the first time that there have been masses of conscious people thinking and judging their lives [and]. . . . the [resulting] disaffection from the nature of modern life is universal . . . In a certain sense I am arguing against education.[21]

Here the subversive patriarch performs his final, perhaps finest role, as the stylish terminator of modern culture itself. Our father, as the cummings poem so beautifully phrases it, has indeed "moved through dooms of love." The question is: after him, can we?

Notes

Index

Notes

Chapter One. *Sacred Mourning*

1. Lionel Trilling, *Prefaces to the Experience of Literature* (New York: Harcourt Brace Jovanovich, 1979), pp. 74–78. Hereafter cited in the text as *PEL*.

2. See Alexander Bloom, *Prodigal Sons: The New York Intellectuals and Their World* (New York: Oxford University Press, 1986).

3. Mark Krupnick, *Lionel Trilling and the Fate of Cultural Criticism* (Evanston: Northwestern University Press, 1986).

4. Steven Marcus, "The Psychoanalytic Self," *Southern Review*, 22, no. 2 (April 1986), 308–325.

5. See Chapters 2 and 6 for further discussion.

6. See Chapter 4 for further discussion.

7. Alan Wilde, *Horizons of Assent: Modernism, Postmodernism, and the Ironic Imagination* (Baltimore: Johns Hopkins University Press, 1981).

8. Sigmund Freud, "Mourning and Melancholia," *Collected Papers*, Vol. 4, trans. Joan Riviere (New York: Basic Books, 1959). This edition was the one Trilling knew and selected for the Reader's Subscription Book Club. Hereafter cited in the text as "MM".

9. See Marcus, "Psychoanalytic Self," especially pp. 320–325.

10. On this topic see "Discipleship: A Special Issue on Psychoanalysis," *October*, 28 (Spring 1984), especially Joan Copjec, "Transference: Letters and the Unknown Woman," pp. 61–90.

11. The best critiques of professionalism are Magali Larson, *The Rise of Professionalism* (Los Angeles: University of California Press, 1977), and the recent essays in cultural theory by Bruce Robbins, especially "Pragmatism, Professionalism, and the Public" (forthcoming).

12. Jonathan Arac, *Critical Genealogies: Historical Situations for Postmodern Literary Studies* (New York: Columbia University Press, 1987). Hereafter cited in the text as *CG*.

13. See Geoffrey Hartman, *Wordsworth's Poetry, 1787–1814* (New Haven: Yale University Press, 1964).

14. See, for example, my remarks concluding "Nietzsche's Teacher: Paul de Man" in *The Romance of Interpretation: Visionary Criticism from Pater to de Man* (New York: Columbia University Press, 1985), pp. 231–233.

15. e. e. cummings, *A Selection of Poems* (New York: Harcourt Brace Jovanovich, 1965), pp. 119–121.

16. "Notes on E. E. Cummings' Language," *Selected Essays of R. P. Blackmur*, ed. Denis Donaghue (New York: Ecco Press, 1986), pp. 47–70. Hereafter cited in the text as *Blackmur*.

17. See Chapter 5 for Trilling's similar analysis.

18. For useful related discussions of the modern critic's ethic of self-sacrifice, see Donoghue's introduction to this volume, "The Sublime Blackmur," pp. 3–16; and Lionel Trilling's speech at Cornell University, "The Scholar's Caution and the Scholar's Courage" (1962), cited in René Wellek, *A History of Modern Criticism, 1750–1950*, Vol. 6: *American Criticism, 1900–1950*, p. 129.

19. Wellek, *History of Modern Criticism*, 6:140.

20. Ibid., p. 141.

21. For discussions of this recent development, see W. T. J. Mitchell, ed., *Against Theory: Literary Studies and the New Pragmatism* (Chicago: University of Chicago Press, 1985).

22. Robert Boyers, "Too Smart to Be Correct," *New York Times Book Review*, April 13, 1986, p. 19; Mark Shechner, "Trilling Man," *Nation*, May 31, 1986, pp. 767–769.

23. Cornel West, "Lionel Trilling: Godfather of Neo-Conservatism," *New Politics*, n.s. 1, no. 1 (Summer 1986), 233–242. Hereafter cited in the text as West.

24. See Bloom, *Prodigal Sons*, pp. 322–323.

25. Lionel Trilling, "George Orwell and the Politics of Truth," *The Opposing Self* (New York: Harcourt Brace Jovanovich, 1955, 1979), pp. 136–137. Hereafter this volume will be cited in the text as *OS*.

26. For an acute discussion of the essayistic tradition of critical writing, see Jeffrey Cane Robinson, "Lionel Trilling and the Romantic Tradition," *Massachusetts Review*, 22, no. 2 (Summer 1979), 217 ff.

Chapter Two. *Spectral Politics*

1. Lionel Trilling, "Impediments," *Of This Time, Of That Place and Other Stories* (New York: Harcourt Brace Jovanovich, 1979), p. 10. Hereafter this volume will be cited in the text as *OTT*.

2. Lionel Trilling, "Chapter for a Fashionable Jewish Novel," *Menorah Journal*, 12 (June 1926), 280.

3. See the appendix by Diana Trilling, "Lionel Trilling: A Jew at Columbia," in Lionel Trilling, *Speaking of Literature and Society* (New York: Harcourt Brace Jovanovich, 1980), pp. 411–429.

4. "From the Notebooks of Lionel Trilling," in William Phillips, ed.,

Partisan Review: The Fiftieth Anniversary Edition (New York: Stern and Day, 1984, 1985), p. 14. Hereafter cited in the text as "Notebooks."

5. The best studies of this background are by Alan M. Wald. See his "The Menorah Group Moves Left," *Jewish Social Studies*, 38, nos. 3 and 4 (Summer-Fall 1976), 289–320, and "Herbert Solow: Portrait of a New York Intellectual," in *Prospects: An Annual of American Cultural Studies*, Vol. 3 (New York: Burt Franklin, 1977), pp. 419–460.

6. Cited in Elinor Grumet, "The Apprenticeship of Lionel Trilling," *Prooftexts*, 4 (May 1984), 153–173. See p. 164 for quotation from letter.

7. See Diana Trilling, "Lionel Trilling: A Jew at Columbia," pp. 414–416.

8. Ibid., pp. 419–420.

9. See Grumet, "Apprenticeship of Lionel Trilling," pp. 163–165.

10. Ibid., pp. 165–166.

11. See my *Romance of Interpretation*. For different perspectives on this subject see Paul Bové, *Intellectuals in Power: A Genealogy of Critical Humanism* (New York: Columbia University Press, 1986), and Leo Braudy, *The Frenzy of Renown: Fame and Its History* (New York: Oxford University Press, 1986).

12. Marcus Klein, *Foreigners: The Making of American Literature, 1900–1940* (Chicago: University of Chicago Press, 1981). For a poignant account of the loss of this intellectual ideal, see Phillip Lopate, "Remembering Lionel Trilling," *American Review*, 25 (October 1976), 148–178. "And now that he is gone, who is there to *name* me?" Lopate asks apropos the passing of Lionel Trilling (p. 178).

13. Lionel Trilling, "A Light to Nations," *Menorah Journal*, 14 (April 1928), 402–408. Hereafter cited in the text as "Nations."

14. Lionel Trilling, "Flawed Instruments," *Speaking of Literature and Society*, p. 24. Hereafter this volume will be cited in the text as *SLS*.

15. On this topic, see Sander Gilman, *Jewish Self-Hatred: Anti-Semitism and the Secret Language of the Jews* (Baltimore: Johns Hopkins University Press, 1986). Gilman's thesis, persuasively argued and historically sweeping, is that Jewish self-hatred, paradigmatic of this condition generally, arises from the conflict produced in the psyches of members of a repressed group who have incorporated at an early age the ideals and values of both their own excluded community and the hegemonic culture to which they aspire guiltily for entry and status. Consequently, not only do such persons become battlefields of conflicting loyalties, they also are prone to turn against members of either interpretive community who exacerbate this conflict. All of this is expressed by a special language usage which, in most instances, ironically deploys the conventions of good taste and style as a psychic and social defense against open class warfare. My point, of course,

is to discover how Trilling turned this fate to his personal imaginative advantage for his critical survival.

16. See Diana Trilling, "Lionel Trilling: A Jew at Columbia," pp. 419–420, and "Notebooks," pp. 16–21.

17. For two very different versions of "absolute irony" in its New Critical and deconstructive modes, see Paul A. Bové, *Destructive Poetics: Heidegger and Modern American Poetry* (New York: Columbia University Press, 1980), and Wilde, *Horizons of Assent*.

18. See Lionel Trilling's contribution to "The Liberal Mind: Two Communications and a Reply," *Partisan Review*, 16 (June 1949), 649–665.

19. Lionel Trilling, "The Genius of O'Neill," *New Republic*, 88 (September 23, 1936), 176–179.

20. Irving Howe, "The New York Intellectuals: A Chronicle and Critique," *Commentary*, 46, no. 4 (October 1968), 29–51. Hereafter cited in the text as Howe.

21. See my phenomenological formulation of this Faustian motif in *The Romance of Interpretation*. For a deconstructive psychoanalytic reading of this cultural phenomenon, see Neil Hertz, *The End of the Line* (New York: Columbia University Press, 1984).

22. Bruce Robbins, "Professionalism and Politics: Toward Productively Divided Loyalties," *Profession 85*, p. 6.

23. See Robert Boyers, *Lionel Trilling: Negative Capability and the Wisdom of Avoidance* (Columbia: University of Missouri Press, 1977).

24. See West, "Lionel Trilling: Godfather of Neo-Conservatism," pp. 233–242.

25. Henry James, "The Altar of the Dead," *The Turn of the Screw and Other Short Novels*, with a Forward by Willard Thorpe (New York: New American Library, 1960, 1980), pp. 252–290. Hereafter cited in the text as "Altar."

26. See, for example, Stanley Fish, "Professionalism Despise Thyself: Fear and Self-Loathing in Literary Studies," *Critical Inquiry*, 10, no. 2 (December 1983), 349–364.

27. Lionel Trilling, *Matthew Arnold, With an Additional Essay, "Matthew Arnold, Poet"* (New York: Harcourt Brace Jovanovich, 1977). Hereafter cited in the text as *Arnold*.

28. *The Portable Arnold*, ed. Lionel Trilling (New York: Viking, 1949), p. 10. Hereafter cited in the text as *PA*.

29. See "Against Nature: Northrop Frye and Critical Romance," in my *Romance of Interpretation*, pp. 147–204.

30. See Trilling's contribution to "Under Forty: A Symposium on American Literature and the Younger Generation of American Jews," *Contemporary Jewish Record*, 7 (February 1944), 17.

31. Lionel Trilling, "Appendix: Some Notes for an Autobiographical Lecture" (Spring 1971), *The Last Decade: Essays and Reviews, 1965–1975* (New York: Harcourt Brace Jovanovich, 1979), p. 234. Hereafter this volume will be cited in the text as *LD*.

32. Lionel Trilling, "On the Teaching of Modern Literature," *Beyond Culture* (New York: Harcourt Brace Jovanovich, 1965, 1979), p. 12. Hereafter this volume will be cited in the text as *BC*.

33. Raymond Williams, *Culture and Society, 1780–1950* (New York: Columbia University Press, 1958, 1983), p. ix.

34. Trilling uses the introductory verses to *Milton* ("And did those feet in ancient time,") at a key point in his 1947 novel about thirties radicals, *The Middle of the Journey* (New York: Harcourt Brace Jovanovich, 1975), p. 178. Hereafter cited in the text as *MJ*. The Trilling narrator-hero, John Laskell, also intensely reflects upon *Jerusalem*.

35. *The Poems of William Blake*, ed. W. H. Stevenson, text by David V. Erdman (London and New York: Longman/Norton, 1971), pp. 640, 643. Hereafter cited in the text as Blake.

36. I realize, of course, that between "System" as Blake intends the term and "style" as Trilling practices it, there is a considerable difference. And yet my point is that this difference does not preclude an underlying continuity of defensive self-interest. A personal style, as Yeats recognized, may become as mythological and husklike, or entrapping, as any systematic vision—and as enabling at times as well. The major difference lies in the unwillingness of the stylist to make all his assumptions of "taste" known in an argumentative fashion. In a like-minded interpretive community more "style" and less system is likely to flourish. Or so it would appear from the historical record. See Grant Webster, *The Republic of Letters: A History of Post-War American Literary Opinion* (Baltimore: Johns Hopkins University Press, 1979).

Chapter Three. *Worldly Messiah*

1. Lionel Trilling, "Reality in America," *The Liberal Imagination* (New York: Harcourt Brace Jovanovich, 1979), p. 10. Hereafter this volume will be cited in the text as *LI*.

2. An early version of "Freud and Literature " is "The Legacy of Sigmund Freud: Part 2, Literary and Aesthetic," *Kenyon Review*, 2 (Spring 1940), 152–173. All citations from "Freud and Literature" come from the revised collected version in *The Liberal Imagination*.

3. See Helen Vendler's contribution to a special issue of *Salmagundi*, 41 (Spring 1978).

4. Mark Sheckner, "Psychoanalysis and Liberalism: The Case of Lionel Trilling," *Salmagundi*, 41 (Spring 1978), p. 8.

5. Ibid., p. 31.

6. T. J. Jackson Lears, "The Concept of Cultural Hegemony: Problems and Possibilities," *American Historical Review*, 90, no. 3 (June 1985), 567–593.

7. R. P. Blackmur, "The Politics of Human Power" (1950), in *The Lion and the Honeycomb* (New York: Harcourt Brace Jovanovich, 1955). Hereafter cited in the text as Blackmur. This is still the best single essay on Trilling. Joseph Frank's "Lionel Trilling and the Conservative Imagination" in *The Widening Gyre* (New Brunswick: Rutgers University Press, 1963), while more controversial, is far less insightful. Of the book-length studies by William Chace (*Lionel Trilling: Criticism and Politics* [Stanford: Stanford University Press, 1980]), Edward Joseph Shoben, Jr. (*Lionel Trilling* [New York: Ungar, 1981]), Robert Boyers (*Lionel Trilling: Negative Capability and the Wisdom of Avoidance* [Columbia: University of Missouri Press, 1977]) and Krupnick (*Lionel Trilling and the Fate of Cultural Criticism*), the best so far are the last two.

8. See Paul de Man, *The Resistance to Theory* (Minneapolis: University of Minnesota Press, 1986). See also de Man's "Phenomenality and Materiality in Kant" in Gary Shapiro and Alan Seca, eds., *Hermaneutics: Questions and Prospects* (Amherst: University of Massachusetts Press, 1984), pp. 121–144. Before his untimely death in December 1983, de Man discovered that it is the prosaic materiality of the letter, what I am calling throughout this study the authority of the commonplace, which underlies, as an abyss of indeterminant (because so overdetermined) meaning, the permutations of the aesthetic ideology of vision since Kant. For more on this topic see my "Paul de Man: Nietzsche's Teacher" in *The Romance of Interpretation*.

9. See the editor's introduction by Alan Wilde in *Critical Essays on E. M. Forster* (Boston: Twayne, 1985).

10. Lionel Trilling, *E. M. Forster* (New York: New Directions, 1943, 1964) p. 4. Hereafter cited in the text as *EMF*.

11. As quoted in Boyers, *Lionel Trilling*, p. 15 from Chase's *The American Novel and Its Tradition* (New York: Doubleday, 1957).

12. See Boyers, *Lionel Trilling*, pp. 16–19.

13. See Diana Trilling, "The Other Night at Columbia: A Report from the Academy," *Partisan Review*, 26 (Fall 1959), 214–230.

14. See Trilling's remarks before his own story in the *Prefaces to the Experience of Literature* and my commentary in Chapter 5.

15. Friedrich Nietzsche, *On the Genealogy of Morals and Ecce Homo*, ed. and trans. Walter Kaufmann (New York: Vintage, 1967), p. 34. Hereafter cited in the text as *GM*.

The second section of Nietzsche's untimely essay "On the Advantage and Disadvantage of History for Life," trans. Peter Prauss (Indianapolis: Hackett, 1980), pp. 14–19, contains the classic characterization of "monumental history" (what I refer to throughout as "monumental criticism"). "Monumental history" is the first of three modes of history (the other two are the "antiquarian" and the "critical"). These three modes of history correspond to three kinds of needs or "relations" of "the living man" to life: insofar as "he is active and striving"; insofar as "he preserves and admires"; and insofar as "he suffers and is in need of liberation" (p. 14). All three modes, like all three needs, interact and overlap, and prove useful and effective in the proper combination and order, depending on the circumstances of the time. "Monumental history" is needed primarily by the man who requires "models, teachers and comforters and cannot find them among his associates and contemporaries" (p. 14). In the quest to do the great work and leave his inspiring "monogram" for posterity's sake and achieve immortal fame, such a man discovers in the past the spectacle of genius that suggests that all ages are linked by a chain of genius, and that what once was indeed may be again—through the creation of this very man (pp. 15–16). The danger of "monumental history" is that, especially in artistic matters, envious critics incapable of genius or the noble appreciation of genius may resentfully use the canon of past art to condemn present artists, and so rob life of its future aesthetic justifications (pp. 16–17). My argument is that we can learn from Trilling how to pursue and achieve the most appropriate use of "monumental history," which equates different ages on the basis of some underlying metaphorical similarity (or critical fiction and myth), and thereby overcomes the excess of suspicion that afflicts the profession of literary study at the present time. That is, we can see operating in Trilling at his best and at considerable cost a critical humanism worthy of the name.

16. Diana Trilling, "Other Night at Columbia," p. 230.

17. "Under Forty: American Literature and the Younger Generation of American Jews," *Contemporary Jewish Record*, 7 (February 1944), 201.

18. "Notebooks," p. 21. See Chapters 1 and 2 for discussions of Trilling's radical ambivalence.

19. Sigmund Freud, "Repression," *Collected Papers*, Vol. 4 (New York: Basic Books, 1959), p. 84.

20. Hertz, *End of the Line*, p. 161.

21. See Edward W. Said, "Opponents, Audiences, Constituencies, and Community," *Critical Inquiry*, 9, no. 1 (Fall 1982).

22. See Edward W. Said, "Traveling Theory," *The World, the Text, and the Critic* (Cambridge: Harvard University Press, 1983).

23. As cited in *Nathaniel Hawthorne* by Henry James, collected in Henry

James, *Literary Criticism: Essays on Literature, American Writiers, English Writers*, ed. Leon Edel (New York: Library of America, 1984), p. 325. Hereafter
cited in the text as *NH*. James on Hawthorne informs my views here
considerably, as he did Trilling's. See the latter's "Hawthorne in Our Time"
in *Beyond Culture* and my commentary in Chapter 5. I cite from James's
citation of Hawthorne to highlight this connection and to direct those
interested in pursuing it for themselves to do so easily.

24. The best discussion of the novel in its generic context and of its
reception is Joseph Blotner's in *The Modern American Political Novel* (Austin:
University of Texas Press, 1966), pp. 315–332. The most devastating review,
which perceptively accuses Trilling of arguing with his own characters
owing to his too intimate identification with John Laskell, is that by Robert
Warshaw, "The Legacy of the Thirities," *The Immediate Experience* (Garden
City: Doubleday, 1962).

25. "The State of American Writing, 1948: A Symposium," *Partisan
Review*, 15 (August, 1948), as collected in *Speaking of Literary and Society*
where it is entitled "The State of Our Culture: Expostulation and Reply,"
p. 246.

26. "The Jewish Writer and the English Literary Tradition: A Symposium," *Commentary*, 8 (October 1946), 368.

27. "The Liberal Mind: Two Communications and a Reply," [Richard
Chase, Lionel Trilling, and William Barrett]. *Partisan Review*, 16 (June 1949,
656.

28. Lionel Trilling, "The Repressive Impulse," *Partisan Review*, 15 (June
1948), 718.

29. See Webster, *Republic of Letters*.

30. See Norman Podhoretz, "The Arnoldian Function in American Criticism," *Scrutiny*, 18 (June 1951, 59–65).

Chapter Four. *Subversive Patriarchy*

1. See, for example, Frank, "Lionel Trilling and the Conservative Imagination," and Krupnick, *Lionel Trilling and the Fate of Cultural Criticism.*

2. See, for example, the final chapter, in Jonathan Arac's *Critical Genealogies*, pp. 281–315.

3. On this topic of the willful irrelevance of much contemporary criticism, see Paul A. Bové's "Intellectuals at War: Michel Foucault and the
Analytics of Power," in *Intellectuals in Power*.

4. On these two topics see, respectively, Gerald Graff, *Professing Literature* (Chicago: The University of Chicago Press, 1986), and Harold Bloom,
"Sublime Crossing and the Death of Love," *Agon: Towards a Theory of Revisionism* (New York: Oxford University Press, 1982).

5. See also Terry A. Cooney, *The Rise of the New York Intellectuals: Partisan Review and Its Circle* (Madison: University of Wisconsin Press, 1986).

6. Howe, "New York Intellectuals," p. 36. See also Delmore Schwartz, "The Duchess' Red Shoes," *Selected Essays*, ed. Donald Davie and David Zucker (Chicago: University of Chicago Press, 1970); Mark Krupnick, "Lionel Trilling: Criticism and Illusion," *Modern Occasions*, 1, no. 2 (Winter 1971), 282–287; and Nathan Scott, Jr., *Three American Moralists: Mailer, Bellow, Trilling* (Notre Dame, Ind.: University of Notre Dame Press, 1973).

7. See the discussion of "Notes of a Departure" and "The Changing Myth of the Jew" in Chapter 2.

8. "Seven Professors Look at the Jewish Student: A Symposium," *Commentary*, 12 (December 1951), 526–529 (Trilling's contribution).

9. "Art and Morals," *Arts Digest*, 27 (May 15, 1953), 19–20 (Trilling's contribution).

10. See Webster, *Republic of Letters*.

11. See, Lionel Trilling, "A Speech of Robert Frost: A Cultural Episode," *Partisan Review*, 26 (Fall 1959), 445–452 (hereafter cited in the text as "Frost"); *Newsweek*, 54, no. 27 (July 27, 1959); M. L. Rosenthal, "The Robert Frost Controversy," *Nation*, 188 (June 20, 1959), 559–561; and "The Art of Poetry II: An Interview with Robert Frost," *Paris Review*, 24, no. 2 (Summer–Fall 1960), 88–120.

12. At roughly the same time, the early 1950s, Trilling gives up graduate teaching (see the Notes to Chapter 2). As Paul Bové has reminded me, this does not mean Trilling had no association with graduate students at Columbia University. By the time Trilling became University Professor in the early 1970s, shortly before his death, graduate students would flock to his courses, swelling their ranks to the point that seminars often turned, de facto, into lecture courses. Similarly, I must remind the reader that while Trilling never wrote again on American writers, especially contemporary figures, with the one notable exception "Hawthorne in Our Time," he does occasionally refer to contemporary figures, especially novelists such as Bellow. See, for example, "The Fate of Pleasure" in *Beyond Culture*.

13. See Chapter 1 for a discussion of Jewish self-hatred in this context.

14. Lionel Trilling, "The Morality of Inertia," *A Gathering of Fugitives* (New York: Harcourt Brace Jovanovich, 1956), pp. 34–44. Hereafter this volume will be cited in the text as *GF*.

15. See the essays on these writers in *A Gathering of Fugitives*.

16. See *Romance of Interpretation*; Hertz, *End of the Line*; Julia Kristeva, *Powers of Horror: An Essay on Abjection*, trans. Leon S. Roudiery (New York: Columbia University Press, 1982); and, last but far from least, de Man, *Resistance to Theory*.

17. T. W. Adorno, *Aesthetic Theory*, trans. C. Lenhardt, ed. Gretel

Adorno and Rolf Tredemarin (London: Routledge and Kegan Paul, 1984), p. 97.

18. Martin Jay, *Adorno* (Cambridge: Harvard University Press, 1984), p. 156.

19. I am deeply indebted not only to Kristeva's *Powers of Horror* but to Neil Hertz's discussion of her essay "The Abject of Love" in *The End of the Line*, which has been incorporated into Kristeva's book in its first two chapters: "Approaching Abjection," pp. 1–31, and "Something to be Scared Of," pp. 32–55. These theorists bear no responsibility, of course, for my "patriarchal" development of their work.

20. "The Demiurge's Laugh," *The Poetry of Robert Frost*, ed. Edward Connery Latham (New York: Holt, Rinehart and Winston, 1964, 1967), p. 25.

Chapter Five. *Normal Mysticism*

1. For Trilling's role see, especially, Richard M. Pells, *The Liberal Mind in a Conservative Age: American Intellectuals in the 1940s and 1950s* (New York: Harper and Row, 1985), pp. 135–138.

2. Donald Pease, *Cold War Texts* (forthcoming). See also his *"Moby Dick and the Cold War"* in Donald Pease and Walter Benn Michaels, eds., *The American Renaissance Reconsidered* (Baltimore: Johns Hopkins University Press), pp. 113–155.

3. It should be noted that Trilling supervised the one-volume abridgment of Ernest Jones's three-volume biography. See Ernest Jones, *The Life and Work of Sigmund Freud*, edited and abridged in one volume by Lionel Trilling (New York: Basic Books, 1961).

4. Lionel Trilling, *Freud and the Crisis of Our Culture* (Boston: Beacon, 1956). This monograph essay appears in a cut and revised form as "Freud: Within and Beyond Culture" in *Beyond Culture*. All citations from the former will be given in the text as *FCOC*.

5. For Hegel, the significance of the Penates lies in their being a more abstract, less personal representation of the absolute in a Stoic form.

6. See, especially, Paul Ricoeur, "Fatherhood: From Phantasm to Symbol," *The Conflict of Interpretations* (Evanston: Northwestern University Press, 1973).

7. One way of viewing Trilling's later career is as a quest for a principle of necessity adequate to his belief in the power of mind.

8. Similarly, see Trilling's curious 1955 lecture to the National Institute of Arts and Letters "On Not Talking," reprinted in *A Gathering of Fugitives*, pp. 153–163.

9. For a fuller discussion of this revisionary tactic in the contexts of neo-

Freudian and neo-Marxist critical theory, see my "The Reality of Theory: Freud in His Critics" in Joseph Buttigieg, ed., *Criticism without Boundaries* (Notre Dame: University of Notre Dame Press, 1987).

10. John Dewey, *Art as Experience* (New York: Perigee Books/Putnam, 1934, 1980). See, especially, p. 22: "Experience is the result, the sign, and the reward of that interaction of organism and environment which, when it is carried to the full [in art], is a transformation of interaction into participation and communication." That is, experience per se, outside of the formative powers of human organization such as the languages of art and everyday practices, can never really occur. Experience is always already on the way to being what it is potentially: a signifying form of life. It is in this sophisticated and complex sense that Trilling uses the term in entitling his anthology *The Experience of Literature*.

11. I am indebted for this anecdote to Paul A. Bové, now of the University of Pittsburgh, formerly a colleague of David S. Shapiro at Columbia.

12. See the following special issues: "The Politics of Interpretation," *Critical Inquiry*, 9, no. 1 (September 1982), 1–280; and "Canons," *Critical Inquiry*, 10, no. 1 (Fall 1983), 1–250.

13. This term, "cultural literacy," originally put into circulation by E. D. Hirsch in his recent work, has been taken up by William Bennett, the secretary of education under Reagan, in a variety of speeches around the country over the past several years. Just as there are "basics" of reading and writing English, so there are fundamental masterworks of the Western tradition, ignorance of which makes one as culturally "illiterate" as the inability to read and write English is said to make one "illiterate" in the old sense. That there are some questions to be raised about this "old" sense of illiteracy as well as the new—and specious—cultural analogy now being circulated goes without saying, especially given its academic and governmental sources and purveyors.

14. See West, "Lionel Trilling: Godfather of Neo-Conservatism."

15. For the most sensitive and probing exploration of this problematic, a legacy of poststructuralism, See Paul A. Bové, "Critical Negation," *Intellectuals in Power*.

16. See, for instance, Donna Pryzbylowicz, "D. H. Lawrence's *The Plumed Serpent*: The Dialectics of Ideology and Utopia," *Boundary 2*, 13, nos. 2 and 3 (Winter/Spring 1985), 289–318. This issue is volume 2 of the special issues "On Humanism and the University" edited by William V. Spanos.

17. See Braudy, *Frenzy of Renown*.

18. See Chapter 4 for a brief discussion of some of these ways of theorizing the sublime and as well my book *The Romance of Interpretation*. See, finally, the discussion of Freud's "Mourning and Melancholia" in Chapter 1 here.

19. See Frank Lentricchia's now classic study of postmodern criticism, *After the New Criticism* (Chicago: University of Chicago Press, 1979), for a particularly insightful critique of Harold Bloom's revisionism which Lentricchia rightly blasts as "the spirit of revenge" incarnate.

20. See Chapter 1 and my critique of Arac and West, two of the finest of contemporary cultural critics, for just such willed blindness.

21. See Trilling's "The Situation of the American Intellectual" in *A Gathering of Fugitives*, pp. 65–84.

22. Freud revises what Neitzsche in *On the Genealogy of Morals* characterizes as the ascetic will of religion and secularizes it. Unlike the related revisionary secularization of this will to nothingness found in modern science and art with their devotion to "truth" and "the criticism of life," Freud's refuses to substitute science or art, even the artful science of psychoanalysis, for the intellectual bankruptcy of religion. Freud preserves the "seriousness" and "weight" of traditional religion in the fateful—and often fatal—primacy he gives to loss in the compensatory formations of the individual ego and the collective subject of such groups as the church and the military. See, especially, *Group Psychology and the Analysis of Ego*. In short, Freud takes death and the illusions of desire seriously, as if the life of a client or of a people hung in the balance.

23. For an extended discussion of this topic, see Paul A. Bové, "The Last of the Latecomers" (pts. 1 and 2) on Erich Auerbach in *Intellectuals in Power*, pp. 79–130 and 131–208.

24. Trilling's point, and mine after him, is that what Grant Webster in *The Republic of Letters* terms the bourgeois avant-gardists have become the academic heirs of Gabriel Conroy insofar as they have remained stubbornly loyal to modernism in the arts—the half of that union of Marxism and modernism which *Partisan Review* once promoted.

25. See the discussions of the apocalyptic bell and Trilling's comments on this matter in Chapter 2.

Chapter Six. *Infectious Apocalypse*

1. For further discussion of this relation between Kant and Nietzsche, see Bové, *Intellectuals in Power*, especially the last chapter, "Critical Negation."

2. Jean-Jacques Rousseau, *Reveries of the Solitary Walker*, trans. Peter France (New York: Penguin, 1979). Hereafter cited in the text as *RSW*.

3. That is, what appears to be at one and the same time a sublimely disruptive *and* constituting force can be read as "the sentiment of being" or the "play" of indetermination or the "power" of discussive practices, depending upon the intellectual frame and social constraints operative at

any particular historical conjuncture. Elaine Scarry in *The Body in Pain: The Making and Unmaking of the World* (New York: Oxford University Press, 1985) can even read this force as her title and subtitle suggest. At the risk of appearing both superfluous and reductive, I suppose this force, however interpreted, to be representative of the experience of the will—both one's own and the massed wills of the people—that doing a work, laboring, entails once it is subjected to the processes of memory and fantasy.

4. Lionel Trilling, *Sincerity and Authenticity* (Cambridge: Harvard University Press, 1971, 1972), p. 66. Hereafter cited in the text as *SA*.

5. Trilling here (*SA*, p. 22) makes surprising reference to Lacan and his famous essay on "the mirror stage."

6. Denis Diderot, *Rameau's Nephew and Other Works*, trans. Jacques Barzun and Ralph H. Bowen (Indianapolis: Bobbs-Merrill Educational Publishing, 1956), pp. 84–85. Hereafter cited in the text as *RN*. This is the edition that Trilling cites in *Sincerity and Authenticity*.

7. The finest survey of the question of the postmodern is Jonathan Arac's introduction to a volume he edited, *Postmodernism and Politics* (Minneapolis: University of Minnesota Press, 1986), pp. ix–xliii, which is reprinted in *Critical Genealogies* as the last chapter.

8. See also my discussion of Arac in Ch. 1.

9. That is, at least three generations of twentieth-century Anglo-American critics have been refighting their version of the English Civil War!

10. See my book *The Romance of Interpretation*.

11. The best study of postmodern literature to date is Alan Wilde's *Horizons of Assent*.

12. A crucial distinction must be underscored here. The new subjectivities generated by postmodern texts are ephemeral effects of a deconstructive textual logic so long as they are not situated in history by means of a reformation of institutional and social practices. Texts from any period may produce the fragments of various possible subjects. That any one or other persists through time is a political decision in the broadest sense.

13. For a detailed discussion of this subject, see my essay "The Reality of Theory: Freud in His Critics."

14. See Charles Altieri, "Ecce Homo: Narcissism, Power, Pathos, and the Status of Autobiographical Representations," in Daniel O'Hara, ed., *Why Nietzsche Now?* (Bloomington: Indiana University Press, 1985), pp. 389–413.

15. That this is also Foucault's point in *Madness and Civilization* goes without saying. That Trilling never directly attacks Foucault's work—only Cooper's introduction to the English edition—should be noted.

16. See *The Middle of the Journey*, p. 302. Maxim says to John Laskell, Trilling's ironic surrogate: "You have been sitting there opposite me with

a little core of safety, a little center of moral certainty because of what you did this evening. You ran after Caldwell, [to explain that his daughter's death wasn't his fault], not in rage but in charity. I've mentioned Paul once and I'll take the chance of mentioning him again. If you don't mind too much—do you know his text for Pharisees and revolutionaries? 'Though I bestow all my goods to feed the poor, and though I give my body to be burned and have not charity, it profiteth me nothing.' Do you know what charity means—infinite dearness, the sense of how costly and valuable a human life is." For the finest recent study of the political novel, See Robert Boyers, *Atrocity and Amnesia: The Political Novel Since 1945* (Evanston, Ill.: Northwestern University Press, 1986).

17. See Bloom, *Prodigal Sons*, pp. 381, 383–384.

18. See my discussion of contemporary narcissism, critical style, in Chapter 1.

19. For a contrary view, see Fredric Jameson, "Periodizing the Sixties," in Sohnya Sayres et al., eds., *The Sixties without Apology* (Minneapolis: University of Minnesota Press, 1984), pp. 178–209. See also Jameson's companion pieces: "The Politics of Theory: Ideological Positions in the Postmodernism Debate," *New German Critique*, 33 (1984), 53–65; and "Postmodernism, or the Cultural Logic of Late Capitalism," *New Left Review*, no. 146 (1984), 53–92.

20. See, for instance, Edward W. Said, "Secular Criticism," *World, the Text, and the Critic*.

21. "Sincerity and Authenticity: A Symposium," *Salmagundi*, no. 41 (Spring 1978), 109 and "Culture and the Present Moment: A Round-Table Discussion," *Commentary*, 58, no. 6 (December 1974), 47–48. See also Lopate, "Remembering Lionel Trilling," especially the conclusion (p. 178): "Of course [his death] had nothing to do with me. . . . But I had to work my way into his death somehow. I even imagined my book on his night table, by the deathbed, his last reading! Anything to prolong the connection. . . . And now that he is gone, who is there to *name* me?" See also Ahab's comment in the Quarterdeck scene: "If man will strike, strike through the mask," *Moby-Dick*, ed. Harrison Hayford and Hershel Parker (New York: W. W. Norton, 1967), p. 144.

Index

Wellek, Rene, 296*nn18, 19, 20*; his aesthetic purity, 131
Wells, H. G., 283, 285
West, Cornel, 26–27, 296*n23*, 298*n24*, 305*n14*, 306*n20*
Wharton, Edith, 146, 243
Whitman, Walt, 21, 144, 242–43, 258; as cultural critic, 76; Trilling's "Sermon on a Text from Whitman," 89, 121, 147; Wallace Stevens as modern revision of, 138; discovery of self through death in, 161, 191
Wilde, Alan, 295*n7*, 298*n17*, 300*n9*; and the "aesthetics of crisis," 8; on postmodernism, 263, 307*n11*
Wilde, Oscar: his conscious insincerity, 263, 265; his masks, 287
Will, George, 142
Williams, Raymond, 64, 299*n33*; as cultural critic, 76
Wilson, Edmund, 97, 102, 185, 216
Wolfe, Thomas, 134, 149
Wollstonecraft, Mary, 15–16
Wordsworth, Dorothy, 16
Wordsworth, William, 21, 59, 73, 150, 174, 237, 256, 258, 295*n13*; Arac's reading of "Nutting," 13–18, 78–79; Trilling's essay on Wordsworth, 52, 125, 152–55, 160–61, 209, 238, 260; union between nature and culture envisioned in preface to *The Excursion*, 85; and theory of attachment to first pleasures, 126;

and the "morality of inertia," 146–47, 149; his poetic materialism, 164; as figure of the "opposing self," 174; his "Resolution and Independence," 177, 212, 242; as example of original revisionary psychology, 188; discussed by Trilling in "The Fate of Pleasure," 202–5, 209; and the Preface to the *Lyrical Ballads*, 244; his figures of "old man," 246
Woolf, Virginia, 249
Wyatt, Sir Thomas, 219

Yeats, W. B., 96, 118, 132, 171, 179, 186–87, 194. 201, 213, 235, 264, 272, 280, 281, 299*n36*; as Celtic Bard, 133; as modern author with belief, 134; as modernist master, 152, 222; his aestheticism in "Lapis Lazuli," 158; as model of the "opposing self," 174; his definition of demonic imagination, 184; as discussed by Trilling in "The Fate of Pleasure," 202; his prophetic vision in "The Second Coming," 215; Trilling's preface to "Sailing to Byzantium," 219–20; Trilling's preface to *Purgatory*, 223–27; his "Celtic Twilight gothic romanticism," 240; and "daemonic soul-making," 287; his sense of the past, 289–90

Zucker, David, 303*n6*

DATE DUE

	261-2500		Printed in USA